EVIDENCE THAT YOU ARE TRULY CHRISTIAN

Keep Testing Yourselves to See If You Are In the Faith—Keep Examining Yourselves

EDWARD D. ANDREWS

i

EVIDENCE THAT YOU ARE TRULY CHRISTIAN

Keep Testing Yourselves to See If You Are In the Faith—Keep Examining Yourselves

Edward D. Andrews

Christian Publishing House

Cambridge, Ohio

Christian Publishing House
Professional Christian Publishing of the Good News!

Unless otherwise stated, Scripture quotations are from *The Holy Bible, Updated American Standard Version (UASV)*®, copyright © 2016 by Christian Publishing House, Professional Conservative Christian Publishing of the Good News!

EVIDENCE THAT YOU ARE TRULY CHRISTIAN Keep Testing *Yourselves to See If You Are In the Faith—Keep Examining Yourselves* by Edward D. Andrews

ISBN-13: 978-0692562307

ISBN-10: 0692562303

EVIDENCE THAT YOU ARE TRULY CHRISTIAN

Edward D. Andrews

Table of Contents

PREFACE

Are we sure that we are truly walking in the truth? What kind of self-examination is fitting for servants of God? The Apostle Paul exhorted the Christians at Corinth to "Keep testing yourselves to see if you are in the faith. Keep examining yourselves!" (2 Cor. 13:5) Why should Paul's admonition to the Corinthians be of interest to us? We can do the same today. It will protect us from being uncertain as to whether we are walking in the truth. What standard do we have for testing whether we are in the faith, and why is that the perfect standard? If we are going to take a test to see whether we are truly in the faith, namely, truly walking with God, we must measure our conduct in light of the Word of God.

William Lange Craig wrote, "Remember that our faith is not based on emotions, but on the truth, and therefore you must hold on to it." What truth? Jesus said to the Father in prayer, "Sanctify them in **the truth**; your word is truth." (John 17:17) By identifying the Scriptures some of which actually say, "You are my disciples if ...," we can know if we are truly Christian. A test that can actually tell us whether we are walking in the truth should never be based on emotionalism, but rather on Scripture. Do our words, our thoughts, our actions, our mind, our heart attitude harmonize with the Scriptures? Within this publication, we will be able to let the Word of God prove who we really are. Let us follow the Apostle Paul's counsel, by testing ourselves to determine whether we are adhering to God's Word.

1

INTRODUCTION Examine Yourselves to See Whether You Are In the Faith

2 Corinthians 13:5 Updated American Standard Version (UASV)

5 Keep testing yourselves to see if you are in the faith. Keep examining yourselves! Or do you not realize this about yourselves, that Jesus Christ is in you, unless indeed you fail to meet the test?

When was the last time that we truly took a good look at ourselves? How did we feel about what we saw? When we ponder over our personality, what are we actually projecting to others? Most of us are very complex people when it comes to our thoughts, feeling and beliefs, so it might be difficult to lock down what kind of personality that we have. As a man, are we faithful like Abraham one moment and then blown back and forth like doubting Thomas the next? As a female, are we submissive like Sarah when we are in public and then like domineering Jezebel in private? As a Christian, are we devoted and energetic for the truth on Christian meeting days and then loving the world like Demas[1] the other days out of the week? As a Christian, have we entirely taken off the old person with its practices and clothed ourselves with the new person? – Colossians 3:9-10; Ephesians 4:20-24.

Some women are known to spend much time every morning, 'putting on their face,' as it is commonly expressed. So much so, it has been commonly joked about, and men know not to interfere until the project is over. However, truth be told, men are very much concerned with how they look when going out into public. Thus, all of us are conscious of whether our hair is out of place, if we have a pimple or a cold sore, or if there is something about us that is unkempt, ruffled, scruffy, or messy. We want to look our best. What we may have not considered is, our personality, is always showing as well. The deeper question though is "are we putting on our personality to cover over before we go out in public while our real personality is on display in

---

[1] A "fellow worker" with Paul at Rome (Col. 4:14; Philem. 24), who eventually, "in love with this present world," forsook the apostle and left for Thessalonica (2 Tim. 4:10). No other particulars are given concerning him. (ISBE, Volume 1, Page 918)

private?" Is what the public sees, who we really are? Does our real personality bring honor to God?

A man walking the roads of the countryside in a small European country comes to a fork in the road. He is uncertain as to which way he should go. Therefore, he asks several who are passing by for directions, but some told him to take the left fork, and others said to make the right. After receiving contradictory information, he simply did not know what to do, how was he to go on, without knowing for certain which path led to the destination. He was unable to move on until he knew what the right path was. Having doubts about our faith, our walk with God, his Word can influence us similarly. It can actually cause severe emotional turmoil as we go about our Christian life.

There was a similar situation on the first-century Corinthian congregation. Some known as "super-apostles" were actually taking the apostle Paul to task, as to Paul's walk with God, saying, "His letters are weighty and strong, but his bodily presence is weak, and his speech of no account." (2 Cor. 10:7-12; 11:5-6, ESV) Certainly, we can see how a Christian in that congregation could wonder if they were truly walking with God when the apostle Paul himself was being call into question.

Paul founded the Corinthian congregation in about 50 C.E.[2] on his second missionary journey. "When Silas and Timothy arrived from Macedonia, Paul was occupied with the word, testifying to the Jews that the Christ was Jesus. And the Lord said to Paul one night in a vision, 'Do not be afraid, but go on speaking and do not be silent, for I am with you, and no one will attack you to harm you, for I have many in this city who are my people.' And he stayed a year and six months, teaching the word of God among them." (Acts 18:5-11, ESV) The apostle Paul was deeply interested in the spiritual wellbeing of the brothers and sisters in Corinth. Moreover, the Corinthian Christians were interested in their spiritual welfare as well, so they wrote Paul for his counsel on certain matters. (1 Cor. 7:1-40) Therefore, Paul, under inspiration offered them inspired counsel in what would be his second letter to them.

"Keep testing yourselves to see if you are in the faith. Keep examining yourselves! Or do you not realize this about yourselves, that Jesus Christ is in you, unless indeed you fail to meet the test?" (2 Cor. 13:5) If these brothers in the days of having Paul found their

---

[2] B.C.E. means "before the Common Era," which is more accurate than B.C. ("before Christ"). C.E. denotes "Common Era," often called A.D., for *anno Domini*, meaning "in the year of our Lord."

congregation, who spent sixteen months under the guidance of the greatest, inspired Christian, needed to self-examine themselves, how much more should we need to do so, as we are 2,000-years removed. If these brothers followed this advice to examine themselves, it would have offered them direction on how to walk with God and let them know if they were on the right path.

Remember, Jesus warned, "Not everyone who says to me, 'Lord, Lord,' will enter the kingdom of heaven, but **the one who does** the will of my Father who is in heaven." (Matt 7:21, ESV) In other words, not every Christian was going to enter into the kingdom, even though they felt that they were walking with God. Jesus spoke of their mindset in the next verse, "On that day many will say to me, 'Lord, Lord, did we not prophesy in your name, and cast out demons in your name, and do many mighty works in your name?'" (Matt. 7:22, ESV) Yes, these ones, who felt that they were walking with God, on that day they were supposing that they were truly Christian, were in for a rude awakening. What is Jesus going to say to these ones, "And then will I declare to them, 'I never knew you; depart from me, you workers of lawlessness.'" (Matt. 7:23) What were and are these ones lacking?

Jesus said they were **not doing the will of the Father**, even though they believed they were. Notice that in 98 C.E., the apostle John, the last surviving apostle, in one of his letters offered that same warning too. He wrote, "The world is passing away, and its lusts; but the one who does the will of God remains forever." (1 John 2:17) Thus, we can see the wisdom of the apostle Paul's counsel to 'Keep testing ourselves to see if you are in the faith. Keep examining ourselves!' Thus, the next question is, what do we need to do to follow this advice? How does one test whether or not they are in the faith? In addition, what does it mean to 'keep examining ourselves after we have tested ourselves?

Keep Testing Yourselves

In a **test**, there is an examination of a person or an object to find something out, e.g. whether it is functioning properly or not. In this **test**, there must be a standard by which the person or object is measured. For example, the "normal" human body temperature is 98.6°F (37°C). Therefore, if we were testing our temperature, it would be measured against the normal body temperature. Anything above or below that would be considered high or low. Another example is the normal resting heart rate for adults, which ranges from 60 to 100 beats a minute.

However, our test in this publication is to see if we are truly Christian. However, what we are looking for when we 'test ourselves, to see if we are in the faith,' is **not** the faith, that is the basic Bible doctrines. In our test, we are the subject. What we are testing is, if we are truly walking with God. If we are to test our walk as a Christian, we need to have a perfect standard. Our perfect standard by which to measure ourselves is,

Psalm 19:7-8 Updated American Standard Version (UASV)

⁷ The law of Jehovah is perfect,
　restoring the soul;
the testimony of Jehovah is sure,
　making wise the simple.
⁸ The precepts of Jehovah are right,
　rejoicing the heart;

Yes, the Word of God, the Bible is the standard by which we can measure our walk with God. On this, the author of Hebrews wrote, "For the word of God is living and active and sharper than any two-edged sword, and piercing as far as the division of soul and spirit, of both joints and marrow, and able to judge the thoughts and intentions of the heart." (Heb. 4:12) Thus, we must test our walk with God by examining our life course as outlined by Scripture, to find his favor, to be in an approved standing, to be declared righteous before him. Herein, each of the twenty chapters will have a text that they will be built around, a text that defines **what we should be** in the eyes of God. For example, several times Jesus says 'if we are doing _____, we are truly his disciples.' Well, the objective would be to discover what all is involved in doing _____.

Keep Examining Yourselves

The phrase keep *examining yourselves* is self-explanatory, but it involves a self-examination. We may have been a Christian for a number of years, but how many times have we had a spiritual checkup. Every six months we are to go in for a dental cleaning and unless there is a problem, we should get a health screening once a year. The problem with our spirituality is it is far more susceptible to injury than we are physically. The author of Hebrews warns us, "We must **pay much closer attention** to what we have heard, lest we **drift away** from it." (2:1) One chapter later, we are told, **"Take care**, brothers, lest there be in any of you *an evil, unbelieving heart*, leading you to **fall away** from the living God. But exhort one another every day, as long as it is called "today," that none of you may be **hardened by the deceitfulness of sin**." (3:12-13) This same author warns us about falling away (6:6), becoming sluggish (6:12), and growing weary or fainthearted (12:25).

Why would this be the case? If we are saved, why is it necessary that we keep examining ourselves? Why would we still be susceptible to bad behaviors to the point of drifting away, to the point of having an unbelieving heart, falling away, becoming sluggish, growing weary or fainthearted?

There are four reasons. **(1)** First and foremost, we have inherited sin, which means that we are missing the mark of perfection. **(2)** In addition, our environment can condition us into the bad thinking and behavior. **(3)** We have our human weaknesses, which include inborn tendencies that we naturally lean toward evil, leading us into bad behaviors. **(4)** Moreover, there is the world of Satan and his demons that caters to these human weaknesses, which also leads us down the path of bad thinking and behaviors. After our self-examination, what is needed if we are to overcome any bad thinking or behaviors and how are we to avoid developing them in the future? We will offer more on this in each chapter as well as two appendices at the end, but we offer this for now. It is paramount that we fully understand what all is involved in our human imperfection and never believe that we are so strong spiritually that we would never fall away, slow down, or becoming sluggish in our walk with God.

Obviously, this should be of the greatest concern to each one of us. We may be a person of good character, and believe that in any situation, we will make the right decisions. However, the moment that **innocent appearing situation** arises, we are plagued with the inner desire toward wrong. We need to address more than what our friends, or our workmates or our spouse may see. We need to look into our inner self, in the hopes of determining, who we really are, and what do we need to do to have a good heart (i.e., inner person).

As we know, we could not function with half a heart. However, we can function, albeit dysfunctional, with a heart that is divided. Yes, we have things outside of us that can contribute to bad thinking, which id left unchecked will lead to bad behavior, but we also have some things within. The apostle Paul bewailed about himself, "For I do not do the good I want, but the evil I do not want is what I keep on doing. Now if I do what I do not want, it is no longer I who do it, but sin that dwells within me." (Romans 7:19-20) This is because all of us are mentally bent toward the doing of wrong, instead of the doing of good. (Gen 6:5; 8:21; Rom 5:12; Eph. 4:20-24; Col 3:5-11) Jeremiah the prophet informs us of the condition of our heart (our inner person), "The heart is deceitful above all things, and desperately sick; who can understand it?" These factors contribute to our being more vulnerable to the worldly desires and the weak human flesh than we may have thought. One needs to understand just how bad human imperfection is before they can fully implement the right **Christian Living Skills**.

Returning to the book of Hebrews, we are told, "solid food belongs to the mature, to those who through practice have their discernment trained to distinguish between good and evil." (5:14) We will have evidence that we are one of the mature ones by training ourselves to distinguish between good and evil. We likely believe that we are already spiritually mature, which may very well be the case. Nevertheless, we are told by Paul to carry out this self-examination and to keep on examining ourselves, to remain that way, and even to improve upon what we currently have by way of maturity. Just as a man or woman in a marathon must continually train their muscles to surpass others in the sport, our discernment (perception) needs to be trained through regularly and rightly applying the Word of God. Throughout this publication, we will apply the inspired words of James, Jesus' half-brother.

James 1:22-25 Updated American Standard Version (UASV)

22 But be doers of the word, and not hearers only, deceiving yourselves. **23** For if anyone is a hearer of the word and not a doer, he is like a man who looks intently at his natural face[3] in a mirror.

24 for he looks at himself and goes away, and immediately forgets what sort of man he was. **25** But he that looks into the perfect law, the law of liberty, and abides by it, being no hearer who forgets but a doer of a work, he will be blessed in his doing.

When we are inundated in the Word of God, it serves as the voice of God, telling us the way in which to walk.

Review Questions

(1) How can we test whether we are truly Christian?

(2) What warning did Jesus and the apostle John give to those who believed they were doing the right things?

(3) What is involved in examining what we ourselves are?

---

[3] Lit *the face of his birth*

(4) Why must we keep testing ourselves?

(5) Why must we keep examining ourselves?

(6) Why do we need to understand just how bad human imperfection is before we can fully implement the right Christian Living Skills?

CHAPTER 1 Faith Without Works Is Dead

James 2:14-26 Updated American Standard Version (UASV)

¹⁴ What use is it, my brothers, if someone says he has faith but he has no works? Can that faith save him? **¹⁵** If a brother or sister is without clothes and lacks daily food, **¹⁶** and one of you says to them, "Go in peace, be warmed and be filled," and yet you do not give them what is necessary for their body, what good⁴ is that? **¹⁷** Even so faith, if it has no works, is dead in itself.

¹⁸ But someone will say, "You have faith and I have works." Show me your faith apart from your works, and I will show you my faith by my works. **¹⁹** You believe that God is one. You do well; the demons also believe, and shudder. **²⁰** But do you want to know, O foolish man, that faith without works is useless?

What use is it, my brothers, if someone says he has faith but he has no works? Can that faith save him? (2:14)⁵

James uses the term **what use is it, my brothers,** to ask a rhetorical question to highlight or emphasize his point. James asks **if someone says he has faith, but he has no works, can that faith save him?** Faith is an assurance and confidence in what is believed in based on the knowledge of that particular object. Faith is not blindly hoping for something or someone, but rather knowing and trusting with complete certainty. Rather faith is based on knowledge of something that can be known. It is putting faith **into** something or someone. The Christian faith it is not blind at all since it is in an all-powerful and holy God. Instead, Christianity is built upon the knowledge of God who is the creator of the universe and all of humanity itself.

The major issue here is in the fact that one is merely claiming to have faith. They are giving nothing more than a verbal affirmation to a belief that consists only of the framework of their mind, but has not yet affected the nature of their will and produced proper actions. James makes it clear that faith is not just some head knowledge alone, but true faith is manifested in the fact that it produces appropriate actions

---

⁴ Or "*benefit*"

⁵ This chapter is from the CPH Christian Living Commentary by Brent A. Calloway

http://www.christianpublishers.org/apps/webstore/products/show/5575711

consistent with what one claims to profess. James here asks the question for his audience to ponder and think about to come to their conclusion as he states **can such faith save him**?

Faith does not just begin and end at a mere profession of Christ. Good works in one's life then must evidence it. These works are not done as a way to earn salvation, but rather out of gratitude of a heart that has been changed by the power of Christ that made one a new creation in Christ. Good works are to be done out of the overflow of the heart that has been redeemed by the power of God through Christ. The answer to James question, as he will explain in the following verses, is faith without works is not true saving faith.

If a brother or sister is without clothes and lacks daily food, and one of you says to them, "Go in peace, be warmed and be filled," and yet do not give them what is necessary for their body, what good is that? (2:15-16)

James has just got through asking the question as to whether or not faith that has no works is a saving faith or not. James now is going to give an example to answer his question as to whether saving faith is one that produces no good works. James gives them a hypothetical situation of **a brother or sister is without clothes and lacks daily food**. It is clear that the individual is without clothing and daily food, in other words, the individual did not have the essentials of life. The Jews would have known from the Old Testament about the importance and the necessity of showing hospitality. It was written in Leviticus 19:9-10, "Now when you reap the harvest of your land, you shall not reap to the very corners of your field, nor shall you gather the gleanings of your harvest. Nor shall you glean your vineyard, nor shall you gather the fallen fruit of your vineyard; you shall leave them for the needy and for the stranger. I am the Lord your God." James does not describe how this brother or sister got into the condition in which they found themselves but merely gives the reality of the condition.

James unfolds the progression of the situation and says **one of you says to them, go in peace**. Now the problem with what is happening here is that the Christians who were saying **go in peace, be warmed, and filled**, were content with just lip service. The problem is that what they were saying to the individual needed to be supported by actions. True faith would not just have said go in peace, because how could this person honestly go in peace when they were daily worrying about how to keep warm and be fed. There would have been daily anxiety and fear of not knowing where the next meal would come from or how to keep warm. Real faith not only expresses kind wishes to the individual in need, but takes action to see those needs come true.

These believers saying be warmed were telling the individual to do something that they were unable to do on their own. This individual they were telling to keep warm would benefit nothing from their merely good wishes. Real faith would not just make good wishes to keep warm but seek the resources to help the individual to keep warm. The whole point in the person coming to these believers was to try to get warm, and mere lip service does nothing without being accompanied by actions that would have enabled the individual to be warm and fed.

One more time we see that simple words are meaningless in this situation, for how can one be filled, if he has no means by which to be filled. You will note that the word "be" is used twice in this passage when James says be warmed and be filled. The emphasis on the word is put on the one coming to them to be fed and clothed. This was suggesting that it was in power of the one who was hungry and needed clothes to be able to do these things. However, they cannot in their current situation because they have no means by which to do so. Here again, real saving faith in this context would seek to get the individual the food that they needed or try to get them filled in some way.

It is for this reason that James says **and yet do not give them what is necessary for their body, what good is that**? James has given his readers a compelling example. Kind words and best wishes ring hollow when they are not supplemented by physical aid when he is capable of helping materially. In fact, this is ridiculously inadequate and does nothing but generate more heartache and pain for the one suffering. (See Proverbs 3:27-28) The result is, one with this so-called faith who does nothing to bring any kind of relief to those in need, nor at least moves others to demonstrate their faith, is worthless. Anyone, who says, "go in peace," while offering nothing to this destitute one, leaving the helping to others, would be known as one who has no love or kindness about him. In addition, this faithless one would bring reproach on God and Christianity. Those from outside of Christianity looking in, would ask themselves, "Who would want to be a part of such a religion?"

Even so faith, if it has no works, is dead in itself. (2:17)

James is now connecting his example of what he has just said on how it relates to faith. It is pointless to say peace and keep warm and well fed when one takes no action to help alleviate the situation. The fact that one does not act in accordance with his words, therefore, proves his

11

words to be dead and false. To just claim to have faith but **has no works, is dead in itself**. The word that James uses for dead is *nekros*, which means "*inactive, inoperative.*" (Vine 1996, 148) This believer's mere lip service to faith without the outward expression of faith through works is inactive. James is making it clear that without works, his faith is dormant and dead and, therefore, proves that he truly does not have faith. Jesus himself said that many would be judged for the supposed claim of faith without works on judgment day with the parable of the sheep and the goats. – Matthew 25:31-46.

But someone will say, "You have faith and I have works. Show me your faith apart from your works, and I will show you my faith by my works. " (2:18a)

James now is going to deal with a statement that he foresees being raised because he said faith without works is dead. James makes the statement, **will say you have faith, and I have works**. Some may claim that they do not need any faith to do good works. This was the issue with the Pharisees of Jesus' day: it was all about knowing the law of God and interpreting it, but they never applied it to their lives. In fact, Jesus said to them in John 5:39-40, "You search the scriptures because you think that in them you have eternal life; and it is these that witness of me, and you are unwilling to come to me, that you may have life."

James twice uses the word show, signifying the fact that the only way true faith is authenticated is by works. James says **show me your faith apart from your works**, in other words, faith without works is impossible because faith is only known through works. Faith is not divided separately between works and faith, but rather they are inseparably linked together. James asks the reader here to show them faith without works because he knows that it is impossible to do. Anybody could claim that he believes in God and yet have a wicked and evil heart and still be able to affirm verbally that he loves God. That is as far as it goes with just a verbal affirmation that produces no evidence of faith being true although they can deceive themselves into thinking they do have faith. It is for this reason that James says **I will show you my faith by my works** because works are the only way to evidence the authentication of faith.[6] Good works cannot save you; one does good

---

[6] Thomas D. Leas writes, "We have no room for some people to emphasize faith while others stress deeds. You must have both. Genuine commitment to Jesus Christ demonstrates its presence by deeds. Faith produces works. You can't have one without the other." (Lea 1999, p. 287)

works because it is an evident demonstration of who he is, a truly born-again Christian, with a genuine faith.

You believe that God is one. You do well; the demons also believe, and shudder. (2:19)

James here exposes the reality that having no works is, in fact, a pseudo-faith. James is going to compare the so-called believer, who allegedly has faith as he is without works to nothing more than the faith of a demon. This would have been a strike at the heart of those, who would have been reading his letter, comparing their faith without works to that of a demon. James says **you believe that God is one.** James then tells these believers if they believe that God is one, then the **do well.** However, James is going to make it clear that just merely to believe that God is one is not enough if good works do not accompany it because **demons also believe and shudder**.

Demons are Satan's fallen angels who serve as his agents against humanity to seduce, tempt, and destroy mankind. James tells his audience how the demons are just like them concerning their belief in God in the fact that the demons just like them, believe that God is one. Every Jew in the days of James would have had the word of Moses as recorded in Deuteronomy 6:4-5 embedded in their hearts. This passage was referred to as the Grand Shema and would have been quoted on a daily basis through prayer and petitions by all Jews living in the days of James. It reads in Deuteronomy 6:4-6 "Hear, O Israel! Jehovah, our God, is one Jehovah! You shall love Jehovah your God with all your heart, with all your soul, and with all your might. These words, which I am commanding you today, shall be on your heart." This was perhaps the essence of all the spiritual life of every Jew to love God, who had chosen them as his people. He was to be praised and honored in this way because he was the one and only true God, the Creator of heaven and earth and all humanity.

James states that the demons also believe that God is one and is no different from any believer that claims the same thing. However, what the demons lack is actionable evidence that there is something beyond their belief, i.e. a genuine faith. We know from several other parts of scriptures that the demons know and believe in God. In fact, they knew that Jesus Christ himself was the Son of the highest God. The demons clearly evidence their understanding of who Jesus is in the Gospels. – Mark 5:6-7; Mark 1:23-24; Luke 4:40-41.

It is interesting to note that here in his passage James uses the word shudder, which is the only time that this word is used in the entire New Testament. James is making it clear that not only do the demons believe in God, but also it causes a great disturbance and fear among them because they know his power and authority that he has over them. The problem with the demons is that their belief in God consists of just an awareness of his existence and his great power, never drawing close to him. They shudder out of fear because of the authority that they know God has over them, but that is as far as it goes for them. Even though they know God's great power, they continue to serve Satan.

But do you want to know, O foolish man, that faith without works is useless? (2:20)

The man spoken of here in verse 20 of chapter 2 applies to any Christian, male or female. This man has not taken in "the knowledge of God" by way of his Word. (Jam. 1:18, 21) Both his mind and heart are empty because no genuine faith exists there. The demons even fared better than this man did because the "faith" or belief that they possess at least generated the emotion of fear, which caused them to shudder, tremble uncontrollably at the thought of God's great power and authority. However, those demons and Christians such as this man, lack genuine faith that would move them toward salvation, it was categorically having no action, i.e., unproductive.

James 2:21-26 Updated American Standard Version (UASV)

21 Was not Abraham our father justified[7] by works when he offered up Isaac his son on the altar? **22** You see that faith was working together with his works, and by the works the faith was perfected;[8] **23** and the Scripture was fulfilled that says, "Abraham believed God, and it was counted to him as righteousness,"[9] and he was called a friend of God. **24** You see that a man is justified by works and not by faith alone. **25** And in the same way was not also Rahab the prostitute justified by works when she received the messengers and sent them out by another way?

---

[7] "Verse 21 concludes that Abraham showed his righteousness by his willingness to offer Isaac on the altar. KJV translates "justified" instead of niv's **considered righteous.** Paul uses the same Greek word in Romans 3:28; 4:2, 5; and 5:1 ("justified") to describe the righteousness God credits to a believer through faith in Jesus Christ. James uses the word to describe the righteousness we show to others as we obey Jesus." (Lea 1999, p. 289)

[8] Or *completed*

[9] Quoted from Gen. 15:6

26 For as the body apart from the spirit[10] is dead, so also faith apart from works is dead.

Was not Abraham our father (2:21a)

James here now does something very significant to argue his point about faith and works by stating **was not Abraham, our father**. James makes his argument from the Old Testament scriptures using Abraham, who the Jews considered the father of their nation and perhaps the most respected man in all Old Testament history. The Jews took pride in their ancestry and could trace their lineage back to Abraham as the Father of the Jewish nation, which is why James says "Abraham, our father." The Jewish nation of Israel was God's chosen people, and that nation stemmed from the seed of Abraham, which God promised would happen.

The Jews highly esteemed their ethnicity and the father of their nation because they were God's chosen that came through the lineage of Abraham. For this reason, the Jews looked at Abraham as the most prominent figure in their history, since he was the father of their nation. It is because of this that James would select Abraham to make his point that faith and works must exist together for it to be true saving faith. James purposely used one of the most significant men in Jewish history to make his point. This way, the Jewish audience he was writing to would be more apt to listen and take heed to what he was saying.

justified by works when he offered up Isaac his son on the altar? (2:21b)

Here James says that Abraham our father was **justified by works**. However, Paul wrote, "For by works of the law no human being will be justified." (Rom 3:20) How is it that these two were not contradicting one another? In Romans 4:2-3 Paul writes, "For if Abraham was justified by works, he has something to boast about, but not before God. For what does the Scripture say? 'Abraham believed God, and it was counted to him as righteousness.'" Paul is here quoting that same exact verse from Genesis 15:6 that James refers to in verse 23 of chapter 2. This verse that both are using was about Abraham's faith some 35 years before he ever attempted to offer up his son Isaac. This is the same event that James is referring to here in verse 21 of chapter 22. Thus, how are these two inspired New Testament authors in harmony?

---

[10] Or *breath*

If we look at the context of Genesis 15:1-6, we find that Abraham was declared righteous because of his trust in God's promise to make his offspring number like the stars of the heaven, even though Sarah was decades past being able to have a child. Therefore, how is it that James can say that Abraham was justified by works? Abraham's actions confirmed what God already knew was true of him. By Abraham's action, he proved, confirmed, demonstrated, beyond question that his faith in God for decades had been and was still real, i.e. genuine. Abraham evidenced that he had a living faith, not a dead one. It was not Abraham's works in and of themselves that made Abraham righteous, but rather his works were a result of his genuine faith, which God confirmed by declaring him righteous by way of this pronouncement or verdict.[11]

You see that faith was working together with his works, and by the works the faith was perfected; (2:22)

James is calling his believers attention to Abraham's faith stating **you see that faith was working together with his works.** Abraham's faith was authenticated not because he believed intellectually but was authenticated in the fact that he was willing to follow through with the act of sacrificing his son. It for this reason that James says **by the works the faith was perfected**. God told Abraham to sacrifice his son, and yet it was the very son, which God promised would bring him his descendants. Therefore, if Abraham was to offer up his son then how could he bring about descendants if he was dead?

Abraham would not have been sure how this would happen either, but he truly trusted God enough to follow through with the act of killing his son. Abraham believed that God would somehow allow descendants to come despite whether or not he sacrificed his son, and he was willing to trust God at all costs. Abraham's act of attempting to offer up his son authenticated his faith in God, which was evidenced by his actions of obedience. The word for perfection means complete or finished.

---

[11] Was God tempting or testing Abraham? Andrews writes, "God does **not** tempt us, but he does allow us to go through temptations. As we know from Abraham, God can test us, but never tempt us with sin ... The Greek word (*Peirazo*) can be rendered either as 'tempted' or 'tested,' and it is the context that determines which word should be chosen. In the case of Satan with Jesus in the wilderness, it should be rendered 'tempt.' However, in reference to God, in some very limited cases in history, he has put some to the test, i.e., Abraham, even his Son."–Hebrews 2:18.

16

Abraham's faith was complete in the fact that works, which made his trust in God complete by his actions of obedience, accompanied his faith.[12]

and the scripture was fulfilled that says, "Abraham believed God, and it was counted to him as righteousness," and he was called a friend of God. You see that a man is justified by works and not by faith alone. (2:23-24)

James says, **and the scripture was fulfilled that says Abraham believed God and it was counted to him as righteousness.** Here James is referring to Genesis 15:6 about Abraham. In Genesis 15:4, God had told Abraham that he would provide an heir and many descendants from his seed. Then in Genesis 15:5, to confirm his promise, God asked Abraham to go out and count the stars. In the same way, the stars were too numerous to count so would Abraham's descendants be through the promised child. Despite being old and against all odds, it says in Genesis 15:6, "Then he believed in the Lord, and He reckoned it to him as righteousness." Abraham had not seen his son and the child was not even conceived in the womb at this point. However, Abraham still believed God would carry out his promises. Since Abraham believed, what God said was firm and trustworthy, he was willing to kill his son, and as a result, be declared righteous in God's sight. The word righteousness here, as stated before, carries with it the idea of being right, moral, and just.

Abraham not only believed in God but was also willing to put that into practice by killing his son; he was declared right in God's sight. God declared him right in the fact that Abraham acted upon his faith through his actions. As a result, he was also called **a friend of God**, which is the only time in the Bible where someone is called a friend of God. Abraham was first called a friend of God in Jehoshaphat's prayer in 2 Chronicles 20:7, "Did you not, O our God, drive out the inhabitants of this land before thy people Israel and give it to the descendants of Abraham thy friend forever?" Isaiah also makes mention of Abraham as a friend of God in Isaiah 41:8, "But you Israel, My servant, Jacob whom I have chosen, descendant of Abraham my friend."

---

[12] An analogous situation might be a wealthy father testing his daughter's fiancé. The father offers the fiancé $50,000 to leave his daughter. This test will tell the father whether the poor fiancé is in love with his daughter, or after the father's money. Keep in mind, God never intended for Abraham to offer his son up, as he foreknew what Abraham would do in such a situation decades before even. Let us adapt apologist William Lane Craig's words to this situation. 'God had morally sufficient reasons for permitting the test, which he placed on Abraham.'

Abraham's belief and actions were working together in a real, genuine faith and Abraham became a friend of God. James reaffirms the argument that he has been making by saying you see. James wants his readers to have a focused view of what he has been talking about in regards to faith and action. He has just offered Abraham as his example that faith is justified when accompanied by works. As a result, these Jews would have a hard time arguing against their forefather. Faith and works must go together, they are inseparably linked, and we cannot have one without the other. For this reason, as James says **a man is justified by works and not by faith alone**.

And in the same way was not also Rahab the prostitute justified by works when she received the messengers and sent them out by another way? (2:25)

In the same manner that Abraham's faith was evidenced by his actions, **was not also Rahab the prostitute justified by works**. The story of Rahab is found in the Old Testament book of Joshua chapter 2, shortly after Moses died, and Joshua took over in leading the nation of Israel. It would be Joshua, who would guide the nation of Israel into the promised land of Canaan. However, to get there many obstacles would be in their way and that through the power of God they would have to overcome. One of these major obstacles would be conquering the city of Jericho.

The problem is that Jericho had very thick and high walls that surrounded their city, and it was nearly impossible to penetrate. Joshua summoned two men who were to go and spy out the city and come to report to Joshua what they had seen and learned. When the spies got into the city, they went to the home of a prostitute whose name was Rahab. The king of the town somehow caught wind that the spies had come into town and were at Rahab's home, and he sent to have them killed. Rahab knew that the king wanted to kill the spies and so decided to hide them on the roof of her home under stalks of flax. The king's officials arrived at the house, but Rahab told them that the spies had already left. The king's officials went off trying to find the direction of the men to kill them.

When the king's officials had left, Rahab asked a favor of the spies found in Joshua 2:8-14, "Now therefore, please swear to me by the Lord, since I have dealt kindly with you, that you also will deal kindly with my father's household, and give me a pledge of truth, and spare my father and my mother and my brothers and my sisters, with all who belong to them, and deliver our lives from death." Therefore, the men said to her, "Our life for yours if you do not tell this business of ours; and it shall

18

come about when the Lord gives us the land that we will deal kindly and faithfully with you."

The spies told Rahab that they would indeed spare her life if she tied a scarlet cord in her window. The scarlet cord was what Rahab used to let the spies down out of the city to spare their lives. Rahab could have just told the spies to get out of her house and never have let them in. Because she feared God and believed in the God of the spies, she took the risk of letting the men stay in her home. Rahab's belief in God was authenticated in that **she received the messengers and sent them out by another way**. It would be a direct result of the action of Rahab saving the spies that would help in giving Joshua the victory over the city of Jericho.

For the body apart from the spirit is dead, so also faith apart from works is dead. (2:26)

When a person (a soul) dies (beyond clinical death), there is no longer any animating force or "spirit" within any single cell out of the body's one hundred trillion cells. Many of us have seen the animation video in science classes at school, where the cell is shown to be like a microscopic factory with an enormous amount of work taking place. Therefore, no work is taking place within the lifeless body, as all of the cells that were animated by the spirit are dead. The body is not good for anything. This is the similarity that James is trying to draw as a faith that lacks works is just as lifeless, producing no results and of no use as a corpse. The literal eye cannot see faith; however, works is an evident demonstration that faith can be seen. When one has is not moved to good works, it is all too clear that this one has no real faith. Alternatively, any Christian that is motivated to good works possesses a genuine faith.

Review Question

- **[vs 14]** Do the faith/works that Paul was talking about contradict the faith/works that James discusses? How did Jesus touch on faith and works?

- **[vs 15-16]** What point is James making here in verses 15-16?

- **[vs 17]** Why is faith if it has no works, dead in itself?

- **[vs 18]** How can we know that a person has genuine faith?

- **[vs 19]** Why do the demons believe and shudder over belief in God and how should that impact us?

- **[vs 20]** Why are we foolish if we **do not** believe that faith without works is useless?

- **[vs 21]** What does Paul say about Abraham being declared righteous?

- **[vs 22]** How was faith working together with Abraham's works? How did the works of Abraham perfect his faith?

- **[vs 23]** How do we know that Abraham had faith in God all along? How did Abraham become God's friend?

- **[vs 24]** Why is it that a man is justified by works and not by faith alone?

- **[vs 25]** How does the account about Rahab add to the conversation of faith and works?

- **[vs 26]** Why is a dead body a good analogy of faith without works? How do the works of Christians evidence that they have a genuine faith?

CHAPTER 2 You Keep His Commandments

1 John 5:3 Updated American Standard Version (UASV)

³ For this is the love of God, that we keep his commandments. And his commandments are not burdensome.

When we look at the world around us today, what we find is a conflicting message. Dictators, who abuse their people in a socialistic setting, run much of the third world. However, if any of these ones escape that environment and make it to the United States, they start voting for politicians that believe in a bigger government with greater authority in a socialistic setting. The European countries are almost all liberal-progressive and quasi-socialist in nature. Moreover, virtually all of them have a cradle to grave handout system by the government and are on the verge of an economic crash. Nevertheless, when election time comes around, the people in these countries tend to elect another Democratic liberal-progressive candidate because they have become so used to the mentality of the handouts. What do all of these people have in common? The liberal-progressive desires of a bigger government that controls every human facet of life is actually at odds with the same individuals, who truly want absolute freedom, with not authority telling them what they can and cannot do.

No one today wants anyone to have the right to tell them how they out to behave. Teenagers are rebelling against their parents. Society is rebelling against the government and law enforcement. Employees are rebelling again big business. No one wants to submit to the will of another. Nevertheless, most in this world are "conformed to this world" by the government that they are under. (Rom. 12:2, ESV) Moreover, instead of independence, "they themselves are slaves of corruption," i.e., they are slaves to their sinful tendencies, namely, their fleshly desires. (2 Pet. 2:19, ESV) This world is "following the prince of the power of the air, the spirit that is now at work in the sons of disobedience, among whom we [Christians] all once lived in the passions of our flesh, carrying out the desires of the body and the mind, and were by nature children of wrath, like the rest of mankind." – Ephesians 2:2-3, ESV.

Christian View of Authority

Our view of authority, as Christians, is different from those who walk blindly in this world. Christian children follow the authority of their parents and school. Christian adults follow the authority of their spouse, their employers, and the government under which they live. Paul says, "Children, obey your parents in the Lord, for this is right." (Eph. 6:1-3, ESV) He also wrote, "Wives, submit to your own husbands, as to the Lord. For the husband is the head of the wife even as Christ is the head of the church, his body, and is himself its Savior." (Eph. 5:22-23, ESV) Paul also tells every Christian, "Let every person be subject to the governing authorities. For there is no authority except from God, and those that exist have been instituted by God." (Rom 13:1, ESV) However, the question begs to be asked, "Are Christians to just blindly do whatever they are asked by their government, workplace or spouse?" No, Christians can ignore any authority if it is at odds with the Word of God. In the first-century, the Jewish religious leaders had commanded the Christians to sop witnessing about Jesus. However, this was against Jesus command to proclaim the good news, to teach, and make disciples. (Matt. 24:14; 28:19-20; Ac 1:8) Peter and John took the position that is the balancing principle for all Christians, even today, "We must obey God rather than men." – Acts 5:27-29

At present, while this book is being penned, the United States has legalized marriage between the same sex, i.e., man marrying man and woman marrying woman. This is in conflict with God's Word that clearly states homosexual relationships are a gross sin and contrary to nature. (Lev. 18:22; Rom 1:24-27' 1 Cor. 6:9; Jude 1:7) This United Sates ruling by the Supreme Court is placing Christians in the position of having to obey God or obey man. For example, some Christians who own bakeries have refused to make wedding cakes for homosexual weddings. They have not refused homosexuals from coming into their store and purchasing baked good, but they feel that to make a cake for a homosexual wedding is participating in that wedding, which would be contrary to Scripture. Paul warned Timothy against 'sharing in the sins of others.' (1 Tim. 5:22, HCSB)

The world as we speak is quickly moving away from any sort of good moral values. Nevertheless, while we want to be courageous in the face of persecution, this does not give us the right to be stubborn because we have an unreasonable spirit. There is the other case, where a city official was jailed for refusing to give out a marriage license to homosexual couples. She had taken a job that is subject to change with the world because government by nature is of the world. If the government refuses to make exceptions for a Christian official, the only recourse for the Christian is to find another line of employment.

It is not our Christian obligation to repair Satan's World. If it is possible to win a legal case, overturning a law that infringes on the rights of Christians, this is perfectly fine. Many cases have been won in the United States Supreme Court that have granted Christians more freedom or have removed restrictions that were there. However, if we cannot obey a law, we must not involve ourselves in that line of work. As wise Solomon said, there is "a time to be silent and a time to speak." (Eccl 3:7, NASB) The principle is that we accept God's authority over any human. We do so, even in a "Christian" household, if a husband asks his wife to do anything that violates Scripture, she can refuse. The same would be true of parents that may ask Christian children to violate Scripture. Again, 'we obey God rather than man,' any man.

The United States of America is Not God's Kingdom

The United States has served Americans and the rest of the world well and will likely do so right up into the Great Tribulation. However, conservative Christians need to take note of the fact that at present, we are the majority and prayer without an evident demonstration of our faith in that prayer is not going to halt the socialist direction that the United States is heading. In other words, Paul encourages,

1 Timothy 2:1-2 Updated Standard Version (UASV)

[1] First of all, then, I urge that entreaties and prayers, petitions and thanksgivings, be made on behalf of all men, [2] for kings and all who are in high positions, that we may lead a peaceful and quiet life, godly and dignified in every way.

We pray for our government leaders to make decisions that will allow us to "lead a peaceful and quiet life, godly and dignified in every way." However, prayer is not enough. We must act on our prayers by voting for the lesser of the two evils, which we did not do in McCain versus Obama in 2008 or in Romney Versus Obama in 2012. The United States is greatly weakened after eight years of a quasi-socialist president, not because the Democrats, liberal, and atheists are now the majority, but rather because many conservatives sat at home, because their choice in a candidate was not selected to run against Obama. Remember, it is Christ and his Kingdom that we seek, but we can hold a measure of stability longer if we are united against the liberal, progressive, socialist movement of this world.

Godlessness in the Last Days Means the Kingdom is Closer

John 18:36 Updated Standard Version (UASV)

36 Jesus answered, "my kingdom is not of this world. If my kingdom were of this world, then my servants would be fighting so that I would not be handed over to the Jews; but as it is, my kingdom is not of this world."

2 Timothy 3:1-7 Updated American Standard Version (ASV)

1 But realize this, that in the last days difficult times will come. **2** For men will be lovers of themselves, lovers of money, boastful, arrogant, revilers, disobedient to parents, ungrateful, unholy, **3** unloving, irreconcilable, malicious gossips, without self-control, brutal, not loving good, **4** treacherous, reckless, conceited, lovers of pleasure rather than lovers of God, **5** having the appearance of godliness, but denying its power; avoid such men as these. **6** For among them are those who enter into households and captivate weak women weighed down with sins, led on by various desires, **7** always learning and yet never able to come to an accurate knowledge[13] of truth.

The balanced biblical view of authority is that we pray and take what actions are possible within whatever authority we as Christians are under while awaiting Christ's kingdom. If we can vote for a conservative candidate that make not be perfect (because who is), we still vote for him or her as opposed to a liberal progressive vote. If a conservative sits at home, it is a vote for the liberal progressive. Even so, if one is sitting at home because their Christian conscience tells them not to involve themselves in politics, this is different and acceptable.

We as Christians use whatever legal system is available to win cases that will allow us to "lead a peaceful and quiet life [while we await Christ's second coming], godly and dignified in every way." We as Christians also use whatever branch of government that is that is available to legislate a bill into a law so that we may "lead a peaceful and quiet life [while we await Christ's second coming], godly and dignified in every way." However, we are no so focused on changing Satan's world, which is due to be removed [i.e., wicked people that is], forgetting that Jesus

---

[13] *Epignosis* is a strengthened or intensified form of *gnosis* (*epi*, meaning "additional"), meaning, "true," "real," "full," "complete" or "accurate," depending upon the context. Paul and Peter alone use *epignosis*.

gave us but one great commission. He commanded that we proclaim the good news of the kingdom in all the inhabited earth, teaching biblical truths, to make disciples until his return. The overall principle again is, we obey God as ruler rather than man, meaning that if man asks us to do anything that conflict with God's Word, then we obey God. We give Caesar's things to Caesar and we give God's things to God. However, if Caesar starts asking for what belongs to God, we are not to make any concessions in any way. – Matthew 22:20-22.

We as Christians have accepted God's authority as our supreme authority. We apply the words as stated at Proverbs 3:5-6, "Trust in Jehovah with all your heart, and do not lean on your own understanding. In all your ways acknowledge him, and he will make straight your paths." We know that if we follow God's Word to the best of our ability, generally speaking, things will work out for our good.[14]

Deuteronomy 10:12 Updated Standard Version (UASV)

[12] "And now, O Israel, what does Jehovah your God require from you, but to fear Jehovah your God, to walk in all his ways and love him, and to serve Jehovah your God with all your heart and with all your soul, [13] and to keep Jehovah's commandments and his statutes which I am commanding you today for your good?

Isaiah 48:17-18 Updated American Standard Version (UASV)

[17] Thus says Jehovah,
    your Redeemer, the Holy One of Israel:
"I am Jehovah your God,
    who teaches you to profit,
    who leads you in the way you should go.
[18] Oh that you had paid attention to my commandments!
    Then your peace would have been like a river,
    and your righteousness like the waves of the sea;

Scripture is quite clear that while we know Christians are not immune from the effects of living in imperfection within Satan's world, it is always in our best interests to obey the Word of God. The pint that follows is very important. As long as we have a correct understanding of what the Bible says on a matter, we must obey, even if, at present, we do

---

[14] We say "generally speaking" because bad things happen to good people in an imperfect world run by Satan.

not understand the reasons as to why. This is not gullibility or naiveté; it is trusting in the one and only True God.

Discernment Trained

Returning to the book of Hebrews, we are told that we need to have our "discernment trained to distinguish between good and evil." (Heb. 5:14) Therefore, we are not to obey God's laws, rules and principles simply because they are there without being a human being with thoughts and feelings. In order to be able to 'discern between right and wrong,' we have to think, so Got does not want us to be some automaton robot that just follows his laws because he says so. We want to understand and appreciate the wisdom behind what God says. If acquire the mind of Christ, we will be able to say, "I delight to do your will, O my God; your law is within my heart." – Psalm 40:8, ESV.

If we are going to be like the Psalmist, to have the mind of Christ, who said, "I have come down from heaven, not to do my own will but the will of him who sent me" (John 6:38), we will need to ponder on what the Bible authors meant by what they wrote. We might ask ourselves, "How do I apply this verse of 'do not get drunk with wine' (Eph. 5:18, NASB), with say beer as Paul did not mention beer?" "Why is law or that principle to be applied in different circumstances?" On the other hand, "in what all circumstances does it apply?" "Why is it best for me to obey God's Word?" "If I obey God's Word will everything always work out for me?" If our Christian mind and heart are in harmony with the mind of Christ, we will then make decisions based on a biblical worldview. Right before the above verse on wine, Paul wrote, "So then do not be foolish, but **understand what the will of the Lord is**." (Eph. 5:17, NASB) Let us revisit "give back to Caesar what is Caesar's," which is not always easy to determine.

We just spoke of the Kentucky County clerk, who was refusing to hand out marriage licenses to same-sex couples. The liberal media was trying to use the Bible to evidence that the Christian clerk had no choice but to obey the Supreme Court ruling. They quoted Matthew 22:21, "give back to Caesar what is Caesar's." Well, this verse does not even apply to these circumstances. First, the liberal commentators leave out the second half of the verse. It reads, "and to God what is God's." The question was raised before, what if Caesar (governmental authorities) asks for something that belongs to God? We do not give what belongs to God to Caesar. We reiterated this issue to make our point about having a correct understanding of the Bible. The *Critical and Exegetical Hand-Book to the Gospel of Matthew*, by Heinrich Meyer, explains: "By [Caesar's things] … we are not to understand merely the *civil tax*, but everything to which Caesar was entitled in virtue of his legitimate rule." Yes, everything we are to give Caesar everything he is entitled to, but not what God is entitled to from us, such as obedience.

Satan Attempts to Undermine God's Authority

From the time of the Garden of Eden, Satan has sought to undermine God's authority and sovereignty (right to rule). He chose to be independent of God's authority in his rebellion, which independence, a lack of respect for authority has been the way of humanity after Adam, and Eve joined him. It used to be that marriage was a divine institution. Now, we have couples that just choose to live together. Moreover, the United States one of the last conservative Judeo-Christian countries had their Supreme Court alter the definition of marriage from a man and a woman, to include same-sex couples. In addition, the divorce rate, even among Christians is over fifty percent. While this serves as just one example, we should ask, "Do I respect God's authority to establish marriage to be between man and woman, for live and to hate a divorcing as much as he?" "Have I allowed the world around me to affect my thinking toward marriage?"

Many young ones in the Christian Church are falling away from the faith because Satan has singled them out as a special group. Satan does this by undermining God's authority. The apostle Paul warns young ones to "flee youthful passions and pursue righteousness, faith, love, and peace, along with those who call on the Lord from a pure heart." (2 Tim. 2:22) It is Satan's world, which caters to the youthful passions, and the peer pressure of worldly children, which lead young ones to see God's Word as oppressive. They need to understand fully and appreciate the wisdom behind God's Word. We are all told to "flee from sexual immorality" (1 Cor. 6:18), but this counsel is especially poignant to the young one's today. In the 1980s, it was common to find a teenage boy and girl kissing under the bleachers at a basketball or football game. We now live in a world where teenagers culturally believe that oral sex is the same as kissing. What a stark contrast in just in thirty-five years!

There are "3 in 10 teen American girls will get pregnant at least once before age 20. That is nearly 750,000 teen pregnancies every year. Parenthood is the leading reason that teen girls drop out of school. More than 50% of teen mothers never graduate from high school. About 25% of teen moms have a 2nd child within 24 months of their first baby. Less than 2% of teen moms earn a college degree by age 30. The United States has one of the highest teen pregnancy rates in the western industrialized world."[15] Young ones ask yourselves, 'Why is the command to flee from sexual immorality wise?' 'If you obey the command, how will it benefit you?' Certainly, young ones, you see pregnant teens walking around your schools, you see that they eventually drop out. This author is aware of numerous cases where there is an eighteen-year-old with three children. While the children are precious, the young girl, a child herself, is ignoring God's Word and has paid the price. Certainly, it is best to accept God's authority as the Creator of humanity, who knows what is best for his creation.

Avoid an Independent Spirit

In our world, that values an independent spirit above all else, we must be on guard to not adopt the same attitude, as accepting God's authority will be called into question. If we begin to think of ourselves more than we ought to, it can becomes self-assurance, i.e., believing that your views and abilities are of greater value than say our spouse, our school, our parents, our employer, the government, or even our Creator. After Jesus had spoken of figuratively feeding on his flesh and drinking his blood (spiritual sense),[16] many of his disciples turned back and no longer walked with him. Therefore, Jesus said to the twelve apostles, "Do you want to go away as well?" Simon Peter answered him, "Lord, to whom shall we go? You have the words of eternal life." – John 6:52-68.

If we are accepting God's authority, it means that we will be taught by it, we will be reproved by it from time to time, corrected by it, trained in righteousness by it, so that we may be complete, being equipped for every good work. (2 Tim. 3:16-17) In these last days, we will also follow Paul's counsel, "let us not sleep, as others do, but let us keep awake and be sober." (1 Thess. 5:6) Who are **the others**, who are **sleeping**? It could be a reference to the unbelievers in the world, who are sleeping through

---

[15] 11 Facts About Teen Pregnancy - Do Something,

https://www.dosomething.org/facts/11-facts-about-teen-pregnancy (accessed September 21, 2015).

[16] Jesus was talking about the cross—the spiritual act whereby we accept his death on our behalf in order to gain access to his offer of eternal life. In the spiritual sense, that is the real food and the real drink. (Gangel 2000, p. 129)

this important time because the Word of God is mere foolishness to them. However, it may also apply to Christians who is uninterested. "Falling asleep is a picture of what can happen to us spiritually, ethically, or morally if we are not watchful. We simply drift off. Drowsiness begins, we become comfortable, our hearts become insensitive. Spiritual drowsiness slowly paralyzes the spirit. The person who was once vibrant and wide awake in following Christ can become lethargic and lazy about issues of the spirit." We, on the other hand, "are to be alert and self-controlled. To be alert is the opposite of being asleep. An alert person is aware, sensitive to life around him, and morally and spiritually awake." (Larson 2000, p. 70)

1 John 2:15-17 Updated American Standard Version (UASV)

¹⁵ Do not love the world or the things in the world. If anyone loves the world, the love of the Father is not in him. ¹⁶ For all that is in the world, the lust of the flesh and the lust of the eyes and the boastful pride of life, is not from the Father, but is from the world. ¹⁷ The world is passing away, and its lusts; but the one who does the will of God remains forever.

Humility is Important

Humility will help us to appreciate always that Jesus "is the head of the body, the church." (Col. 1:18) Humility will also help us to accept the direction and guidance from those taking the lead n our church. Paul wrote, "we ask you, brothers, to respect those who labor among you and are over you in the Lord and admonish you, and to esteem them very highly in love because of their work. Be at peace among yourselves." (1 Thess. 5:12-13, ESV) However, the leaders can evidence their humility as well, accepting that it is Christ's congregation not theirs, that they may learn from Paul and first-century leaders "not to go beyond what is written" in the Word of God. – 1 Corinthians 4:6.

Yes, it is not "glorious to seek one's own glory." (Pro. 25:27) The apostle John had to deal with a serious case of one who suffered from this pitfall. He wrote, "I have written something to the church, but Diotrephes, who likes to put himself first, does not acknowledge our authority. So if I come, I will bring up what he is doing, talking wicked nonsense against us. And not content with that, he refuses to welcome the brothers, and also stops those who want to and puts them out of the church." (3 John 9-10, ESV) While progressing spiritually is exactly what all of us need to be reaching for, selfish ambition is something entirely different. Ambition is having a strong desire to be successful in life, always seeking an angle to get ahead of others. Solomon wrote, "When pride comes, then comes disgrace, but with the humble is wisdom. (Pro. 11:12, ESV) He also wrote, "Pride goes before destruction, and a haughty spirit before a fall." (Pro. 16:18, ESV) We never want to take our relationship with God for granted. In every aspect of our lives, we must reject the independent spirit of this world and accept God's authority.

Review Questions

* What all is involved in accepting God's authority?

How is the Christian view of authority different from those living in Satan's World?

What evidence is there that the Kingdom of God is closer?

• How is training our discernment connected to accepting God's authority?

• How is Satan trying to undermine God's authority?

• Why is humility Connected to our accepting God's authority?

CHAPTER 3 You Must Love One Another

John 13:34-35 Updated American Standard Version (UASV)

³⁴ A new commandment I give to you, that you love one another, even as I have loved you, that you also love one another. ³⁵ By this all men will know that you are my disciples, if you have love for one another."

Sharing the good news of the Kingdom is something that Christians have been doing since Pentecost 33 C.E. Many millions of Christians have been persecuted, even martyred for sharing the hope that dwells in them. Nevertheless, the identifying marker of being a true Christian in this chapter is what motivated these ones to share their faith. These ones loved God with all their heart, with all their soul, and with their entire mind. Yet, they also loved their neighbor as themselves. (Matt. 22:37-39) This is why Paul's words are so crucial for our walking with God. He wrote that we are to "walk in love, just as Christ also loved you¹⁷ and gave himself up for us, an offering, and a sacrifice as a sweet fragrance to God." – Ephesians 5:2.

The love evidenced in true Christianity cannot be equaled by any other religion. A magnet is a piece of metal that has the power to draw iron or steel objects toward it and to hold or move them. This is true of true Christianity as well, as its love is able to draw people toward it in sincere, unified, true worship, moving them to love another just as Christ has loved them. Christlike love is not to be confused with emotionalism. Emotionalism is an exaggerated or undue display of strong feelings. While being emotional is fine, this emotionalism or mental imbalance is of false Christianity and is an instance in which "Satan disguises himself as an angel of light" to deceive. (1 Cor. 13:8, 11; 2 Cor. 11:14, NASB) True love is,

1 Corinthians 13:4-7 Updated American Standard Version (UASV)

⁴ Love is long suffering and kind; Love is not jealous, it does not brag; it is not puffed up,¹⁸ ⁵ does not behave indecently;¹⁹ is not seeking its own interests, is not provoked, does not keep a record of wrong, ⁶ does not rejoice over unrighteousness, but rejoices with the truth; ⁷ bears all things, believes all things, hopes all things, endures all things.

---

¹⁷ One early ms reads *us*

¹⁸ I.e., self-important or made proud

¹⁹ Or *is not rude*

True Christian love is not temporary and should not be taken for granted. If we think of a group of Christians on a cold night, sitting around a warm campfire, the chill in the air draws them nearer the fire, bringing them comfort and warmth. What happens if those Christians do not continue to add fuel to the fire? It will go out, leaving them in the cold. The same is true of the Christian congregation and the bond of love shown there. It will go out unless there are true Christians adding fuel to the fire of love. Unlike false emotionalism, true love has strong emotion, especially righteous anger against Satan and his world, as well as having a strong zeal for truth and righteousness, evidenced in their love for God and neighbor. Paul told us to "**walk in love**, just as Christ also loved you." (Eph. 5:2) The question that begs to be asked is, "how can we **continuously walk in love** until the second coming of Christ?

Widen Our Hearts

The ancient Corinthian congregation received the second letter from Paul, which said, "We have spoken freely to you, Corinthians; our heart is wide open. You are not restricted by us, but you are restricted in your own affections. In return (I speak as to children) widen your hearts also." (2 Cor. 6:11-13) Why was Paul asking the Corinthians to 'widen their hearts'?

For the answer, we must go to the fall of 50 C.E., when the apostle Paul arrived in Corinth. Even though Paul had some difficulties with his preaching work in the beginning, he never gave up on the Corinthians. "He stayed a year and six months, teaching the word of God among them." Many would put faith in him. (Acts 18:5, 6, 9-11) The Christians in Corinth had many reasons for loving and respecting Paul. Nevertheless, some chose to abandon him because he was very direct in his counsel to them. (1 Cor. 5:1-5; 6:1-10) Then, there were those, who were known as the super-apostles, who was slandering Paul, which contributed to others leaving him as well. (2 Cor. 11:5-6) He had done nothing but bring the Corinthians love and kindness, hoping that his brothers and sisters would reciprocate. Therefore, he implored them 'widen their hearts' toward him and others.

How might we apply that same counsel today? How might we show brotherly and sisterly love toward others? Generally, whether, in the congregation or outside, there are human tendencies to draw closer to those like us, in say ethnic background or age. Then, there are those that have similar things in common, like recreation, who bond and spend more time together. Yes, we may stop and idly chitchat (i.e., small talk) for a few seconds before and after meetings but this is only superficial. However, these similarities are actually pulling us apart into what is known as clicks because we easily communicate or work together well. This is nothing wrong about us; like-minded people tend to gravitate toward one another. However, this is why we need to 'widen our hearts' toward others. Do we do anything entertainment wise with anyone outside of our social group? Are there certain ones at the congregation that I have failed to draw close to for more than a few seconds of conversation? Have we been to their house, or have they been to ours? Have we eaten out together before? Have we done anything fun together? Have we shared in any sort of ministry together? Do I honestly talk with the older ones, or if we are older, do I talk to the younger ones?

Paul exhorted us to "**welcome** one another as Christ has welcomed you, for the glory of God." (Rom. 15:7.) The Greek word (*proslambanesthe*) translated "welcome" means "to receive kindly or hospitably, admit to one's society and friendship."[20] (Acts 28:2; Rom. 14:1, 3; 15:7) In Bible times, hospitality was very important. When ones came into the home of another, the host went out of their way to welcome them and make them feel at home. Jesus has welcomes us similarly into his flock and we are to do the same for others.

When we are around fellow Christian, be it at a get-together or a meeting, we can make a special effort to speak with ones that we have not spoken with lately. We can go over and spend a few minutes catching up from the last time we spoke with them. If it is at a Christian meeting, this means coming early as opposed to the last minute and staying after instead of rushing out. Once we get to know all of our brothers and sisters, it will be easy to engage any of them in a conversation. Of course, there is no need to try to have conversations with everyone in one meeting. Select a new person each meeting to talk with for a few minutes before the meeting and choose a different person to speak with after the meeting.

Give of Ourselves to Others

We want anyone in the congregation to feel comfortable to approach us for conversation. Jesus was this way. Even little children felt

---

[20] προσλαμβάνω | Teknia, https://www.teknia.com/greek-dictionary/proslambano (accessed September 22, 2015).

comfortable around him. "And [people in the crowds] were bringing children to him that he might touch them, and the disciples rebuked them. But when Jesus saw it, he was indignant and said to them, 'Let the children come to me; do not hinder them, for to such belongs the kingdom of God. Truly, I say to you, whoever does not receive the kingdom of God like a child shall not enter it.' And he took them in his arms and blessed them, laying his hands on them." (Mark 10:13-16, ESV) We can only imagine the joy in the hearts of those children.

As a Christian, we must examine ourselves, asking, "Do I give of myself to others?" On the other hand, "Do I come off as always being busy"? "Am I always in my own little world?" "Am I always deep in conversation with my social group"? "Am I always using my cell phone?" While certain patterns of behavior might not be wrong in and of themselves, they may be a blockade to being approachable. Wise Solomon wrote there is "a time to be silent and a time to speak." (Eccl. 3:7) If ones see us always involved with certain ones, or with our face shoved in a cell phone, or sitting off in a corner researching something, they may feel that we do not like talking to others.

When we buy out the time to be upbuilding in conversation with others, we are contributing to their well-being and spirituality. There are many older ones in Christ, who have had a tremendous impact on the lives of thousands throughout the decades of their lives. However, if we ask them, they will say it is others when they were younger, who took time to speak with them. The words of encouragement can mean so much to a young mind and hearts, making them feel even more welcome in the house of God. We need to imitate this buying out the time for other.

Peace Makers Possess Humility

Euodia and Syntyche, two Christian sisters in ancient Philippi, clearly "differences had arisen between them on some subject, we know not what." "At Philippi the gospel was first preached to women (Ac 16:13), and the church was first formed among women—evidently in the house of Lydia (Ac 16:15, 40). Paul here makes a request of Euodia and Syntyche. He requests the word is never used of prayer from us to God, he asks, he beseeches. Euodia, and then he repeats the word, he beseeches Syntyche, to be of the same mind in the Lord. But whatever the subject in dispute was, it had become so serious that, instead of the breach being healed, matters had become chronic; and news regarding this lack of forbearance between Euodia and Syntyche had been carried to Paul in his captivity in Rome."[21]

Paul entreats them, as "the state of Christian life in the church at Philippi gave Paul almost unmingled satisfaction. He regarded with joy their faith and steadfastness and liberality. There was no false teaching, no division; among them. The only thing, which could cause him any uneasiness, was the want of harmony between Euodia and Syntyche. He beseeches them to give up their differences and to live at peace in the Lord. Such is the motive which he puts before them with a view to bringing about their reconciliation; to live in dispute and enmity is not worthy of those who are "in the Lord," who have been redeemed by the Lord, and whose whole life should be an endeavor to please Him."[22]

Paul asks "a certain person, unnamed, but whom he terms "true yokefellow" to assist them, that is, to assist Euodia and Syntyche; for each of them, he says, "labored with me in the gospel." It is uncertain what is meant by "true yokefellow." He may refer to Epaphroditus, who carried the epistle from Rome to Philippi. Other names have been suggested-- Luke, Silas, Timothy. It has been thought by some that Paul here refers to his own wife, or to Lydia. But such a suggestion is untenable, inasmuch as we know from his own words (1Co 7:8) that he was either unmarried or a widower. And the idea that the "true yokefellow" is Lydia, is equally wrong, because the word "true" is in the Greek masculine Another suggestion is that "yokefellow" is really a proper name—Syzygus. If so, then the apostle addresses Syzygus; or if this is not so, then he speaks to the unnamed "true yokefellow"; and what he says is that he asks him to help Euodia and Syntyche, inasmuch as their work in the gospel was no new thing. Far from this, when Paul brought the gospel to Philippi at the first, these two Christian women had been his loyal and earnest helpers in spreading the knowledge of Christ."[23]

It was truly "sad then that any difference should exist between them. How sad that it should last so long! He asks Clement also, and all the other Christians at Philippi, his fellow-laborers, whose names, though not mentioned by the apostle, are nevertheless in the book of life, to assist Euodia and Syntyche; he asks them all to aid in this work of

---

[21] Euodia - International Standard Bible Encyclopedia, http://www.biblestudytools.com/encyclopedias/isbe/euodia.html (accessed September 23, 2015).

[22] IBID

[23] IBID

reconciliation. Doubtless, he did not plead in vain."[24] What we learn from this brief account is that even true Christians, with impeccable records of accomplishment of working for Christ, are not immune to having differences, even disputes. Clearly, God makes available to us the help and determination to overcome any disputes and repair friendships. Yes, personal differences will arise, but they are overcome with humility. – James 4:10.

Esau was a Son of Isaac, twin brother of Jacob. "The young Esau was fond of the strenuous, daring life of the chase—he became a skillful hunter, 'a man of the field' ('ish sadheh). His father warmed toward him rather than toward Jacob because Esau's hunting expeditions resulted in meats that appealed to the old man's taste (Ge 25:28). Returning hungry from one of these expeditions, however, Esau exhibited a characteristic that marked him for the inferior position, which had been foretokened at the time of his birth. Enticed by the pottage which Jacob had boiled, he could not deny himself, but must, at once, gratify his appetite, though the calm and calculating Jacob should demand the birthright of the firstborn as the price (Ge 25:30-34). Impulsively he snatched an immediate and sensual gratification at the forfeit of a future glory. Thus he lost the headship of the people through whom God's redemptive purpose was to be wrought out in the world, no less than the mere secular advantage of the firstborn son's chief share in the father's temporal possessions. Though Esau had so recklessly disposed of his birthright, he afterward would have secured from Isaac the blessing that appertained, had not the cunning of Rebekah provided for Jacob. Jacob, to be sure, had some misgiving about the plan of his mother (Ge 27:12), but she reassured him; the deception was successful and he secured the blessing. Now, too late, Esau bitterly realized somewhat, at least, of his loss, though he blamed Jacob altogether, and himself not at all (Ge 27:34, 36). Hating his brother on account of the grievance thus held against him, he determined upon fratricide as soon as his father should pass away (Ge 27:41); but the watchful Rebekah sent Jacob to Haran, there to abide with her kindred till Esau's wrath should subside."[25] – Genesis 27:42-45.

Esau, who was about forty, "had taken two Hittite wives, and had thus displeased his parents. Rebekah had shrewdly used this fact to induce

---

[24] IBID

[25] Esau - International Standard Bible Encyclopedia,

http://www.internationalstandardbible.com/E/esau.html (accessed September 23, 2015).

Isaac to fall in with her plan to send Jacob to Mesopotamia; and Esau, seeing this, seems to have thought he might please both Isaac and Rebekah by a marriage of a sort different from those already contracted with Canaanitish women. Accordingly, he married a kinswoman in the person of a daughter of Ishmael (Ge 28:6, 9). Connected thus with the 'land of Seir,' and by the fitness of that land for one who was to live by the sword, Esau was dwelling there when Jacob returned from Mesopotamia. While Jacob dreaded meeting him, took great pains to [appease or pacify] him, and made careful preparations against a possible hostile meeting, very earnestly seeking Divine help, Esau, at the head of four hundred men, graciously received the brother against whom his anger had so hotly burned. Though Esau had thus cordially received Jacob, the latter was still doubtful about him, and, by a sort of duplicity, managed to become separated from him, Esau returning to Seir (Ge 33:12-17). Esau met his brother again at the death of their father, about twenty years later."[26] – Genesis 35:29.

In Jacobs meeting with Esau in Genesis chapter 33, it had been some twenty years sin the bitter dispute over the birthright, and all Jacob knew was that his brother wanted to kill him. Meeting after all that time, "Jacob was greatly afraid and distressed." He knew it was possible that Esau was going to assault him. Therefore, Jacob, the one who had the birthright, who, in essence was the head of the patriarchal family, he humbly bowed "to the ground seven times, until he came near to his brother." What happened next? "Esau ran to meet him and embraced him and fell on his neck and kissed him, and they wept." – Genesis 27:41; 32:3-8; 33:3-4.

The Bible contains outstanding guidance on overcoming conflicts. (Matt. 5:23, 24; 18:15-17; Eph. 4:26-27) If we cannot humble ourselves to the point of applying that guidance, making peace is highly unlikely. Many times it becomes a waiting game, both waiting for the other to humble themselves, when both hold the key (God's Word), to overcoming differences.

What are we to do if we take the initiative and humbly seek peace to only be rebuffed? Well, Jacob spent twenty years apart to allow Esau's rage to simmer. Certainly, no one is seeking to kill us and there is no need for twenty years, but time does heal wounds. Therefore, we should not give up, but rather, allow some time to pass, so the other can work through their feelings. In time, the heart can be repaired and our sincere

---

[26] IBID

interest in reconciling and restoring our friendship will be seen. If we do not have and make peace among ourselves in the fallen world, the Christian congregation will lose its unity and joy will be no more. – Colossians 3:12-14.

In Deed and Truth

1 John 3:18 Updated American Standard Version (UASV)

[18] Little children, let us not love with word or with tongue, but in deed and truth.

Nisan 14, 33 C.E., In Jerusalem, Just before Jesus' death, in an act of great humility, after the Passover feast had been eaten, Jesus washes the feet of his apostles. (Joh 13:1-20) At that point, Jesus said, "For I gave you an example that you also should do as I did to you." (John 13:15, NASB) This was no mere ritual and it was not some act of kindness. Consider the words of the apostle John, just before he tells of the feet washing account. He wrote, "Now before the Feast of the Passover, when Jesus knew that his hour had come to depart out of this world to the Father, having loved his own who were in the world, he loved them to the end." (John 13:1) Washing the apostles feet was a service that would have normally been carried out by a slave, which evidences his great love for his disciples. This act of humility was an example that they too must now follow, as they show love for one another throughout the first-century, setting up a Christian congregation that would be over a million just after John died in 100 C.E. In these last difficult days, we need to possess genuine brotherly love, which will move us to exhibit affection, compassion, and empathy for the whole of our Christian brothers and sisters.

While Peter did not initially appreciate what Jesus had done for him by washing his feet, he would later as he would grow to become one of the leading apostles. On this, he wrote, "Having purified your souls by your obedience to the truth for a sincere brotherly love, love one another earnestly from a pure heart." (1 Pet. 1:22, ESV) The apostle John, who has his feet washed as well, wrote, "Little children, let us not love with word or with tongue, but in deed and truth." (1 John 3:18) We need to develop such a heart condition that will move us to express our brother love in deed.

Review Questions

- How can we "widen our hearts" in brotherly and sisterly love?
- How can we give of ourselves to others?
- How does humility play an important role in making peace?
- Why should we care deeply for our fellow believers?

CHAPTER 4 You Must Pursue Peace With All Men

Hebrews 12:14 Updated American Standard Version (UASV)

¹⁴ Pursue peace with all men, and the sanctification without which no one will see the Lord.

If we think of the steps, leading up to a house wherein the wood is old, dry rotted and cracked after years of many seasons. It definitely needs to be restored or replaced to guarantee safety and to preserve the steps.

This is true of our relationships with others over many years, which can become dry rotted and cracked in these difficult times. The apostle Paul tells us in his letter to the congregation that they were dealing with ones who had different viewpoints. He wrote, "let us not pass judgment on one another any longer, but rather decide never to put a stumbling block or hindrance in the way of a brother." (Rom. 14:13, NASB) Thus, he counsels, "So then we pursue the things which make for peace and the building up of one another." (Rom. 14:19, NASB) So, then, why is it essential to "pursue the things which make for peace"? How are we do we effectively and fearlessly pursue peace?

Pursue Peace

If untreated, those decaying, dry rotted board can become weakened and dangerous. Imagine walking on them one day, when suddenly, we fall through and catching our side or stomach on a nail or sharp board, ripping through as we fall to the ground. If we leave personal difference to go on without being repair, it could very well cost us or another eternal life. The apostle John writes, "If someone says, 'I love God,' and hates his brother, he is a liar; for the one who does not love his brother whom he has seen, cannot love God whom he has not seen." (1 John 4:20, NASB) If a difference goes on long enough, it could cause fellow Christians to end up hating one another.

Jesus made it clear that if we have an unresolved issue with our Christian brothers and sisters, our worship is unacceptable. He said, "If you are presenting your offering at the altar, and there remember that your brother has something against you, leave your offering there before the altar and go; first be reconciled to your brother, and then come and present your offering." (Matt. 5:23-24) Even above the fact that it is right for us to pursue peace, to restore our relationships, it should be our love for God, which is our biggest motivator.

In the previous chapter, we learned of Euodia and Syntyche, who were there at the foundation of the Philippian congregation. They offer us the other major reason for pursuing peace. As we may recall there was an unspecified reason problem between these two Christian sisters. However, their problem became the congregations problem, because it was removing the peace within the congregation. (Phil. 4:2-3) When an unresolved difference between two members of the congregation becomes public, people begin to take sides. Thus, we work to pursue peace with fellow believers for the sake of the congregation and its unity.

Jesus said, "Blessed are the peacemakers, for they shall be called sons of God." (Matt. 5:9, NASB) When we restore peace where there was previously none, it brings us untold joy. "Peace is, first and foundationally, internal and spiritual. It is not primarily physical, military, or political. Peace for the nations flows from peace in the hearts of individuals. Peacemakers are not power brokers but people lovers. The promised kingdom is characterized by peace, as described in Isaiah 9:6–7; 66:12–13; Micah 4:3." (Weber 2000, p. 61) Moreover, peaceful relations make us healthier, as "a tranquil heart is life to the body." (Pro. 14:30) Alternatively, doctors have said that feeling of anger and resentment can lead to physical illnesses.

Remaining Calm

If we are restoring our relationship from some minor crack, like a weathered porch, we can simply sand it down and water stain it and then paint. For minor issues with our brothers and sister, we can simply cover over the grievance. On this, the apostle Peter wrote, "Above all, keep loving one another earnestly, since love covers a multitude of sins." – 1 Peter 4:8.

What if the problem is more serious, one that just cannot be dismissed? Let us look at a hyperbolic example from the history of the Israelite nation. Remember that there were twelve tribes of Israel and after conquering, the land of Canaan God was assigning each tribe their area of the Promised Land. The tribes of Reuben, Gad, and East Manasseh reached the western side of the Jordan River valley and built a huge altar there beside the river. When the rest of the Israelites heard what these tribes had done, they believe the altar had been set up for idolatrous worship. They could not just cover over this problem. The Israelite men met at Shiloh to get ready to attack the two and a half tribes. – Joshua 22:9-12.

After all the Israelites had been through over the last forty years while wondering in the wilderness, this may just be it for some, who felt is best to do a sneak attack. However, cooler heads prevailed, and some leaders decided it best to talk with their brothers first. They sent a priest, Phinehas the son of Eleazar, to speak with the two and a half tribes. Each of the tribes at Shiloh sent the leader of one of its families along with Phinehas. They asked, 'why you are unfaithful to our God. You have turned your backs on our God by building that altar. Why are you rebelling against him?' (Josh. 22:16) As it turned out, those who built the altar were not being unfaithful.

However, should they now be just as upset as the ones who had initially thought they were unfaithful? I mean, instead of asking what they were doing, these ones straight out **accused them of wrongdoing**: namely, idolatrous worship, turning their backs on God, rebelling, not carrying about the whole nation and that their actions could lead to many deaths. No, rather the tribes of Reuben, Gad, and East Manasseh that were being accused **replied mildly** to some serious accusations that were undoubtedly leveled in anger. They started that God was great and that they had asked him to be their witnesses at their reasons for building an altar. They explained that they did not build the altar to rebel and turn their backs on God. They did not even build it so we could offer animal or grain sacrifices on it. They built that altar because they were worried that someday their descendants might forget all that they had been through, and they wanted the altar to serve as a memorial, as a reminder.

Thus, the lesson here is not to presume the others actions or words had evil intentions, or that their heart condition or motivations were bad. It is best to investigate but not interrogatively, but rather in brotherly love. The other lesson is, when someone comes to us, we should not take it as an accusation even if the tone comes off as angry. We should respond in a mild voice and with loving concern for our Creator and our brothers (Josh. 22:13-34) On this, Wise King Solomon writes, "Do not be eager in your heart to be angry, For anger resides in the bosom of fools." (Eccl. 7:9, NASB) If we are going to follow the Bible's counsel, we must deal with personal differences through mild and honest discussion. Do we honestly believe that we have God on our side if we are boiling with anger, as we privately continue to keep in mind an emotion or thought that the other person has wronged us, so we refuse to approach?

Again, what if we are the one that our Christian brother or sister comes to us, accusing us of some wrongdoing, especially if we are not guilty? The Bible states, "A gentle answer turns away wrath, But a harsh word stirs up anger." (Pro. 15:1, NASB) We need to follow the example of the Israelite tribes, who mildly and in clear, concise words, explained what they were doing, which turned away wrath. If we are, the one approaching another we need to ponder what we might say and how may we say it, to pursue peace.

Taming the Tongue

God is well aware of our human weakness as the designer of our human body and mind, so he knows we need to express our pent up feelings. If a personal difference goes without being dealt with, the most common reaction is to share those feeling with a friend. Here is where the problem could lie, as we feel comfortable with our friend, in whom we can unload our hard feelings, so we may tend to be critical of the one with whom we have a difference. Proverbs 11:11 tells us, "By the blessing of the upright a city is exalted, But by the mouth of the wicked it is torn down." In the same way, critical speech can just as easily tear down our city like congregation.

Nevertheless, our pursuit of peace does not mean that we must bottle our feeling up inside. The apostle Paul wrote, "Let no unwholesome word proceed from your mouth, but only such a word as is good for edification according to the need of the moment, so that it will give grace to those who hear ... Let all bitterness and wrath and anger and clamor and slander be put away from you, along with all malice. Be kind to one another, tender-hearted, forgiving each other, just as God in Christ also has forgiven you." (Eph. 4:29-32, NASB) Would it not be easy on our part to apologize to a brother or sister, who was offended by something we said or did, if we know he or she has spoken positively about us to others in the past? Thus, the lesson is, if we have a pattern of speaking well of our brothers and sisters, it will make restoring peace so much easier of the occasion arises. – Luke 6:31.

Serving God Shoulder to Shoulder

Considering our human weaknesses and imperfection, the normal course would be to back away from one who has offended us, removing ourselves from a difficult situation. However, as a people that are one in

Christ, we need to be determined to 'serve God shoulder to shoulder.' – Zephaniah 3:9.

Our zeal for pure worship should outweigh what another has said or done and should never weaken our unity of purpose. Jesus had roundly condemned the Jewish leaders and the Jewish system of things (Judaism) of his day just before his execution because they rejected the Son of God for their own selfish glory. However, just a few days before his execution, which would begin the end of the Israelite nation being the only true wat to God, 'he saw a poor widow put in two small copper coins into the offering box, she out of her poverty put in all she had to live on.' Did Jesus rush over and try and stop her because he knew in a few short years, the only way to God would be Christianity? No, rather he commended her, 'I tell you, this poor widow has put in more than all of those that contributed out of their abundance.' (Luke 21:1-4) She was giving her all to support God and at that moment, he was working through the Jews. The unrighteous acts of the Jewish leaders did not remove her obligation to support the worship of God.

Even if we feel strongly that a fellow brother or sister in the faith has acted wrongly toward another or us, it is how we react that will make the difference. Will we allow another to impact out worship of the only true God? No, we will want to make right and differences that we may have, to pursue peace. The apostle Paul counsels, "If possible, so far as it depends on you, live peaceably with all." (Rom. 12:18, ESV) May we heed Paul's inspired word for the sake of the path that leads to life.

Restoring Our Brother

Matthew 18:15 Updated American Standard Version (ASV)

15 "If your brother should sin, go reprove him between you and him alone. If he listens to you, you have gained your brother.27

While some take Jesus' words to refer to something inconsequential, his words actually apply to a more serious sin. Jesus said, "If your

---

27 "'Church discipline' is commonly thought to refer only to those 'official' cases in which the sin is extremely serious and the entire church becomes formally involved in the effort to correct the sinning brother or sister. In reality, church discipline is more biblically understood as covering every effort by any individual or group of individuals in the church to turn a straying believer back to righteous living. (Weber 2000, p. 291)

brother[28] should sin," is referring to one action.[29] The Greek term for sin is hamartano, which could refer to and mistaking or falling short. However, if we look at the context, it is obvious that Jesus is referring to a more serious sin. The sin was so serious that Jesus said if he remained unrepentant, he was to be viewed as "a Gentile and a tax collector." What does that suggest?

Jesus was speaking to a Jewish audience, and so we must consider their mindset when analyzing how Jews would view Gentiles and tax collectors. No Jewish person would socialize with any Gentile (John 4:9; 18:28; Acts 10:28), nor would they have a tax collector as an associate let alone a friend, both being despised. Zondervan Bible Background notes, "The fourth step of discipline is to treat the sinning brother like a pagan (lit., "Gentile," ethnikos) or a tax collector, the common titles for those who are consciously rebellious against God and his people ... Jesus ... focuses on spiritual exclusion from the fellowship of the church, which is symbolic of spiritual death." (Arnold 2002, p. 115) Clearly, the sin must be serious that if the person does not repent, he can be expelled from the Christian congregation into a spiritual death, as opposed to some personal offense, which could just be forgiven. – Matthew 18:21-22.

While all sin results in death, the Bile does qualify sin as some being more serious than others are, referring to them as gross sin. Certainly, common sense tells us that murder is more serious than stealing. Under the Mosaic Law, some sins were not the sort that was just forgiven by the one offended. Blasphemy, apostasy, idolatry, and sexual sins such as fornication, adultery, and homosexuality were to be handed over to the priests. This is also true of the Christian congregation, but would be handed off to the elders or pastors. (Lev. 5:1; 20:10-13; Num. 5:30; 35:12; Deut. 17:9; 19:16-19; Pro. 29:24) Thus, the sin Jesus refers to is not a sin that can just be dismissed but it also is not so serious that the offended has to take it straight to the congregation leaders, but rather he can deal with it himself. For example, a fellow Christian may have slandered the brother; it may be financial matters involving a degree of

---

[28] This process applies to females as well as brothers.

[29] The Greek verb hamartese (Root: hamartano) is in "the aorist verb tense is used by the writer to present the action of a verb as a "snapshot" event. The verb's action is portrayed simply and in summary fashion without respect to any process. In the indicative mood, the aorist usually denotes past time, while an aorist participle usually refers to antecedent time with respect to the main verb. Outside the indicative and the participle, the aorist does not indicate time." (Lukaszewski, Dubis and Blakley 2013)

deceit, fraud, or trickery of some sort. While these examples are serious enough to get an unrepentant person expelled, they are at the level where they can be dealt with personally. Thus, we need to take the initial step.

Notice that the first step is to "go reprove him between you and him alone." The brother will feel less embarrassed as he need not share his words or deeds with anyone, but the one has offended. Some points to keep in mind are that we need to understand fully the wrong ourselves, so we can help him see how he has strayed. It is best if we not procrastinate, stewing at how we were wronged because this will affect our tone and demeanor once we do talk with him. Moreover, we should not be sharing what has happened to us with others because this is gossip. It certainly does not make sense that we would counsel our brother on his sin against us while at the same time, sinning against him.

Our goal is to sin our brother back, not make ourselves look better or try to make him look bad or ruin his reputation. If he has committed the sin that we are coming to him with, he must worry about his relationship with God. We will have far more success if we consider what want to say beforehand and consider out tone once we do approach him. We do not want to come off as harsh or accusatory. We must always keep in mind that we are an imperfect human as well, and it may be that someday another may be coming to us. (Rom. 3:23-24) When he realizes that you have not shared his sin with another, he will be more receptive, realizing you are coming to him out of love. Moreover, it may be discovered that both played a role in the situation, or that there was simply some misunderstanding. – Proverbs 25:9-10; 26:20; James 3:5-6.

If we can help him to see where he has sinned, he may repent, turn around, and not repeat the behavior again.[30] However, pride is difficult for the best of us to overcome. (Pro. 16:18; 17:19) Therefore, if he fails to admit to things initially, we may allow a few days or a week and, then, try again. Jesus said, "Go reprove him between you and him alone." "Go is in the Greek present tense (imperative mood), implying a gentle, patient series of confrontations." (Weber 2000, p. 292) Yes, we can try more than once to help our brother see where he has wronged us. What,

---

[30] "Done correctly in the environment of a trusting relationship, one-on-one confrontation will often result in a positive response. Let us start by believing in the power of God to turn a heart and the longing of every believer for the fulfillment and security of holy living." (Weber 2000, p. 293)

though, if he just refuses to see the sin that he has committed and will not respond to us?

Take Others

Matthew 18:16 Updated American Standard Version (ASV)

[16] But if he does not listen, take along with you one or two more, in order that at the mouth of two or three witnesses every word might stand.

If he fails to listen to us, Jesus says, "Take along with you one or two more." Remember that we are still trying to save our brother. Again, just because we are now taking more, this does not give us the right to talk to others about the wrongdoing. What we have to realize at this point is, biblically, the wrongdoing has not been officially established yet. We would not want to run around telling others of a wrongdoing, to find that we were actually mistaken in our understanding of the situation. (Pro. 16:28; 18:8) The question now is, why is Jesus asking us to take others along and who are we to take?

Our objective is to help our brother to see his sin, so we can gain a brother and restore his relationship with God. If our brother actually committed this wrongdoing in front of others, these would be the ideal "one or two more." These ones would have insight into what had been done or not done. If there were no witnesses to the matter, and if it is a business matter where one was wronged, it might be best to find the "one or two" that has experience in that area, to establish if a wrong has even been committed. Moreover, these ones need to be selected because they will also serve as congregation witnesses on what was said during the discussion. (Num. 35:30; Deut. 17:6) These are not simply friends taken along to gang up on the supposed offender.

It is not necessary that these ones be elders or pastors in the church. Nevertheless, they need to be mature ones, who know the Word of God well, and should fit the spiritual qualifications of a servant. Thus, an elder or pastor may be the best choice depending on the circumstances. (Isa. 32:1- 2) On this Stuart Weber writes, "The purpose of the additional witnesses is primarily: (1) to bring added loving persuasion to the straying brother so he will realize the seriousness of his sin; (2) to prepare for the possibility of the straying brother's continued resistance (in this event, there would be third-party testimony concerning what happened in the confrontation); and (3) to provide one or two "referees" or moderators in the continued confrontation between the original confronter and the straying brother. It is possible the witnesses might conclude that the accuser was wrong. Again, the hope is that the two or three witnesses will be able to cooperate in the Father's zealous pursuit of the straying brother in order to bring him back from the danger of destruction (18:12–14)." (Weber 2000, p. 293) What though if the accused still refuses to see the wrongdoing.

Speak to the Congregation

Matthew 18:17 Updated American Standard Version (ASV)

¹⁷ If he should refuse to hear to them, speak to the congregation. If he does not listen even to the congregation, let him be to you as a Gentile and a tax collector.

If step two does not work, the elder or pastor of the congregation is definitely involved in the third step. Jesus said, "If he should refuse to hear to them [the one or two], speak to the congregation." Thus, if the elder or pastor was initially involved during the "one or two," there is no need to rehash the matter so to speak. The meeting with the offender would be in a more official capacity this time. There is nothing here to suggest that they are to meet in front of the whole congregation to expose the wrongdoing. Even under the Mosaic Law, the whole nation did not hear a man's sins. Instead, the elders would deal with in on behalf of the nation as a whole. The same should be true within the Christian congregation, two or three elders or pastors can deal with the sin on behalf of the entire congregation.

They have the same goal as the initial steps, to save their brother from becoming rebellious. They are to help him humbly repent of any wrongdoing if possible. They want to reestablish biblically that there is a sin or an ongoing sin, even if the offending brother refuses to recognize it. The congregation leaders must now worry about saving the spirit of the congregation. (1 Cor. 2:12; 5:5-7) They must "must hold firm to the trustworthy word as taught so that he may be able to give instruction in sound doctrine and also to rebuke those who contradict it." (Titus 1:9, ESV) It is hoped that the wrongdoer will not be rebellious like the nation of Israel. God said of them, "I called, you did not answer; when I spoke, you did not listen, but you did what was evil in my eyes and chose what I did not delight in." – Isaiah 65:12.

If the help is continuously rejected, Jesus says, "Let him be to you as a Gentile and a tax collector." Jesus is here not recommending that Christians now treat the offender inhumane as the Jews treated the Gentiles and tax collectors, looking down on them in disdain. However, he is saying the unrepentant sinner is to be expelled from the congregation, and no one is to associate with or even speak to him. (1 Cor. 5:11-13) This is not punitive but rather is corrective. The goal remains the same, i.e., winning the brother back. If the person comes to his senses and is repentant, he can return to the congregation by attending the meetings again. However, no congregation member is to associate or speak with him until he has been reinstated back into the congregation leaders. This may take a few months or even longer. His regular meeting attendance and meetings with the elder or pastor will evidence his repentant heart.

Review Questions

- Why is it important that we pursue peace and what illustration can make this point?

- How does remaining calm help us to restore peace? What historical example evidences this?

- How can we tame our tongue?

- How does our serving God shoulder to shoulder make the bigger picture clear?

- Principally, what sort of sin is Jesus dealing with in Matthew 18:15-17 apply?

- How should we approach the first step?

- What should we consider if we must go to the second step?

- Who are to be involved if it must be taken to the third step? What is our goal through all three steps and what attitude will help us meet that goal

CHAPTER 5 You Must Be Holy In All Your Conduct

1 Peter 1:15-16 Updated American Standard Version (UASV)

14 but like the Holy One who called you, you also be holy in all your conduct; **16** because it is written, "You shall be holy, for I am holy."

Why would the apostle Peter offer the above direction? Because he was aware of imperfect human weaknesses and the need to focus on being in step with God's holiness, personality, standards, ways, and will, in word, in deed or knowing the right thing to do and failing to do it, or in mind or heart attitude. Thus, in the two previous verses, Peter wrote, "gird the loins of your mind,[31] and being sober-minded, set your hope fully on the grace that will be brought to you at the revelation of Jesus Christ. As children of obedience,[32] do not be conformed according to the desires you formerly had in your ignorance." – 1 Peter 1:13-14.

We likely took not that these "desires" are those that feed the flesh, our senses, and our emotions. When we do not dismiss inappropriate desires, our thoughts take control over us, which leads to a sinful action. If our Christian conscience has been trained well by the Word of God, it will quickly identify wrong desires, giving us an opportunity to dismiss it. However, if we ignore our conscience, it will become callused, meaning that we will no longer be warned as to right and wrong, good and bad. This is why we need our God given power of reason to control our desires. Paul wrote, "I urge you, brothers, by the mercies of God, to present your bodies a living and holy sacrifice, acceptable to God, which is your reasonable service.[33]" – Romans 12:1.[34]

---

[31] I.e., *prepare your minds for action (mental perception)*

[32] I.e., *obedient children*

[33] Lit *the reasonable (or rational, logical) service of you*

[34] Today most interpreters understand the adjective [*Logiken*] as spiritual, which makes good sense and is certainly in mind. But it is hard to think that the connection with "reason" has been completely lost, and there is something to be said for "intelligent worship" (Phillips) or JB's "that is worthy of thinking beings". – Leon Morris, *The Epistle to the Romans, The Pillar New Testament Commentary* (Grand Rapids, MI; Leicester, England: W.B. Eerdmans; Inter-Varsity Press, 1988), 434.

On Romans 12:1, Kenneth Boa and William Kruidenier write,

The reason that offering oneself to God is both reasonable and **spiritual** is based partly on the meaning of *logikos* and partly on Paul's context. *Logikos* derives from *logos*, the Greek term for word or reason. But Paul is also drawing a contrast here between the physical sacrifices of the Old Testament and the spiritual sacrifice of the New Testament. The **spiritual act of worship** which Paul is encouraging is one that springs from the inner man, the realm of the mind (see v. Heb. 12:2). It is therefore a reasonable as well as **spiritual** form of **worship**.

"**Worship** has always been accompanied by sacrifice, but the form of sacrifice has changed under the new covenant:

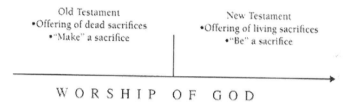

Old Testament
•Offering of dead sacrifices
•"Make" a sacrifice

New Testament
•Offering of living sacrifices
•"Be" a sacrifice

WORSHIP OF GOD

In the Old Testament, there were sacrifices for sin as well as sacrifices of gratitude and praise. Christ has obviously fulfilled the sacrifice for sin once for all (Heb. 9:26; 10:10, 12,14), and there is nothing that the believer can add to that sacrifice. But **living sacrifices** of gratitude and praise are the appropriate (reasonable, spiritual) sacrifices to be made by those who live only by the mercy of God. These sacrifices are as much the **act of worship** of the believer today as the sacrifices of dead animals were the **act of worship** of Old Testament Israelites. *Latreia* is the word Paul used for the worship practices of Israel in Romans 9:4, so he obviously has the same concept in mind for New Testament believers. The root of worship is *latreuo*, to serve. God was served in the Old Testament by sacrifices of property owned by the believer, but he is served in the New Testament by the sacrifice of the believer himself or herself. Paul does not tell believers to "make" a sacrifice, but to "be" a sacrifice.[35]

---

[35] Kenneth Boa and William Kruidenier, Romans, vol. 6, Holman New Testament Commentary (Nashville, TN: Broadman & Holman Publishers, 2000), 363.

Romans 12:2 Updated American Standard Version (UASV)

² And do not be conformed to this world, but be transformed by **the renewing of your mind**, so that you may prove what the will of God is, that which is good and acceptable[36] and perfect.

On Romans 12:2, Leon Morris writes, "The transformation is to take place *by the renewing of your mind*. The believer, whose life is that of the new age, does not think like an unbeliever. The reference to the mind is important. Paul does not envisage a mindless emotionalism, but a deeply intelligent approach to life, as characteristic of the Christian who has been renewed by the Holy Spirit. The term *mind* is not confined to intellectual pursuits (it includes an important moral element), but it certainly embraces them. The force of the present tense should not be overlooked; Paul envisages a continuing process of renewal."[37]

Because of our human imperfection, if we are to 'be holy in all our conduct' (Peter), if we are 'to present our bodies a living and holy sacrifice, we must use 'renewing our minds' (Paul), to control our thoughts, which will affect the way we feel, and in turn determine our behaviors. The apostle Paul encourages us to use our "power of reason" to be molded by God's thinking, not by the world of humankind alienated from God. This does not mean that we are to go around emotionless; it just means that irrational thinking will result in irrational emotions, while rational thinking will result in rational emotions. If it is our desire to possess the fruit of the Spirit as opposed to the works of the flesh, we must have Christ's way of thinking. – Galatians 5:22-23; Philippians 2:5.

Holy Precious Blood of Christ

There is a reason Peter was so focused on the need for Christians to be holy. He knew of the Holy precious blood of Christ that bought back any human that freely chose to trust in Jesus. He wrote, "knowing that you were ransomed from the futile ways inherited from your forefathers, not with perishable things such as silver or gold, but with the precious blood of Christ, like that of a lamb without blemish or spot." (1 Pet. 1:18-19) The source of holiness, our heavenly Father, which Isaiah referred to

---

[36] Or *well-pleasing*

[37] Leon Morris, *The Epistle to the Romans*, The Pillar New Testament Commentary (Grand Rapids, MI; Leicester, England: W.B. Eerdmans; Inter-Varsity Press, 1988), 435.

as holy, holy, holy, sent "the only begotten Son," "the Holy One of God," to earth, "to give his life a ransom for many." (Isaiah 6:3; John 1:18; 3:16; 6:69; Exodus 28:36; Matthew 20:28, ASV) This ransom sacrifice made it possible for all of us to restore our relationship with God.

Nevertheless, it is quite difficult to live a holy life within Satan's world that caters to the fallen human flesh. Satan is busier trying to stumble the true Christians off the path to life than he is keeping the unbeliever on the path that leads to death. (1 Pet. 5:8; Eph. 6:12; 1 Tim. 6:9-10) The temptations that surround the Christian mind could never be greater with the internet, the smartphone, tablet, and television that have streaming set to tour schedule. Advertising and marketing are far more sensual than just 20-yrears ago, and it is everywhere. The pressures of daily life, such as the workplace, family members that see Christianity as foolish, bullying of our children in school, peer pressure, makes it paramount that we are spiritually strong, if we are to remain holy. This means that our regular, personal Bible study, our preparation for Christian meeting, so that we may fully participate when opportunities present itself, our being prepared to share our faith with others, are all important. Paul counseled Timothy, who had just spent 15-years traveling with him, growing and strengthening congregations throughout the then known world. If Timothy needed to be advised, it would seem that we would need to even more so. Paul counseled, "Hold fast to the pattern of sound words[38] which you heard from me, in the faith and love that are in Christ Jesus." – 2 Timothy 1:13, LEB.

Family Life That Is Holy

Peter's Word from above, "You shall be holy, for I am holy," is a quote from Leviticus 11:44. The Greek word behind "holy" is *hagios*, which "fundamentally signifies "separated" (among the Greeks, dedicated to the gods), and hence, in Scripture in its moral and spiritual significance, separated from sin and therefore consecrated to God, sacred."[39] Our extended family is no different than the rest of the world if they are sinful

---

[38] The true gospel is founded upon the prophets, the words of Jesus, and apostolic teaching. Acutely aware of the damage inflicted by false teachers, Paul returned to the need for orthodoxy as revealed through Christ to Paul. It is this pure doctrine which is the pattern of sound teaching. – (Larson 2000, p. 270)

[39] W. E. Vine, Merrill F. Unger, and William White Jr., *Vine's Complete Expository Dictionary of Old and New Testament Words* (Nashville, TN: T. Nelson, 1996), 307.

unbelievers. If we are to separate ourselves from sin, would this not mean separating ourselves from family reunions or get-togethers where there is cursing, smoking, immoral talk and drunkenness? We can have dealing with such ones at our home, where we can control who is invited and what is served.

How though do we apply separating ourselves from our Christian family of father, mother and children? We do so by separating ourselves from qualities that are unchristian, such as lying, anger, jealousy, bad language, sexual immorality, and any other unclean practices of this world. Just as "God is love" (1 John 4:8), we too are to have self-sacrificing love toward our family. (1 Cor. 13:4-8; Eph. 5:28, 29, 33; 6:4; Col. 3:18, 21) When we see a family come to the Christian meetings, are we seeing who they really are, or are we seeing only what they want us to see?

Do the teenagers of that family have a secret life at school, on the internet of which the parents are not aware? Does the husband love his wife just as he loves himself at the meeting, but hits his wife and mentally mistreats her in the home? Is he jealously yelling at her, controlling her ever move? Does the wife weep and nag the husband to get her way? Is the wife overly critical of the husband? Is sexual relations withheld as a form of punishment or revenge? Do the family members take into their minds things that are morally unclean, graphically violent, or use of bad language? This can take place through the internet, television, and movies. Moreover, maybe worldly friends outside of the Christian meetings further influence the family. If cameras were secretly put up in our home, car, workplace, school, places of recreation, what would people see about us? Let us look at just one verse that should govern our actions, as an example of how Scripture should govern us.

The apostle Paul counseled, "**No rotten word** [Greek, *logos sapros*, "impure, foul, unwholesome speech,"[40] "defiling speech,"[41] i.e., unholy] **must proceed from your mouth**, but only something good for the building up of the need, in order that it may give grace to those who

---

[40] Johannes P. Louw and Eugene Albert Nida, *Greek-English Lexicon of the New Testament: Based on Semantic Domains* (New York: United Bible Societies, 1996), 229.

[41] W. E. Vine, Merrill F. Unger, and William White Jr., *Vine's Complete Expository Dictionary of Old and New Testament Words* (Nashville, TN: T. Nelson, 1996), 49.

hear." (Eph. 4:29, LEB) This counsel from Paul applies to the family in the home, which would also include the children.

On this verse Max Anders writes, "This is the Bible's version of, "If you can't say something nice, don't say anything at all." We are to speak only words that build up and encourage others. This one passage, if consistently obeyed, would eliminate the overwhelming majority of life's conflicts. Words of a mature Christian seek to help the listener, not harm him. Thus the ministerial gifts of Christ's grace achieve their purposes, and the unity of the body of Christ is preserved and enhanced."[42]

Peter Thomas O'Brien helps us to appreciate the extent that Ephesians 4:29 covers. He writes, "Christians should keep their lips free not only from lying (v. 25) but also from unwholesome language of any kind. Paul's exhortation is comprehensive: it is directed to all his readers[43] who have put on the 'new man', and stresses that *no* word they utter should be harmful.[44] The adjective is used elsewhere in the New Testament in the literal sense of 'decayed' trees which produce 'rotten' fruit (Matt. 7:17–18), and in relation to 'rotten' fish (Matt. 12:33–34). Here the word is employed figuratively to denote language that is 'harmful' or 'unwholesome'.[45] What is prohibited, then, is harmful speech of any kind (cf. Col. 3:8; Eph. 5:4), whether it be abusive language, vulgar speech, or slander and contemptuous talk. Lips given to this kind of utterance not only defile the speaker (Matt. 15:11) but are also destructive of communal life. Our Lord had already warned that people would have to render account on the final day for every careless word they speak (Matt. 12:36).[46]

---

[42] Max Anders, *Galatians-Colossians*, vol. 8, Holman New Testament Commentary (Nashville, TN: Broadman & Holman Publishers, 1999), 156.

[43] The singular for mouth (στόμα) is a Semitic distributive singular relating to each member of the group. All are to heed the apostolic command.

[44] The πᾶς ('every, each') before an anarthrous substantive, λόγος ('word'), indicates that Paul wishes to stress that 'every word' is to be wholesome, not simply some important words (cf. BDF §275[3]; BAGD, 631).

[45] So Louw and Nida §20.14, who add that σαπρός stands in contrast to ἀγαθός. The latter means 'good' in the sense of 'building up what is necessary', and thus 'helpful'. By contrast, σαπρός means 'harmful' or 'unwholesome'. BAGD, 742, has 'evil'.

[46] Peter Thomas O'Brien, *The Letter to the Ephesians*, The Pillar New Testament Commentary (Grand Rapids, MI: W.B. Eerdmans Publishing Co., 1999), 344–345.

Looking at Ephesians 4:29, William Hendriksen and Simon J. Kistemaker help us to appreciate the difficulty of overcoming the worldly personality as we put on the new personality. They write, "Corrupt speech is that which is putrid, rotten; hence also corrupting, defiling, injurious (Matt. 15:18). We may well assume that for many years these rather recent converts to the Christian faith had been living in an impure environment, where foul conversation, at feasts and other social gatherings and parties, had been the stock in trade of everyone present. The change from this toxic environment to the pure and wholesome atmosphere of Christian fellowship must have been nothing short of revolutionary. Even believers who are well advanced in sanctification have at times complained about the fact that it was difficult for them to cleanse their minds entirely from the words and melody of this or that scurrilous drinking song. They hated it, fought against it, were sure at last that they had expelled it forever from their thoughts, and then suddenly there it was again, ready to plague and torture them by means of its reappearance. Thus also certain vile phrases or catch-words, sometimes even profanity, all too common in the pre-conversion period of life, have the habit in unguarded moments to barge right in and to befoul the atmosphere. Think of Simon Peter who, although a disciple of the Lord, "began to curse and to swear" when he thought that his life was in danger (Matt. 26:74). Here, too, the only remedy, in addition to prayer, is to fill mind and heart with that which is pure and holy, in the spirit of Gal. 5:22 and Phil. 4:8, 9.[47]

Now Ephesians 4:29 is but one verse that helps Christians to guide their behavior as to being holy as God is holy. All day, the children of the family are around the worldly children spewing the most unholy "impure, foul, unwholesome speech," "defiling speech." We can only imaging the young mind and how easily it can absorb bad behavior, which they too try to hide by being different at home. However, if it slips out on occasion, we can assume that away from the house they are imitating the unholy and bad-mannered talk of their worldly fellow-students! It is far more difficult for the children to remove themselves from the presence of these bad influences, as will result in isolated loneliness, not to mention their peers will ostracize them (i.e., give coldshoulder), if not bully them. While the objective of this book is not to find solutions but simply to point out the evidence of whether we are truly Christian, it is suggested

---

[47] William Hendriksen and Simon J. Kistemaker, *Exposition of Ephesians*, vol. 7, New Testament Commentary (Grand Rapids: Baker Book House, 1953–2001), 220–221.

that the parents find some material on how to cope with and prepare the children for such a battle for the faith.

William Lain Craig warns Christian parents, "I think the church is really failing [our] kids. Rather than provide them training in the defense of Christianity's truth, we focus on emotional worship experiences, felt needs, and entertainment. It's no wonder they become sitting ducks for that teacher or professor who rationally takes aim at their faith. In high school and college, students are intellectually assaulted with every manner of non-Christian philosophy conjoined with an overwhelming relativism and skepticism. We've got to train our kids for war. How dare we send them unarmed into an intellectual war zone? Parents must do more than take their children to church and read them Bible stories. Moms and dads need to be trained in apologetics themselves and so be able to explain to their children simply from an early age and then with increasing depth why we believe as we do. Honestly, I find it hard to understand how Christian couples in our day and age can risk bringing children into the world without being trained in apologetics as part of the art of parenting."[48]

Craig continues, "Of course, apologetics won't guarantee that you or your children will keep the faith. There are all kinds of moral and spiritual factors that come into play, too. Some of the most effective atheist Web sites feature ex-believers who were trained in apologetics and still abandoned the faith. But when you look closely at the arguments they give for abandoning Christianity, they are often confused or weak. I recently saw one Web site where the person provided a list of the books that had persuaded him that Christianity is bunk— followed by the remark that he hopes to read them someday! Ironically, some of these folks come to embrace positions that are more extreme and require more gullibility—such as that Jesus never existed—than the conservative views they once held.[49]

Craig closes with, "But while apologetics is no guarantee, it can help. As I travel, I also meet many people who have been brought back from the brink of abandoning their faith by reading an apologetics book or watching a debate. Recently I had the privilege of speaking at Princeton University on arguments for the existence of God, and after my lecture a young man approached me who wanted to talk. Obviously trying to hold

---

[48] Craig, William Lane (2010-03-01). On Guard: Defending Your Faith with Reason and Precision (Kindle Locations 267-274). David C. Cook. Kindle Edition.

[49] IBID, (Kindle Locations 276-281).

back the tears, he told me how a couple of years earlier he had been struggling with doubts and was almost to the point of abandoning his faith. Someone then gave him a video of one of my debates. He said, 'It saved me from losing my faith. I cannot thank you enough.' I said, 'It was the Lord who saved you from falling.'"[50]

As Christians, there should be no filthy speech of any sort coming out of our mouths regardless of where we are. (Eph. 5:4) Rather, 'our speech should always be with grace, as though seasoned with salt,[51] so that we will know how we should respond to each person.' – Colossians 3:8-10; 4:6.

Holy Life Among the Unbelieving Family

Certainly, our objective is to live a truly holy life; however, being holy does not mean that we become sanctimonious, self-righteous, and superior when we interact with unbelieving family members. When our unbelieving side think about us, talk about us to friend, we want them to reference our Christlike conduct. We want them to see that we stand out as different from today's perception of what a Christian is like. – Luke 10:30-37.

The principle that Peter laid out for the Christian wives toward their unbelieving husbands, can be applied to all unbelieving family members. "You wives, be submissive to your own husbands so that even if any of them are disobedient to the word, **they may be won without a word by the behavior** of their wives, as they observe your chaste and respectful behavior." (1 Peter 3:1-2) Wifely submission is not simply set aside because the husband is an unbeliever. We treat our unbelieving relatives as though they were going to be our future spiritual relatives. We can make Christianity more appealing to our unbelieving relatives if our Christian conduct is genuine and always on display. If anyone can identify a false Christian personality, it will be a relative. We do not snub our relatives because we have Christian obligations.

---

[50] IBID, (Kindle Locations 282-287).

[51] We need "to continue in prayer and to conduct [ourselves] in a worthy manner toward others. Believers' conduct and speech should be carefully controlled and used with great wisdom and love. – David S. Dockery, "The Pauline Letters," in *Holman Concise Bible Commentary*, ed. David S. Dockery (Nashville, TN: Broadman & Holman Publishers, 1998), 592.

What about the leaders in the congregation, how can they play a role in the lives of our unbelieving family members? If a wife has an unbelieving husband, the elders or pastors can get to know them on a social level. This way, the husband can see that Christian men are normal, good people who have the same interests in life as other people do (e.g., sports, current events, cars, motorcycles, fishing, hunting, and the like). Being holy does not mean that Christians must be prudish, narrow-minded, some goody-goody as many are viewed or having a one-track mind (i.e., every time going straight to the Bible to witness). We can witness by conduct and drawing close in friendships. – 1 Corinthians 9:20-23.

Holy Life in the Congregation

Satan the Devil is a slanderer. The Greek behind "Devil" is "*diabolos* , an adjective, "slanderous, accusing falsely," is used as a noun, translated "slanderers" in 1 Tim. 3:11, where the reference is to those who are given to finding fault with the demeanor and conduct of others and spreading their innuendos and criticisms in the church." (Vine 1996, Vol. 2, p. 580) Paul tells Timothy, "Women must likewise be dignified, not malicious gossips, but temperate, faithful in all things." (1 Tim. 3:11, NASB) Just as Satan has falsely slandered God's good name, we would never want to slander the good name of our brothers and sisters in the congregation. Gossip is conversation about the personal details of other people's lives, whether rumor or fact, especially the malicious kind. Slander is even more serious, it is saying something false or malicious that damages somebody's reputation. Wise King Solomon wrote, "A perverse man spreads strife, and a slanderer separates intimate friends." (Pro. 16:28, NASB) If we are truly Christian, our speech should always be upbuilding, loving, respectful, and kind. We want to focus our attention on the good qualities of our brother and sisters not the bad qualities. It is easy to criticize another. If someone is gossiping in our ear about another, he or she is likely gossiping in the ear of another about us. – 1 Timothy 5:13; Titus 2:3.

If we are going to keep our congregation holy, we must have the mind of Christ, as his prevailing quality is live. Paul directed the Colossians to be kindhearted like Christ. "So, as those who have been chosen of God, holy and beloved, put on a heart of compassion, kindness, humility, gentleness and patience; bearing with one another, and forgiving each other, whoever has a complaint against anyone; just as the Lord forgave you, so also should you. Beyond all these things put on love, which is the perfect bond of unity. Let the peace of Christ rule in your hearts, to which indeed you were called in one body; and be thankful." – Colossians 3:12-15.

Holy Life in the World

How are we to deal with our neighbors, strangers, people with whom we have infrequent interactions? Well, again, the first question is, if they were to describe us as a person, what would they say? When our Christian personality is on display, does it come across as a joyful life or some burden that we must carry? James, Jesus' half-brother wrote, "Consider it a great joy, my brothers, whenever you experience various trials, knowing that the testing of your faith produces endurance. But endurance must do its complete work, so that you may be mature and complete, lacking nothing."

THE BOOK OF JAMES: CPH CHRISTIAN LIVING COMMENTARY addresses this joy. "The joy is not in the fact that one is going through the trial, but rather in what that trial will be able to produce in their lives. James wants his readers to realize that if they can understand that God is the one who allowed imperfection to come into humanity for a particular reason then they can consider any trial with a response of joy, i.e., an opportunity for them to show an evident demonstration of their faith. Do not believe that God placed these trials here to grow their faith, but rather, because the trials (difficult times) are here because of human imperfection, here was their opportunity to grow from difficult times." (Calloway 2015, p. 13)

We can demonstrate our holiness by simply being neighborly. There are times when we can help each other in need, even take part in some kind of neighborhood cleanup. What if the neighbor's car breaks down, are we close enough that he would think to call us? What if he needed to run out for an emergency, would he trust us to watch his children in a pinch? Unbelievers have questions about God whether they make it known or not; therefore, simple be the good neighbor, and when the time comes for him to ask a Bible question, do not overwhelm him. Find him a reasonable, rational, biblical answer to his inquiry and leave it at that. If we do that and he realizes he is not going to get a two-hour sermon every time he has a small Bible question, he will ask more often.

Holy Life at Work

The apostle Paul wrote the Corinthians about 55 C.E., one of the most unholy cities of his day. He offered them the following counsel. "I wrote you in my letter not to associate with immoral people; I *did* not at all *mean* with the immoral people of this world, or with the covetous and swindlers, or with idolaters, for then you would have to go out of the world." (1 Cor. 5:9-10) On this the Holman New Commentary says,

> Paul clarified one aspect of his instruction that may have been easily misunderstood. He referred to a previous letter in which he had written that believers were **not to associate with sexually immoral people**. This instruction could easily have been misunderstood (or purposefully twisted) to mean that believers should withdraw entirely from all immoral people. Paul ridiculed this misunderstanding of his earlier words by noting that avoiding all immoral people can only happen if Christians **leave this world**.
>
> Since Christians must minister to the world, they must not separate themselves from all who are **greedy and swindlers, or idolaters**. These people are the church's mission field (see Matt. 9:10–13; Luke 15:1–32).
>
> Possibly, those in Corinth who opposed Paul used this misunderstanding to undermine Paul's ministry and authority. They may have suggested that Paul called Christians to stay away from all sinners, and on that basis discounted all his teaching. Paul treated the Corinthians harshly for this misunderstanding for three reasons: it stemmed from a wrong reading of his prior letter; it had led to wrongful pride and corruption in the church; and it had allowed the church's toleration of the incestuous man. (Pratt Jr 2000, p. 77)

This is a quandary for Christians that must be in the world but be do part of the world. Day in and day out, they must interact with immoral people. This will certainly put one's integrity to the test. Think of the amount of time two co-workers of the opposite sex must spend together in a certain work environment, one is Christian and one is not. In this setting, we do not want to come across as normal. We want to be friendly, loving, respectful, but we must wear our Christianity on our shoulder, so no one would even consider acting worldly with us. For example, many Christians have experienced an unbeliever accidently saying a curse word in front of us and he stops himself and immediately apologizes profusely, as though he had cursed in front of God. If this is how they see us, this means they respect us. We want to stand out as different, coming across as a truly Christian. – Matthew 5:3; 1 Peter 3:16-17.

Holy Life at School

Our children to be need protected from a school system that is designed to undermine their faith from the first day. Many teachers are skeptics, atheists, agnostics, humanistic, liberal-progressive in their worldviews. The new atheist is not like the atheist of 1950. In those days, the atheist just did not believe in God, and he did not share those beliefs with others, it was a "live and let live" atmosphere. Today we have an atheist, who is not content with keeping his views private. In fact, they are on an atheist revival like those the Christian revivals had in the 19th- and 18th-centuries (John Wesley, Charles Wesley and George Whitefield in England and the Great Awakening in America). This is an enormous increase in activity, from enraged persons, who have an interest in try to persuade Christians and non-Christians to their point of view, both nationally and globally. Even the agnostic[52] is in the line of fire of the atheist, for the new atheist will not allow there to be any doubt as to the existence of a god or creator. Our children are in the crosshairs of their agenda to evangelize the worldview. We have already discussed the importance of preparing them well.

Then, there are the unbelieving children, whose minds are feeding on the filthiest material, who are most eager to influence the lives of Christian children. Most young people today are very much influenced by hip-hop, rap, and heavy metal music, as well reality television, celebrities, movies, video games, and the internet, especially social media. Parents are now allowing their children to receive life-altering opinions, beliefs, and worldviews from the likes of Snooki, a cast member of the MTV reality show *Jersey Shore*. Kim Kardashian and her family rose to prominence with their reality television series, *Keeping Up with the Kardashians*.

The ABC Family channel (owned by Disney) comes across as a channel that we would want our children watching. However, most of the shows are nothing more than dysfunctional families, promotions of homosexuality as an alternative lifestyle, and young actors and actresses

---

[52] Agnostics believe that it is impossible to know whether God exists.

that are playing underage teens in high school, running around killing, causing havoc, and having sexual intercourse with multiple characters on the show. In August 2006, an all-new slogan and visual style premiered on ABC Family: A New Kind of Family. The channel shows such programming as Pretty Little Liars, Twisted, The Fosters, Melissa & Joey, Switched at Birth, The Lying Game, Bunheads and Baby Daddy.

The world has added new words to their vocabulary, like "sexting," which is the act of sending sexually explicit messages and/or photographs, primarily between cell phones. The term was first popularized in 2007. Then, there is "F-Bomb," which we are not going to define fully other than to say that the dictionary considers it "a lighthearted and printable euphemism" for something far more offensive. If all of the above is unfamiliar to you as a parent, and you have a teen or preteen child, you may want to Google the information.

Regardless of the degree of the relationship, these relationships often influence the thinking of a young life. It is important that we do not allow the wrong persons to influence us or our children. The truth is our thinking, and our actions are a direct result of bad associations, be it the wrong friends, music, celebrities, video games, or social media. The same holds true of good associations, like our parents, teachers, coaches, and good friends. Paul warned, "For there are many **rebellious men**, **empty talkers** and **deceivers**," from whom we should watch out! – Titus 1:10

In the end, with help from God's Word, the Christian congregation, the pastor, and especially the family, our Christian children have a reasonable expectation that they will not act on the desires of the flesh. Moreover, if they put on the new personality and possess a deeply engrained mind of Christ, the fleshly desires will be controlled. Self-control is the way of things until God brings this wicked age to an end. The final warning offered herein is this. Do not allow charismatic religious rhetoric to suggest that the laying on of hands can save our Christian children from bad influences. This will only leave them more vulnerable, as they will then let down their guard, and not seek the help that they need. What charismatics espouse is just not how it works and is not biblical.

Parents, make certain you visit the schools, getting a sense of the atmosphere. Also, build rapport with the teachers and school administration. Make time, so you are aware of the jungle of violence, immorality, drugs and sex that our child must weave through. Paul counseled, "Fathers, do not exasperate your children so that they will not lose heart." (Col. 3:21) Our children will "lose heart" if we do not fully appreciate what their life is like at school or any social function of the school. Overcoming the temptations begins in the Christian home. – Deuteronomy 6:6-9; Proverbs 22:6.

Holiness is paramount for all Christians, as it protects us from Satan and his world. Go; be in the world but no part of the world because you do not use it to its fullest extent. The objective is to have a biblical worldview to the point that every decision that is made is something that Jesus would have done, had he been in our place.

Review Questions

- Why is Peter's counsel for Christians on holiness important?
- What is it about us in this condition and at this point that makes living a holy life so difficult?
- How can we live a holy life in the family?
- How can we live a holy life among the unbelievers?
- How can we live a holy life in the congregation?
- How can we live a holy life in the workplace?
- How can we live a holy life at school?

CHAPTER 6 You Must Forgive Others Their Trespasses

Matthew 6:14-15 Updated American Standard Version (UASV)

¹⁴ For if you forgive others their trespasses, your heavenly Father will also forgive you. ¹⁵ But if you do not forgive others their trespasses, neither will your Father forgive your trespasses.

The apostle Paul says that we are to continue "putting up with one another and forgiving one another. If anyone should have a complaint against another, forgiving each other; as the Lord has forgiven you, so you also must forgive." In addition, Peter asked Jesus, "how often shall my brother sin against me and I forgive him? Up to seven times?" (Matt. 18:21, NASB) It is likely that Peter thought he gave a good answer and that he was being quite generous with his suggestion of seven times. The rabbinic tradition in later Judaism was that one did not have to forgive more than three times for the same offense.[53] However, Jesus said to Peter, "I do not say to you, up to seven times, but up to seventy times seven." (Matt. 18:22, NASB) Jesus was not giving us a specific number for us to keep track of, but rather that it was unlimited.

The ability to forgive offenses is a quality that does not come readily and easily. When someone injures our feelings it seems so unfair that we can barely look at them or even think of their name let alone forgive them. Maybe we shared a very private secret with someone and then he or she shared it with another until many in the congregation are now aware of our private information. (Pro. 11:13) When this person is one of our close friends, their betrayal is so much more hurtful. (Pro. 12:18) In our imperfect condition, the natural reaction is that we become angry. When we arrive at the meetings, we avoid the offender and never intend to speak again. The idea of forgiving such a betrayal seems as though we are letting him get away with such a heinous offense. However, by cultivating bitterness, we are only going to cause ourselves more hurt.

Thus, we must be prepared to forgive an indefinite number of offenses if we are to follow Jesus' teaching, which would never allow us

---

[53] "Later Judaism recognized that repeat offenders may not really be repenting at all, and drew the line at how many times a person could seek restoration and forgiveness: 'If a man commits a transgression, the first, second and third time he is forgiven, the fourth time he is not (Yoma 86b, 87a).'" (Wilkins and Evans 2013)

to be further harmed. Reasonably, Jesus knows that we are far better off by forgiving others than holding in all of that pent up anger. Before delving in the why of forgiveness, we should clarify what forgiveness is and what it is not. If we fully understand what the Bible means by forgiveness, it may help us to feel more comfortable doing so.

When we forgive someone this does not mean that we are excusing or trivializing their offense. Moreover, it does not mean that we are allowing others to take advantage of us. When God forgives us, are we to believe that he is trivializing our transgression, and he would never allow sinful humans to take advantage of his mercy. According to *Vine's Complete Expository Dictionary of Old and New Testament Words*, forgiveness "signifies the remission of the punishment due to sinful conduct, the deliverance of the sinner from the penalty divinely, and therefore righteously, imposed; secondly, it involves the complete removal of the cause of offense; such remission is based upon the vicarious and propitiatory [covering over] sacrifice of Christ." (Vine 1996, Vol. 2, p. 251) Vine goes on to point out that, "Human 'forgiveness' is to be strictly analogous to divine 'forgiveness,' e.g., Matt. 6:12.[54] If certain conditions are fulfilled, there is no limitation to Christ's law of 'forgiveness,' Matt. 18:21, 22. The conditions are repentance and confession, Matt. 18:15-17; Luke 17:3."

We Must Forgive

One reason that we must forgive others is specified at Ephesians 5:1, "Therefore be imitators of God, as beloved children." In what way are we supposed to be "imitators of God"? The adverb "therefore" connects verse one with the preceding verse. Ephesians 4:32 reads, "bearing with one another, and forgiving each other, *whoever has a complaint against anyone; just as the Lord forgave you, so also should you*." First, we want to remember that we have been pardoned from a death since because of Adam's sin. Moreover, God forgives us daily for our transgressions, even the egregious ones. As a child of God, we want to imitate our heavenly Father, freely forgiving others. Certainly, it must warm God's heart to see us forgive others freely when he knows that in our imperfection, we actually lean toward evil, and yet we still forgive out of love for our heavenly Father and neighbor. – Luke 6:35-36; See Matthew 5:44-48.

---

[54] forgive us our debts, as we also have forgiven our debtors.

We must understand, though, we are unable to imitate God perfectly in our ability to forgive, but this should not prevent us from continuing to try. Ponder for a moment on the difference between our forgiving someone and God forgiving us. (Isa. 55:7-9) We know that when we forgive someone for their sin against us, it is only a matter of time before someone will need to forgive us for our sin against them. We can appreciate why we need to forgive others because we are in the same situation as them. We suffer from inherited sin (missing the mark of perfection), human weaknesses, meaning that we are unable to go without sinning, it will happen in time, and no matter how much we wish it not to, no matter what preventions we put in place. Therefore, a human forgiving another human is perfectly understandable based on this alone. God on the other hand **never** needs to be forgiven; he is always the one forgiving others. – Matthew 6:12.

What we must further recognize is that a lack of forgiveness on our part, when mercy is required means that we now jeopardizing our relationship with God. We must realize that God is expecting us to forgive others; it is not as though he is asking us to forgive others. Jesus tells us, "For if you forgive others their trespasses, your heavenly Father will also forgive you." (Matt. 6:4, ESV) On another occasion, Jesus said, "And whenever you stand praying, forgive, if you have anything against anyone, so that your Father also who is in heaven may forgive you your trespasses." (Mark 11:25, ESV) We just learned in the above from Paul, "as the Lord has forgiven you, so you also must forgive." (Eph. 4:32, ESV) The apostle John wrote, "If God so loved us, we also ought to love one another." (1 John 4:11, ESV) Therefore, if we refuse to forgive others when there are legitimate reasons for doing so, how are we to expect God to forgive us? – Matthew 18:21-35.

Another reason for us to forgive others is that it is the wise course of action. God is well aware of the human body and mind, as our Creator. Therefore, when he inspires Paul to write, "Leave room for the wrath of God"[55] (i.e., do not be wrathful, leave it to God if such wrath is needed), he has good reasons. Anger, especially if it is carried over time, will become all-consuming, which may turn into wrath and will undoubtedly affect us physically, emotionally and mentally, not to mention spiritually. (Pro. 14:30) What is even worse, the one who put us in the provoked state may not even be aware of what all we are putting ourselves through, and he is carrying nothing. God knows how we were made and

---

[55] Romans 12:9, NASB

what is in our best interests. He knows that we need to forgive freely those who are worthy of such mercy.

Putting Up With One Another

When we compare physical injuries with emotional ones, it can help us to see the range of attention needed in caring for them. If we get a scratch on our hand, we do not go to the emergency room, we simply put some Neosporin on it, and within a couple days, all is well. The same holds true when our feeling receive a minor scratch, what can we do to easily overcome that, is there some spiritual Neosporin? Yes, there actually is. We will get to that in a moment. When we forgive minor frustrations, affronts, and displeasures, we need not go to the emergency room of making it a big deal. If we are a bit of a recluse and are easily offended at every trivial distress, who then wants this big formal apology or we will never speak to them again, people will start avoiding us.

Rather, let us become Paul's counsel, "Let your reasonableness be known to everyone." As we all are living in human imperfection, so it is expected that our Christian brothers and sisters will use the wrong words occasionally. Moreover, it is guaranteed that we will do the same. Paul told the Colossians that they needed to be "**putting up with one another and forgiving one another**. If anyone should have a complaint against anyone, just as also the Lord forgave you, thus also you do the same." This means that we have to develop patience as a quality, so we can be long-suffering toward them, even living with personality traits of others that may grate against our personality. Paul tells us that our "every action must be done with love." (1 Cor. 16:14, HCSB) This love will help us deal with those scratches on our feelings. Of course, prayer is paramount and really ties into that spiritual Neosporin of which we spoke. Prayer need not be bent over piously saying well thought-out words to God. Prayer can also be openly talking with God, telling him how we feel and walking through our feelings. Our next heading can be used for trivial affronts to us and the deeper wounds which we will discuss thereafter.

Prayer and Rational Self-Talk

Self-talk is what we tell ourselves in our thoughts. In fact, it is the words we tell ourselves about people, self, experiences, life, in general, God, the future, the past, the present. It is all the words that we say to ourselves all the time. Actually, if we regularly cultivate and entertain slights against us or the deeper personal affronts, it can lead to destructive depression, mood slumps, our self-worth plummeting, our body feeling sluggish, our will to accomplish even the tiniest of things is not to be realized, and our actions defeat us.

Intense negative thinking will always lead to at least a minor depressive episode or simple painful emotion. Our thoughts based on a good mood will be entirely different from those based on our being upset. Negative thoughts that flood our mind are the actual contributors of our self-defeating emotions. These very thoughts are what keep us sluggish and contribute to our feeling frustrated, angry, or worthless. Therefore, this thinking is the key to our relief.

Every time we feel down about something, attempt to locate the corresponding negative thought that contributed to our feeling down. It is these thoughts that have created our feelings of frustration, anger, or low self-worth. By learning to offset them and replace them with rational thoughts, we can actually change our mood. Remember the thoughts that move through our mind, with no effort, this is the easiest course to follow as these are established pathways to our way of thinking. It is so subconscious that they even go unnoticed. Therefore, if we have a negative way of thinking, we will continue down that path until we establish a new positive pathway in our thinking.

The centerpiece to it all is the mind. Our moods, behaviors and body responses result from the way we view things. It is a proven fact that we cannot experience any event in any way, shape, or form unless we have processed it with our mind first. No event can depress us; it is our perception of that event that will depress us or make us angry. If we are only sad over an event, our thoughts will be rational, but if we are depressed, wrathful, or anxious over an event, our thinking will be bent and irrational, distorted and utterly wrong.

It may be difficult for each of us to wrap our mind around it, but we are superb at telling ourselves outright lies and half-truths, repeatedly throughout each day. In fact, some of us are so good at it that it has become our reality and leads to annoyance, stress, irritation, anger, even depression, and anxiety. This section should be a beginning in helping us to start identifying these lies and half-truths.

Lies about Self

- I am dumb
- I am unattractive

- No one really likes me
- I have no talent
- I am miserable
- This always happens to me
- This is the story of my life
- Life is never going to change
- I am so lonely
- I am no good

Lies about Others

- He always makes dumb comments
- He is always saying things like that
- No one really likes him
- He has no respect
- He makes me miserable
- He always making me unhappy
- Why does he always do that
- He is never going to change
- He should …
- He is no good

DEGRADING SELF

1. Self-degrading:

I am so stupid

I never get anything right.

Everything I do seem to fail. Even when I do all I can to make someone love me; they just end up rejecting me.

2. Situation Degrading:

Life is the same every day; I do not even know why I bother getting up!

Life just kicks me in the face every day—it stinks!

3. Future Degrading:

I am never going to make it in life; I do not know why I even try. It is a waste of time!

DEGRADING OTHERS

1. Degrading Others:

He is always saying rude things

He never goes a day without insulting me

Everything word out of his mouth seems to be meant for me. Even when I do all I can to make things right, he just keeps hurting my feelings.

2. Situation Degrading:

He treats me the same every day; I do not even know why I bother trying to remain friends!

He makes life miserable for me–He is not worth my efforts!

3. Future Degrading:

I am never going forgive him again; I do not know why I even try. It is a waste of time!

I will never talk with him again. Forgiveness, what is that!

I will avoid him like everyone else that mistreats me. Forgiveness? Never!

We must appreciate that our thinking can deceive all of us, contributing to our belief that the negative mood, which has been created, because of our thinking, is reality, when it is not. If we have established a negative way of thinking, an irrational way of thinking, our mind will simply accept it as truth. Within a moment, we can alter our mood, and it is not even likely we notice it taking place. These negative feelings seem as though they are the real thing, which only reinforces to the deceptive thinking.

If we are under mental distress, and we find ourselves having anger issues or mild depression and are unhappy much of the time, we need to be in prayer for Holy Spirit. However, we need to act in behalf of our prayers as well. Remember, the Bible is the Spirit-inspired Word of God, so applying it is actually acting in behalf of our prayers. It is likely that we can combine our spiritual pursuits with some self-help cognitive-behavioral therapy. Our recommending cognitive therapy principles is not replacing God's Word with modern day psychology, as cognitive-behavioral therapy was in the Bible thousands of years before man discovered this way of dealing with irrational thinking. If things have become more involved, we may want to speak with the elder or pastor. However, if we are moderately depressed, where things feel unbearable because we are having feelings of despair, we need to get some professional help from a Christian counselor. Our recommendation of a placed to find a great Christian counselor is found in the footnote below.[56]

Romans 15:13 Updated American Standard Version (UASV)

[13] Now may the God of hope fill you with all joy and peace in believing, so that you will abound in hope by the power of the Holy Spirit.

Dr. David Burns wrote, "feelings are not facts!" We can be easily tricked by our own thinking. Regardless of what deception our depressed brain tells us, we will accept it as total truth. In fact, it does not take but a partial second to establish these irrational thoughts with ourselves. Therefore, in many cases we are unlikely even to notice it taking places. These negative thoughts feel so right and give credibility to the lie.

Self-Defeating Thoughts

While many are well aware that self-defeating thoughts and behavior(s) are harmful to themselves, they also know that resisting and overcoming them is another story. Self-defeating thoughts and behaviors can become deeply rooted over the years and can be extremely resistant to efforts to change them. Trying to curb such thinking can be exhausting and even painful, spiraling into depression in and of itself.

Humans being in the state of imperfection should not expect perfection in this endeavor. Our genetic heritage, inborn weaknesses, and experiences make it impossible for us to avoid all self-defeating thoughts and behaviors. Therefore, lovingly, we do not demand perfection of ourselves, nor should we of others.

However, this consideration on our part does not absolve us of our responsibility to control our thinking and thus our feelings that lead to moods and behaviors. Behavioral scientists say that self-defeating

---

[56] www.aacc.net/

thoughts, like good ones, are learned and developed over time. If that is correct, then self-defeating thoughts can just as surely be **un**learned! Of course, ridding ourselves of self-defeating thoughts that may have dominated our lives for years will be difficult. We should not underestimate the struggle ahead of us. There will certainly be setbacks and failures. However, rest assured, things usually get easier with time. The more we work at it, the more our new behavior will become a part of us. How?

Life: Common everyday events, both positive and negative

Thoughts: Each of these events is interpreted by your thinking throughout the day.

Mood: It is developed not by the day's events; no, it is developed by our perception of those events, by our thinking.

Every bad feeling that we have are a direct result of our bent thinking. If one finds themselves embedded in day-in-and-day-out of negative thinking, there is most certainly going to be an outburst of anger or some mild depressive episode will follow. We will not be so bold as to use the word "cause," but instead we will say *contribute*. Thus, we will find that those continual negative thoughts will contribute to an emotional spiral until it arrives at the bottom floor of a depressive episode.

Breaking Away From Bent Thinking

1. Identify and own our bent thinking. We have to self-analyze our days. We must slow down and identify what thinking error we are having and write it down. This is called mental journaling. If we are careful and wisely analyze, we can keep track of the thinking stimulus that sets off our feelings, followed by our actions. In our prayerful conversations with God, we can identify the thinking error, and internally discuss the irrational thought with God. Why is it irrational thinking? What would be the rational thought?

2. Replace the bent (irrational) thinking with rational thinking. We start self-branding ourselves: "I am no good," "I am lazy." Or we self-brand others: "he is always saying things like ..." He is rude." We should immediately stop and start to rationally reason with ourselves. "No I am not no good, this is doing nothing but making me feel worse, I am a good person who makes mistakes like everyone else." Or, "Well, he isn't always saying bad things and we all slip in what we say at times."

Positive self-talk should be done at length, keeping it honest, and aloud if possible.

3. Keep Records. Each day we need to write down the episodes of negative self-abuse, bent thinking that we go through, as well as the forms. In addition, the time spent in rationalizing with the negative thoughts. At the end of the day, summarize it in a short paragraph. We should see a decrease almost immediately in our first week.

4. Let others know. Keep our friends and family in the loop of what we are attempting to do. Periodically ask them if they notice a change in attitude and mood. Explain to them that it is best if they are honest with us. Also, prepare mentally for a possible negative feedback. Simply use the feedback as an instrument and know that more work is needed.

5. The most important key is to be practical and balanced. It took many years to achieve our way of thinking; it is not going to change overnight. In addition, if we put 50% into the putting on a new person, we will get 50% out of it. If we put 100% in, we will get 100% out of it. We should notice a small difference in a week, but we should see tremendous changes in about a four months period, some maybe six months to a year.

6. Pray to God. We need to bring God into the picture, for him, nothing is impossible.--Psalm 55:22; Luke 18:27

Read the list below of Twelve Distorted Thoughts. These were developed with the idea of focusing on the culprit that is guilty of the distortion (self), and what it is (thinking). As we work our way through this book or any self-help book, we should have the Twelve Distorted Thoughts in front of us (mentally, i.e., memorized).

Twelve Distorted Thoughts

1. SELF-ABSOLUTE (THINKING)

With this frame of mind, there is no middle ground. One who has a setback in life will see it as nothing more than a life-ending result. To receive one bad mark on a work evaluation is the same as receiving all bad marks. To receive a "D" on a school report card will be viewed as a life-ending grade. For these ones, absolute thinking is only applicable when it comes to bad thing, they do not seem to have the same over the top thinking when they receive an "A+" on their report card.

2. SELF-SWEEPING (THINKING)

If a bad event happens to us, we say, "This is the story of my life." We see our life as a never-ending series of negative events. For us one bad event might as well be a thousand because we blow it up in our mind.

3. SELF-BRANDED (THINKING)

We own every negative event that happens in our life as being our fault. We carry the weight of the world on our shoulders. If something positive happens it is a freak accident, because nothing good happens to us.

4. SELF-CLASSIFYING (THINKING)

As these negative events unfold on us, we own those that are not even ours, we begin to classify ourselves as "losers," "total failures," "disappointments," "let downs." It is to the point that we even begin to question why we were even born.

5. SELF-RATIONALIZING (THINKING)

We perceive life in a negative manner, even though, much of our lives may be just fine. We refuse to acknowledge the good in our lives, or the possibility of it becoming good.

6. SELF-PROPHECY (THINKING)

We see everything as ending negatively, so we end up fulfilling our own negative thinking. A negative event happens to us and we have already mapped out in our mind the dreadful course, followed by a tragic ending. John calls to say he **cannot** make the dinner date tonight. At once, Lisa is offering reasons as to why he has broken off the date: 'he doesn't like me;' 'he has found someone else' and on and on.

7. SELF-PSYCHIC (THINKING)

We regularly have a feeling that someone is thinking badly of us or talking badly about us without any evidence. We assume that bad things just always happen to us.

8. SELF-AMPLIFYING (THINKING)

Small negative things, events that happen to each of us every day, are amplified to unrealistic measures by our overactive thinking. This has such an impact that, if one small thing happens in the morning, it can impact the rest of the day because this one will self-fulfill their prophecy that this is how their entire day will go.

9. SELF-FOCUS (THINKING)

We focus in on the negative details, seeing nothing else. We refuse to see the bright side of any situation. If one attempts to point to some positive aspect of anything, we negate them and their audacity even to consider such a thing.

10. SELF-PROJECTING (THINKING)

Jim should have done this. Jane should have said this. Mark should not have done that. This is simply projecting us on everyone else.

11. SELF-LABELING (THINKING)

I am no good! I am not a good mother. I am a poor student. I am stupid.

12 SELF-PERSONALIZING (THINKING)

With no evidence, we make ourselves the scapegoat because we will always blame ourselves for everything. Lisa thinks, 'If only I were a better wife!' Lisa, as a verbally abused wife, thinks, 'it's my fault; I must be doing something wrong.' On the other hand, Lisa may scream at her husband habitually, so much so that he loses his self-esteem, "I can never do anything right.'

Dealing with Our Imperfections

Mental distress is not a part of healthy living. The important aspect is that it can be overcome by learning some simple methods that will elevate our moods. The techniques of having rational self-talk with God and identifying our irrational thinking will reduce the symptoms of a variety of mental distresses (frustration, anger, jealousy, anxiety, etc.). The idea of how we think is how we feel has been in psychology books for over one hundred years. However, it has been in God's Word, many Bible books, for about 2,000 – 3,000 years. God's Word and cognitive therapy can help us control the symptoms that lead to mental distress and help us to recreate a completely new personality. Paul calls it putting on the new person and removing the old person.

1. Swift Improvement of Thinking Errors: For those suffering from a milder form of mental distresses such as moodiness or anxiety, control of thinking and the new personality can be achieved in as little as three to six months, depending on the level of effort placed into oneself.

2. The Ability to Fully Grasp: In the end, by way of deep study in God's Word, we will fully grasp exactly why our moods alter and have at our disposal, numerous principles to apply in controlling these mood swings. We will understand the difference between bent-thinking and rational thinking and be able to recognize the level of our mood.

3. Control Not Removal: Our irrational thinking is a part of the person that is imperfect; it can only be controlled, not cured. However, there will be new life-skills that we will learn to cut off and control the distorted thinking and emotion before they consume us.

4. New Person: This new person can be maintained, but we have to always be aware of the symptoms, events and situations that can contribute to a setback.

First, one needs to recognize that ALL of their moods are brought on by our internal self-talk. This is based on the way one looks at something: perceptions, mental attitudes, and beliefs. The way we feel at this very moment is based on the self-talk that is going on between our ears.

Second, when one is distressed mentally, such as mild depressed frustration, anger, jealousy, or anxiety; really any negative mood, their thoughts are dominating the mood. We perceive not only ourselves but also the entire world in such a way that it regulates our moods. Moreover, we will buy into this false reality. If we have hit a low, we will move into the stage, believing that 'this is who I am and it has and will always been this way.' As we reflect on the past, only those bad moments will surface. In addition, we will project this bad past as an ongoing reality for our future, creating a feeling of hopelessness.

Third, we must realize that the thinking that creates our moods is really a gross distortion of reality; this is why we are so affected by them. Although they appear valid at present, we will find that they are irrational and just downright wrong. Our mind is like a transmission in a car, where our thinking is a result of mental slippage and not accurate perception. As we progress in rational thinking and we begin to master methods that will help us identify this mental slippage, we will begin to remove that way of thinking and we will begin to feel better for longer periods of time, until it is the norm.

Fourth, we will begin to use the Scriptures in an entirely new way. It is paramount that we take note of how the Scriptures offer us far more than the mere surface knowledge that we have grown accustomed to, and see that by our having an accurate, deep understanding, with application, we can begin to alter our old person into an entirely different person. It is highly recommended that the reader consider three other publications by this author as well.[57]

Dealing with Deeper Wounds

What are we to do, though, if others sin against us causing deeper wounds? If the sin is not that deep, we may simply apply Paul's words to the Ephesians, "forgiving one another, as God in Christ forgave you." (4:32, ESV) This eagerness to forgive is found in Peter's counsel as well, "Above all, keep loving one another earnestly, since love covers a multitude of sins." (1 Pet. 4:8, ESV) If we can keep the fact that we too are sinners to the forefront of our thinking, this will make it easier for us to forgive others. We can do as God does for us; we make allowances for human imperfection. When we do forgive the other, it is completely releasing them from our mind, calling their sin to mind no more, not holding onto the resentment. If we can do this, we can resume our relationship with the offender as though they had never sinned against us. Moreover, this level of forgiveness will help us to maintain peace in the congregation. – Romans 14:19.

However, if the offender sin to the point of serious injury, deeply hurting us, we may need to take more steps that simply freely forgiving him. If the circumstances permit, our first step would be speaking with the offender. If we are taking this approach, it is best not to procrastinate, as time will allow the wounds to deepen. Paul exhorted, "Be angry, and yet do not sin; do not let the sun go down on your anger." (Eph. 4:26, NASB) In other words, get it done within a day, i.e., quickly. – Matthew 5:23-24.

How are to approach the person that sinned against us? We can apply Peter's counsel to "seek peace and pursue it." Thus, we want to set aside our anger and seek peace with our brother. Such an approach

---

[57] PUT OFF THE OLD PERSON WITH ITS PRACTICES And Put On the New Person, By Edward D. Andrews

http://www.christianpublishers.org/apps/webstore/products/show/4832713

APPLYING GOD'S WORD MORE FULLY IN YOUR LIFE How to Broaden and Deepen Your Understanding of God's Word by Edward D. Andrews

http://www.christianpublishers.org/apps/webstore/products/show/4676315

WALK HUMBLY WITH YOUR GOD: Putting God's Purpose First in Your Life by Edward D. Andrews (Apr 29, 2013)

http://www.christianpublishers.org/apps/webstore/products/show/4676342

means that we choose our words carefully, not wanting to use tough, harsh or accusatory words or body language. If we do, this will likely cause him to return in kind and things will escalate. (Pro. 15:18; 29:11) Remember the section above that spoke of distorted thoughts. Number 8 was SELF-AMPLIFYING (THINKING), Small negative things, events that happen to each of us every day, are amplified to unrealistic measures by our overactive thinking. Number 10 SELF-PROJECTING (THINKING), Jim *should* have done this. Jane *should* have said this. Mark *should* not have done that. This is simply projecting us on everyone else. While these are not a perfect fit here because someone has done us wrong, the principle still applies. If we are trying to pursue peace, we do not want to use exaggerated statements, such as "You *always* do this ...!" "You *never* ...!" These types of comments will do one thing, place him on the defensive because no one does or says anything every time.

Rather, we want to allow our tone of voice and body language to speak for us as well, conveying that it is our desire to resolve what has caused us pain. We do not want to come across as ambiguous, though, as they may not realize the extent that we were hurt, so we need to be specific. We also need to give them an opportunity to explain their side of things. (Jam. 1:19) We want to listen carefully to what they have to say. It is common for people to rationalize, minimize and justify their bad behavior, so this is to be expected as a possibility. However, do not approach it by saying things like, "You are just making excuses." Rather, express how it makes us feel. "When you say ..., it makes me feel like you are not seeing how it has hurt me." Proverbs 19:11 explains, "A person's insight gives him patience, and his virtue is to overlook an offense." (HCSB) We need to get at the feelings the real reasons behind his committing the offense. This will help us overcome and negative feelings on our part.

When we forgive others, are we obligated to forget what happened? Is it even possible to forget what happened? How does God deal with the forgiveness of our sins? "I, I am he who blots out your transgressions for my own sake, and I will not remember your sins."[58] (Isaiah 43:25)

---

[58] This verse is one of the highest points of grace in the OT. In spite of Israel's utter unworthiness, the Lord in His grace has devised a way that He can forgive their sins and grant righteousness (see note on 61:10) without compromising His holiness. This redemption He would accomplish through the work of His Servant (53:6). In spite of her failures, Israel will always be God's chosen people. – MacArthur, John (2005-05-09). *The MacArthur Bible Commentary* (Kindle Locations 28881-28884). Thomas Nelson. Kindle Edition.

Repentant King David said: "My sin I finally confessed to you, and my error I did not cover. I said: I acknowledged my sin to you, and I did not cover my iniquity; I said, "I will confess my transgressions to the Lord," and you forgave the iniquity of my sin." (Psalm 32:5, ESV) How completely does God forgive?

Psalm 103:12 Updated American Standard Version (UASV)

¹² As far as the east is from the west,
so far does he remove our transgressions from us.

We will notice in Psalm 103:12, that God removes the sins of the repentant one as far as the east is from the west. The picture being painted is, to the human mind that is the farthest we can remove something, as there is no greater distance.

Isaiah 38:17 Updated American Standard Version (UASV)

¹⁷ Look, it was for my welfare
    that I had great bitterness;
but in love you have delivered my soul
    from the pit of destruction,
for you have cast all my sins
    behind your back.

In Isaiah 38, we are given another visual, God throwing our sins behind his back, meaning he can no longer see them, as they are out of sight, thus out of mind.

Micah 7:19 Updated American Standard Version (UASV)

¹⁹ He will again have compassion on us;
    he will tread our iniquities underfoot.
You will cast all our sins
    into the depths of the sea.

In Micah, our last example, we see that God hurls all of the sins of a repentant person into the depths of the sea. In the setting of the ancient person, this meant that retrieving them was literally impossible. In other words, God has removed them, to never be retrieved or brought to mind ever again. This was the viewpoint that he had before Jesus ever even offered himself as a ransom sacrifice. While all three examples seem to point to completely forgetting, we know that it is impossible for God to forget out sins. All of these cases are making the point that he simply does not call them to mind no more. In other words, once he forgives, he never again raises those sins against us.

Similarly, a criminal can get his record expunged, which is defined as getting rid of something completely, or do away with something. Does the court 'get rid of the crime completely'? No. they lay a sheet of paper over the file that states it is expunged. However, when one applies for a job, they are legally allowed to answer that they have never committed a crime; it is as though they never broke into the store. When the prospective employer does a background check, it will come back that the person has no criminal history. Is the court unaware of that crime? No, they know it is there, but it is to never be used against the offender again. Even if that offender down the road commits another breaking and entering, the expunged one will not be brought up in court. That expunged crime can never be weighed against the offender again; it is as though it never happened.

Likewise, when we forgive a brother or a sister, it is not as though we cannot remember the offense, but once we forgive them, it cannot be thrown up at them at some future time. Moreover, we would never talk about it to other (i.e., gossip) because it has been expunged from history. It is true that this may not be something we can do overnight because the wounds are fresh, so it may be in our mind each time we see him, it is at the forefront of our thinking. This is where our self-talk prayer with God comes in, so we can rationalize our irrational thinking. As time passes, the wound will heal. In time, the closeness that we shared prior to the offense will be restored. – Luke 17:3.

Deepest of Wounds from the Unrepentant

What are we to do, though, if the offender commits a serious offense against us, wounding us deeply but refuses to acknowledge his sin? What is he does not even evidence any form of repentance? What are we to do, if the offender refuses to apologize? (Pro. 28:13) Well, we have been imitating God through the escalation of this discussion, so we stay on that course. Scripture shows that God does not forgive unrepentant sinners. (Heb. 6:4-6; 10:26-27) Therefore, we are not obligated to forgive an unrepentant sinner, as they are God's enemies. Let no one tell us that we are to forgive one who commits a malicious, willful sin against others or us and is not repentant. – Psalm 139:21-22.

Even though we are not obligated to forgive such ones who have committed cruel acts against us, remember that to hold onto frustration, anxiety and anger will only be harmful to us. If we sit around waiting on some apology that will never come, this will simply cause us more mental distress, i.e., more victimization at our own hands. If we focus on the injustice of his seeming to get away with hurting us, it will serve to damage us even more emotionally, spiritually, mentally and even physically. What we would be doing is allowing an offender, who likely has not given us a second thought, to continue hurting us. We need to apply the Psalmists words, "Refrain from anger, and forsake wrath!" (Ps. 37:8, ESV) This type of forgiveness is not about forgetting or expunging the wrongdoer, it is about ceasing to hold onto the resentment, refusing to allow him to control our emotions, and leaving the justice in God's hands. – Psalm 37:28.

When we are wounded deeply, if we cannot deal with it, it will affect how we live our lives, refusing to trust those who are worthy of our trust. While we may not be able to remove the sting of the sin, it will dissipate with time. Understanding the levels of forgiveness, appreciating the way God forgives and walking with God, will ease the pain and give us some semblance of normalcy now. Moreover, God promises that soon he "will wipe away every tear from their eyes, and death shall be no more, neither shall there be mourning, nor crying, nor pain anymore, for the former things have passed away." (Rev. 21:4) While we will remember at that time, it will cause us no pain at all. – Philippians 4:7.

Review Questions

- Paul and Jesus said what about forgiving others.

- Why is it so difficult for us to forgive others

- Why forgive others?

- How should we deal with minor irritations from others?

- What does it mean by putting up with one another?

- What is prayer and rational self-talk?

- What are self-defeating thoughts?

- How do we break away from bent thinking?

- What are some of the twelve distorted thoughts?

- How do we deal with our imperfections?

- How are we to deal with deeper wounds?

- How are we to deal with the deepest of wounds from unrepentant ones?

- How does God forget and why should we try to imitate such forgiveness?

- What type of forgiveness are we to have for the unrepentant wrongdoer?

CHAPTER 7 You Must Crucify the Flesh with Its Passions and Desires

Galatians 5:24 Updated American Standard Version (UASV)

²⁴ And those who belong to Christ Jesus have crucified the flesh with its passions and desires.

On this verse, The Holman News Testament Commentary has, "The struggle between our flesh and our new nature is real ... When Christ died, our flesh was judged. This does not mean our propensity to sin has been eradicated or rendered inoperative. We must accept that our old nature has died with Christ and that as new people we have an increasing power to resist sin (Rom. 6:10–12)." (Anders 1999, p. 66) While it is, true that our old nature died and we are truly new persons, having increased power to resist sin; this does not mean that our old nature is ineffective and that we have some magical power so that we do not need to worry about the desires for inappropriate pleasure. This power comes from God's Word. If we do nothing with God's Word our power will be negligible. If we do not possess a correct understanding of God's Word; then, our power will also be insignificant.

Just because we are born again Christians, this does not mean that we are no longer imperfect, suffering with human weaknesses, or that we are no longer living in imperfect flesh. Wrong desires are gratifying to our imperfect human flesh, and they are not easily set aside. "Those who belong to Christ Jesus have crucified the flesh with its passions and desires."[59] (Gal. 5:24) Being crucified in the days of Jesus was an extremely harsh way to be executed and more painful than we will ever want to know. Therefore, we still need to take harsh measures with ourselves to set aside and deaden the body members to improper desires, before they have taken root in our heart and mind. A simple example is the modern day immorality of television and movies. If a television show

---

[59] "The struggle between our flesh and our new nature is real. Yet there is more truth to help us win this battle. Paul explains that those who know Jesus Christ do not have to respond to the flesh because they have crucified the [flesh] with its passions and desires. This crucifixion refers to our identification with Christ in his death and resurrection (Gal. 2:20). When Christ died, our flesh was judged. This does not mean our propensity to sin has been eradicated or rendered inoperative. We must accept that our old nature has died with Christ and that as new people we have an increasing power to resist sin (Rom. 6:10–12)." (Anders 1999, p. 66)

or movie were to excite sexual arousal in us, we should turn it off immediately. When we ignore our Christian conscience, it becomes callused. In time, we would no longer be warned by it as to what is good and what is bad. Another example would be that we need to be conscious of our conversations with unbelievers at the workplace or in school and how we look at those of the opposite sex. – Matthew 5:28-30; Colossians 3:5.

Ephesians 4:24 Updated American Standard Version (UASV)

[24] and put on the new man,[60] the one created according to the likeness of God in righteousness and loyalty of the truth.

> This means, we are to allow the new self to govern our activities. We are to begin living the lifestyle that corresponds to who we have become in Christ. This new holy self shows we are maturing, growing in unity with the body, and doing our part of the body's work.[61]

God is "the Father of lights," and "there is *no* darkness in him at all." (James 1:17; 1 John 1:5) The Son said of himself, "I am the light of the world. Whoever follows me will **not** walk in darkness, but will have the light of life." (John 8:12) Christian worshipers of the Father and the Son have the illumination: mentally, emotionally, morally, and spiritually, as "they shine as lights in the world." (Phil 2:15) Jesus said to his followers in the Sermon on the Mount, "Let your light shine before others, so that they may see your good works and give glory to your Father who is in heaven." (Matt. 5:16) Jesus also said,

John 3:19-21 Updated American Standard Version (UASV)

[19] And this is the judgment: that the light has come into the world, and men loved the darkness rather than the light, because their works were wicked. [20] For the one who practices wicked things hates the light and does not come to the light, so that his works may not be exposed. [21] But the one who practices the truth comes to the light, in order that his works may be revealed that they are accomplished in God.

Some 2,700 year ago, the Prophet Isaiah gave this coming contrast,

---

[60] An interpretive translation would have, "put on the new person," because it does mean male or female.

[61] (Anders, Holman New Testament Commentary: vol. 8, Galatians, Ephesians, Philippians, Colossians 1999, p. 155)

Isaiah 60:2 Updated American Standard Version (UASV)

2 For, behold, darkness shall cover the earth and thick darkness the peoples; but Jehovah[62] will arise upon you, and his glory will be seen upon you.

Some 700 years later, the apostle Paul spoke of the condition of all humanity, who is alienated from God,

Ephesians 6:12 Updated American Standard Version (UASV)

12 For our struggle[63] is not against flesh and blood, but against the rulers, against the powers, against the world-rulers of this darkness, against the wicked spirit forces in the heavenly places.

"The reason this spiritual armor is needed is that **our struggle is not against flesh and blood**. The picture of warfare here implies that we do not face a physical army. We face a spiritual army. Therefore our weapons must be spiritual." This list "seems to suggest a hierarchy of evil spirit-beings who do the bidding of Satan in opposing the will of God on earth."[64] Paul was very concerned about this darkness outside of God's sovereignty, exhorting Christians on how they were to remain free from such darkness,

Ephesians 4:17 (UASV)	Ephesians 5:8 (UASV)
17 This, therefore, I say and bear witness to in the Lord, that you no longer walk as the Gentiles also walk, in the futility of their mind,	8 for you were formerly darkness, but now you are light in the Lord; walk as children of light

Here in 4:17, Paul speaks of "the futility of their mind." What did he mean? According to The Anchor Bible, it "implies emptiness, idleness, vanity, foolishness, purposelessness, and frustration." What Paul wanted his first century readers of Ephesus to realize was, the fame and glory of the Greek culture and Roman Empire, may have seemed striking, remarkable and extraordinary, but to pursue them was 'empty, vanity, foolish, and purposeless.' This mindset was merely immediate

---

[62] For those unfamiliar with the use of the divine name, Jehovah of the Old Testament is a reference to the Father.

[63] Lit., "wrestling."

[64] (Anders, Holman New Testament Commentary: vol. 8, Galatians, Ephesians, Philippians, Colossians 1999, p. 191)

gratification, a showy display of one's life, which would end in frustration and regret. If this were true of that ancient world, how much more true would it be of our narcissistic world of today? In Ephesians 5:8, Paul helps his readers to appreciate that they were freed from the darkness of this world; therefore, they were/are obligated to "walk as children of light."

Come to Know Jesus Christ

Paul goes on to describe the unclean world of his day, as well as the worthless pursuits, before returning to the Ephesian Christians.

Ephesians 4:20-21 Updated American Standard Version (UASV)

20 But you did not learn Christ in this way, 21 if indeed you have heard him and have been taught in him, just as truth is in Jesus

The apostle had spent close to three years in the city of Ephesus, preaching and teaching. Therefore, he would have known many in the Ephesian congregation. (Acts 20:31-35) Thus, when he said, "that is not the way you learned Christ," he evidenced just how well he knew the Ephesian Christians, that they had not be taught some lenient, diluted, wishy-washy truth that would condone the types of serious wrongdoing that he had described in 4:17-19. He knew that they had been given an accurate knowledge of the real Christian way of life, which was exemplified by Jesus Christ. As a result, the Ephesians no longer walked in the darkness of the Roman world that surrounded them. Rather, they 'walked as children of light.'

Considering verses 20-21 of Ephesians chapter 4, we notice that Paul implied a study process of sorts, with his expressions: 'to 'learn,' 'to hear' and 'to be taught.' Of course, we cannot learn from Jesus directly, like those throughout his three and half year ministry. However, we can "learn Christ" through the Word of God, and the many helpful study tools that are available to us today. Yet, this is only possible, if we buy out the time for diligent personal Bible study at home, and take the time to prepare for Christian meetings. Moreover, we need to put faith in the things that we learn, which is evidenced by our applying them into our daily lives. Then, we can honestly say, that we "have heard about him and were taught in him."

Note too, that after the study process, Paul said, "As the truth is in Jesus." We should observe that Paul hardly ever uses the personal name *Jesus* in his writings, without also using *Christ* or just Christ alone. In other words, he says either Jesus Christ, or Christ. In fact, out of 47 references to Jesus Christ in the book of Ephesians, this is the only time that he uses *Jesus* by itself. Generally, a reference to the personal name Jesus alone is to the person of Jesus, his human side, while a reference to Christ alone is a reference to his office, the anointed one. Jesus had said of him, "I am the way, and the truth, and the life." (John 14:6) Paul elsewhere tells us that in Jesus "are hidden all the treasures of wisdom and knowledge." Jesus did not say, 'I am the teacher of the truth,' but rather "I am … the truth." He was the greatest teacher who has ever lived, but he also lived the truth and was the epitome of the truth, i.e., was the embodiment of the truth, the personification of the truth. Therefore, being a true Christian is not just having a head full of knowledge and wisdom, but it is also a way of life, the essence of who we are. When we "learn Christ," this means that we pattern ourselves after him, imitating him, following in his steps closely, by living the truth. Paul helps us to appreciate how we can "learn Christ" and "walk as children of light, as he went on to say,

Take Off the Old Man

Ephesians 4:22-24 Updated American Standard Version (UASV)

22 *that* you **take off**, according to your former way of life, the old man, who is being destroyed according to deceitful desires,23 and to be renewed in the spirit of your minds, 24 and **put on** the new man,65 the one created according to the likeness of God in righteousness and loyalty of the truth.

The often-used metaphorical image of 'putting off' and 'putting on' reminds us of taking of and putting on an article of clothes. (Rom. 13:12, 14; Eph. 6:11-17; Col. 3:8-12; 1 Thess. 5:8) If we carry the metaphor a little further, the article of clothing is taken off once it has been soiled, and a new article of clothing is put on. If we are out eating and spill some soup down the front of our shirt, we rush to change it. Certainly, our spirituality is far more critical than an article of clothing.

How does one go about taking off that old person? If we look at the Greek verb behind "put off," we will notice that it is in the aorist tense. The aspect66 of the aorist is like that of a snapshot photo, while other

---

65 An interpretive translation would have, "put on the new person," because it does mean male or female.

66 **Tense** refers to a grammatical temporal reference; that is referring to a particular time frame is intrinsic with the meaning of tense.

verbs, such as the present and the imperfect, are more like an ongoing movie. Buist Fanning describes aspect in this way: "The action can be viewed from a reference-point *within* the action, without reference to the beginning or end-point of the action, but with a focus instead on its internal structure or make-up. Or the action can be viewed from a vantage-point *outside* the action, with focus on the whole action from beginning to end, but without reference to its internal structure."[67]

The "aorist aspect was used when the Greek writer didn't want you to pay any attention to the duration or the completion of the action. ... The action itself could have taken years, but that's not the point." (Black 1998, 96) The action here of 'putting off" the old person is a onetime snapshot, or 'once and for all.' 'The old person, as well as our former manner of life,' must be removed with a certain and conclusive action, carefully and completely. In other words, this is not something we can simply consider, dither or even waver in doing. Why?

The expression "being corrupted" is evidence that "the old self" is in a constant and progressive decline into a moral ruination, continuously deteriorating. Yes, as we subtly feed the desires of the flesh, our moral compass that God gave us is weakened, until it no longer warns of the wrongs that we practice. Yes, they become our new norms. Those of humanity who reject the Word of God will continue in this not caring about good behavior or morals, i.e., downward spiral. They will believe that they do have values, moral and good behavior, but this is because they have ruined their moral compass and are unable to recognize the difference between good and bad. These have "become hardened by the deception of sin." (Hebrews 3:13) This is what is known as innocent appearing situations, where they place themselves in harm's way spiritually, not even realizing the dangers, like an animal that is boiled alive, because the heat is turned up so slow, they do not realize that they are being cooked. If we allow ourselves to ignore the Scriptures, the path is the same for us as well. The end of those *things is* death."--Romans 6:21

Aspect refers to viewpoint – how the action is viewed: perfective (from the outside, as a whole, from afar), or imperfective (from the inside, reference to internal structure and its details).

Aktionsart refers to how an action takes place – what sort of action it is: once-occurring, instantaneous event (punctiliar); repeated over and over (iterative); focuses on the beginning (ingressive)

[67] Buist M. Fanning, Verbal Aspect in New Testament Greek (Oxford Theological Monographs; Oxford: Clarendon, 1990), 27.

Romans 8:13 Updated American Standard Version (UASV)

¹³ for if you are living according to the flesh, you must die; but if by the Spirit you put to death the deeds of the body, you will live.

On this verse, the Holman New Testament Commentary has that "Paul begins by saying that believers are under obligation—but **not to the sinful nature**. Rather, our obligation is to the Spirit. The believer is indwelled by the Spirit;[68] the believer's spirit has been regenerated by the Spirit; and the believer's body will be resurrected from the dead by the Spirit. That puts the believer under an obligation to **put to death the misdeeds of the body**. What believer, understanding the implications of the presence of the Spirit that Paul has just enumerated, could feel the slightest freedom to indulge the sinful desires of the flesh? We are under a holy obligation. And if we do not put to death **the misdeeds of the body?** It is a sign that no obligation to do so is felt, which is a sign of the lack of the presence of the Spirit, which is a sign that **you will die**." (Boa and Kruidenier 2000, p. 254)

Be Renewed in the Spirit of Your Mind

If we have gotten our clothes soiled with dirt, grease and sweat while, at work, we do not just come home and take off our clothes, and put on clean clothes. No, we take a shower, cleaning our body thoroughly before we put on clean clothes.[69] This is what Paul makes clear in the second half of his spiritual illumination, saying, 'be renewed in the spirit of our mind. (Eph. 4:23) Back in verses 17-18 of this chapter Paul said that the worldly were 'walking in the futility of their mind,' "being darkened in understanding." The *mind* is the center of consciousness that generates thoughts, feelings, ideas, and perceptions, and stores knowledge

---

[68] For a biblically correct understanding of the indwelling of the spirit, please see this free chapter online.

http://www.christianpublishers.org/holy-spirit-indwelling

Also, see: **The Work of the Holy Spirit**,

http://www.christianpublishers.org/holy-spirit-the-work-of

As well as **The Holy Spirit in the First Century and Today**

http://www.christianpublishers.org/holy-spirit-then-and-now

[69] Allowing sweat (perspiration) to sit on our flesh inspires bacterial growth, which may contribute to an outbreak on the surface of the skin that is often reddish and itchy.

and memories. This is what must be renewed. How does this renewal process work?

"According to Ephesians 4:23, the sphere in which the renewal takes place is 'the spirit of your mind,' an unusual expression which has no analogy in the rest of ancient Greek literature. Many regard the phrase as a reference to the Holy Spirit and render the verse, 'Be renewed by the Spirit in your mind'. No, this is not the case, the phrase "renewed in the spirit of your mind," literally reads, "to be renewed in the spirit of the mind of you." (Marshall 1993, p. 768-9) Nowhere in Scripture is the Holy Spirit spoken of as belonging to humans, or as a part of a human. Here the meaning is "a person's emotional dispositions considered collectively and understood by the seat of emotional faculties, the soul; especially as positively or negatively disposed toward God." (Boisen, et al. 2014) In other words, the inclination causes a person to exhibit a particular attitude, outlook, or feeling or to act in a certain way or follow a certain course. Therefore, the "spirit of the mind" is the force that sets our mind into motion, i.e., our inclinations, predisposition, leanings, likings, or dispositions.

Because of human imperfection, the "spirit of the mind" or the force that sets our mind into motion is toward the desires of his or her imperfect flesh. (Eccl. 7:20; 1 Cor. 2:14; Col. 1:21; 2:18) Some Christians have taken of the old person, and have given up their former bad practices, but have not overcome their sinful mental inclinations, leanings, predisposition, likings, or dispositions. This means, they will eventually return to those bad practices if their mental inclinations go unchanged. An example would be those who have given up smoking or abusing alcohol or drugs. If they have not made any effort toward being made new in the force that sets their mind into motion, they will eventually return to their former ways. If there is to be real change, they must 'be transformed by the renewal of their mind.' – Romans 12:2.

Do we play a role in making the force that sets our mind into motion new, so that our inclinations, predisposition, leanings, likings, or dispositions are toward good? The Greek verb ananeousthai (to be renewed) is in the present tense, which is expressing continuous action.[70] What continuous action is needed? We need to have a personal Bible study program, as well as a family Bible study if we have a family. This

---

[70] The verb tense where the writer portrays an action in process or a state of being with no assessment of the action's completion. Michael S. Heiser, *Glossary of Morpho-Syntactic Database Terminology* (Logos Bible Software, 2005).

study needs to be more involved than just surface reading of the Bible. We also need to be preparing for each Christian meeting, so that we can fully participate. What does this accomplish? It is by our taking in this knowledge, which is inspired by God (2 Tim. 3:16), generated by the Holy Spirit (2 Pet. 1:21), and is brought back to our minds by the Holy Spirit. Let us take a quick look at the science of how memories are stored in our brain.

How Memories are Stored in the Brain

Researchers have been able to trace memory down to the structural and even the molecular level in recent years, showing that memories are stored throughout many brain structures in the connections between neurons, and can even depend on a single molecule for their long-term stability.

The brain stores memories in two ways. Short-term memories like a possible chess move, or a hotel room number are processed in the front of the brain in a highly developed area called the pre-frontal lobe, according to McGill University and the Canadian Institute of Neurosciences, Mental Health and Addiction.

Short-term recollection is translated into long-term memory in the hippocampus, an area in the deeper brain. According to McGills, the hippocampus takes simultaneous memories from different sensory regions of the brain and connects them into a single "episode" of memory, for example, you may have one memory of a dinner party rather than multiple separate memories of how the party looked, sounded, and smelled.

According to McGill, as memories are played through the hippocampus, the connections between neurons associated with a memory eventually become a fixed combination, so that if you hear a piece of music for example, you are likely to be flooded with other memories you associate with a certain episode where you heard that same music.[71]

In some ways, a memory implanted in our brain is like writing on the hard drive of our computer (i.e., storing and retrieving digital

---

[71] Live Science: http://www.livescience.com/32798-how-are-memories-stored-in-the-brain.html

information), which is relatively permanent. The reason we run the disk defragmenter is to keep the information in its proper place. As we work with our computer throughout the day, it is like taking books off the shelf at the library, and then putting in back in the wrong place. At the end of the day, the librarian is tasked with putting them back in the right place. Our disk defragmenter accomplishes the same thing, so the information can be found faster. When the memory is created in our brain, it leaves an imprint, which is accessed faster and faster each time that it is used. If the information that is stored is the Bible and Bible study tools, it will begin to create new patterns of thinking within us. Within our brain lies our worldview. A worldview is a comprehensive and usually personal conception or view of humanity, the world, or life.

Everything from the day that we were born plays a role in developing our worldview. Such things that develop our worldview are life experiences, parents, teachers, news media, entertainment, work experiences, politics, as well as our religious experiences. Literally, everything that enters our minds develops our worldview. Therefore, as we take in spiritual food, we are developing our biblical worldview, developing a new pattern of thinking, i.e., we are being renewed in the spirit of our mind. Now, if we barely fed on the Word of God, we would have a very weak biblical mindset, just as we would have a very weak body if we barely ate food. In addition, if we ate nothing but junk food, we would not have a healthy body. Additionally, if we ate foods that were harmful to our body (allergic), it could kill us. Therefore, if we take in junk food type information or harmful information into our brain, it could affect our spiritual health even causing spiritual shipwreck. – Philippians 4:8.

Put On the New Man

Ephesians 4:24 Updated American Standard Version (UASV)

[24] and **put on** the new man, the one created according to the likeness of God in righteousness and loyalty of the truth.

We take off the old man; clean ourselves up from the practicing of any sin, renewing the spirit of our mind, putting on the new man. This "new" man is not a *new* version of us, it is a completely *new* us, "in accordance with God." Paul told the Colossians, "put on the new person who is being renewed to accurate knowledge[72] according to the image of the one who created him" (3:10) How does this completely new man come about?

Adam and Eve were created in the image of God (Gen. 1:26-27), meaning that they possessed a perfect moral compass and spiritual qualities, which imperfect humans still possess to a degree. Once we accept Jesus Christ, to the point of complete trust in his ransom sacrifice, we will take off the old man, and we "will be set free from its bondage to corruption and obtain the freedom of the glory of the children of God." (Rom 8:19-21) If we truly 'belong to Christ Jesus we will have crucified the flesh with its passions and desires.' – Galatians 5:24.

Romans 6:6 Updated American Standard Version (UASV)

⁶ knowing this, that our old man was crucified together with *him*, in order that the body of sin might be done away with, so that we would no longer be slaves to sin.

Those who are truly Christian are "no longer be slaves to sin," carrying out "the works of the flesh." Rather, they are entertaining "the fruit of the Spirit." (Gal. 5:19-23, ESV) Those who are truly Christian realize that the old person is counted as being "dead" by God, so they put forth much effort in keeping the fallen flesh under subjection. They keep the apostle Paul's words in mind. "In him also you were circumcised with a circumcision made without hands, by putting off the body of the flesh, by the circumcision of Christ, having been buried with him in baptism, in which you were also raised with him through faith in the powerful working of God, who raised him from the dead." – Colossians 2:11-12, ESV.

Take Off the Old Person and Put On the New Person

Colossians 3:5-7 Updated American Standard Version (UASV)

⁵ Deaden, therefore, your members on the earth: sexual immorality,[73] uncleanness, lustful passion,[74] evil desire, and greediness,

---

[72] *Epignosis* is a strengthened or intensified form of *gnosis* (*epi*, meaning "additional"), meaning, "true," "real," "full," "complete" or "accurate," depending upon the context. Paul and Peter alone use *epignosis*.

[73] Gr *porneia*

which is idolatry. **6** On account of these the wrath of God is coming [upon the sons of disobedience],[75] **7** and you once walked in these things when you were living in them.

We might just be entering into the Christian faith from the world of humankind alienated from God. On the other hand, we may have been a Christian for some time, but have stumbled in our faith with a serious sin and are working toward recovering spiritually. If so, we need to put to death our body members, which is no easy task considering that we are mentally bent toward evil (Gen 6:5; 8:21, AT), and our heart [inner person, seat of motivation] "is deceitful above all things, and desperately sick." (Jer. 17:9, ESV) Therefore, we must be determined if we are to win this battle over the fallen flesh. We begin with sober, intense and deep prayer for God's help, followed by acting in behalf of that prayer. If we understand the level of our fallen condition and have an accurate knowledge of Scripture, which needs to be applied, we can reject wrong desires and pursue righteousness and godly devotion even though we live in Satan's world that caters to our human weaknesses.

Sexual fantasies can infect our worship of God. This is why Paul exhorted us to "deaden, therefore, your members" in relation to "sexual immorality,[76] uncleanness, lustful passion,[77] evil desire, and greediness, which is idolatry." Paul is connecting lustful passion with greediness [covetousness], which is to have a strong desire to possess something that belongs to somebody else. Why is covetousness or greediness a form of idolatry? Because the one craving puts his desires before everything else in his life, for example, his family, the congregation and God. Sexually explicit material will stimulate "lustful passion" for something that belongs to somebody else. This need not be to the extreme of pornographic images per se, but can be scantily dressed character in a television show,

---

[74] Lit *passion*; Gr *pathos*

[75] The longer reading, "upon the sons of disobedience," has good early documentary support, but it is also absent from some very good early witnesses as well. In all likelihood, early scribes felt that something should have been a direct object after "the wrath of God is coming" upon whom? Thus, they likely made it to conform to the parallel passage of Eph. 5:6. Paul informs his readers as to why the wrath is coming (4:5), but not who the object of that wrath is. Of course, it would be upon those who are disobedient. We retained it in square brackets because it is found in the Untied Bible Society and the Nestle-Aland Greek text.

[76] Gr *porneia*

[77] Lit *passion*; Gr *pathos*

or the lust can be for someone we know. Whatever one lusts after, he worships it.

Colossians 3:8 Updated American Standard Version (UASV)

⁸ But now you must put them all away: anger, wrath, malice, slander, and obscene talk from your mouth.

On this verse, the Holman New Testament Commentary has, In verse 8, Paul switches metaphors. The exhortation remains the same, but the picture changes. The imagery behind the call to **rid yourselves**, in verse 8, and **take off** and **put on**, in verses 9 and 10, is that of taking off clothes. Believers are to discard their old, repulsive habits like a set of worn-out clothes. They are then to adorn themselves with the kind of behaviors that will make them well dressed and appropriately fashionable.

"Not only are perverted passions to be eliminated (vv. 5–7), believers must also **rid [themselves]** of a hot temper. **Anger** (*orge*) is a settled feeling, the slow, seething, smoldering emotion that boils below the surface. **Rage** (*thumos*) is a quick, sudden outburst, the blaze of emotion which flares up and burns with intensity."

"Between the sins of the hot temper (anger, rage) and the sins of the sharp tongue (slander, filthy language), Paul mentions **malice**. The Greek term (*kakian*) refers to "ill will, the vicious, deliberate intention of doing harm to others." This ill will may work itself out through angry outbursts or sinful speech."

Slander (*blaspemian*) is basically defamation of character. To slander someone is to injure their reputation. This term is sometimes used in reference to God; but in this context, it probably refers to slanderous speech against another person. **Filthy language** refers to "obscene or abusive speech."[78]

Colossians 3:9-11 Updated American Standard Version (UASV)

⁹ Do not lie to one another, seeing that you have put off the old man[79] with its practices ¹⁰ and have put on the new man[80] who is being

---

[78] Max Anders, *Galatians-Colossians*, vol. 8, Holman New Testament Commentary (Nashville, TN: Broadman & Holman Publishers, 1999), 330.

[79] Or *old person*

[80] Or *new person*

renewed through accurate knowledge[81] according to the image of the one who created him, **11** where there is not Greek and Jew, circumcised and uncircumcised, barbarian, Scythian, slave, free; but Christ is all, and in all.

The Human Mind

Before discussing what Paul meant by the words that he used, let us consider how the human mind works. Science has certainly taken us a long way in our understanding of how the mind works, but it is only a grain of sand on the beach of sand in comparison to what we do not know. However, we have enough in these basics to understand some fundamental processes. When we open our eyes to the light of a new morning, it is altered into and electrical charge by the time it arrives at the gray matter of our brain's cerebral cortex. As the sound of the morning birds reaches our gray matter, it arrives as electrical impulses. The rest of our senses (smell, taste, and touch) arrive as electrical currents in the brain's cortex as well. The white matter of our brain lies within the cortex of gray matter, used as a tool to send electrical messages to other cells within other parts of the gray matter. Thus, when anyone of our five senses detects danger, at the speed of light, a message is sent to the motor section, to prepare us for the needed action of either fight or flight.

Here lies the key to altering our way of thinking. Every single thought, whether it is conscious or subconscious makes an electrical path through the white matter of our brain, with a record of the thought and event. This holds true with our actions as well. If it is a repeated way of thinking or acting, it has no need to form a new path; it only digs a deeper, engrained, established path. This would explain how a factory worker who has been on the job for some time, gives little thought as they perform their repetitive functions each day, it becomes unthinking, automatic, mechanical. These repeated actions become habitual. There is yet another facet to be considered; the habits, repeated thoughts and actions become simple and effortless to repeat. Any new thoughts and actions are more difficult to perform, as there needs to be new pathways opened up.

The human baby starts with a blank slate, with a minimal amount of stable paths built in to survive those first few crucial years. At the boy grows into childhood, there is a flood of pathways established, more than all of the internet connections worldwide. Our five senses are

---

[81] See Romans 3:20 ftn.

continuously adding to the maze. Ps. 139:14: "I will give thanks to you, for I am fearfully and wonderfully made. . . ." (NASB) So, it could never be overstated as to the importance of the foundational thinking and behavior that should be established in our children from infancy forward.

Human Nature Transformed

It is really possible to overcome many of the worst traits of human nature that we may have picked up throughout our life before having become a Christian? Again, Paul, in his letter to fellow Christians at Colossae, wrote, "put off the old man with its practices and have put on the new man who is being renewed through accurate knowledge according to the image of the one who created him." As we saw from the above, Paul lists some of the practices of the old person (lit. man) that we tend to gravitate toward, yet must be removed and controlled. In 3:5, he mentions sexual immorality, uncleanness, lustful passion, evil desire, and greediness, which is idolatry. In 3:8, Paul mentions anger, wrath, malice, slander, and obscene talk.

The apostle Paul urged at Ephesians 4:22, "that you take off, according to your former way of life, the old man, who is being destroyed according to **deceitful desires**." Yes, we are not to try and patch up our old person, but rather we are to take off our old person. Notice why we are to take off instead of patch up, it is because of our "**deceptive desires**," which linger in our heart [inner person, seat of motivation] that is deceitful above all things, and desperately sick, which we cannot understand.' (Jer. 17:9, ESV) Sadly, some Christians have rationalized the fact that they are more like the world and less like Christ by saying their forms of entertainment does not bother their conscience, so it is not wrong. What they have not considered is that their conscience is wrong. In other words, their **deceptive desires** of their **deceitful** and **sick** heart are misleading them.

Just because our conscience does not bother us over something, does not in and of itself mean that our course is Scriptural. Even the apostle Paul wrote of himself, "I find it to be a law that when I want to do right, evil lies close at hand. For I delight in the law of God, in my inner being, but I see in my members another law waging war against the law of my mind and making me captive to the law of sin that dwells in my members." (Rom. 7:21-23, ESV) He then asks, "Wretched man that I am! Who will deliver me from this body of death?" (7:24) The answer, "Thanks be to God through Jesus Christ our Lord! So then, I myself serve

the law of God with my mind, but with my flesh I serve the law of sin."
(7:25) Elsewhere, he wrote, "For I am conscious of nothing against
myself, yet I am not by this acquitted; but **the one who <u>examines</u> me** is
the Lord." (1 Cor. 4:4, NASB) The conscience of the first century Christians
had become callused, unfeeling to the point that they could tolerate
immorality among themselves, even boasting about it. – 1 Corinthians 5:1,
2, 6; Titus 1:15; 1 Timothy 4:2.

It is a slippery slope of sorts. We become a Christian and in the
beginning, we are very strong spiritually because everything is new and
our senses are attuned to anything that might be biblically wrong. In fact,
during this period, we are usually overly sensitive and are not doing
things that are actually allowed. However, once we mature and realize
the extent of our biblical freedoms, we start to practice things that we
formerly viewed as being wrong when we were a spiritual babe.
However, some take it a step further when their conscience lets them
know that a song, a movie, a game or some activity is wrong, they ignore
their conscience and soon it becomes unfeeling at level of wrongness.
Then, we began ignoring our conscience at higher and higher levels of
wrongness. While we need to be *spiritually mature* about our Christian
freedoms, we also need to remain *spiritually strong* to set aside the tidal
wave of immorality and violence sweeping over the world. While we
cannot change the world, for Paul said it will only go from bad to worse,
we can improve our *spiritual strength* to battle it. We do this with the
Word of God, the body of Christ, the Holy Spirit, and prayer.

We need to have a daily personal Bible study and a weekly family
study. Joshua wrote, "This book of the law shall not depart from your
mouth, but you shall meditate on it [God's Word] day and night [i.e.,
regularly], so that you may be careful to do according to all that is written
in it; for then you will make your way prosperous, and then you will
have success." – Joshua 1:8.

Bible study will help us to 'be transformed by the renewal of our
mind, that by testing we may discern what is the will of God, what is
good and acceptable and perfect. ' (Rom. 12:2) For instance, if we
practice "the works of the flesh," we "will not inherit the kingdom of
God." These include such things as, "sexual immorality, impurity,
sensuality, 20 idolatry, sorcery, enmity, strife, jealousy, fits of anger,
rivalries, dissensions, divisions, 21 envy, drunkenness, orgies, **and things
like these**." (Gal. 5:19-21) Yes, Paul mentions other *things like these*, like
Colossians 3:5, he mentions sexual immorality, uncleanness, lustful
passion, evil desire, and greediness, which is idolatry. In Colossians 3:8,

Paul mentions anger, wrath, malice, slander, and obscene talk. In Ephesians 5:3-5, the Paul mentions 'sexual immorality, and all uncleanness, or greediness, must not even be named among you, as is proper among holy ones; and there must be no filthiness nor foolish talk nor crude joking, which are not fitting, but rather giving of thanks. For this you know with certainty, that no sexually immoral or impure person or covetous man, who is an idolater.' (Eph. 5:3-5) Furthermore, neither the sexually immoral, nor idolaters, nor adulterers, nor men who practice homosexuality, nor thieves, nor the greedy, nor drunkards, nor revilers, nor swindlers will inherit the kingdom of God." – 1 Corinthians 6:9-10.

When Paul uses the phrase "things like these," he is showing that none of his lists is exhaustive. In other words, if it is like these examples, it is a part of the list even though he did not specifically mention it. If one were to remove all of these practices, it would certainly mean a much more wholesome life. However, taking off the old person (lit. man) is only the beginning. We also need to put on the new person (lit. man), which Paul describe with another list. He wrote, "A heart of compassion, kindness, humility, meekness, and patience, putting up with one another and forgiving one another. If anyone should have a complaint against another, forgiving each other; as the Lord has forgiven you, so you also must forgive. And above all these things put on love, which is a perfect bond of union." (Col. 3:12-14) We will discuss these verses more fully in a moment.

Here is where the Holy Spirit comes in, as without the help of the Spirit it is impossible to become the new Christlike person. "The fruit of the Spirit is love, joy, peace, patience, kindness, goodness, faithfulness, gentleness, [and] self-control." Jesus said the two greatest commandments are, "You shall love the Lord your God with all your heart and with all your soul and with all your mind. This is the great and first commandment. And a second is like it: You shall love your neighbor as yourself." (Matt. 22:37-39, ESV) James, Jesus half-brother wrote, "If you really fulfill the royal law according to the Scripture, 'You shall love your neighbor as yourself,' you are doing well." – James 2:8.

If we are to become *spiritually mature* and *spiritually strong*, we also need God's people in the Christian congregation. On this, the apostle Paul[82] wrote, "let us consider how to stimulate one another to love and

---

[82] **Who Authored the Book of Hebrews: A Defense for Pauline Authorship**

http://www.christianpublishers.org/who-authored-hebrews

good deeds, not forsaking our own assembling together, as is the habit of some, but encouraging one another; and all the more as you see the day drawing near." (Heb. 10:24-25, NASB) The fourth piece of the process to being *spiritually mature* and *spiritually strong* is prayer. Paull tells us to "not be anxious about anything, but in everything by prayer and supplication with thanksgiving let your requests be made known to God." (Phil. 4:6, ESV) He further tells us, "Rejoice in hope, be patient in tribulation, be constant in prayer." (Rom. 12:12, ESV) He says that we are to "pray without ceasing." (1 Thess. 5:17, ESV) We are to "put on the whole armor of God, that you may be able to stand against the schemes of the devil ... praying at all times in the Spirit, with all prayer and supplication." (Eph. 6:11-18, ESV) Bear in mind that God only listens to the praters of the righteous ones. If we expect our prayers to be heard by God, we must be doing our best to live by God's Word. (Pro. 15:29; 28:9) We must have a humble heart when we pray. (Lu 18:9-14) We need to act in behalf of what we ask of God. God will answer our prayers if it is according to his will and purposes. – Hebrews 11:6.

Seek New Behavior

Colossians 3:12-14 Updated American Standard Version (UASV)

¹² Therefore, put on as God's chosen ones, holy and beloved, a heart of compassionate, kindness, humility, meekness, and patience, ¹³ putting up with one another and forgiving one another. If anyone should have a complaint against another, forgiving each other; as the Lord has forgiven you, so you also must forgive. ¹⁴ And above all these things put on love, which is a perfect bond of union.

On these verses, the Holman New Testament Commentary has the following. Verses 12–17 contain the virtues that stand in contrast to the vices mentioned in the preceding verses. With the old discarded, the character of Christ is to be displayed in its place. The transformation process includes more than don'ts. There are some dos as well.

Since the old humanity has been **put off** and the new community has been **put on**, believers are **therefore** to **clothe** themselves with the kind of behavioral apparel that fits their new life. The famous story "The Emperor's New Clothes" by Hans Christian Andersen has many possible applications for believers. One of them would be the simple lesson that we are not to be foolish like the emperor and take off our old clothes and put nothing back on. Before listing the appropriate attire, Paul reminds believers that they are **God's chosen people, holy and dearly loved.**

These are exalted titles formerly used as designations for the nation of Israel (Deut. 4:37; 7:7–8) but now applied to the new community in Christ (1 Pet. 2:9–10).

William Barclay has an insightful comment on the nature of the virtues listed now:

> 'It is most significant to note that every one of the virtues and graces listed has to do with personal relationships between man and man. There is no mention of virtues like efficiency, cleverness, even diligence and industry—not that these things are not important. But the great basic Christian virtues are the virtues which govern and set the tone of human relationships. Christianity is community' (Barclay, 188).

"The first piece in the believer's fashionable wardrobe is **compassion**, which refers to "heartfelt sympathy for those suffering or in need." The next item in the believer's wardrobe is **kindness**, the friendly and helpful spirit which meets needs through good deeds. This is the concrete action of compassion. If the believer is to be fully dressed, other Christlike characteristics are to be worn as well. The believer is to be clothed with **humility**, which is a proper estimation of oneself (Rom. 12:3). **Humility** is not a self-debasing attitude (like the "false humility" of 2:18 and 2:23) but an attitude that is free from pride and self-assertion. The believer is to be clothed with **gentleness**, sometimes translated "meekness." **Gentleness** has been described as "power under control"; the picture of a powerful horse under the control of its master is a helpful image. The attitude behind **gentleness** is an attitude of refusing to demand one's rights. The believer is to be clothed with **patience** which is the capacity to bear injustice or injury without revenge or retaliation."

"The idea of putting up with the abuses and offenses of others continues with Paul's call to **bear with each other**. Believers are to go beyond quiet resignation positively to **forgive whatever grievances [they] may have against one another**. Believers have been fully forgiven by Christ (2:13–14), and the forgiven are obligated to become forgivers. The standard for this forgiveness is Christ himself."

"Paul saves the most important item of clothing for last. Without love, all the other virtues may amount to mere moralism and little else (a thought found also in 1 Cor. 13:1–3). When love is present, there is harmony and unity in the community. It is not clear whether **love** binds the virtues together, completing a lovely garment of Christlike character, or whether **love** binds the members of the community together in mature

102

oneness. Perhaps the ambiguity is intentional. Both ideas make good sense."[83]

Colossians 3:15 Updated American Standard Version (UASV)

[15] And let the peace of Christ rule in your hearts,[84] to which also[85] you were called in one body. And be thankful.[86]

What if we have some within our Christian congregations, who have shortcomings that grate against our personality, to the point that it irritates us? How are we to remain calm in such an environment? The apostle Paul provides us with inspired counsel that will help us to maintain **a perfect bond of union** (v. 14), allowing **the peace of Christ rule in [our] hearts**. The Greek word behind rule literally means, "**to be acting as umpire.**" When there are differences between two people, we simply allow **the peace of Christ** to make the call as an umpire would. This **peace** is the calmness, the composure that we gain when we become disciples of **Christ**. This peace is there because we know for a certainty that we are loved and accepted by the Father and the Son. Our being **thankful** will also add much toward maintaining peace with our Christian brothers and sisters. Therefore, we do well to cultivate a spirit of gratitude.

Colossians 3:16 Updated American Standard Version (UASV)

[16] Let the word of Christ[87] dwell in you richly, in[88] all wisdom, teaching and admonishing[89] one another with psalms and hymns and spiritual songs, singing with grace in your hearts unto God.

After Paul exhorts us to be **thankful** (v. 15), he writes, **Let the word of Christ dwell in you richly, in all wisdom**. This means that we are to let the whole of Jesus' teaching, really the whole of the Word of God to become a part of our mindset, our way of thinking, embedded

---

[83] Max Anders, *Galatians-Colossians*, vol. 8, Holman New Testament Commentary (Nashville, TN: Broadman & Holman Publishers, 1999), 331–332.

[84] Or *control your hearts*

[85] Or *indeed*

[86] Or *show yourselves thankful*

[87] The Christ P46 א2 B C2 D F G Ψ 1739 Maj it copsa; the Lord א* I copbo; God A C* 33

[88] Or *with*

[89] Or *encouraging*

in our inner person. The interpretive paraphrase, *J. B. Phillips New Testament*, puts it this way, "Let Christ's teaching live in your hearts, making you rich in the true wisdom." If the entirety of God's Word is to take up residence in us, we must be familiar with it to the point that we are absorbed with the truth. When this takes place, the Holy Spirit guides us because God inspired all Scripture, as the Spirit moved along men to pen the very Word of God. If **the word of Christ** dwells in us richly, we will be encouraging and upbuilding toward our brothers and sisters in the faith.

Colossians 3:17 Updated American Standard Version (UASV)

[17] And whatever you do, in word or deed, do all in the name of the Lord Jesus, giving thanks to God the Father through him.

If we are to have the joy and contentment in all aspects of our lives, that Jesus' half-brother spoke of (Jam. 1:2-4), we must have all the factors that Paul spoke of, if we are to preserve the peace. We are disciples of Jesus Christ first and foremost, at all times of our life, not just Christian meetings. This is why the apostle Paul wrote: "whatever you do, in word or deed, do all in the name of the Lord Jesus, giving thanks to God the Father through him." Therefore, in every facet of our lives, in word and in deed, we are a representative of the Son of God, and we should be grateful for the opportunity to speak in his place.

Earlier we considered Paul's words at Ephesians 4:17-24, which has given us much to ponder. Verses 17-19 are an apt description of the world that we live in, alienated from God, and heading down the path of death. These ones have refused to accept the knowledge that leads to eternal life. While they may seem to succeed in a fallen world, this is short-lived. They do not even realize that they are wallowing in moral and spiritual ruin.

In verses 20-21 of chapter 4,[90] Paul stresses that we need to learn the truth, which is found in Jesus. Lastly, in verses 22-24, we saw that we are to take off the old man and to put on the new man, determinedly and purposefully. As long as we live in this fallen world, under the pressures of Satan and his demon horde, we must continue to feed our minds spiritual food, "for God, who said, "Let light shine out of darkness," has shone in

---

[90] "In contrast to this former way of life, the Ephesian Christians were to live righteous lives. Paul says, 'This is not how you learned from Jesus to live!' 'Your hearts are no longer darkened. You have learned the truth, which is to be found in Jesus.'" (Anders 1999, p. 154)

our hearts to give the light of the knowledge of God's glory in the face of Jesus Christ." – 2 Corinthians 4:6

Review Questions

- Who are the lights of the world, and what role do Christians play?

- How concerned was Paul about the darkness outside of God's sovereignty, and why does it impose such a threat to our light?

- In 4:17, Paul speaks of "the futility of their mind." What did he mean?

- What did Paul evidence when he said, "that is not the way you learned Christ"?

- What do we need to do so that that we can honestly say that we "have heard about him and were taught in him."

- What can we conclude from Jesus saying of himself, "I am ... the truth"?

- How does one go about taking off that old man (person)?

- Why must one be determined and decisive in taking off the old man?

- Talk about the moral compass that God gave Adam and Eve, and what is an innocent appearing situation?

- How are we to understand Romans 8:13?

- How does this renewal process "in the spirit of our mind" work?

- What role do we play in making the force that sets our mind into motion new, so that our inclinations, predisposition, leanings, likings, or dispositions are toward good?

- How are memories stored in the brain, and what illustrations help us to appreciate how we can get at our biblical memories faster? What is a worldview, and how do we develop our biblical worldview?

- In what sense is the new man new?

- How does this completely new man come about?

- How do we "learn Christ"?

- Why is it important that we put away the old person definitively?

- What is the force that sets our mind into motion, and how is it made new?

- What was Adam given that imperfect humans still have, which needs to be cultivated?

- What is the difference between having the truth in our head, being in the truth superficially, as opposed to having the truth in us?

CHAPTER 8 You Must Remain In My Word

John 8:31-32 Updated American Standard Version (UASV)

31 So Jesus said to the Jews who had believed him, "If you **remain in my word**, you are truly my disciples, **32** and you will know the truth, and the truth will set you free."

Only if we remain in the truth of God's Word, can we be freed from a false faith, false teachings, false relationships, false religion, and false righteousness. Those who are truly disciples of Jesus Christ, have the mind of Christ, which encompasses humility. As a Christian grows in knowledge and understanding of God's Word, there will be times that he or she will have to adjust conclusions that were based on a previous understanding. Yes, more knowledge, or accurate knowledge of what may have only been known partially, may mean that we will have to adjust our thinking, which, again, requires humility. Those who are truly Christian will remain in his word, and they will, therefore, be set free by the truth of that word.

One day, Jesus and his disciples were passing through Samaria, when they came to a town called Sychar, where the well of Jacob was. Tired from the journey, he decided this would be the place to rest. A woman from Samaria came to draw water, and a conversation ensued, which ended with Jesus saying, "God is spirit, and those who worship him must worship in spirit and truth." (John 4:24) We will take a deeper look at this verse in a moment, but for now, this is a clear indication that there is a form of worship, which is acceptable and there are forms of worship, which are unacceptable. Jesus made this all too clear when he said, "Not everyone who says to me, 'Lord, Lord,' will enter the kingdom of heaven, but the one who does the will of my Father who is in heaven. On that day, many will say to me, 'Lord, Lord, did we not prophesy in your name, and cast out demons in your name, and do many mighty works in your name?' And then will I declare to them, 'I never knew you; depart from me, you workers of lawlessness.'" (Matthew 7:21-23, ESV) Toward the end of his life and ministry, Jesus prayed to the Father,

John 17:17 Updated American Standard Version (UASV)

17 Sanctify them in the truth; your word is truth.

If there is a form of worship that is acceptable, it must be in harmony with God's Word. God's Word contains the truth about him, his will and his purposes. "The realm in which the disciples' consecration is to be realized is the truth of God's word and of his name (see 17:11).[91] This involves the work of both Son and Spirit; association with them, the one who in his person is the truth (14:6), and the one who is the "Spirit of truth" (14:17; 15:26; 16:13) who will lead believers into all truth (16:13), will so sanctify believers that they will be equipped for service of God. Critically, such service is ultimately grounded in divine revelation and predicated on an accurate understanding of and response to such revelation (Morris 1995: 647)."[92]

Psalm 119:142 Updated American Standard Version (UASV)

[142] Your righteousness is an everlasting righteousness, and your law is truth.

When we compare the laws of man in the lands throughout the world, which in essence are under the control of Satan the Devil, whom Paul called "the god of this world," with the laws of God, we can agree with the Psalmist, "Your law is truth."

2 Samuel 7:28 Updated American Standard Version (UASV)

[28] And now, O Sovereign Lord Jehovah, you are God, and your words are truth, and you have promised this good thing to your servant.

On this verse, the *Holman Old Testament Commentary* has that "David began the conclusion to his prayer of gratitude with a bold command. He ordered God to keep forever the promise he had made about his servant, the promise to build a house–i.e., a dynasty–for David. In addition, the king asked God to bless the house of his servant, that it might continue forever in his sight. David's courage to make these brash requests rested squarely on the word of God. The king knew that God's

---

[91] Barrett (1978: 510) rightly contends that "truth" here "means the saving truth revealed in the teaching and activity of Jesus." Earlier references to the word in this chapter are 17:6 and 17:14 (see also 17:20, and 14:23–24; 15:3, 20, earlier in the farewell discourse). The present phrase is similar to Ps. 119:142: "Your law is true" (cf. 119:151, 160). David likewise acknowledged, "Your words are trustworthy" (2 Sam. 7:28; cf.Ps. 19:7). D. M. Smith (1999: 315) perceptively observes that the reference to God's word here seems sudden, since according to the prologue it is Jesus who is the Word. As Smith duly notes, however, the difficulty is alleviated by the fact that "after Jesus is named (1:17), he is never again called the Word in the Gospel."

[92] Andreas J. Köstenberger, *John*, Baker Exegetical Commentary on the New Testament (Grand Rapids, MI: Baker Academic, 2004), 495–496.

words are trustworthy. And since the Lord had revealed that he would build a house for him and that it would last forever (v. 16), the king found the courage to make these requests."[93]

Psalm 19:7 Updated American Standard Version (UASV)

[7] The law of Jehovah is perfect,
   restoring the soul;
the testimony of Jehovah is sure,
   making wise the simple.

In the Bible, we find answers to life's most difficult questions. Why are we here? What is the meaning of life? If there is a God and he is good, why so much suffering? What is the purpose of our existence? What is right and wrong and who should determine it? Will world peace ever be achieved? Will poverty ever end? How can we be happy? What is true freedom and does it exist? What happens after we die? Is there such a thing as **absolute truth**? Therefore, we discover that we have a Creator and why such a loving Creator would allow sickness, old age and death, with much suffering all throughout our limited lives.[94] We also learn the truth about why we are here, what our Creator expects of us, and how his decisions in our behalf have been for our good. – Isaiah 48:17.

Proverbs 2:6 Updated American Standard Version (UASV)

[6] For Jehovah gives wisdom;
   from his mouth come knowledge and understanding;[95]

If it is the truth, which sets us free, how can we know what the truth is? The most basic rule of biblical interpretation in arriving at the correct meaning of a text is; the text means what the author meant by the words he used, as should have been understood by his intended readers. While we will not take the time to be bogged down in how to correctly interpret God's Word, we will touch on it briefly below, by first offering the Bible advice as to **the level of effort needed**, and recommending

---

[93] Andrews, Stephen J.; Bergen, Robert D. (2009-06-01). *1, 2 Samuel (Holman Old Testament Commentary)* (p. 246). B&H Publishing. Kindle Edition.

[94] **Suffering & Evil - Why God?**

http://www.christianpublishers.org/suffering-evil-why-god

[95] "The words of His mouth are contained in Scripture. It is there that God speaks (cf. Heb. 1:1, 2; 2 Pet. 1:20, 21). True wisdom comes only by revelation." – MacArthur, John (2005-05-09). The MacArthur Bible Commentary (Kindle Locations 24777-24778). Thomas Nelson. Kindle Edition.

the best book for learning the truly conservative evangelical way of interpreting Scripture, that is, grammatical-historical method of interpretation.

Proverbs 2:1-5 Updated American Standard Version (UASV)

¹ My son, if **you** receive my words
 and treasure up my commandments with **you**,
² making **your** ear attentive to wisdom
 and inclining **your** heart to discernment;[96]
³ For if **you** cry for discernment[97]
 and raise **your** voice for understanding,
⁴ if **you** seek it like silver
 and search for it as for hidden treasures,
⁵ then **you** will understand the fear of Jehovah
 and find the knowledge of God.

God has chosen to convey an extremely important message to the human family, one that is a matter of life and death. In his book of 66 smaller books, we find God's will and purpose for us, as well what role we need to play in his purposes. Sir Matthew Hale, lord chief justice of England, once said, "The Bible is the only source of all Christian truth; the only rule for the Christian life; the only book that unfolds to us the realities of eternity."[98]

If we are to know God, it only makes sense; we must know his Word, the Bible. Jesus Christ makes this all too clear for us when he said in prayer to his Father: "This is eternal life: that they may know You, the only true God, and the One You have sent—Jesus Christ." (John 17:3, HCSB) Therefore, here we see that "eternal life" is closely related to our knowing (having a relationship with) God and his Son, Jesus Christ. It is the apostle John who answers the why: "And the world with its lust is passing away, but *the one who does God's will remains forever*." – 1 John 2:17, HCSB

In order to know "*the will of God*," we must recognize and trust that the Bible as our only guide in this matter. Each Christian should ". . . be *filled with the knowledge [lit. accurate or full knowledge] of his will in all*

---

[96] The Hebrew word rendered here as "discernment" (*tevunah*) is related to the word *binah*, translated "understanding." Both appear at Proverbs 2:3.

[97] See 2.2 ftn.

[98] Edward, Tyrone (1966). The New Dictionary of Thoughts: New Delhi: Standard Book Company, p. 40

spiritual wisdom and understanding, *to walk worthily* of the Lord unto all pleasing, bearing fruit in every good work, and increasing in the knowledge [lit. accurate or full knowledge] of God; (Col. 1:9, 10) Is it possible to *"walk worthily"* of God without fully knowing his *will*? Is it possible to know his *will* without first understanding the Bible?

Below are several things that the Bible offers us. The list is in no way exhaustive, but the points help us choose between the wisdom of man as opposed to **the knowledge of God**.

The Bible Gives Us Answers to Questions about Life

The Bible gives us answers to questions about this life and the one to come, which can be found nowhere else, and offers illumination to its readers. Those that take in this life-saving knowledge are freed from the misunderstandings of life that dominate billions of others. For instance, here is one that might come as a shock. We are all **Mentally Bent toward Evil**. See verses below.

Psalm 51:5 Updated American Standard Version (UASV)

5 Behold, I was brought forth in iniquity,[99]
and in sin did my mother conceive me.

King David had his adultery with Bathsheba and the subsequent murder of her husband exposed, for which he accepted full responsibility. His words about the human condition give us one reason for the evil of man. He says, "I was brought forth in iniquity." What is iniquity? The Hebrew word *awon* essentially relates to erring, acting illegally or wrongly.

David stated that his problem was a corrupt heart, saying; **surely, I was sinful at birth**. He entered this world a sinner in nature long before he became a sinner in actions. In fact, this internal corruption predated his **birth**, actually beginning nine months earlier when he was **conceived** in the womb. It was at conception that the Adamic sin nature was

---

[99] Iniquity "signifies an offense, intentional or not, against God's law." (Vine 1996, Vol. 1, P. 122) Really, sin is anything not in harmony with God's personality, standards, ways, and will, which mars one's relationship with God.

transmitted to him. The problem of what he did, sin, arose from what he was, a sinner.[100]

David is not here casting the blame onto his mother, as God never intended mothers to conceive and give birth to children who would sin. Nevertheless, when Adam and Eve rebelled, were expelled from the Garden of Eden, they lost their ability to pass on perfection. Therefore, every child was born missing the mark of perfection. The Hebrew term translated "sin" is *chattath*; in Greek, the word is *hamartia*. Both carry the idea of missing the mark of perfection.

The verbal forms occur in enough secular contexts to provide a basic picture of the word's meaning. In Judges 20:16, the left-handed slingers of Benjamin are said to have the skill to throw stones at targets and "not miss." In a different context, Pro. 19:2 speaks of a man in a hurry who "misses his way" (RSV, neb, KJV has "sinneth"). A similar idea of not finding a goal appears in Pro. 8:36; the concept of failure is implied.[101] Moses tells us in the book of Genesis,

Genesis 6:5 (AT)

[5] When the LORD saw that the wickedness of man on the earth was great, and that the **whole bent of his thinking was** never anything but **evil**, the LORD regretted that he had ever made man on the earth.

Genesis 8:21 (AT)

[21] I will never again curse the soil, though the **bent of man's mind** may be **evil from his very youth**; nor ever again will I ever again destroy all life creature as I have just done.

All of us have inherited a sinful nature, meaning that we are currently unable to live up to the mark of perfection, in which we were created. In fact, Genesis 6:5 says we all suffer from, 'our whole bent of thinking, which is nothing but evil." Genesis 8:21 says that 'our mind is evil from our very youth.' Jeremiah 17:9 says that our hearts are treacherous and desperately sick." What does all of this mean? It means that prior to the fall, our natural inclination; our natural leaning was

---

[100] Anders, Max; Lawson, Steven (2004-01-01). Holman Old Testament Commentary - Psalms: 11 (p. 266). B&H Publishing. Kindle Edition.

[101] G. Herbert Livingston, "638 חָטָא," ed. R. Laird Harris, Gleason L. Archer Jr., and Bruce K. Waltke, *Theological Wordbook of the Old Testament* (Chicago: Moody Press, 1999), 277.

toward good. However, after the fall, our natural inclination, our natural leaning was toward bad, wicked, evil.

We should never lose sight of the fact that unrighteous desires of the flesh are not to be taken lightly. (Rom. 7:19, 20) Nevertheless, if it is our desire to have a righteous relationship before God, it will be the stronger desire. Psalm 119:165 says, "Abundant peace belongs to those who love Your instruction; nothing makes them stumble." We need to cultivate our love for doing right, which will strengthen our conscience, the sense of what is right and wrong that governs somebody's thoughts and actions, urging us to do right rather than wrong. It is only through studying the Bible that we can train the conscience. Once it is trained, it will prick us like a needle in the arm, when we are thinking of doing something wrong. It will feel like a pain in our heart, sadness, nervousness, which is the voice saying, 'do not do this.' Moreover, if we ignore our voice, it will grow silent over time, and will stop telling us what is wrong. – Romans 2:14-15.

James 1:14-15 Updated American Standard Version (UASV)

14 But each one is tempted when he is carried away and enticed by his own desire.[102] **15** Then the desire when it has conceived gives birth to sin, and sin when it is fully grown brings forth death.

We have a natural desire toward wrongdoing, and Satan is the god of this world (2 Cor. 4:3-4), and he caters to the fallen flesh. James also tells us that "each one is tempted when he is carried away and enticed by his own desire. Then the desire when it has conceived gives birth to sin, and sin when it is fully grown brings forth death." (James 1:14-15) We resist the devil by immediately dismissing any thought that is contrary to God's values found in his Word. We do not entertain it for a moment, nor do we cultivate it, causing it to grow. We then offer rational prayers in our head, or better yet, in an undertone, so we can defeat fleshly irrational thinking with rational biblical thinking. The Apostle Peter, referring to the Devil wrote, "Resist him, firm in your faith, knowing that the same kinds of suffering are being experienced by your brotherhood throughout the world." (1 Pet. 5:9) While the Bible helps us better to understand the gravity of our fallen condition, this should not cause us alarm as the Bible also shows us how to control our mental bent toward evil. We can renew our mind (Rom. 12:2), acquire the mind of Christ (1

---

[102] Or "own *lust*"

113

Cor. 2:16)), take of the old person and put on the new person (Eph. 4:20-24; Col 3:9-10), among other things.

The Bible Offers How to Get the Best out of Life Now

Another facet of benefiting from the Bible is that it shows us the way to get the best out of life now, even in imperfection. Again, one basic rule of interpretation is this, there are verses that sound like, "if you do **A**, you will get **B**." This has created some difficulty in many churchgoers because they are treated like absolutes or guarantees; if we do **A** we will get **B**. Scriptures are not to be applied in this sense in an imperfect world, with imperfect people. The best phrase that we can put before the proverb is "generally speaking." Let us look at Proverbs 22:6 as our example, it says, "train up a child in the way he should go; even when he is old he will not depart from it." (ESV) Let us look at a easy version of this, "direct your children onto the right path, and when they are older, they will not leave it." (NLT) Is this an absolute guarantee that, if I raise my children in the best way, when they get older they will not leave it? No. Let us place our phrase in front of it. 'Generally speaking,' if you direct your children onto the right path, and when they are older, they will not leave it.'

1 Timothy 3:2 (UASV)	2 Corinthians 7:1 (UASV)	1 Corinthians 6:18 (UASV)
²Therefore an overseer must be above reproach, the husband of one wife, sober-minded, **self-controlled**, respectable, hospitable, able to teach,	¹ Therefore, having these promises, beloved, let us **cleanse ourselves from all defilement** of flesh and spirit, perfecting holiness in the fear of God.	¹⁸ **Flee from sexual immorality.** Every other sin that a man commits is outside the body, but the sexually immoral person sins against his own body.

What do we discover in these three texts? Is there any doubt that if we possess the quality of **self-control** that we will not have better health and better relationships. Through '**cleansing ourselves from every**

114

defilement of body and spirit,' we evade damaging our health. Finally, the marriage is on safe grounds by our '**fleeing from sexual immorality**.'

The Bible Offers How to Best Live In an Imperfect World

Another aspect of the Bible is that it will help us to find true happiness in this imperfect world that we live in, with the hope of even greater happiness to come. Bible knowledge helps us to discover the innermost harmony and satisfaction that this imperfect life offers, and gives us faith and hopefulness of an even greater one to come. It assists us to develop such pleasing characteristics as empathy, love, joy, peace, kindness, and faith. (Gal. 5:22, 23;[103] Eph. 4:24, 32) Such characteristics will help us to be a better spouse, father or mother, son or daughter, or friend.

The Bible helps us to See What the Future Holds

Another facet of the Bible is its prophecies, which will help us to understand where we are in the steams of time, and what is yet to unfold. Notice the conditions that are coming in the text below.

Revelation 21:3-4 Updated American Standard Version (UASV)

3 And I heard a loud voice from the throne, saying, "Behold, the tabernacle of God is among men, and he will dwell[104] among them, and they shall be his people,[105] and God himself will be among them,[106] **4** and he will wipe away every tear from their eyes, and death shall be no more, neither shall there be mourning, nor crying, nor pain anymore, for the former things have passed away."

---

[103] Godly attitudes that characterize the lives of only those who belong to God by faith in Christ and possess the Spirit of God. The Spirit produces fruit which consists of nine characteristics or attitudes that are inextricably linked with each other and are commanded of believers throughout the NT. – MacArthur, John (2005-05-09). *The MacArthur Bible Commentary* (Kindle Locations 56586-56588). Thomas Nelson. Kindle Edition.

[104] Lit *he will tabernacle*

[105] Some mss *peoples*

[106] One early ms and be *their God*

The Bible helps us Share the Good News

Romans 10:13-17 Updated American Standard Version (UASV)

13 For "everyone who calls on the name of the Lord[107] will be saved.""

14 How then will they call on him in whom they have not believed? And how are they to believe in him of whom they have never heard? And how will they hear without someone to preach?[108] **15** And how are they to preach unless they are sent? As it is written, "How beautiful are the feet of those who declare good news of good things!"[109]

16 But they have not all obeyed the gospel. For Isaiah says, "Lord,[110] who has believed what he has heard from us?" **17** So faith comes from hearing, and hearing through the word of Christ.

The Bible Helps Us Achieve and Maintain Our Spirituality

"The spiritual man is one who walks by the Spirit both in the sense of Gal. 5:16 and in that of 5:25, and who himself manifests the fruit of the Spirit in his own ways ..." (Vine 1996, Vol. 2, P. 595) The apostle Paul wrote, "But a physical man does not accept the things of the Spirit of God, for they are foolishness to him; and he is not able to know them, because they are examined spiritually." (1 Cor. 2:14) It should be noted that Paul, nor any other biblical author ever says that the physical man cannot understand God's Word. If they could not understand it, why would we ever pen books that are geared toward them as an audience? If

---

[107] Quotation from Joel 2:32, which reads, "everyone who calls on the name of Jehovah shall be saved." In other words, Paul was referring to the Father not the Son.

[108] Paul's main point in this series of rhetorical questions is that a clear presentation of the gospel message must precede true saving faith. True faith always has content—the revealed Word of God. Salvation comes to those who hear and believe the facts of the gospel. — MacArthur, John (2005-05-09). *The MacArthur Bible Commentary* (Kindle Locations 52264-52265). Thomas Nelson. Kindle Edition.

[109] Romans 10:15 : Cited from Isa. 52:7; [Nah. 1:15; Eph. 6:15]

[110] Quotation from Isaiah 53:1, which reads, "Who has believed our message? And to whom has the arm of Jehovah been revealed?"

they cannot understand it, why would we ever spend time evangelizing them? The physical man can understand the Word of God, it is just that he sees it as foolish, i.e., having no significance or value, so he places not trust in it.

Matthew 4:4 Updated American Standard Version (UASV)

⁴ But he answered, "It is written,

"'Man shall not live by bread alone,
but by every word that proceeds out of the mouth of God.'"[111]

Matthew 5:3 Updated American Standard Version (UASV)

³ "Blessed[112] are the poor[113] in spirit, for theirs is the kingdom of the heavens.

> In any century, a poor person has little reason to be happy, based on outward circumstances. Jesus, however, clarified in the first words of his sermon that he was not speaking of physical poverty, but spiritual poverty–**poor in spirit**. The beginning of repentance is the recognition of one's spiritual bankruptcy–one's inability to become righteous on one's own. The blessing or happiness that belongs to the poor in spirit is because such a person is, by his admission, already moving toward participating in God's kingdom plan, acknowledging his need for a source of salvation outside himself. Old Testament uses of this concept would have been familiar to Jesus' listeners and Matthew's readers. (Familiar Scriptures would have included Pss. 40:17; 69:29–30, 33–34; Isa. 57:15; 61:1; 66:2, 5.)[114]

Yes, we need to be aware of our spiritual needs. We were created with the need of developing a friendship with our Creator. One thing is for certain, humans may fail us, but God never will. Therefore, we can feel secure in that friendship, like no other.

---

[111] Deut. 8:3

[112] I.e. fortunate or prosperous

[113] "Blessed are those who [are poor in spirit] recognize they are spiritually helpless ..." (GOD'S WORD Translation) The Greek word *ptochos* means "beggar." The "poor in spirit" is an alternative literal rendering. The meaning is that the "beggar/poor in spirit" is aware of his or her spiritual needs, as if a beggar or the poor would be aware of their physical needs.

[114] http://biblia.com/books/hntc61mt/Mt5.3

The Bible Helps Us Understand the Will and Purposes of the Creator

When we enter the pathway of walking with our God, we will certainly come across resistance from three different areas. **Our greatest obstacle** is **ourselves**, because we have inherited imperfection from our first parents Adam and Eve. The Scriptures make it quite clear that we are mentally bent toward bad, not good. (Gen 6:5; 8:21, AT) In other words, our natural desire is toward wrong. Prior to sinning, Adam and Eve were perfect, and they had the natural desire of doing good, and to go against that was to go against the grain of their inner person. Scripture also tells us of our inner person, our heart.

Jeremiah 17:9 Updated American Standard Version (UASV)

⁹ The heart is more deceitful than all else,
and desperately sick; who can understand it?

Romans 7:21-24 Updated American Standard Version (UASV)

²¹ I find then the law in me that when I want to do right, that evil is present in me. ²² For I delight in the law of God according to the inner man, ²³ but I see a different law in my members, warring against the law of my mind and taking me captive in the law of sin which is in my members. ²⁴ Wretched man that I am! Who will deliver me from this body of death?

1 Corinthians 9:27 Updated American Standard Version (UASV)

²⁷ but I discipline my body and make it my slave, so that, after I have preached to others, I myself will not be disqualified.

Paul is describing his approach that he used to correct himself. He disciplined his imperfect human nature with well-directed blows of counsel in the Scriptures. Initially, seeking God's direction in applying the Scriptures, he would go to God in prayer; thereafter, he would work in harmony with the Scriptures to improve himself. We can follow this example to remove any inclinations we might have.

Ephesians 4:1 Updated American Standard Version (UASV)

¹ Therefore I, the prisoner of the Lord, implore you to walk in a manner worthy of the calling with which you have been called,

We need to **walk** in a way that evidences we are truly Christian. Many times, we know that long-suffering will be involved. However, we must fully understand what long-suffering is. It means more than simply suffering some kind of pain, discomfort, or difficulty for an extended period. If someone has chronic pain from arthritis, he will suffer for a long period, but it is not as if he has a choice. The Christian, by his biblical choices, his conscience, makes decision that willfully places him in a position to face mistreatment for indefinite periods. All the while, he does not retaliate or get irritated. He is slow to anger because he has measured control.

Ephesians 5:15-17 Updated American Standard Version (UASV)

¹⁵ Therefore be careful how you walk, not as unwise men but as wise, ¹⁶ buying out¹¹⁵ the time, because the days are evil. ¹⁷ Therefore do not be foolish, but understand what the will of the Lord is.

There are horrific dangers and deceptions that lie within the world that is under the influence of Satan. God recognizes that we are imperfect, knowing that we have human weaknesses that he originally did not intend, meaning that he is aware of how difficult it is to walk in godly wisdom. He is aware that we are all missing the mark of perfection, and that we are all mentally bent toward evil. He knows that our natural desire is to do wrong, and our heart (inner self) is treacherous and we cannot even know it. It is for this reason that he makes allowances for our imperfection. Jesus Christ offered himself as a ransom, covering our Adamic sin and our human weaknesses when we stumble at times, but only if we demonstrate trust in him.

We need to walk not as **unwise** but as **wise**. What does Paul; mean by 'wise' and 'unwise' in this text? God has made known to us his plan of salvation, which was a mystery up until the time of Paul's writings. At that time, he had lavished upon them/us, "in all wisdom and insight making known to us the mystery of his will, according to his purpose, which he set forth in Christ." (Eph. 1:8-9) Yes, God has afforded his people wisdom, "that the God of our Lord Jesus Christ, the Father of glory, may give you the Spirit of wisdom and of revelation in the knowledge of him, having the eyes of your hearts enlightened, that you may know what is the hope to which he has called you." (Eph. 1:17-19) It would take a wise person to understand and appreciate the mystery of salvation, and the fact that they are required to bring their life into harmony with God's magnificent plan of saving the world of mankind who are receptive to accepting Christ. To

---

¹¹⁵ (an idiom, literally 'to redeem the time') to do something with intensity and urgency (used absolutely)—'to work urgently, to redeem the time.'– GELNTBSD

be wise also means that these ones fully grasp the will of the Father (Matt. 7:21), and are carrying that out to the best of their ability. Therefore, the wise accept, value, and see the significance of wisely walking worthily with God. On the other hand, the unwise are those of the world of humankind who are alienated from God, living their life in the moment, walking in the desires of the flesh, because they see God's Word as foolish.

Turning our attention to verse 16 of Ephesians chapter 5, we see that the wise knows how to buy out the opportune time from the world, by living in the world, but they do not use it to the fullest extent, unlike the unwise. Why, because they know that the world of wicked mankind is passing away. The wise one buys time back from this wicked world. Some of the areas that can be bought from are watching less television, less time playing on the computer, other forms of entertainment, not always working overtime, or maybe even not taking a promotion that would cause him to miss Christian meetings, so he can focus on the better things. Some of these better things are personal family time, family Bible study, personal Bible study, religious services, sharing the Good News with others, congregational responsibilities, and so on. Notice below that we were formerly the unwise, but are now the wise.

Ephesians 2:1-3 Updated American Standard Version (UASV)

¹ And you being dead in the trespasses and your sins, ² in which you formerly walked according to the age of this world, according to the ruler of the authority of the air, the spirit now working in the sons of disobedience. ³ Among whom also we all formerly lived in the desires of our flesh, doing the desires of the flesh and of the thoughts, and were by nature children of wrath, even as the rest.

Help in Understanding the Bible

The irony is that hundreds of millions of Christians are humble enough to recognize that the Bible is difficult to understand, it is a deep and complex book. There are tens of millions, who believe they understand everything they read, and for them, the Bible is easy to understand. The sad part is that many of the latter do not understand it any better than the former; they are simply putting a modern-day twist on Scripture and having it say what they want it to say. Even Peter in the first century, one of the pillars of the early church, an apostle of Christ, viewed the Apostle Paul's letters as difficult to understand.

2 Peter 3:15-16 Updated American Standard Version (UASV)

[15] and regard the patience of our Lord as salvation; just as also our beloved brother Paul, according to the wisdom given him, wrote to you, [16] as also in all his letters, speaking in them of these things, in which are some things hard to understand, which the untaught and unstable distort, as they do also the rest of the Scriptures, to their own destruction.

If we are to appreciate and apply the Bible in our lives, we must first fully understand it. We must know what the author of a Bible book meant by the words that he used, as should have been understood by his original intended audience. Then, we will be able to attach the significance that it has in our lives. If we are unaware of the correct way of interpreting the Scriptures, grammatical-historical interpretation, then we are going to be one of those ones who Peter spoke of as, "the ignorant and unstable twist to their own destruction." Hundreds of millions of Christians unknowingly share an incorrect understanding of Scripture, because they are not aware of the principles of interpretation, and how to apply them correctly.[116]

Our **first step** is *observation*, to get as close to the original text as possible. If we do not read Hebrew or Greek; then, two or three literal translations are preferred (ESV, NASB, HCSB). The **second step** is *interpretation*, i.e., what did the author mean by the words that he used, as should have been understood by his original audience. A part of this second step would be what are the differences between the biblical audience and us? As mentioned above, the Christian today is separated from the biblical audience by differences in culture, language, situation, time, and often covenant. The **third step** is the *implications* or *principles* in this text? This is perhaps the most challenging step. In it, we are looking for the implications or principles that are reflected in the meaning of the text we identified in the second step. Part of this third step is making sure that we stay within the pattern of the original meaning when we determine any implications for us. The **fourth step** is *application*. How should individual Christians today live out the implications and principles?

---

[116] Basic Bible Interpretation, Jan 1, 1991 by Roy B. Zuck

A BASIC GUIDE TO BIBLICAL INTERPRETATION Understanding the Correct Methods of Interpretation by Edward D. Andrews (Apr 22, 2014)

http://www.christianpublishers.org/apps/webstore/products/show/4818742

Certainly, no one would suggest that God intended such division and confusion. If each of us can give our own meaning to a text; then, it has no meaning at all, and has lost all authority over our lives.

What does the Bible really teach? For example, is the Bible completely without errors of any kind, or is it only error free on matters of faith? **(Inerrancy)** Was the universe and man created within the past 6,000 to 10,000 years, or are the days creative periods. Or rather, is there a large gap of time between Genesis 1:1 and 1:2, or the literary framework view correct that asserts that God was not having Moses address how He created the world, nor the length of time in which to do such? This view holds that this account in Genesis 1 is merely a literary outline that summarizes a theology of creation. **(Creation Account)** Is God sovereign over all things, or does God limit his control by granting freedom? **(Providence)** Is the image of God our soul, or is the image of God our God-given authority, or is it our relations? **(Divine Image)** Are we made up of a body and soul, or body, soul and spirit, or are we the person a soul? **(Human Constitution)** Did Christ die in our place, or is it that Christ destroyed Satan and his works, or that Christ displayed God's wrath against sin? **(Atonement)** Did God from eternity in the past predestine some to salvation, and others to eternal damnation, or is it that God loves everyone, and we can choose to accept or reject that love, with God not coercing them, while they must maintain an approved standing? **(Salvation)** Is sanctification a declaration by God, or a holiness in Christ and personal conduct, or resting-faith in the sufficiency of Christ, or is it entire sanctification in perfect love? **(Sanctification)** Do we retain our security in the Power of God, or do we need to persist in faith? **(Eternal Security)** Are infants to be baptized, or are only believers to be baptized? **(Baptism)** Is speaking in tongues a true sign of faith, or did speaking in tongues die out after the first century C.E.? **(Gifts)** Is there to be a rapture before the reign of Christ, or are we working toward and waiting for a coming reign of peace, or is the thousand-year conquest of Satan symbolic? (Millennium) These sorts of questions could go on for hundreds of pages.

Help in Teaching the Bible

If we are to fulfill the great commission, that Jesus gave to every Christian, to proclaim and to teach the Good News, we must accurately understand it ourselves first. It was in the spring of 31 C.E., and Jesus was about to speak to a very large, mixed crowd on a mountainside, who were anxiously awaiting what he would teach them. He did not let them down in the least, as he was nothing short of astounding in what and how he taught them. "And when Jesus finished these sayings, the crowds were astonished at his teaching." What was special about his way of teaching, in comparison to what they had been hearing from the Jewish religious leaders? He taught with authority from the Scriptures. He quote or referred to the Old Testament, to support what he was saying. The Jewish religious leaders referred to other Rabbis as their authority.

At the end of his ministry here on earth, he told all of his disciples that they too were to be teachers. He said, "Go therefore and make disciples of all nations ... teaching them to observe all that I have commanded you." (Matthew 28:19-20, ESV) The apostle Paul also exhorted Hebrew Christians of their responsibility to teach when they were trying to slide by on doing the minimum possible. "Though by this time you ought to be teachers, you need someone to teach you the elementary truths of God's word all over again. You need milk, not solid food!" (Hebrews 5:12, NIV) Paul also told Timothy, "the Lord's servant must not be quarrelsome but kind to everyone, table to teach, patiently enduring evil." – 2 Timothy 2:24, ESV.

What about us? Sadly, survey after survey over the last 35 years has shown that 93 percent of Christians today are in the same position as what Paul had said to the Hebrew Christians. "Though by this time you ought to be teachers, you need someone to teach you the elementary truths of God's word all over again. You need milk, not solid food!"

Joshua 1:8-9 Updated American Standard Version (UASV)

8 This Book of the Law shall not depart from your mouth, but you shall meditate on it day and night, so that you may be careful to do according to all that is written in it; for then you will make your way prosperous, and then you will have good success. 9 Have I not commanded you? Be strong and courageous! Do not be afraid, and do not be dismayed, for Jehovah your God is with you wherever you go."

Let us test just how much we can pull from a verse that is informing us of what was said in the opening paragraphs. First, we see that we need to **meditate** on it **day and night** (Psalm 1). The day and night is really hyperbole for reading it every day. The Hebrew word behind meditate (*haghah*) can be rendered "mutter." In other words, as we read, we are to read in an undertone, slightly out load, like muttering to oneself. The process of hearing the words increases our retention of the material dramatically. As Bible students we read to understand and remember what we read, and we are obligated to share this good news with others.

Gesenius' Hebrew and Chaldee Lexicon (translated by S. Tregelles, 1901, p. 215) says of haghah: "Prop[erly] to speak with oneself, murmuring and in a low voice, as is often done by those who are musing."—See also Ps 35:28; 37:30; 71:24; Isa 8:19; 33:18.

The last phrase in verse 8, "you will have good success" can be rendered to "act with insight." How was Joshua to acquire this ability "to act with insight"? He was to meditate on God's Word day and night. What is the equation of Joshua 1:8? If Joshua were to read meditatively (in an undertone) from God's Word daily, applying it in his life, he would be able to act with insight, resulting in his prospering. Of course, the prospering is not financial gain. It is a life of joy and happiness in an age of difficult times. It is avoiding the pitfalls that those in the world around us suffer daily. Moreover, it does not mean that we are to prosper or be successful in an absolute sense because bad things happen to good people. We must add the qualifier, "generally speaking," if we follow God's Word we will have success.

2 Timothy 3:15-17 Updated American Standard Version (UASV)

¹⁵ and that from infancy[117] you [Timothy] have known the sacred writings, which are able to make you wise for salvation through trust[118] in Christ Jesus. ¹⁶ All Scripture is inspired by God and profitable for teaching, for reproof, for correction, for training in righteousness; ¹⁷ so that the man of God may be fully competent, equipped for every good work.

Today we have self-help books by the tens of thousands. We have magazines that offer advice on healthy living, fitness training, parenting, the family, men only, women only, and everything else imaginable. We have mental health doctors on television, offering counsel on everything from dieting, to bipolar disorder. We have professional counselors, covering a variety of walks of life, even Christian counselors. We also have the social worker, psychologist, and psychiatrist, to mention just a few. Nevertheless, tens of millions of people still look to a book, made up of sixty-six smaller books, which were written over a 1,600-year period, by forty different authors, who were inspired by the Creator of all things, THE BIBLE. Where do we go for guidance on the everyday decisions

---

[117] *Brephos* is "the period of time when one is very young—'childhood (probably implying a time when a child is still nursing), infancy." – GELNTBSD

[118] *Pisteuo* is "to believe to the extent of complete trust and reliance—'to believe in, to have confidence in, to have faith in, to trust, faith, trust.' – GELNTBSD

(where to eat), to the major decisions of life (which school to send our kids to)?

Basics in Biblical Interpretation

Step 1: What is the historical setting and background for the author of the book and his audience? Who wrote the book? When and under what circumstances was the book written? Where was the book written? Who were the recipients of the book? Was there anything noteworthy about the place of the recipients? What is the theme of the book? What was the purpose for writing the book?

Step 2a: What would this text have meant to the original audience? (The meaning of a text is what the author meant by the words that he used, as should have been understood by his readers.)

Step 2b: If there are any words in our section that we do not understand, or that stand out as interesting words that may shed some insight on the meaning, look them up in a word dictionary.

Step 2c: After reading our section from the three Bible translations, doing a word study, write down what we think the author meant. Then, pick up a trustworthy commentary, like Holmen Old or New Testament commentary volume, and see if we have it correct.

Step 3: Explain the original meaning down into one or two sentences, preferably one. Then, take the sentence or two; place it in a short phrase.

Step 4: Now, consider their circumstances, the reason for it being written, what it meant to them, and consider examples from our day that would be similar to theirs, which would fit the pattern of meaning. What **implications** can be drawn from the original meaning?

Step 5: Find the pattern of meaning, the "thing like these," and consider how it could apply in our modern day life. How should individual Christians today live out the implications and principles?

We know that Scripture makes it all too clear that there is only one acceptable way of worshiping God, the way outlined in God's Word. Everything that we believe and do needs to be based on that Word, and our understanding of that Word needs to be accurate. There are 41,000 different Christian denominations, and clearly not all are on the path of doing the will of the Father as outlined in the Bible, for Jesus said, in that day he will say to some, "depart from me, you workers of lawlessness." (Matt 7:23) Either we can place our trust in man, who bickers and argues over what the Word of God means, or we can take the Bible's point of view itself. After all, it is the inspired Word of God, which is profitable for teaching, for reproof, for correction, and for training in righteousness, so that the man of God may be complete, equipped for every good work." (2 Tim. 3:16-17) We cannot build our hope for the future on the unstable foundation of human promises; however, we can trust the Word of our loving Creator.

Proverbs 3:5-6 Updated American Standard Version (UASV)

⁵ Trust in Jehovah with all your heart,
   and do not lean on your own understanding.
⁶ In all your ways acknowledge him,
   and he will make straight your paths.

Milton H. Terry wrote, "It is an old and oft-repeated hermeneutical principle that words should be understood in their literal *sense* unless such literal interpretation involves a manifest contradiction or absurdity."[119] Robert L. Towns writes, "The Bible is the best interpreter of itself. As we study the Bible, we should learn to compare the Scriptures we are studying with other relevant passages of Scripture to interpret the Bible."[120] These are a couple of the principles, which this series of books will live by, so that we can trust that these Basic Bible Teachings are from the Word of God, not the Word of man. Moreover, what is offered herein will live by the rules below. Lastly, we can take advantage of the book we recommended by Roy B. Zuck, Basic Bible Interpretation or A BASIC GUIDE TO BIBLICAL INTERPRETATION Understanding the Correct Methods of Interpretation by Edward D. Andrews (Apr 22, 2014), so that we are not entirely dependent on the interpretation of others. In other words, we will be able to do as the Bereans did with the Apostle Paul, and for which he commended them,

Acts 17:10-11 Updated American Standard Version (UASV)

Paul and Silas in Berea

¹⁰ The brothers immediately sent Paul and Silas away by night to Berea, and when they arrived, they went into the synagogue of the Jews. ¹¹ Now these were more noble-minded than those in Thessalonica,

---

[119] Robert L. Thomas. *Evangelical Hermeneutics: The New Versus the Old* (p. 280). Kindle Edition.

[120] Towns, *AMG Concise Bible Doctrines* (AMG Concise Series) (Kindle Locations 1011-1012). AMG Publishers. Kindle Edition.

for they received the word with great eagerness, examining the Scriptures daily to see whether these things were so.

Note that they **(1)** "received the word with all eagerness," and then went about **(2)** "examining the Scriptures daily to see if these things were so." If the apostle Paul was to be examined to see if what he said was so, surely uninspired commentators must be examined as well.

LIVE BY THE RULES

The Rule is to Remember Context

As we know, the context is the surrounding verses and chapters, to the text under consideration, as well as the book, and the entire Word of God. Is the interpretation we have come away with, in harmony with the context? Does this interpretation fit the **pattern of meaning** (see Image 1, below), of the historical setting? For example, Psalm 1:1-3 tells us that if we do not walk in the counsel of the wicked, or stand in the path of sinner, nor sit in the seat with scoffers, but delight in the Word of God, 'whatever he does, he will prosper.' Is that how we are to understand this, WHATEVER we do, we will prosper, if we only follow that counsel? No. again, this is important, in psalms, proverbs and other genre, there is an invisible "generally" before these absolute statements. In other words, 'generally speaking, whatever we do, we will prosper, if we follow the counsel correctly.'

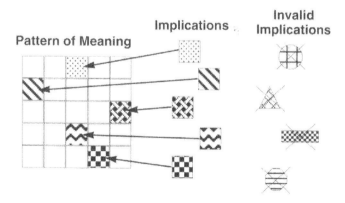

The Rule is Know the Whole of the Word of God

Below, we have repeated a basic interpretation principle for the third time. This is for emphasis because millions violate it. One needs to be familiar with the whole of the Word of God, to not be misled when someone presents us with Scriptures that are out of context. Too many people take a verse by what it says, without looking at what comes before or after it. For example, Jesus said at John 15:7, "ask whatever you wish, and it will be done for you." This brings up to immediate questions: (1) can we simply ask for anything and God will give it to us, (2) and even if it is according to His will and purposes, are we guaranteed of getting it? First, the context of the first part of that verse qualifies what is being talked about here, as Jesus said, "If you abide in me, and my words abide in you . . ." Thus, you must be doing **A** to get **B**. Second, this is not an absolute, which has the invisible "generally speaking" before it. In other words, "generally speaking," if we are abiding in Jesus and his words, the Father will answer our prayer if it is in harmony with His will and purposes.

The Rule is to Remember that Scripture Will Never Contradict Itself

If something is said in one place in Scripture that is at odds with another text in Scripture, it is being misinterpreted, or the context is being violated or misunderstood. There are verses that say the earth will be here forever, and then 2 Peter 3:7 says "the heavens and earth that now exist are stored up for fire." This would seem like a contradiction to the many other verses that say the earth will be here forever. However, if we look at the second half of that verse, it lets us know who is going to be destroyed, "destruction of the ungodly." Therefore, two rules: Scripture will not contradict itself and the context will help us.

The Rule is to Not Hang Our Doctrinal Beliefs on Texts that are Hard to Understand

Do not be ashamed of struggling with passages that are hard to understand, because the apostle Peter even felt this way about some of the Apostle Paul's letters. ". . . Our beloved brother Paul also wrote to you according to the wisdom given him, as he does in all his letters when he speaks in them of these matters. There are some things in them that are hard to understand, which the ignorant and unstable twist to their own destruction, as they do the other Scriptures." – 2 Pet 3:15-16.

The Rule is Literal Interpretation

The Bible is to be interpreted literally, in accordance with what it meant to the original audience at the time of its being written. We are to seek the obvious meaning of the words that the author used, and in the context, he used them, as well as the language he used. This rule does not mean that we are to be ignorant regarding idiomatic,[121] hyperbolic,[122] symbolic[123] or figurative[124] language, where Jesus says he is a door, and Jehovah says he is a rock. Herein, we still take it literally, as to what the figurative language means. In other words, we get a correct understanding of the idiomatic, hyperbolic, symbolic or figurative words, and this is what we take literally. For example, if Jesus meant that he is the way, it is through him that we receive life, we take that message literally, not that we actually believe he is literally some movable barrier used to open and close the entrance to a building, room, closet.

The Rule is what the Author Meant by the Words He Used

This rule will be stressed throughout this book. The meaning is what the author meant by the words that he used, as should have been understood by his readers, at the time of writing. We must understand that descriptive history to move the text along is not necessarily prescribing what we should do. For example, in Judges Chapter 6, Gideon, desiring evidence that God was with him, requested that a fleece be exposed at night on the threshing floor and be wet with dew the next morning but that the floor be dry. This does not mean that we follow this as an example, to see if God wants us to do something. This was descriptive not prescriptive.

The Rule is that Not All Commentaries are Created Equal

Sadly, not all commentaries are equal. Sadly, theological bias affects us all, some more than others do. Therefore, it is good to find a few dependable companies and rely on them, until we discover others just as dependable.

Walk by Spirit and Truth

John 4:24 Updated American Standard Version (UASV)

[24] God is spirit, and those worshiping him must worship in spirit and truth."

---

[121] "Flowing with milk and honey" (Exodus 3:8)

[122] "You blind guides, who strain out a gnat and swallow a camel!" (Matt. 23:24)

[123] "... Israel committed adultery ..." (Jer 3:8-9) How does a nation commit adultery? Adultery is symbolic of idolatry.

[124] Jesus said to his disciples, "You are the light of the world." (Matt. 5:14)

What does it mean to worship in spirit? In spirit is not a reference to the Holy Spirit, but more of an attitude, a mental disposition, a way of thinking, or a mindset. We worship in "spirit" when we following our hearts, which are filled with faith and love of God and his Word. We worship in "spirit" when the inspired Word of God, trains our Christian conscience, the inner law that helps us to determine what is right, and leads us to recognize what is wrong. We worship in "spirit" when our worship is pure, based on an accurate knowledge of God's Word, having grateful hearts. We worship in "spirit" when we apply God's Word in our lives, having our spirit; mental disposition in harmony with the Holy Spirit's leading.

What does it mean to worship in truth? It means honestly, biblically, centered on the Word of God. In other words, we study the Word of God, having biblical truths revealed to us through the study, and then we worship according to that truth. In addition, it means that we are to be obedient to the truths revealed. This would include "truth of the gospel," which focuses on Jesus Christ and his efforts in the vindication of the sovereignty of his Father. (Galatians 2:14) God will allow a strong delusion to fall on those that "refuse to love the truth," 'condemning those who do not believe the truth.' (2 Thess. 2:9-12) Therefore, salvation only belongs to those, who upon hearing the Gospel, accept it as truth, and begin to walk in that truth. — 2 Thessalonians 2:9-12; Ephesians 1:13-14.

All true Christians should strive to be "fellow workers for the truth." They would certainly want to follow in the steps of John and Gaius as they defend the truth (Jude 1:3; 1 Pet 3:15), and like "children are walking in the truth." (3 John 3-8) They are doing so by going out into the community, proclaiming the Gospel, bringing people into the truth. They were to stay committed to the Gospel that they had heard in the beginning when they were first brought into the truth.

Be Aware of Spiritual Needs

We need to strengthen ourselves spiritually, recognizing our spiritual needs. Our spiritual strength needs to grow stronger each day, because if we can be steadfast in the small trials, we will endure the more difficult trials that may lie in our path.

Imagine the faith it must have required for those Israelites, who celebrated the first Passover and then took some of the blood and smeared it on the sides and tops of the doorframes of the houses. (Exodus

12:1-28) Even after their firstborn sons surviving that night, many lost their faith shortly thereafter when the Pharaoh's army was closing in on them at the Red Sea. (Exodus 14:9-12) However, after they walked the night through on the dry seabed to the other side of the Red Sea, then they looked back as the 80 feet walls of water fell in on the Egyptian army, killing them all. "Then they believed his words; they sang his praise." (Psa. 106:12) Yes, once again, they had faith. These Israelites were truly unsure about their relationship with God, whether he was truly with them or not, which caused them to be unstable. Certainly, they could not have any peace of mind, as in one moment; they would have a surge of hope, and in the next, a moment of despair.

James 1:5-8 Updated American Standard Version (UASV)

5 But if any of you lacks wisdom, let him ask of God, who gives to all generously and without reproaching,[125] and it will be given to him. **6** But let him ask in faith, without any doubting, for **the one who doubts is like a wave of the sea that is driven and tossed by the wind**. **7** For that man should not to expect that he will receive anything from the Lord; **8** he is a double-minded[126] man, unstable in all his ways.

If we tire our or grow weary in our walk with God, we can develop an uncertainty of belief that leaves us struggling or worse still, stumbling. Let us not be "double-minded" and "unstable" in prayer or in other ways. We should pray sincerely, with a steadfast sureness that God will hear our entreaties and that he will answer them in his own good time, in his way, and according to his will and purposes. Keep in mind that the answer may also be no answer.

Digging Deeper

Psalm 92:5 Updated American Standard Version (UASV)

5 How great are your works, O Jehovah! Your thoughts are <u>very deep</u>.

1 Corinthians 2:10 Updated American Standard Version (UASV)

10 For to us God revealed them through the Spirit; for the Spirit searches all things, even the depths of God.

There is no doubt that God's thoughts are deep, these deeper things of God are very complex at times, and as Peter tells us, they are not easy

---

[125] Without *criticizing*

[126] Or "*indecisive*," i.e., wavering in mind

to understand. Therefore, we must dig deeper by the use of the many wonderful tools on the market, along with prayerful reflection as we carry on in our studies. It is not a speed-reading contest, to see how many books we can read. Please, ponder the section below on hot to read/study a book. It may seem slow moving at first but in the end, it is worth it.

Psalm 139:17-18 Updated American Standard Version (UASV)

17 How precious to me are your thoughts, O God!
  How vast is the sum of them!
18 If I should count them, they would outnumber the sand.
  When I awake, I am still with you.

Psalm 119:160 Updated American Standard Version (UASV)

160 The sum of your word is truth,
  and every one of your righteous judgments endures forever.

As was true of the Psalmist, we should view God's sharing His thoughts as very precious. We should be very thankful and appreciative that we have access to 'the sum of God's Word' as being truths that He has revealed to us, and therefore, we must dig deeper in the sum of God's Word.

All of God's commandments, as recorded in his written Word, are for our living by and faithfully defending the truth. They are given for keeping us in accord with the truth. To receive God's blessing we should make the truth our own and share it everywhere to his glory and praise.

Tools Needed

Proverbs 2:1-6 Updated American Standard Version (UASV)

1 My son, if you receive my words
  and treasure up my commandments with you,
2 making your ear attentive to wisdom
  and inclining your heart to discernment;[127]
3 For if you cry for discernment[128]
  and raise your voice for understanding,
4 if you seek it like silver
  and search for it as for hidden treasures,

---

[127] The Hebrew word rendered here as "discernment" (*tevunah*) is related to the word *binah*, translated "understanding." Both appear at Proverbs 2:3.

[128] See 2.2 ftn.

⁵ then you will understand the fear of Jehovah
and find the knowledge of God.
⁶ For Jehovah gives wisdom;
from his mouth come knowledge and understanding;

Deep Bible study is like digging in a mine, it takes much effort on our part if we expect to find the treasure. Please, reread the above proverbs again, and this time, look for the active verbs, which emphasize the effort needed, to acquire divine knowledge, wisdom, and discernment.

Spiritual, educational study also requires a good study process. Solomon wrote, "If the axe is dull, and one does not sharpen its edge, then one must exert more strength; however, the advantage of wisdom is that it brings success." (Eccl. 10:10, HCSB) If a worker uses a blade that is not sharp or if he does not use it proficiently, he will squander his power and his work will be substandard.

When an artisan begins his workday, he will get out the tools needed for the task and place them before him. In the same way, when we embark on a period of study, we should decide on which tools we will need in our individual library. Recall too that study is a mental task and requires effort; therefore, it is also best to assume a fitting posture. The idea is to stay mentally attentive, so being at a table in a chair would be more prudent than a recliner, or lying on a bed. It is best to take a short break every 20 minutes or so, walking in another room, stretching or getting some fresh air from outside.

Many great study tools are also available to us today, because of software programs. Foremost among these is the Bible, God's Word. It is recommended that we use a literal translation (ASV, ESV, NASB, HCSB, and UASV in 2016), as well as a couple dynamic equivalent translations (NIV, NET, NLT). The tools listed here are the bare basics that any Bible student should have: several Bibles, concordance, Bible dictionary, Bible handbook, Old and New Testament survey or introductions, wordbooks (Mounce), Bible encyclopedia, and at least a one or more volume commentary, a Bible atlas, and a one-volume commentary on Bible backgrounds.

How to Study

Progressing in our personal study requires us to become skilled at how to study. First, it would be best to write a schedule on our calendar, seven days per week that will not interfere with life's responsibilities, buying out the time to study, possibly at least a half hour each time, twice a day. Better yet, it might be best to have one hour of study, in the early morning, to start our day. Second, we will need to decide beforehand what we will study during the time we have set aside. By setting reasonable goals down on paper and in our mind, we will be much more apt to make the study time far more beneficial than if we had no goal. As an aside, we do not want to sidetrack ourselves by trying to dig deeper for the curiosities that come up during our study. Write these down and do them outside of our regular study.

In order to bring our study to the next level, we must become skilled at using our tools. As is true with everything, skill will only come about by use, use and more use. We will need to acquire skill at searching for background information from maps and Bible dictionaries. Also, using our concordance to see how a word is used throughout the Bible book we are studying, or throughout the New or Old Testament. It can be very helpful in directing us to supplementary information.

When we come upon Bible locations, it is time to use our maps to have a mental picture of Bible lands. An example would be Paul's missionary tours, or the exodus of the Israelites. Seeing where the Israelites were held captive in Babylon, how the huge cedar logs were gotten from the Mountains of Lebanon to Jerusalem, can add meaning to our study. Consider cases when the text says, for example, Samson ripped out the gates of Gaza, which likely weighed several hundred pounds, and then it states that he carried them to the top of Hebron. Our in-depth study will discover that was a 37-mile hike, uphill! – Judges 16:3.

These suggestions will be of no advantage to us unless we have a wish to learn. Without that longing, we will not be motivated to seek the wisdom of God's Word. We will not be motivated to dig for knowledge and understanding. This desire should be the possession of all dedicated Christians. If we are a newly interested one, a desire for a better understanding of God's Word, a longing for it, can be developed. We should crave to be taught about our Creator and about the things, he caused to be written in his Word. As we take in knowledge and understanding, our thirst for these deeper things should grow. "A discerning mind seeks knowledge." – Proverbs 15:14.

An environment that breathes study is very important as well. Some people have convinced themselves that they can study with the radio blaring, or even playing quietly in the background. Silence is the best friend for serious study. This gives our mind the opportunity to meditate and ponder whatever we are considering. If we have children, it may be best to choose a study time when they are in school, or at an activity. The phone should be ignored during this time, not allowing outside distractions.

It is only by being absorbed in our material that we can really profit from the hard effort that we have put forth in our study. While it is true, we live in stressful times, we should follow Jesus' advice to 'seek first the kingdom of God and his righteousness, and all these others things will be taken care of' by applying the very Bible principles that we are learning, by not having a divided mind that is attempting to compete with today's troubles. It is no easy task to dismiss the world around us, but with prayerful efforts, it will come in time. Otherwise, we will find that we have read five pages and have no idea what we just read. Poor concentration is the killer of an advanced study. Yawning, feeling sleepy may not be because we tossed and turned last night, but because we are simply not interested in what lies before our very eyes. However, interest can be achieved by knowing just how we want to use the information that we are studying: our personal life, to help our child, to strengthen our relationships, to grow and mature, to defend what we believe. If we can find a reason for the information, the interest will peak, our concentration will improve, and our study will come to the point where it is not only interesting, but also exciting and captivating.

Study Process

We have just purchased a new book; it has just come in the mail, or downloaded to our Kindle or Nook. How should we go about studying our new book? The first thing is to read the back cover that will give us an overview of the book. Stop for a moment and consider what we know about this subject area. Now, as we would walk around and kick the tires before buying a car, we should investigate before we get into the study of the book. Open the book, and look at the table of content and read the list of chapters and headings, see the progression the book is following, its line of thought. Now, turn to each chapter and look at the subheadings that run through each chapter, to get a feel for the depth that we are going to go into, to be excited by this subject area.

First, read the preface and introduction of the book. Now that we are ready to begin, turn to chapter one. Each topic sentence usually is a summary of the whole paragraph and it generally is the first sentence, so pay special attention as we read in an undertone [slightly aloud], each sentence throughout the chapter. After reading those first sentences, attempt to see how the paragraphs build on that sentence, and the following ones as well. As we work our way through the chapter, look for the topic sentence, and underline it, this way we are mentally outlining the chapter.

As we are reading, do not just read each word individually, but in a group of thought content. This will not only speed up our reading, but will help us to take hold of the content. As we grow in knowledge and understanding, we will encounter terms and subject matter that are new. Initially, this will be quite often, and will taper off as our knowledge deepens. New terms and subject matter is not an area where rapid reading should continue. It is here where we should slow down, because we are attempting to grasp each word at a time and how the joining of them together makes sense. In addition, we may wish to have a dictionary handy as well.[129] After we feel we have grasped this new thought, look up from the page and restate it in our own words.

We may wish to view subheadings as stop signs. At each one, we should give thought to, 'what did I just cover?' Can we recall the whole of what was shared, or is it too muddled? If we feel that, it is too foggy, go back and reread the topic sentences that we had underlined, and it should restore our memory. When we read something that sounds worth repeating, as it may be used to help another, overturn false reasoning, or expounding on a Scripture, attempt to explain it aloud in our own words. If we stumble in expressing it, reread the point, and attempt to explain it again aloud. Before the day is out, share it with another, which will help us retain it. Now we are off to the next subheading, following the same process, as we continue throughout the chapter, keep the title in mind, former subheadings and a progression of what we have taken in. This process should be followed throughout the whole book.

If this is a book that we bought not a library book, hold a pencil (or highlighter) in one hand as we read, underline our topic sentences, exceptional bits and pieces of information, and any key words that may catch our attention. Do not overdo this, as it will defeat the purpose. After each chapter, take a moment to read the subheading, to see if we recall what we have read. If we have, a point that we believe we will

---

[129] The beauty of the Kindle PC software that allows us to download eBooks is threefold: (1) We can highlight the important thoughts, (2) we can add notes right into the book, and (3) it has a dictionary that pops up when we right click a word, which will save us a tremendous amount of time, not to mention convenience. Moreover, the stopping to pick up a dictionary and locate a word will cause us to lose the flow of thought, and many times, we will have to reread the section again. This is avoided with the Kindle PC.

need in the future; go to the front of the book, and create a small phrase that captures the essence of that material, and put the page number where it can be found later. Two years later, we may want to find it again, so we recall what possible books, then we simply look in the front and the phrases will be there. The most important study principle is looking up Scriptures. The rule is if it is not quoted in the book we are studying, look it up every time, unless we can quote it verbatim. If we ever stumble in quoting it, look it up every time we come across it, until we do not stumble in quoting it. Below is a quick overview of how to read/study a book.

STEPS TO READING/STUDYING A BOOK

- Ponder the title and subtitle for a moment

- Read the book description on the back as we keep the title and subtitle in mind

- Read the Table of Content, considering how it relates to the title and subtitle.

- Read the Preface, which will tell us the author's intentions

- Read the Introduction that will help break us into what is coming

How to Read the Chapters

- Ponder the chapter title

- Read the headings and subheading of the chapter and see how it relates to the chapter title

- Get out a legal pad and write the headings and subheadings on the legal pad as questions, which will be our review questions

- Read the next heading and paragraph(s), asking ourselves the heading as a question and answer it in our own words.

- Read the next heading and paragraph(s) and do the same. Continue this until we are done with the chapter.

- Close the book and go through the heading questions. If there are any that we stammer on, reread that material.

- Finally, read the chapter title, the headings and subheadings to refresh the mind, and then write a summary paragraph of the entire chapter

An active mind while reading will enable us to retain so much more at the end of the book. Attempt to picture the material, as we are moving through it. Pay special attention to the basic truths that we are learning. As we work our way through any book, see if we can look into ourselves, to see if there are areas that the information could be applied our lives. Ponder over the material, looking for information that we can use in our ministry of preaching and teaching others.

A motivating factor is the simple fact that one could never teach another if he does not fully understand the subject matter himself. Worse still, it will only alienate those we are preaching to, because they want the confidence that a person teaching them is not stumbling through their answers. If we fully understand something, we will be able to give reasons for it, in our own words. Therefore, the more we know and understand the better will be when the time comes to share that information, giving reasons for the hope that we possess. Moreover, it may be information that we need to personalize, something that will help us to make better decisions. In addition, we will be building our faith up to withstand the agnostic, atheistic, liberal, progressive skeptics and critics that wish only to tear down. As we grow in our understanding of God's Word, it will enable us to have the confidence to speak to others, to grow spiritually, and get on the path that leads to everlasting life.

The objective of our study is to give a half hour each day to Bible reading as laid out in this book, as well as a half hour to the book reading program as explained herein. We can give a half hour to each them in the morning, or we can split it up: one in the morning and the other in the afternoon, or evening. It is recommended that we do both in the morning.

Review Questions

- What questions does the Bible answer?
- What can the Bible offer us now?
- What can the Bible answer as to our future?
- What is the Good News and, who are obligated to share it?
- How does the Bible help us with our spirituality?

- How can we better understand and teach the Bible?
- What rules do we live by?
- What is meant by walk in the spirit and the truth?
- Why should we be aware of our spirituality?
- How do we read-study a book?

CHAPTER 9 You Must Love Jesus More Than Your Family

Luke 14:26 Updated American Standard Version (UASV)

26 "If anyone comes to me and does not hate his own father and mother and wife and children and brothers and sisters, yes, and even his own life, he cannot be my disciple."

How are we to make sense of Jesus telling us that we are to **hate** our relatives? In Bible times, this was an expression, which simple meant *to like less*, not literally hate. (Gen. 29:30-31) Remember, Jesus told us that we are to love our enemies. (Matt. 5:44) Would it then make sense for him to say love your enemy but hate your mother and father? Therefore, being truly Christian means that we love our relatives less than we love Jesus Christ. – Matthew 10:37.

Mark 12:29-30 Updated American Standard Version (UASV)

29 Jesus answered, "The foremost is, 'Hear, O Israel! The Lord our God is one Lord; **30** and you shall love the Lord your God with all your heart, and with all your soul, and with all your mind, and with all your strength.'

And one of the scribes came up and heard them disputing with one another, and seeing that he answered them well, asked Jesus, "Which commandment is the most important of all?" Jesus being the great teacher that he was, he turned to the Word of God. Jesus quoted from Deuteronomy 6:4–5, which reads, "Hear, O Israel! Jehovah our God is one Jehovah! You shall love Jehovah your God with all your heart and with all your soul and with all your might."

This should prove to be no surprise on two fronts: (1) Jesus constantly turned to the Scriptures as his authority.[130] (2) If we look at the Gospel of John, Jesus talked about the Father more than he talked about anything else. For example, at John 5:30, Jesus said, "I can do nothing on my own. As I hear, I judge, and my judgment is just, because I seek not my own will but **the will of him who sent me [i.e., the Father]**." The personal name of the Father in the Hebrew Old Testament is Jehovah.

---

[130] If we took Jesus words out of all three Gospels and looked at all that he said, it would come out to about three hours of talking with over 120 quotations, paraphrases and references to Scripture.

Therefore, if we are to obey the most important commandment of them all, we are to love and obey the Father.

In fact, in speaking of Christians who thought they were truly Christian, Jesus said, "I never knew you; depart from me, you workers of lawlessness." (Matt. 7:23, ESV) Why would he say that to these ones? Jesus said "On that day many will say to me, 'Lord, Lord, did we not prophesy in your name, and cast out demons in your name, and do many mighty works in your name?'" (Matt. 7:22, ESV) However, Jesus told them who were going to benefit by the Kingdom of God, "the one who does the will of my Father." (Matt. 7:21, ESV) The apostle John reiterated this in one of his letters, saying, "The world is passing away along with its desires, but whoever does the will of God remains forever." (1 John 2:17) Therefore, some of us are walking around believing we are truly Christian. However, if we are not doing the will of the Father, we are going to be told, "I never knew you; depart from me, you workers of lawlessness."

Thus, the question to be asking is, "what is the will of the Father." Suffice it to say, we cannot delve into all of that in this chapter, but it is highly important that we discover the will of the Father. In short, we can say that we are to obey both the Father and the Son. We will also not that the greatest commission that was given to all Christians was, 'to proclaim God's Word, to teach God's Word and to make disciples.' (Matt. 24:14; 28:19-20; Ac 1:8)[131] Jesus was sent to the nation of Israel, to do on a small scale, what he commended that we do on a grand scale, proclaim, teach and make disciples. However, he faced **opposition** from the religious leaders, but also **from his family.** (Matt. 16:21-23; Mark 3:21; John 8:29) Are there family members that are against us as

---

[131] *CONVERSATIONAL EVANGELISM Defending the Faith, Reasoning from the Scriptures, Explaining and Proving, Instructing in Sound Doctrine, and Overturning False Reasoning*

http://www.christianpublishers.org/apps/webstore/products/show/5749015

THE CHRISTIAN APOLOGIST: Always Being Prepared to Make a Defense

http://www.christianpublishers.org/apps/webstore/products/show/5273691

THE EVANGELISM HANDBOOK: How All Christians Can Effectively Share God's Word in Their Community

http://www.christianpublishers.org/apps/webstore/products/show/4676258

OVERCOMING BIBLE DIFFICULTIES: Answers to the So-Called Errors and Contradictions

http://www.christianpublishers.org/apps/webstore/products/show/6172711

Christians? In some cases, it is distant cousins, so the impact is small. However, in others, it might be our spouse, who is in opposition to us as a Christian. In others, it might be our parents, or our brothers and sisters. These ones might want us to give up being a Christian, as they see belief in God as foolish. Will we obey God or man? Do we put the will of the Father and the Son first by obeying them, even if our greatest human love opposes God?

The Difficulty of Family Opposition

Jesus did not rationalize or excuse away family opposition to his teachings. He said,

Matthew 10:34-39 Updated American Standard Version (UASV)

34 "Do not think that I came to bring peace on the earth; I did not come to bring peace, but a sword. 35 For I came to set a man against his father, and a daughter against her mother, and a daughter-in-law against her mother-in-law; 36 and a man's enemies will be the members of his household.

37 "He who loves father or mother more than me is not worthy of me; and he who loves son or daughter more than me is not worthy of me. 38 And he who does not take his cross and follow after me is not worthy of me. 39 He who has found his soul[132] will lose it, and he who has lost his soul[133] for my sake will find it.

What are the basic points here? There is no exception for even those closest family members, who opposes Christ. In fact, we can define antichrist as anyone, any group, any organization, or any government that is *against* or *instead of* Christ, or who mistreat his people. Thus, we are not just looking for one person, or one group, or one organization, or one power. The Bible does not refer to just one antichrist. The apostle John wrote in about 98 C.E.,[134] "Children, it is the last hour [John is the last of the 12 apostle and is almost a hundred, close to death]; and as you have heard that antichrist coming, even now **many antichrists** have

---

[132] Or *life*

[133] Or life

[134] B.C.E. means "before the Common Era," which is more accurate than B.C. ("before Christ"). C.E. denotes "Common Era," often called A.D., for *anno Domini*, meaning "in the year of our Lord."

appeared; whereby we know that it is the last hour [of John's protection (the apostolic period), as he dies shortly thereafter]." – 1 John 2:18, ASV.

We notice from 1 John 2:18 that it is "the last hour." It is the last hour, because John is almost one hundred years old, and he is the last of the twelve apostles, of the apostolic period, who could protect the Christians from the great apostasy that was coming. We also notice that John says there are "many antichrists." John refers to these collectively as "the antichrist" in 2 John 1:7 (ASV), "For many deceivers are gone forth into the world, those who do not confess the coming of Jesus Christ in the flesh. This is the deceiver and the antichrist." Should Christians be looking for some future time, to identify some specific antichrist?[135] No, antichrists based on the Bible's definition evidence that antichrists, persons or groups, have been around since Jesus was opposed by the Jewish religious leaders. Therefore, family members can even play that role, if they willfully oppose Jesus Christ in our lives. We also learn from Matthew 10:34-37 that Jesus made it perfectly clear who is to come first in our lives, namely, Jesus Christ. We put the Father first by applying the principles behind the Mosaic Law and by obeying the teachings of the Son. We should love God more than we love anyone, including our own life.

The Father is the Creator of the heavens and the earth, who has given us life and the opportunity at everlasting life, meaning he deserves complete devotion. The apostle John wrote, "Worthy are you, our Lord and our God [the Father], to receive glory and honor and power; for you created all things, and because of your will they existed, and were created." (Rev. 4:11) The apostle Paul wrote, "For this reason I bow my knees before the Father, from whom every family in heaven and on earth is named." (Eph. 3:14-15) The Father created humans in such a way that the love within a family is the greatest bond one can have, aside from the Creator himself. (1 Ki 3:25, 26; 1 Thess. 2:7) However, we saw Satan exploit this love in the Garden of Eden. Adam showed more love for Eve than the very person who created him. Adam ended up rebelling against God, rejecting his sovereignty. Satan has continued to exploit that love for family, in that many Christians have abandoned the faith through the opposition of a spouse, a mother or father, brother or sister. – Revelation 12:9, 12.

---

[135] http://www.christianpublishers.org/antichrist-who

Meeting the Challenge

Some may already be in a family opposition relationship and need to ponder the decisions they have made. If we are not in an opposition relationship at present, we want consider the choice we might make before it prevents itself. While none of our family members might be opposed, it only takes one life-changing event to alter it all. What if our spouse begins to doubt the existence of God and the truthfulness of his Word, until they suffer a spiritual shipwreck?[136] What if a close family member loses a loved one in a tragic accident and they do not understand why God would allow pain, suffering, evil and death.[137] If these ones then turn on us and our Christian faith, will we slowdown in our service to God? Suppose our spouse purposely makes plans for the two of us on meeting days, when there are congregation special events. Will we rationalize that God will not mind if we miss meetings or evens to keep our spouse happy? Will we manipulate Scriptures that say we are to be in in subjection to the husband, or that the husband is to honor and respect the wife? Our having an accurate understanding of Scripture is the difference between our receiving a resurrection or not. – John 17:3; 2 Thessalonians 1:6-8.

Let us use the illustration of a family member, who suffers from a drug addiction. Would it be best for him if we rationalize or condone his behavior? Would we really be bringing peace to the house if we simply gave into his demands, simply ignoring the problem? The answer to all these question is logically, no. The best solution is to continually try and help him overcome his drug problem, even if it means dealing with opposition in the form of being yelled at or intimidation. Most families that have tried to help drug attics have become experts on the subject matter: (1) studying and researching how the problem starts, (2) how to communicate with such ones, and (3) how to overcome such a problem. It is true love that refuses to give into efforts to slow down in our Christian faith. If we abandon the faith; then, both will miss out on everlasting life. It is our standing strong that may win them over to the faith or back to the faith.

---

[136] CRISIS OF FAITH Saving Those Who Doubt the Existence of God and the Truthfulness of His Word

http://www.christianpublishers.org/apps/webstore/products/show/6338461

[137] IF GOD IS GOOD: Why Does God Allow Suffering?

http://www.christianpublishers.org/apps/webstore/products/show/5786449

Some may feel that no one can understand the level of threats, intimidation and pressure we face.[138] However, remember, Satan worked very hard so that Jesus would abandon the will of the Father. Yet Jesus never lost sight of the goal; he endured torture and torment that few gave ever faced for us. Paul tells us that "Jesus Christ [is] our Savior," "who died for us." (Tit. 3:6; 1 Thess. 5:10) Imagine if Jesus had given into the opposition he faced. If he had, we would have no hope of eternal life. – John 3:16, 36; Revelation 21:3, 4.

Saving Those Who Listen

Our maintaining a good standing before our heavenly Father is the only step toward saving the loved one, who is in opposition to us and our faith. If ever he is reached, how will he ever come to have faith, if we abandoned our faith under his pressure? If we have been telling home that God is real and we can trust the Bible, it is not being evidenced that we meant what we said, if we back away from the truth. Paul had some counsel for young Timothy, his 15-year traveling companion, who came from a divided home, as his mother was a Jew and his unbelieving Greek father. (Ac 16:1; 2 Tim. 1:5; 3:14) Paul said, "Keep a close watch on yourself and on the teaching. Persist in this, for by so doing you will save both yourself and your hearers." (1 Tim. 4:16) The Scriptures do not inform us if Timothy's father ever became a believer, but the odds were made better by the faith if Timothy, his mother, and his grandmother.

Paul spoke to the Corinthians about the possibly of saving a person by their remaining in the truth. Paul wrote, "To the rest I say (I, not the Lord) that if any brother has a wife who is an unbeliever, and she consents to live with him, he should not divorce her. If any woman has a husband who is an unbeliever, and he consents to live with her, she should not divorce him ... For how do you know, wife, whether you will save your husband? Or how do you know, husband, whether you will save your wife?" The apostle Peter also commented on how wives could save their husbands, advice that would also apply to husbands saving their wives. He wrote, "Likewise, wives, be subject to your own husbands, so that even if some do not obey the word, they may be won without a word by the conduct of their wives." – 1 Peter 3:1.

---

[138] If there is physical violence, Christians have the right to separate. If there is mental and emotional abuse Christians have the right to separate.

http://www.christianpublishers.org/divorce-scriptural-basis

It is hard to calculate how many hundreds of thousands have come into the faith after years of opposing that faith because the spouse or family member never slowed down in their worship. This is a gift for the steadfast Christian and certainly a blessing for the unbeliever. Many times, it was not overt witnessing but the holy conduct with a few choice words here and there over an extended period. Alternatively, it might be the elder or pastor, who showed an interest in the unbelieving husband. In some cases, it has been a wife enduring the mistreatment of her husband for over a decade, which saved him from himself and satanic influence.

Jesus Set the Example

The one lesson we should most value from Jesus was his steadfastness to the Father. He said, "My food is to do the will of him [the Father] who sent me and to accomplish his work." (John 4:34, ESV) He also said, "For I have come down from heaven, not to do my own will but the will of him [the Father] who sent me." (John 6:38, ESV) Also, "And he [the Father] who sent me is with me. He has not left me alone, for I always do the things that are pleasing to him." (John 8:29, ESV) Even when Jesus was distraught at the idea of dying as a convicted blasphemer (false charge of course), he remain faithful to the end. He said, ""Father, if you are willing, remove this cup from Me [being executed for blasphemy against the Father]; yet not My will, but Yours be done." (Lu 22:42, NASB) Even the Son did not ask the Father to change his will; he is the one that helped John to realize the following. "For this is the love of God, that we keep his commandments. And his commandments are not burdensome." (1 John 5:3) If we are truly Christian, this means that we will always put God's will first in our lives.

This holds true even in the lives where both spouses are Christian. Even Christians can have marital problems. As has been stated in this publication, we are all mentally bent toward evil (Gen. 6:5; 8:21), with a treacherous heart that is desperately sick. (Jer. 17:9)[139] Some have gotten divorced even though there were no grounds for doing so, which is not

---

[139] "The prophet intended to communicate one point to his audience: a person cannot trust his heart completely in major decisions, either morally or spiritually, if it is in a desperately unhealthy state." – Anders, Max; Wood, Fred M.; McLaren, Ross H. (2006-07-01). *Holman Old Testament Commentary - Jeremiah, Lamentations* (p. 172). B&H Publishing. Kindle Edition.

keeping God's commandments.[140] (Matt. 19:9; Heb. 13:4; 1 Cor. 7:12-15) When we do this, we are depending on our human way of thinking, not godly wisdom. If we are truly Christian, both the believing husband and the wife will remain together, using God's Word to work out their marital problems. Thus, they will evade all kinds of sorrows that result when his will is disregarded. - Psalm 19:7-11.

What is the Only Scriptural Basis for Divorce and Remarriage Among Christians?

Matthew 5:31-32 Updated American Standard Version (UASV)

31 "It was said, 'Whoever divorces his wife away, let him give her a certificate of divorce';[141] **32** but I say to you that everyone who divorces his wife, except on the ground of sexual immorality, makes her commit adultery; and whoever marries a divorced woman commits adultery.

Matthew 19:8-9 Updated American Standard Version (UASV)

8 He said to them, "Because of your hardness of heart Moses permitted you to divorce your wives; but from the beginning it has not been this way. **9** And I say to you, whoever divorces his wife, except for immorality, and marries another woman commits adultery."

When Jesus said the only grounds for divorce was/is adultery, the context was his speaking to Jewish men, who were divorcing their wives for insignificant reasons in the extreme, such as cooking a bad meal. In the context and historical setting Jesus dealt with the issue at hand. The context and historical seeing was that Jesus was dealing with a stiff-necked people who were abusing the basis for divorce under the Mosaic Law. Jesus was not dealing with any exceptions to the rule that might come up in life.

Is it lawful for a man to divorce his wife for any and every reason? (19:3). A hotbed of discussion surrounded the various interpretations of Moses' divorce regulations. The leading Pharisaic scholars of Jesus' day debated the grounds for divorce that Moses established, who allowed a man to divorce

---

[140] What is the Only Scriptural Basis for Divorce and Remarriage Among Christians?

http://www.christianpublishers.org/divorce-scriptural-basis

[141] Deut. 24:1

his wife because he "finds something indecent about her" (Deut. 24:1). The debate focused on the meaning of "indecent." The Mishnah tractate Gittin ("Bills of Divorce") reflects back on the debate between different schools of thought among the Pharisees at Jesus' time and records the differing interpretations (m. Giṭ. 9:10). The more conservative school of Shammai held to the letter of the Mosaic law and said, "A man may not divorce his wife unless he has found unchastity in her." The more liberal school of Hillel interpreted "indecency" to mean that "he may divorce her even if she spoiled a dish for him." The esteemed Rabbi Akiba, who belonged to the school of Hillel, later added, "Even if he found another fairer than she," demonstrating that divorce be granted for even the most superficial reasons.[142]

However, the Apostle Paul was in a different context and historical setting. Thus, under the influence of Holy Spirit, he offered an exception. Notice how Paul words things,

1 Corinthians 7:12-16 Updated American Standard Version (UASV)

[12] But to the rest I say, not the Lord, that if any brother has a wife who is an unbeliever, and she consents to live with him, he must not divorce her. [13] And a woman who has an unbelieving husband, and he consents to live with her, she must not send her husband away. [14] For the unbelieving husband is sanctified through his wife, and the unbelieving wife is sanctified through her believing husband; for otherwise your children are unclean, but now they are holy. [15] Yet if the unbelieving one leaves, let him leave; the brother or the sister is not under bondage in such cases, but God has called us in peace. [16] For how do you know, O wife, whether you will save your husband? Or how do you know, O husband, whether you will save your wife?

The first thing to notice is Paul saying, I am inspired by God, so I can say this and the Lord (Jesus), did not touch on this, but I am. Let us take a look at the context and historical setting.

If she does, she must remain unmarried or else be reconciled to her husband. And a husband must not divorce his wife (7:11). Paul lays out the two options available to Christians if they separate from their spouses: either

---

[142] Clinton E. Arnold, Zondervan Illustrated Bible Backgrounds Commentary: Matthew, Mark, Luke, vol. 1 (Grand Rapids, MI: Zondervan, 2002), 117.

remain unmarried or seek reconciliation. Remarriage of a Christian divorcee comes under Jesus' specific teaching (e.g., Luke 16:18). This is in contrast with the Roman legal situation. A divorce settlement from Egypt dated 13 B.C. (after it became a Roman province) declared, "From this day it will be lawful for Zois to marry another man and for Antipater to marry another woman, with neither party being liable to prosecution."[143] [144]

If any brother has a wife who is not a believer and she is willing to live with him, he must not divorce her. And if a woman has a husband who is not a believer and he is willing to live with her, she must not divorce him (7:12-13). Within the Christian community at Corinth, and almost certainly elsewhere, Paul faces the issue of men and women converted to Jesus Christ but the spouse remains an unbeliever. Clearly this may cause tensions within the marriage. If the unbelieving partner is willing to remain married, there should be no move to seek a divorce. The Christians at Corinth may have pointed to Old Testament examples where Jews married non-Jews and brought God's displeasure (e.g., 2 Chron. 21:6) and therefore thought it appropriate for a Christian to seek a divorce.

If the unbeliever leaves, let him do so. [In such cases the brother or sister is not enslaved] God has called us to live in peace (7:15). In a divorce the husband was expected to hand back the dowry he had received over from the bride's family at the time of marriage. For example in a divorce settlement of 13 B.C., the husband had to hand back "the items he received as her dowry, namely, clothing valued at 120 silver drachmas and a pair of gold earrings." A (Christian) husband might try to be difficult and retain such a dowry, but Paul reminds the Christian to live in peace and to let the (unbelieving) wife go.[145]

---

[143] Clinton E. Arnold, *Zondervan Illustrated Bible Backgrounds Commentary: Romans to Philemon.*, vol. 3 (Grand Rapids, MI: Zondervan, 2002), 137.

[144] BGU 1103 (A. S. Hunt and C. C. Edgar, Select Papyri [Loeb Classical Library; Cambridge, Mass.: Harvard Univ. Press, 1956], 6). A translation may be found in Shelton, As the Romans Did, 50, no. 61; Lewis and Reinhold, Roman Civilization, 2:344.

[145] Clinton E. Arnold, *Zondervan Illustrated Bible Backgrounds Commentary: Romans to Philemon.*, vol. 3 (Grand Rapids, MI: Zondervan, 2002), 137.

Under verse 15 of chapter 7, a husband or wife is not enslaved to a spouse who has left him or her and has refused reconciliation. If the husband or wife, who has been left by the other has done his or her due diligence of trying to reconcile (7:10-13), and they have an unbeliever who will never return, nor ever remarry, the brother or sister is not enslaved and are free to remarry under Paul's words, not Jesus, because Jesus was not dealing with this particular circumstance. Jesus and Paul were not contradicting each other, just as Paul and James did not contradict each other over faith and works. Paul is complimenting Jesus' words because he is dealing with an entirely different context and historical setting. However, if anyone argues that Paul was not offering an exception clause to Jesus' words; then, Paul would be contradicting Jesus. There is no reason for Paul to talk about 'not being enslaved' to their husband or wife, if he were not offering an exception clause to Jesus' words about divorce, nor would there be a reason for Paul to say, 'these are not Jesus words, they are mine.' In other words, Jesus did not touch on this circumstance, 'I, an inspired apostle am dealing with it.' Thus, Paul is offering an exception, so there is no contradiction.

The College Press NIV Commentary is correct in its analysis

> Having established a case in 7:14 for remaining married to an unbeliever, Paul now acknowledges **the exceptions**. Beginning in this verse, Paul teaches that his instructions are completely different if the unbelieving spouse is not happily married. That is, if the pagan mate wants to stay married to a Christian, the Christian cannot divorce him or her, but if the pagan mate wants out of the marriage, so be it!

> The very perspectives and divine rules which would keep a Christian married to another Christian (7:10–11) or a Christian married to a happily married pagan (7:12–14) are revoked in the case of a believer married to an unhappily married pagan. Let them have their divorce, Paul writes. In such circumstances the Christian brother or sister need not operate under the same constraints as given in earlier situations. The reason that the Christian is not bound in these situations of inevitable divorce from an uncooperative pagan is that the foundation and principles of a godly marriage are not present. Marriages can be held together by loyalty to God or they can be held together by self-interest, but nothing godly is accomplished by trying to keep a non-believer in a marriage where there is no peace. Peaceful relationships are a two-way matter (cf. Rom 12:18),

and Paul excused the Corinthian believers from any need to coerce non-believing mates into staying in the marriage.[146]

Husbands and Wives

Both husband and wife need to ask themselves, "Do we place God first in our lives, in our family? Do I as truly Christian truly attempt to carry out the family role that God has given to me? Do I apply myself to the best of my abilities to love my spouse, helping him or her to have a good relationship with God?" Applying the Bible applies to children as well. God commands children to obey their parents.[147] (Eph. 6:1-3) He demands that parents teach and correct their children. It is expected that Christian parents would have a home Bible study with their children. They are obligated to care for their physical, emotion, mental and spiritual needs. (Deut. 11:18, 19; Pro. 22:6, 15) Parents are never to correct their children in a severe or painful way. – Colossians 3:21.

Review Questions

- How are we to make sense of Jesus telling us that we are to **hate** our relatives?

- What may be the case as to opposition in many families?

- How have tens of thousands, if not hundreds of thousands of steadfast Christians saved their family members?

---

[146] Richard Oster, *1 Corinthians*, *The College Press NIV Commentary* (Joplin, MO: College Press Pub. Co., 1995), 1 Co 7:15.

[147] "Children are instructed that their role in mutual submission is to **obey your parents in the Lord, for this is right**. Without learning obedience from parents, children would run wild in society. All social order depends on this. **In the Lord** does not mean that children only need to obey Christian parents. Rather, it means that they are obeying the Lord when they obey their parents. Sadly, we are living in a day when child abuse is on the rise. This causes us to mention that the same exceptions which wives have from obeying their husbands, children have in obeying their parents. When children are asked to do something unethical, illegal, or immoral, or when they are harmed or in danger of being harmed, the command to obey would be superseded by higher biblical principles of "obeying God rather than man."' (Anders 1999, p. 189)

- How should true Christians view immorality and divorce?

- What can we learn from the example of Jesus?

- What other grounds is there for a divorce according to Paul?

- What questions should husbands and wives ask themselves?

CHAPTER 10 You Must Carry Your Own Cross and Come After Jesus

Luke 14:27; 9:23 Updated American Standard Version (UASV)

27 "Whoever does not carry his own cross and come after me cannot be my disciple." **23** And He was saying to them all, "If anyone wants to come after me, let him disown himself, and take up his cross day after day and keep following me.

Those viewed as successful in the military or any public sector job are **men and women of dedication**. This characteristic or quality is of even more important for a Christian disciple of Christ. Dedication is defined in *Webster's Collegiate Dictionary* as "an act or rite of dedicating to a divine being or to a sacred use," "devoting or setting aside for a particular purpose," "self-sacrificing devotion,"[148] However, for a Christian, far more is involved.

Jesus said to his disciples, "If anyone wants to come after me, let him deny himself and take up his cross and follow me." (Matt. 16:24, ESV) Devoting oneself to a divine purpose, or as we spoke of in chapter 5, being holy as God is holy, refers to being *"set apart to or by God,"*[149] which is more involved than carrying out an act of worship or going to Christian meetings. A dedication to Christ involves one's entire life. Evidence that we are truly Christian means; we disown ourselves and deny ourselves as we serve God. Moreover, to take up and carry our own cross means that we are brave or tough enough to deal with any unpleasant situation that results from being a follower of Christ.

Jesus Set the Example

In the Gospel of John, Jesus spoke about his dedication to the Father more than any other subject matter. "Consequently, when Christ came into the world, he said, 'Sacrifices and offerings you have not desired, but a body have you prepared for me; in burnt offerings and sin offerings you have taken no pleasure.' Then I said, 'Behold, I have come to do your

---

[148] Frederick C. Mish, "Preface," *Merriam-Webster's Collegiate Dictionary.* (Springfield, MA: Merriam-Webster, Inc., 2003).

[149] Barclay M. Newman Jr., *A Concise Greek-English Dictionary of the New Testament.* (Stuttgart, Germany: Deutsche Bibelgesellschaft; United Bible Societies, 1993), 2.

will, O God, as it is written of me in the scroll of the book.'" (Heb. 10:5-7, ESV) Some would argue that Jesus dedication as a human came at birth because he was born into the nation of Israel and raised by Jewish parents to follow and obey the Mosaic Law. While all of that is true, when Jesus turned thirty and he began his ministry, he offered his life to the Father at his baptism, symbolizing that he was willing to do the Father's will. During his ministry, Jesus said to them, "My food is to do the will of him who sent me and to accomplish his work." (John 4:34, ESV) Jesus also said, "Truly, truly, I say to you, the Son can do nothing of his own accord, but only what he sees the Father doing. For whatever the Father does, that the Son does likewise." (John 5:19, ESV) He went on to say, "I can do nothing on my own. As I hear, I judge, and my judgment is just, because I seek not my own will but the will of him who sent me." – John 5:30, ESV.

Part of the will of the Father was that Jesus would "give his life as a ransom for many." (Matt. 20:28, ESV) Jesus even said that many would believe they were dedicated Christians, "On that day many will say to me, 'Lord, Lord, did we not prophesy in your name, and cast out demons in your name, and do many mighty works in your name?'" (Matt. 7:22, ESV) However, many are going to be disappointed, as Jesus will "declare to them, 'I never knew you; depart from me, you workers of lawlessness.'" (Matt. 7:23) What was it that allowed these ones to believe they were dedicating themselves but were actually failing to the point of being called "workers of lawlessness"? Jesus said, "Not everyone who says to me, 'Lord, Lord,' will enter the kingdom of heaven, **but the one who does the will of my Father** who is in heaven." (Matt. 7:21) What should we know? Yes, Jesus brings it right back to **doing the will of the Father**.

On this William Hendrickson writes,

That there is a connection between these words and the immediately preceding warning against false prophets (verses15–20) is clear. Jesus had told his audience to be on guard against false prophets, those who, while telling lies, pretended to be speaking the truth. Did this mean that if a man proclaims the truth he thereby proves himself to be a true prophet? "Not necessarily," says Jesus as it were. A man who speaks the truth but acts the lie is also in a sense a false prophet. **Let every person therefore examine not only his neighbor but also himself**. As has already been shown, the "fruit" that indicates whether a man is reliable or untrustworthy relates not only to doctrine but also to life. Thus with tremendous force the message is driven home to every heart.

The people whom Jesus condemns are branded as false because in their case life and lip had not been in harmony. Their exclamation "Lord, Lord" had been deceitful. By means of it they also now, on this day of the Great Assize, present themselves as Christ's loyal servants; yet in their previous life they by their actions had constantly been claiming lordship for themselves (Mal. 1:6 ff.; Luke 6:46). But on this day of the last judgment they discover that, whatever may have been their previous success in deceiving others, and perhaps while on earth even *themselves*, they cannot fool the Judge. From the kingdom in its final phase they are excluded.—The lesson is clear: **let everyone examine himself!** What makes introspection important is that there will be many "sayers" who have not been "doers." Jesus says they have not practiced the will of "my Father...." (Bold mine)

After Jesus was baptized, he had a three and a half year ministry that ended with his ransom sacrifice. Jesus did not seek attention for himself, it was always about the Father. He was not interested in raising money to save the poor, or raising money to make himself wealthy, and he was not looking for an easy life. Rather, Jesus life and ministry was his dedication to the will of the Father. He advised his disciples, "But be you seeking[150] the kingdom of God and his righteousness, and all these things will be added to you." (Matt. 6:33) "As [Jesus' ministry] develops, Judea rejects him (John 5:18), Galilee casts him out (John 6:66), Gadara begs him to leave its district (Matt. 8:34), Samaria refuses him lodging (Luke 9:53), earth will not have him (Matt. 27:23), and finally even heaven forsakes him (Matt. 27:46)." (Hendriksen 1973, p. 403) Jesus even said, "Foxes have holes, and birds of the air have nests, but the Son of Man has nowhere to lay his head." (Matt. 8:20) If the false prophet televangelist today can raise hundreds of millions of dollars, we can only manage what Jesus could have accomplished if he had altered his message. Wealth in itself is not intrinsically evil; it is the love of money that is evil. Are we following in the footsteps of Jesus by having a balanced perspective on material things? – Matthew 6:24-34.

Jesus was not concerned about his own desires; rather he sought to do the will of the Father first. If there was ever an example of self-

---

[150] Gr., *zeteite*; the verb form indicates continuous action.

sacrifice, it was Jesus Christ. He was aware of the big picture, as he knew that what the future held was worth far more than a few years of selfish pleasures. There was one occasion when Jesus had been busy all day, even skipping a meal, "when he saw the crowds, he had compassion for them, because they were harassed and helpless, like sheep without a shepherd." (Matt. 9:36; Mark 6:31-34) Jesus, wearied as he was from his journey, was sitting beside Jacob's well. A woman from Samaria came to draw water. Jesus, though tired, decided to teach her. (John 4:6-7, 13-15) Jesus' primary concern was the well-being of those to whom he came to share the good news. (John 11:5-15) Jesus said, "I have come down from heaven, not to do my own will but the will of him who sent me." (John 6:38, ESV) While our commission is not the same as Jesus, we were given a Great Commission by Jesus (Matt 24:14; 28:19-20; Ac 1:8), so we can imitate Jesus by being self-sacrificing toward that commission, being concerned about the eternal well-being of others and the will of the Father and the Son.

Warnings for Us

The prophet Daniel wrote, "All Israel has transgressed your law and turned aside, refusing to obey your voice. And the curse and oath that are written in the Law of Moses the servant of God have been poured out upon us, because we have sinned against him." (Dan. 9:11, ESV) The apostle Paul used this 1,500 years of Israelite history to encourage Christians, "these things happened to them as an example, but they were **written down for our instruction**, on whom the end of the ages has come." – 1 Corinthians 10:1-6, 11.

Paul warned, "Now these things happened as examples for us, so that **we would not crave evil things as they also craved**." (1 Cor. 10:6, NASB) Paul warned the Corinthians against doing what "some of them did." He referred to idolatry, sexual immorality, putting Christ to the test (as they had put the Father to the test), and grumbling. (1 Cor. 10:7-10) Let us quote Richard L. Pratt Jr. at length, to get a sense of the warning examples from the Israelites. However, we will interject a paragraph between his quoted paragraphs, with the citation at the end.

First, the Corinthians were to avoid setting their **hearts on evil things**. This terminology occurs only twice in the Old Testament (Num. 11:34; Prov. 1:22), so Paul may have been alluding to Numbers 11:4–6 where the Israelites valued Egypt's food above loyalty to God. Israel committed so many sins that all but two of the adults who originally left Egypt died in the wilderness (Num. 14:22–30; 32:11–13). Even Moses was not allowed to enter the Promised Land (Num. 20:12).

In general, Paul meant these examples to warn the Corinthians of the conditional nature of God's blessings. If they failed to obey God, if they continued to abuse one another, God might judge them as he had judged Israel. God had already killed some of the Corinthians for these things (1 Cor. 11:30). Specifically, Paul wanted the Corinthians not to allow their desire for meat sacrificed to idols to override their loyalty to God, again to avoid judgment.

Wrong desires of **what is evil** could be compared to the game of Russian roulette,[151] which is not worth the risk of temporary pleasure, yet so many fall victim to the immediate gratification of temporary pleasure. Why? **(1)** We are imperfect and live in an imperfect world, compounded with the fact that God's Word says we are mentally bent and lean toward doing bad. We read, "When the LORD saw that the wickedness of man on the earth was great, and that the whole bent of his thinking was never anything but evil, the LORD regretted that he had ever made man on the earth." (Gen. 6:5, AT) **(2)** We have a wicked spirit creature, Satan the Devil, who is misleading the entire world of humankind. We read, "Be sober-minded; be watchful. Your adversary the devil prowls around like a roaring lion, seeking someone to devour." (1 Pet 5:8, ESV) **(3)** We live in a world that caters to the imperfect flesh. We read, "For all that is in the world—the desires of the flesh and the desires of the eyes and pride in possessions, is not from the Father but is from the world. And the world is passing away along with its desires, but whoever does the will of God abides forever." (1 John 2:16-17) **(4)** We are unable to understand our inner person, which the Bible informs us is wicked: "The heart is deceitful above all things, and desperately sick; who can understand it?" The apostle Paul tells us, "just as sin came into the world through one man, and death through sin, and so death spread to all men because all sinned." There is only one major factor in all four parts that will have an effect on the other two, **you.** – Jeremiah 17:9; Romans 5:12.

Yes, we create our own stress. Because **(1)** we do not understand our true imperfection, and our imperfection is easily mislead by point number

---

[151] Russian roulette is a deadly game in which people take turns firing a revolver loaded with only one bullet at their own heads, after spinning the cylinder. Broadly it can refer to a dangerous or reckless action or activity.

(2), Satan. Moreover, we are easily enticed by point number **(3-4)**, the world and its desires, as well as our heart. We read, "But each person is tempted when he is lured and enticed by his own desire. Then desire, when it has conceived gives birth to sin, and sin when it is fully grown brings forth death." (Jas 1:14-15, ESV) Only by an active faith in Christ, and a true understanding of our imperfection, can we hope to function in an imperfect world, defeat Satan, gain control over our imperfect flesh, allow God to read our heart and help us to **not** fall victim to our own desires of the eyes.

Second, Paul warned believers not to **be idolaters, as some of them were**. Here he had in mind the specific event of Exodus 32:6, and he quoted it to illustrate his point. When Moses went to Sinai to receive the Ten Commandments, Israel began **to indulge in pagan revelry** before the golden calf, which evidently included pagan cultic meals like those the Corinthians ate in pagan temples (8:10). Because of this idolatry God nearly destroyed the entire nation of Israel. As it was, he had three thousand men put to death (Exod. 32:28). Paul warned the Corinthians to take this temptation to idolatrous eating seriously.

We can note that the Israelites never stopped worshiping God; however, they fell to calf worship, which was disgusting to God. After worshiping the golden calf, "the people sat down to eat and drink and rose up to play." (Ex 32:4-6, ESV) Today, many of us may claim that we are worshiping God. However, we need to examine ourselves, to see if we are focused on our dedication to God or the things of this world while working our worship in as best we can. John told us, "Do not love the world or the things in the world. If anyone loves the world, the love of the Father is not in him." (1 John 2:15, ESV) True, "the desires of the flesh and the desires of the eyes and pride of life" (1 John 2:16, ESV) is not the same as worshiping a golden calf, yet the principle applies. If we are letting our fleshly desire lead us as though it were our god; then, we are not committed to our dedication. (Phil. 3:19) Remember, "The world is passing away along with its desires, but whoever does the will of God abides forever." – 1 John 2:17, ESV.

In the third example, Paul warned against **sexual immorality,** referring to the time when **twenty-three thousand of them died** after engaging in idolatry at Baal-Peor and involving themselves in fertility rituals (Num. 25:1–9;31:16). Numbers 25:9 mentions that twenty-four thousand died as a result. Paul approximates this number (just as the original twenty-four thousand was an approximation rather than an exact count), but his point is clear. Many died because of involvement in pagan fertility rites.

Fertility religions believed that participating in religious prostitution and orgies brought health, fertility, and prosperity. The idolatry practiced in Corinth in Paul's day involved similar fertility practices. Paul's warning was plain: eating meat sacrificed to idols may lead to sexual immorality—to which some of the Corinthians were prone (1 Cor. 6:15–16)—and such immorality stirs the wrath of God.

A part of our dedication is the disowning of oneself to carry out the will of the Father and the Son, accepting the moral standards found in the Word of God. (Matt. 5:27-30) The world we live in is filled with immorality in excess, whereas, we as Christians, need to be morally clean, letting God determine what is good and what is bad. (1 Cor. 6:9-11) Dedication to God means that we allow nothing to get in the way of our whole-souled worship. Our hearts belong to God and our Christian conscience is tweaked the moment our eyes set upon anything immoral. In addition, we have a zeal for God that moves us to help any brother or sister who may stumble in the area of immorality, by getting them the help they need.

Fourth, Paul warned the Corinthians **not to test the Lord, as some of them did**, and he mentioned **snakes** which killed many in Israel. This alludes to Numbers 21:4–9 where the people blasphemed God by rejecting his manna. Paul drew upon this parallel because some in Corinth were not satisfied with what God had given them in Christ. As the Israelites before them who desired food other than manna, the Corinthians desired meat so much that they disregarded all other considerations. God's retribution against the Israelites warned the Corinthians against these practices.

As Christians, our desire is to see the return of Christ. When we became a Christian, we likely hoped that it would be soon and the pain and suffering would end. Let us not tire out as the Israelites did. Being dedicated to God was not based on some preconceived time schedule, it was for an eternity, regardless if we grow old and die before Armageddon. So, then, "let us not grow weary of doing good, for in due season we will reap, if we do not give up." – Galatians 6:9, ESV.

Paul's fifth warning was that the Corinthians not **grumble, as some of them did**. Complaining against God and his leaders took place many times in the wilderness (Exod. 15:24; Deut. 1:27). But Paul had in mind a time when **the destroying angel** killed those who grumbled. Although the Scriptures do not mention a particular time when such an angel appeared in the wilderness, similar concepts appear in many places in the Old Testament (Exod. 12:23; 1 Chr. 21:15). The rabbis of Paul's day taught that God had a particular angel who destroyed and killed. Apparently, Paul agreed with this teaching.

Paul may have referred to Numbers 16 where the people rebelled against Moses' leadership and many thousands died, or perhaps to Numbers 14:28–30 where God issued the curse that only Joshua and Caleb would enter the Promised Land. Those who opposed Paul on the matter of meat offered to idols risked committing against him the kind of rebellion against Moses which brought death to the Old Testament Israelites. (Pratt Jr 2000, p. 164-165)

The Israelites failed to appreciate what God had provided them, so **they began to complain**; when, in fact, they had promised they would obey all that he would ask of them. We as faithful servants of our heavenly Father have much to be appreciative of today as well. We have been provided with resources beyond any expectation that we 'may know the only true God, and the one he had sent, Jesus Christ.' (John 17:3) Many of us have been provided church leaders, 'those who spoke to us the word of God. We are told to 'consider the outcome of their way of life, and imitate their faith.' (Heb. 13:7) In fact, the author of Hebrews goes on to say more about these leaders. He writes, "Obey your leaders and submit to them, for they are keeping watch over your souls, as those who will have to give an account. Let them do this with joy and not with groaning, for that would be of no advantage to you." (Heb. 13:17, ESV) Our dedication requires that we appreciate all that God has made available to us and use it wisely. Without taking away from many wonderful leaders, we herein offer our warning too. Not all leaders are the same. Both Jesus and Paul spoke of false ones, so be watchful as the day draws near. – Hebrews 10:25-26; 1 Peter 4:7; 5:8; Matthew 26:41; Romans 12:2; 2 Timothy 4:3-4.

Day After Day

The Israelites fell into many different sinful behaviors over their 1,500-years as God's chosen people. Calf worship was very egregious right at the beginning, but it paled in comparison to child sacrifice to false gods such as Molech.[152] Of course, we are highlighting just how far a group of people can fall by choosing the most serious sins in the nation's history but they also fell into deception, causing discord among each other, sexual sins, taking advantage of the poor, theft, jealousy, fits of anger, orgies, rivalries, dissensions, divisions, envy, drunkenness, even thousands of murders throughout the centuries. Oh, if they had only remained faithful to their dedication, knowing it was unconditional. Unlike the Israelites, Jesus Christ and the apostle and hundreds of thousands of first-century Christians lived up to their dedication daily to the end. This was true in a century where immorality and sinful desires were rampant within the Roman Empire, not to mention outright persecution for even being a Christian.

These early Christians chose "to live for the rest of the time in the flesh no longer for human passions but for the will of God." (1 Pet. 4:2, ESV) The will of the Father and the Son for us today is that "all people to be saved and to come to the knowledge of the truth." Yes, the will of the Father and the Son are one, just as we are to be one with them, united in our dedication and pure worship. Our task in these last days is to 'proclaim the gospel of the Kingdom in the whole inhabited earth for a testimony to all the nations, and then the end will come.' (Matt. 24:14) Our commission is more, though, as we are to take those who are receptive or even though we convert into being receptive and we are to teach them, making them into disciples. The apostle Paul exhorted that Timothy and us by extension to 'Do our best to present ourselves to God as one approved, a worker who has no need to be ashamed, rightly handling the word of truth.' – 2 Timothy 2:15

Rightly Handling the Word of Truth

Evangelism is the work of a Christian evangelist, of which all true Christians are obligated to partake to some extent, which seeks to persuade other people to become Christian, especially by sharing the basics of the Gospel, but also the deeper message of biblical truths. Today

---

[152] Also spelled Moloch, god of the Canaanites and Phoenicians to whom parents sacrificed their children.

the Gospel is almost an unknown, so what does the Christian evangelist do? **Preevangelism** is laying a foundation for those who have no knowledge of the Gospel, giving them background information, so that they are able to grasp what they are hearing. The Christian evangelist is preparing their mind and heart so that they will be receptive to the biblical truths. In many ways, this is known as apologetics.

Christian apologetics [Greek: *apologia*, "verbal defense, speech in defense"] is a field of **Christian theology** which endeavors to offer a reasonable and sensible basis for the **Christian faith**, defending the faith against objections. It is reasoning from the Scriptures, explaining and proving, as one instructs in sound doctrine, many times having to overturn false reasoning before he can plant the seeds of truth. It can also be earnestly contending for the faith and saving one from losing their faith, as they have begun to doubt. Moreover, it can involve rebuking those who contradict the truth. It is being prepared to make a defense to anyone who asks the Christian evangelist for a reason for the hope that is in him or her. – Jude 1.3, 21-23; 1 Pet 3.15; Acts 17:2-3; Titus 1:9.

What do we mean by **obligated** and what we mean by **evangelism** are at the heart of the matter and are indeed related to each other.

EVANGELISM: An evangelist is a proclaimer of the gospel or good news, as well as all biblical truths. There are levels of evangelism, which is pictured in first-century Christianity. All Christians evangelized in the first century, but a select few fit the role of a full-time evangelist (Ephesians 4:8, 11-12), like Philip and Timothy.

Both Philip and Timothy are specifically mentioned as evangelizers. (Ac 21:8; 2 Tim. 4:5) Philip was a full-time evangelist after Pentecost, who was sent to the city of Samaria, having great success. An angel even directed Philip to an Ethiopian Eunuch, to share the good news about Christ with him. Because of the Eunuch's already having knowledge of God by way of the Old Testament, Philip was able to help him understand that the Hebrew Scriptures pointed to Christ as the long awaited Messiah. In the end, Philip baptized the Eunuch. Thereafter, the Spirit again sent Philip on a mission, this time to Azotus and all the cities on the way to Caesarea. (Ac 8:5, 12, 14, 26-40) Paul evangelized in many lands, setting up one congregation after another. (2 Cor. 10:13-16) Timothy was an evangelizer or missionary, and Paul placed distinct importance on evangelizing when he gave his parting encouragement to Timothy. – 2 Timothy 4:5; 1 Timothy 1:3.

The office of apostle and evangelist seem to overlap in some areas, but could be distinguished in that apostles traveled and set up congregations, which took evangelizing skills, but also developed the congregations after they were established. The evangelists were more of a missionary, being stationed in certain areas to grow and develop congregations. In addition, if we look at all of the apostles and the evangelists, plus Paul's more than one hundred traveling companions, it seems very unlikely that they could have had Christianity at over one million by the 125 C.E. This was accomplished because all Christians were obligated to carry out some level of evangelism.

OBLIGATED: In the broadest sense of the term for evangelizer, all Christians are obligated to play some role as an evangelist.

• *Basic Evangelism* is planting seeds of truth and watering any seeds that have been planted. [In the basic sense of this word (euaggelistes), this would involve all Christians.] In some cases, it may be that one Christian planted the seed, which were initially rejected, so he was left in a good way because the planter did not try to force the truth down his throat. However, later he faces something in life that moves him to reconsider those seeds, and another Christian waters what had already been planted by the first Christian. This evangelism can be carried out in all of the methods that are available: informal, house-to-house, street, phone, internet, and the like. What amount of time is invested in the evangelism work is up to each Christian to decide for themselves.

• *Making Disciples* is having any role in the process of getting an unbeliever from his unbelief state to the point of accepting Christ as his Savior and being baptized. Once the unbeliever has become a believer, he is still developed until he has become strong. Any Christian could potentially carry this one person through all of the developmental stages. On the other hand, it may be that several have some part. It is like a person that specializes in a certain aspect of a job, but all are aware of the other aspects, in case they are called on to carry out that phase. Again, each Christian must decide for themselves what role they are to have, and how much of a role, but should be prepared to fill any role if needed.

• *Part-Time or Full-Time Evangelist* is one who sees this as their calling and chooses to be very involved as an evangelist in their local church and community. They may work part-time to supplement their work as an evangelist. They may be married with children, but they realize their gift is in the field of evangelism. If it were the wife, the husband would work toward supporting her work as an evangelist and vice-versa. If it were a single person, he or she would supplement their work by being employed part-time, but also the church would help as well. This person is well trained in every aspect of bringing one to Christ.

• *Congregation Evangelists* should be very involved in evangelizing their communities and helping the church members play their role at the basic levels of evangelism. There is nothing to say that one church could not have many within, who take on part-time or full-time evangelism within the congregation, which would and should be cultivated.[153]

Review Questions

- How did Jesus evidence his dedication to carrying out the will of the Father?

- If we know entertaining wring desires leads to bad thing, why do so many stumble in this area?

- Why examine ourselves as to our desires of the flesh?

- In what way can we avoid letting wrong sexual desires intrude into our lives?

- How does remembering our dedication is "day after day" help us in doing God's will?

- How are we to rightly handle the Word of truth?

---

[153] CONVERSATIONAL EVANGELISM Defending the Faith, Reasoning from the Scriptures, Explaining and Proving, Instructing in Sound Doctrine, and Overturning False Reasoning by Edward D. Andrews

THE CHRISTIAN APOLOGIST: Always Being Prepared to Make a Defense By Edward D. Andrews

OVERCOMING BIBLE DIFFICULTIES: Answers to the So-Called Errors and Contradictions by Edward D. Andrews

THE EVANGELISM HANDBOOK: How All Christians Can Effectively Share God's Word in Their Community by Edward D. Andrews

CHAPTER 11 You Must Renounce All You Have

Luke 14:33 Updated American Standard Version (UASV)

[33] "So therefore, any one of you who does not renounce all that he has cannot be my disciple."

Calculating the Cost

What did Jesus mean that we could not be his disciple, if we do not renounce all that we have? Jesus had said just a few verses earlier, "For which one of you, when he wants to build a tower, does not first **sit down and calculate the cost** to see if he has enough to complete it?" (Lu 14:28) This section of Scripture is dealing with 'sitting down and counting the cost of what it means to truly be a disciple.' While this is not advocating that every Christian must reject all material things and live in isolation as early Christians thought, it is saying that if you are truly Christian, you must be prepared to give up all material things if that is what is called for in a particular situation. For example, suppose we had worked twenty years to build up a great Christian bakery and in the gay marriage climate of the recent United States Supreme Court, we were told by another court that we had to make a homosexual couple a wedding cake, which we had refused to do, or be arrested. What would we do? Would we risk our business that we sunk twenty years of our life into and share in the sins of other by making the cake? Our dedication that we made was to Christ Jesus not to material things. Thus, we must be prepared to 'renounce all that we have' if circumstances call for it or we are not Jesus' disciple.

Therefore, one who is truly Christian, i.e., truly a disciple of Christ, must have **calculated the cost** and have accepted that if there comes a time to **renounce all things**, God will not leave us in a lurch. While the salvation that Jesus offers all is freely given, there may come a time when being a disciple may cost us everything, including our lives, which God can replace, as in the case of Job. Again, leaving one's home, selling off all of one's belongings and giving it to some church, to live in some isolated commune, is not a qualification of being a disciple. However, we gave ourselves as slaves of Christ, meaning we have up our lives and all we own, and if, it comes to a circumstance where we must let our material possession go or be unfaithful, it means that we **renounce all that we**

have. What we have is a loving relationship with the Father and the Son, salvation and a hope at eternal life in the Kingdom of God.

Jesus gave his life on our behalf and for the Kingdom of God. When Jesus stood before Pilate, his life in the hand of this pagan, Roman Governor, he did not waver but stood there steadfast. (John 18:37) Even after being beaten to the point of death, hanging on the cross, he looked to the Kingdom of God, saying to one of the evildoers, "you will be with me in Paradise." – Luke 23:43.

Testify to the Truth

We need to ponder as to why Jesus focused so much attention and concern for the kingdom. Pilate said to Jesus, "So you are a king?" Jesus answered, "You say that I am a king. For this purpose, I was born and for this purpose, I have come into the world, **to testify to the truth**. Everyone who is of the truth hears my voice." (John 18:37) To what truth was Jesus testifying? He was testifying to the truth that the Kingdom of God would rule in righteousness and make it so that the will of the Father could be done on earth as it had been done in heaven. (Matt. 6:10) There is no greater joy than using one's life to help the Father in carrying out his will for humanity, bringing about pur worship earth wide.

The prophet Daniel foretold, "And **in the days of those kings** the God of heaven will set up a kingdom that shall never be destroyed, nor shall the kingdom be left to another people. It shall break in pieces all **these kingdoms** and bring them to an end, and it shall stand forever." (Dan. 2:44) The Father was to establish the Kingdom and the rule of Christ at Jesus second coming, and it would be **in the days of those kings**. What **kings** was Daniel referring to in his prophetic interpretation of King Nebuchadnezzar's dream? Some say Daniel was referring to rulers associated with the ancient Roman Empire, while others believe the kings are the four kingdoms pictured by the statue (i.e., the Babylonian, Persian, Grecian, and Roman empires), still other argue that the kings are from the Greek period, namely, the Seleucids and Ptolemies. Others would argue that Daniel is referring to the Maccabean period where the descents of Mattathias restored pure worship for a time in Israel.

Actually, all of these are wrong. Let us establish the points of the text.

- "In the days of those **kings**" refers to more than one king ruling as a world power because it is plural, i.e., more than one.

- "It shall break in pieces all these **kingdoms**" refers to more than one kingdom also holding sway in the world.

- "In the days of **those** kings," the demonstrative pronoun "those" refers to its immediate antecedent, namely, the kings within the statue.

Everyone agrees, "The God of heaven [the Father] will set up a kingdom [ruled by Christ at his second coming] that shall never be destroyed." How can this be, as the Babylonian, Persian, Grecian, and Roman empires have passed away as world powers? Well, some might take the whole of that statue as the immediate antecedent of the demonstrative pronoun "those" but that is not necessary, nor could it be maintained or defended. Let us look at Daniel 2:32-33, which summarize the statue.

- **BABYLONIAM EMPIRE:** The head of this image was of fine gold,

- **MEDO-PERSIAN EMPIRE:** its chest and arms of silver,

- **GREECIAN EMPIRE:** its middle and thighs of bronze,

- **ROMAN EMPIRE:** its legs of iron,

- **CONTEMPORANEOUS EMPIRES:** its feet partly of iron and partly of clay

Old Testament Bible scholar, John F Walvoord writes, "The fourth kingdom in Nebuchadnezzar's dream represented by the legs and feet of the image is obviously the most important. Daniel gives more attention to this fourth kingdom than to the preceding kingdoms put together."[154] Can we see the mistake he is making? Daniel sections this statue not into four parts, but into five parts. First, let us say there are four chapters in the book of Daniel that have world powers moving through time, creating a timeline that walks us up to the Kingdom of God. These chapters intertwine and are in perfect harmony as to the world leaders on the stage.

CHAPTER 2 THE IMMENSE STATUE (Daniel 2:31-45): The head of gold is Babylonia. The chest and arms of silver is the Medo-and Persia. The middle and thighs of bronze is Greece. The legs of Iron represent Rome.

---

[154] Walvoord, John F (2012-02-01). *Daniel (The John Walvoord Prophecy Commentaries)* (Kindle Locations 1460-1461). Moody Publishers. Kindle Edition.

CHAPTER 7 THE FOUR BEATS (Daniel 7:3-8, 7, and 25): The first beat is Babylonia, the second beast is Medo-and Persia, the third beast is Greece, and the fourth beast is Rome.

CHAPTER 8 VISION OF A RAM, A GOAT AND LITTLE HORN (Daniel 8:1-25): Daniel himself tells us the interpretation, "As for the ram that you saw with the two horns, these are the kings of Media and Persia. And the goat is the king of Greece." (8:20-21) The controversy of this chapter is over the "little horn" that grew out one of the four horns mentioned in verse 8.

CHAPTER 11 KING OF THE NORTH AND KING OF THE SOUTH (Daniel 11:5-45): In Daniel chapter 11 we start with Daniel 11:2, which also begin with Persia and Greece. "And now I will show you the truth. Behold, three more kings shall arise in Persia [(1) Cyrus the Great, (2) Cambyses II, and (3) Darius I], and a fourth [Xerxes I] shall be far richer than all of them. And when he has become strong through his riches, he shall stir up all against the kingdom of Greece." Then Daniel 11:3 reads, "Then a mighty king shall arise [Alexander the Great], who shall rule with great dominion and do as he wills." Daniel 11:4 reads, "And as soon he has arisen, his kingdom shall be broken and divided toward the four winds of heaven [Alexander's four general split the territory[155] after Alexander died suddenly], but not to his posterity, nor according to the authority with which he ruled, for his kingdom shall be plucked up and go to **others besides these**."

Now, Daniel 11:5-6 jump into a battle between the king of the south and the king of the north. Notice that Daniel had told us the four parts of Alexander's kingdom would **not be** a strong as his. That was true, as two of the four generals defeat the other two, leaving Ptolemy to the south and Seleucus to the north. The Ptolemaic and Seleucid dynasties were north and south of what? They were north and south of Israel. These two dynasties would go on for a time before being replaced by a new King of the north and king of the south. The king of the north and the king of the south run all the way down until the second coming of Christ, with one being the lead power for a time, followed by the other taking the power for a time. At his second coming, Jesus, the king of the Kingdom of God will crush whoever is the leading one at time, along with the contemporaneous empires (feet partly of iron and partly of clay). We

---

[155] Cassander ruled Macedonia and Greece. Lysimachus was over Asia Minor and Thrace. Seleucus I Nicator ruled Mesopotamia and Syria. In addition, Ptolemy Lagus ruled Egypt and Palestine.

return to Daniel 2:34, which read, "As you looked, a stone was cut out by no human hand, and it struck the image on its feet of iron and clay, and broke them in pieces." Notice that it was not the head of this statue, nor the chest and arms, or the middle and thighs, or the legs that were to be struck, but rather, it was feet partly of iron and partly of clay, i.e., contemporaneous empires and the king of the north and the south. The *feet partly of iron and partly of clay* is the immediate antecedent of the demonstrative pronoun "those," which refers to the contemporary empires or kingdoms that would rule in the last days, and would be destroyed by the Kingdom of God.

Yes, Daniel 2:45 would seem to shatter all of this because it reads "just as you saw that a stone [the Messianic Kingdom] was cut from a mountain by no human hand [but rather by divine power], and that it broke in pieces the iron, the bronze, the clay, the silver, and the gold. A great God has made known to the king what shall be after this. The dream is certain, and its interpretation sure." Even though the Babylonian (gold), Persian (silver), Grecian (bronze), and Roman empires (iron) had passed away as world powers, their remnants are still in existence today, and they make up contemporary empires, with the king of the north embarking on its final campaign "to destroy and devote many to destruction." – Daniel 11:44.

In the Gospel of Luke an angel named Gabriel said to Mary, the mother of Jesus, "Do not be afraid, Mary, for you have found favor with God. And behold, you will conceive in your womb and bear a son, and you shall call his name Jesus. He will be great and will be called the Son of the Most High. And the Lord God will give to him the throne of his father David, and he will reign over the house of Jacob forever, and of his kingdom there will be no end." (Luke 1:30-33) This is very similar to the prophetic message from Daniel. The Father promised that Jesus would become the King of His Kingdom. During Jesus' life and ministry here on earth, he showed that he would be a kind, just, and perfect Ruler.

When Jesus ascended back to heaven, he was enthroned as King of God's Kingdom right away. However, he did not and has not for some 2,000 years broken into pieces all these kingdoms to an end and has not ended Satan's rule. The apostle Paul tells us, "But when Christ had offered for all time a single sacrifice for sins, he sat down at the right hand of

God, **waiting from that time** until his enemies should be made a footstool for his feet." (Heb. 10:12-13, ESV)[156]

On these verses, Thomas D. Lea writes, "Two features showed the conclusive nature of Christ's sacrifice. First, Christ had offered only a single sacrifice, and this single offering did the job (v. 10). Second, Jesus' job as sacrificial lamb was finished. When Jesus exclaimed, "It is finished" (John 19:30), he really meant it. His enthronement at the right hand of God showed the completion of the task. His seat at God's right hand showed that God had exalted him to the position of highest glory. In Jesus, believers have access to unlimited grace and power. The present era is a waiting period as Christ anticipates a final victory over his enemies. We have been living in this era since the time of Jesus' exaltation to heaven. Christ has already won the victory, but we do not yet see the complete defeat of Christ's spiritual enemies. Rather than complaining about the delay, we should see this time as a day of grace to allow outsiders to experience God's mercy and forgiveness. We have no doubt or question about the ultimate outcome. Although this verse [10:12-13] does not directly quote Psalm 110:1 (see Heb. 1:13), that passage is clearly in view. Jesus is portrayed as our High Priest, assuming the kingship. As a king, Christ will enjoy full victory over his enemies. He will make a final display of triumph over evil at the end of history (see 1 Cor. 15:22–28)." (Lea 1999, p. 184)

I would like to qualify Dr. Lea's last comment, which says, "He [Jesus] will make a final display of triumph over evil at the end of history." This does not mean the earth is being destroyed, just that the wicked are being destroyed and Satan and his demons will be abyssed for a thousand years. The original intention of the Father for the earth, righteousness will be realized and all of humanity, who will then be in perfection, will accept the sovereignty of God. Since 33 C.E., Jesus has ruled in heaven as the Father's appointed King. The Father and the Son have also selected some faithful men and women from the earth to go to heaven. They will rule with Jesus as kings, judges, and priests over humankind. Jesus said to his apostle, "You are those who have stayed with me in my trials, and I assign to you, as my Father assigned to me, a kingdom, that you may eat and drink at my table in my kingdom and sit on thrones judging ..." (Lu 22:28-30, ESV) On Jesus co-rulers, the apostle

---

[156] **Who Authored the Book of Hebrews: A Defense for Pauline Authorship**

http://www.christianpublishers.org/who-authored-hebrews

John wrote, "Worthy are you [Jesus] to take the scroll and to open its seals, for you were slain, and purchased for God with your blood men from every tribe and language and people and nation, and you have made them a kingdom and priests to our God, and they shall reign over the earth."[157] – Revelation 5:9-10.

One day soon Jesus will judge humanity, separating the like a shepherd separates sheep from goats. The sheep are those who are truly Christian. They have evidence that they have s genuine faith. They have been loyal subjects to the king and his kingdom. They will receive eternal life on earth, which will be ruled over by Jesus and his kingdom of co-rulers. The goats on the other hand will be those who have rejected Jesus Christ. (Matt. 25:31-34, 46) What are to happen to the goat like ones? Jesus and his co-rulers will destroy these ones. The apostle Paul answers,

2 Thessalonians 1:5-9 Updated American Standard Version (UASV)

5 This is evidence of the righteous judgment of God, that you may be considered worthy of the kingdom of God, for which you are also suffering. **6** since indeed God considers it just to repay with affliction those who afflict you, **7** and to give relief to you who are afflicted along with us when the Lord Jesus will be revealed from heaven with His mighty angels in flaming fire, **8** in flaming fire, inflicting vengeance on **those who do not know** God and on **those who do not obey** the gospel of our Lord Jesus. **9 These ones will pay the penalty of <u>eternal destruction</u>**, from before the Lord[158] and from the glory of his strength,

Do Not Be Anxious

Certainly, living within Satan's world that caters to the imperfect human flesh is no easy task. Jesus said, "I tell you, do not be anxious about your life." (Matt. 6:25, ESV) What should be our main focus? Jesus said, "Seek first the kingdom of God and his righteousness, and all these things will be added to you. Therefore, do not be anxious about tomorrow, for tomorrow will be anxious for itself. Sufficient for the day is its own trouble." (Matt. 6:33-34) Jesus set the example of putting the kingdom first in his life, and it was no easy task for him either. Those who are truly Christian will have to prioritize their life, knowing that each of us

---

[157] **Resurrection Hope - Where?**

http://www.christianpublishers.org/resurrection-hope-where

[158] Lit *from before the face of the Lord*

have different responsibilities, so not everyone can give as much of themselves to the kingdom as another. Therefore, we should not compare ourselves to anyone else. Jane might be a single mother with four children, while Lisa has a husband to help with only two children. John might be eighty-four years old, while Kenney is only twenty-three years old. Samantha and her husband might be living in poverty, while Denise and her husband are upper middle class.

Walking in the footsteps of Jesus means that we are willing to carry a cross and all that might be involved in being a disciple. If we are counting the cost of our service, this means that we are prepared to give up any material possessions for the kingdom. Lu 14:27-28, 33) No matter the events of our country, those who are truly Christian are obligated to share the good news with others, whenever the opportunity presents itself. The hope of attaining eternal life under the kingdom of Christ is what helps us to keep our focus, as we keep our eyes on the prize. – Matthew 13:44-46.

We must ask ourselves, 'do we allow secular activities to crowd out our service to God. Have we taken a job promotion that causes us to miss more of our Christian meetings? Do we skip our daily personal Bible study to do things with friends? Are we working voluntary overtime, which keeps us from the meetings? Are we considering a job that would mean we miss weekly meetings and our personal Bible study (e.g., truck driver)? We should do everything within our power to have a daily Bible study program, attend every meeting each week, to prepare for those meetings, to be able to participate, and to have some share in preaching the gospel to unbelievers. (Col. 3:23-24) Yes, if a family is in poverty, a father or mother needs to take whatever job can pull them out of poverty. Jesus does not expect us to leave our children in poverty because we are zealous for the kingdom. However, if we have to take a job that cuts into our worship, we should keep our eye out for another that will not cause us to set aside our worship. The congregation is strengthened by the presence of all of us.

Plan Ahead

Those who are truly Christian would do well to **live as though** Jesus second coming is tomorrow [maintain righteous standing], **plan as though** it is 50-years away [prepare life so one can evangelize to the extent possible]. What about pur young ones though who are soon to be out of high school. They should be planning now, and parents need to prepare them if they are going to go onto higher education. We have already discussed in previous chapters of the liberal progressive professors that are more evangelistic about atheism than most Christians are about the kingdom. Thus, studying some apologetic material prior to attending college is highly recommended. Whether our young ones are going to college or not, they still need to maintain the same level of worship.

Satan's world has a way of sucking the vitality out of us if we are willing to slave for it, as opposed to slaving for Christ. If our children are heading to college, they must consider the debt, which if much is accumulated, it will take many years to repay such. Do they really need to attend a big named university for the name alone? This may mean the difference between $15,000 a year, as opposed to $65,000 a year. Consider what that means after 4-6 years of college and university. In addition, consider eternal life. If we truly believe in eternal life, what difference does it make after we are millions of years into eternity, looking back on these few decades of imperfection?

Review Questions

- What does it mean that we cannot be a disciple of Jesus unless we renounce all that we have?

- Why did Jesus focused so much attention and concern for the kingdom?

- Explain the four chapters in the book of Daniel that have world powers moving through time.

- When did Jesus begin to rule and what are we awaiting?

- What did Jesus mean by our not needing to be anxious and why not?

- How do we evidence that the kingdom is first in our lives?

- Why is it important that we plan?

CHAPTER 12 You Must Love the Lord

1 Corinthians 16:22 Updated American Standard Version (UASV)

22 If anyone does not love the Lord, **he is to be accursed.**

Here the apostle Paul places a curse on anyone who does not love the Lord. Likewise, in Galatians 1:9, Paul wrote, "As we have said before, so now I say again: If anyone is preaching to you a gospel contrary to the one you received, **let him be accursed.**" While Paul clearly knew that most Christians accepted the gospel and loved Jesus Christ, he also knew that false teachers, deceptive men and liars had slipped into the congregation as well. He had warned the Ephesian elders, "Take heed to yourselves and to all the flock, in which the Holy Spirit has made you overseers, to care for the church of God which he obtained with the blood of his own Son. I know that after my departure fierce wolves will come in among you, not sparing the flock; and from among your own selves will arise men speaking perverse things, to draw away the disciples after them." (Acts 20:28-30, RSV) Paul is telling us that the Lord even curses people in the Christian congregation if they do not love him. Notice the motive of some deceivers is **to draw away <u>the disciples</u>** [i.e., Jesus' disciples] after them. Paul even prayed that these deceptive ones who brought trouble would be punished.

Your Love Is Important

Matthew 22:34-40 Updated American Standard Version (UASV)

34 But when the Pharisees heard that Jesus had silenced the Sadducees, they gathered themselves together. **35** And one of them, versed in the Law,[159] tested him by asking, **36** "Teacher, which is the great commandment in the Law?" **37** And he said to him: "'You must love the Lord[160] your God with your whole heart and with your whole soul and with your whole mind.'[161] **38** This is the greatest and first commandment. **39** The second, like it, is this: 'You must love your

---

[159] I.e. an expert in the Mosaic Law

[160] This is a reference to the Father, I.e., Jehovah of the Old Testament

[161] A quotation from Deut. 6:5

neighbor as yourself.'[162] [40] On these two commandments the whole Law hangs, and the Prophets.'"

If the Pharisees were surprised by Jesus answer, Scripture does not say. However, it would not be unexpected if they were because they knew Jesus was a carpenter's son and had not attended the rabbinic schools, nor had he studied under anyone like Gamaliel.[163] Therefore, they likely thought Jesus being called a teacher by his disciples was not to be taken serious and they could easily trip him up. Anyway, Jesus knew that the most important aspect of pure worship was/is the love of God, even though the Jewish religious leaders of his day failed to display it. In the synagogue, the Shema (Deut. 6:4-9), the Jewish statement of faith was often recited.

Deuteronomy 6:6-9 Updated American Standard Version (UASV)

[6] "Hear, O Israel! Jehovah our God is one Jehovah! [5] You shall love Jehovah your God with all your heart and with all your soul and with all your might. [6] These words, which I am commanding you today, shall be on your heart. [7] You shall teach them diligently to your sons and shall talk of them when you sit in your house and when you walk by the way and when you lie down and when you rise up. [8] You shall bind them as a sign on your hand and they shall be as frontlets bands between your eyes.[164] [9] You shall write them on the doorposts of your house and on your gates.

---

[162] A quotation from Lev. 19:18

[163] Gamaliel was a "Jewish scholar. This man lived in the 1st century A.D. and died 18 years before the destruction of Jerusalem in A.D. 70 by Titus, the Roman general. Gamaliel is mentioned in Acts 22:3 as the rabbi with whom the apostle Paul studied as a youth in Jerusalem. Traditionally Gamaliel is considered to be the grandson of Hillel, and was thoroughly schooled in the philosophy and theology of his grandfather's teaching. Gamaliel was a member of the Sanhedrin, the high council of Jews in Jerusalem, and served as president of the Sanhedrin during the reigns of the Roman emperors Tiberius, Caligula, and Claudius. Unlike other Jewish teachers, he had no antipathy toward Greek learning. The learning of Gamaliel was so eminent and his influence so great that he is one of only seven Jewish scholars who have been honored by the title "Rabban." He was called the "Beauty of the Law." The Talmud even says that "since Rabban Gamaliel died, the glory of the Law has ceased." (Elwell, Baker Encyclopedia of the Bible 1988, P. 839)

[164] I.e. on your forehead

While it is true that burnt offerings and animal sacrifices were a major part of the Mosaic Law, it was the love that the servant had for his Creator that mattered.

Micah 6:6-8 Updated American Standard Version (UASV)

⁶ "With what will I come before Jehovah,
  and bow myself before God on high?
Shall I come before him with burnt offerings,
  with year-old calves?
⁷ Will Jehovah take delight in thousands of rams,
  with ten thousands of rivers of oil?
Shall I give my firstborn son for my transgression,
  the fruit of my body for the sin of my soul?"
⁸ He has told you, O man, what is good;
  and what does Jehovah require of you
but to do justice, and to love kindness,
  and to walk humbly with your God?

As Micah shows, the cost of the sacrifice does not matter if it is presented in love and godly devotion. One could offer tens of thousands of the most costly animal sacrifices, but if it is not done in love, it is to not avail, i.e., worthless. Consider the account of a poor widow's offering at the temple, Jesus pointed out that with her two small coins, she put in more than all those who are contributing to the offering box. For they all contributed out of their abundance, but she out of her poverty has put in everything she had, all she had to live on." (Mark 12:41-44) Her contribution was given out of love and godly devotion. Think for a moment, what has the greatest value to God is something that we all can possess, regardless of our situation, our love for him.

The apostle Paul importance of love and the superior love to the Corinthians. He wrote, "If I speak in the tongues of men and of angels, but have not love, I am a noisy gong or a clanging cymbal. And if I have prophetic powers, and understand all mysteries and all knowledge, and if I have all faith, so as to remove mountains, but have not love, I am nothing. If I give away all I have, and if I deliver up my body to be burned, but have not love, I gain nothing." (1 Cor. 13:1-3) Plainly, love is vital if we are caring out pure worship and are truly Christian. Moreover, without love it is impossible to please God. However, what are some different ways can we express our love for God?

Showing Your Love for God

While it is true that love is an emotion and it is spoken of as though we lacked control over it. For example, people have said, "you cannot help who you falling in love with." However, love is far more, which is regarded as an action in the Bible. The apostle Paul refers to love as "a still more excellent way" and as something we need to "pursue." (1 Cor. 12:31; 14:1, NASB) In fact, those, who are truly Christian, are encouraged to "let us not love with word or with tongue, but **in deed and truth**." – 1 John 3:18, NASB.

We are not to love the world. The apostle John writes, "Do not love the world nor the things in the world. If anyone loves the world, the love of the Father is not in him. For all that is in the world, the lust of the flesh and the lust of the eyes and the boastful pride of life, is not from the Father, but is from the world." (1 John 2:15-16, NASB) The psalmist tells us the same saying that we are love God but "hate evil." (Ps. 97:10) Love moves us to be obedient. John writes, "For this is the love of God that we keep his commandments, and his commandments are not burdensome." (1 John 5:3) Then, there is the love of neighbor. Yes, we show love for God by expressing our love for our neighbors as well. Jesus tells us that we are to 'love our neighbor as ourselves.' (Matt. 19:19) While caring for the sick, the needy, and the unfortunate is quite virtuous, helping them to find the path to eternal life is what God expected. – Matthew 24:14; 28:19-20; Acts 1:8.

Jesus voluntarily because of his love for the Father, love for humanity, and simply what is right, 'found himself in human form, humbling himself by becoming obedient to the point of death, even death on a cross.' (Phil. 2:8) This is evidence of one's love for the Father. Paul showed that it was by obedient love that we could have a righteous standing before God. Paul wrote, "As through the one man's [Adam's] disobedience the many were made sinners, even so through the obedience of the One [Jesus] the many will be made righteous." – Romans 5:19, NASB.

Therefore, we demonstrate our love for God by being obedient. "This is love that we walk according to His commandments. This is the commandment, just as you have heard from the beginning that you should walk in it." (2 John 1:6) Our love also means that we desire his guidance in our lives. Those who are truly Christian know that the way of man is not in himself, that it is not in man who walks to direct his steps." (Jer. 10:23) Therefore, we 'received the word with all eagerness, examining the Scriptures daily.' In other words, we work in behalf of our loving prayers with the Father, by looking to the Scriptures, to see more fully what his will and purposes are.

As Jesus said, we need to 'love the Lord our God with all our heart and with all our soul and with all our mind and with all our strength.' (Mark 12:30) Such love originates from our heart, comprising our feelings, desires, and our mindset, and we passionately desire to please the Father. Our love also originates in our thinking abilities as well, for our godly devotion is not motived by blind faith. We know who God is: his standards, qualities, will and purpose. We know that he is real trustworthy and true. We know and understand why he has allowed this temporary pain, suffering, old age and death within humanity. We know Him!

Why Do You Love God?

"God is live" and we were 'made in the image of God. Therefore, we naturally love fellow humans and especially our Creator. Of course, inherited sin has hampered this natural love for God and neighbor (more on developing this love below), yet it remains within each one of us. The sovereignty of God, the right to rule or the righteousness of God's rule is found in God's desire for us to serve him out of love not dreadful fear. In other words, we appreciate the life we have now and the life that is to come, and we love the righteousness of his rule.

If we ae to love God to the extent that Scriptures show, he cannot just be some distant being outside of the created universe. He is a person, who is spirit (i.e., invisible), but a real person, who spent 1600 years, sixty-six book and forty human authors revealing his love for us. He brought Noah through the flood. He brought Abraham into the land that his descendants would own. He brought Moses and millions out of slavery in Egypt. He rescued his people from one threat after another, even though they were the most unruly child for more than a millennium. He even disciplined them in love. He sheltered, sustained, and cherished the Israelites. He even gave the only begotten Son as a ransom, so that some might be saved, so our faith and hope might be in Him. Thus, we love our Father and neighbor, because he first loved us. – 1 John 4:19.

Developing Your Love for God

The apostle John tells us "no one has seen God at any time." (John 1:18) This is because "**God is spirit**." (John 4:24) Nevertheless, we are invited by James to 'draw near God.' (Jam 4:8) How is it even possible to draw near to an invisible spirit person? If we walk into a mall, there are hundreds of people walking around. Just because we can see all of those people, does that mean we love them? No. What is it that makes us love another person? It is by our getting to know him, right? As we get to know a new person, we draw close to them in friendship. Was not Abraham called God's friend? (James 2:21-23) The apostle John wrote, "This is eternal life: that they may **know** you, the only true God, and the One you have sent, Jesus Christ." The Greek (*ginosko*) behind our English "they may know," is referring not to head knowledge but rather indicates a relationship. Therefore, the more we know about the Father and the Son and our love for them will develop over time.

When we watch a movie, we get emotionally involved with characters that we do not even know. However, as any avid book reader will tell you, a great novel will draw us into the lives of the characters and the plot even more than a movie. In a book, we see these characters through our heart, to the point that we will get angry or cry when a beloved character loses their life, or is even spoken of in a disparaging way. We also find joy when our main character succeeds. We literally have four novels of the life and ministry of Jesus Christ.

Jesus tells us, "Whoever has seen me has seen the Father." (John 14:9) We could read the gospels through, where we would find the compassion that Jesus showed to a widow when he resurrected her only son. (Lu 7:11-15) As we work through the gospels, see the power, the strength, and wisdom of this one man, to find him washing the feet of his disciples. (John 13:3-5) Could we not draw close to such a great man, who also took out time to be with the children? (Mark 10:13-14) If we read the four gospels, we too can feel like those that Peter wrote to in his first letter. "Though you have not seen him, you love him. Though you do not now see him, you believe in him and rejoice with joy that is inexpressible and filled with glory." (1 Pet. 1:8) As our love for Jesus grows, so will our love for the Father. As we read the Old Testament, we will be emotionally moved as we draw close to the Father, which means drawing close to the Son as well.

Paul tells us; God "did not leave himself without witness, for he did good by giving you rains from heaven and fruitful seasons, satisfying your hearts with food and gladness." (Acts 14:17, ESV) In a letter to the Christians in Rome, Paul writes, God's "invisible attributes, namely, his eternal power and divine nature, have been clearly perceived, ever since the creation of the world, in the things that have been made." Therefore, we have yet another way that we can develop our love for God. We can appreciate all that he has provided us, as well as the beauty of his creation, and how wonderfully we were made to not just live in our earthly home but to fully enjoy the beauty of it. For example, pondering the human eye alone can help draw closer to God.

Taylor Richardson writes, "For many years, scientists have compared the eye to the modern manmade camera (see Miller, 1960, p. 315; Nourse, 1964, p. 154; Gardener, 1994, p. 105). True, the eye and camera do have many things in common, if the function of the camera demands that it was "made," does it not stand to reason that the **more complex** human camera, the eye, also must have had a Maker? Alan Gillen explained it best when he wrote: 'No human camera, artificial device, nor computer-enhanced light-sensitive device can match the contrivance of the human eye. **Only a master engineer with superior intelligence could manufacture a series of interdependent light sensitive parts and reactions**' (p. 99, emp. added). That master engineer was God. The writer of Proverbs knew this when he wrote, 'The hearing ear and the seeing eye, the Lord has made them both' (20:12)."[165]

The more we take in from his Word the Bible as well as the physical universe, the more we learn of God's endless goodness and generosity. Another gift that he has given humans is prayer. He could have just created humans, a far inferior creature than even his angelic creations, and he could have just left us to enjoy his creation. Nevertheless, he gave us a way to communicate with him, namely, prayer. He even went a step further and made prayer a part of our worship. God expects us in our private prayers to speak about whatever lies on our hearts, anything that affects our relationship with him. We can literally talk to God whenever our heart motivates us to do so. The only condition of being heard, we must be making some effort to carry out his will and purposes. The Father listens to every prayer and he knows each of us personally and intimately. King David said, "O you who hear prayer, to you shall all flesh come." – Psalm 65:2.

---

[165] Apologetics Press - Seeing is Believing: The Design of the Human Eye (accessed October 12, 2015).

http://www.apologeticspress.org/APContent.aspx?category=9&article=1412

Once we fully accept the existence of God and the truthfulness of his Word, we can also draw close to him by considering what he has in store for humankind and our planet earth.[166] What can we learn from Scripture? God created the earth to be inhabited, to be filled with perfect humans, who are over the animals, and under the sovereignty of God. (Gen 1:28; 2:8, 15; Ps 104:5; 115:16; Eccl 1:4) Sin did not dissuade God from his plans (Isa. 45:18); hence, he has saved redeemable humankind by Jesus ransom sacrifice. It seems that the Bible offers two hopes to redeemed humans, (1) a heavenly hope, or (2) an earthly hope. It also seems that those with the heavenly hope are limited in number, and are going to heaven to rule with Christ as kings, priests, and judges either on the earth or over the earth from heaven. It seems that those with the earthly hope are going to receive everlasting life here on a paradise earth as originally intended. Ponder the words of Walter A. Elwell,

> In the O[ld] T[estament] the kingdom of God is usually described in terms of a redeemed earth; this is especially clear in the book of Isaiah, where the final state of the universe is already called new heavens and a new earth (65:17; 66:22) The nature of this renewal was perceived only very dimly by OT authors, but they did express the belief that a humans ultimate destiny is an earthly one.[15] This vision is clarified in the N[ew] T[estament]. Jesus speaks of the "renewal" of the world (Matt 19:28), Peter of the restoration of all things (Acts 3:21). Paul writes that the universe will be redeemed by God from its current state of bondage (Rom. 8:18-21). This is confirmed by Peter, who describes the new heavens and the new earth as the Christian's hope (2 Pet. 3:13). Finally, the book of Revelation includes a glorious vision of the end of the present universe and the creation of a new universe, full of righteousness and the presence of God. The vision is confirmed by God in the awesome declaration: "I am making everything new!" (Rev. 21:1-8).

> The new heavens and the new earth will be the renewed creation that will fulfill the purpose for which God created the universe. It will be characterized by the complete rule of God and by the full realization of the final goal of redemption: "Now the dwelling of God is with men" (Rev. 21:3).

---

[166] http://www.christianpublishers.org/resurrection-hope-where

The fact that the universe will be created anew[16] shows that God's goals for humans is not an ethereal and disembodied existence, but a bodily existence on a perfected earth. The scene of the beatific vision is the new earth. The spiritual does not exclude the created order and will be fully realized only within a perfected creation. (Elwell, Evangelical Dictionary of Theology (Second Edition) 2001, pp. 828-29)

Therefore, once we get to know God fully through his Word and his Creation, our love for him will grow to the point that we like Jesus, would lay this life down for him, knowing that we have a resurrection hope awaiting us. As we continue to grow in this life saving knowledge, our love for God will only continue to be strengthened, especially as he directs and guides us through the landmines of Satan's world. If our love is to grow, it must be cultivated and maintained through prayer, personal Bible study, family study, preparing for our Christian meetings, telling others what we have learned, and enjoying the life that God gave us. Moses said some 3.500 years ago, "I call heaven and earth to witness against you today, that I have set before you life and death, blessing and curse. Therefore choose life, that you and your offspring may live, loving the Lord your God, obeying his voice and holding fast to him, for he is your life and length of days, that you may dwell in the land that the Lord swore to your fathers, to Abraham, to Isaac, and to Jacob, to give them." – Deuteronomy 30:19-20, ESV.

Review Questions

- Why is your love for God so important?
- How can you show love for God?
- Why do You Love God?
- How might you develop your love of God?

CHAPTER 13 You Must Love Others

Mark 12:31 Updated American Standard Version (UASV)

[31] The second is this: 'You shall love your neighbor as yourself.' There is no other commandment greater than these."

The twenty first century has become the "Self-First" generation. Nick Gillespie writes, "Seventy-one percent of American adults think of 18-to-29-year-olds – millennials, basically – as "selfish," and 65% of us think of them as "entitled." That's according to the latest <u>Reason-Rupe Poll</u>, a quarterly survey of 1,000 representative adult Americans. If millennials are self-absorbed little monsters who expect the world to come to them and for their parents to clean up their rooms well into their 20s, we've got no one to blame but ourselves — especially the moms and dads among us."[167]

The apostle Paul told the Ephesian elders, "In all things I have shown you that by working hard in this way we must help the weak and remember the words of the Lord Jesus, how he himself said, 'It is more blessed to give than to receive.'" (Acts 20:35, ESV) Kenneth O. Gangel writes about this verse, "Like Paul, the Ephesian elders should not covet material things nor expect such from the congregation. One can only assume that these were hardly full-time vocational pastors but lay leaders who served others through hard work. Paul's concern for the weak and the needy is well documented in his epistles (Rom. 15:1; 1 Thess. 5:14; Eph. 4:28; Gal. 6:2). He particularly turns to this theme in dealing with the elders (1 Tim. 3:3, 8; Titus 1:7, 11), perhaps because false teachers in Asia so frequently acted in greed and love of material things. Would God that modern church leaders, many of whom live in opulence far exceeding that of their parishioners and constituents, would pay heed to this simple teaching from Miletus. The greed against which Paul warned the Ephesian elders seems to be an assumed trait of many popular figures in the modern church." (K. O. Gangel 1998, p. 345)

The trend is toward selfishness today. Some young parents today will put drugs before their children. This author is aware of a young woman who did several thousands of dollars of heroin throughout her entire pregnancy. Her father pled with her about the dangers to the baby, and

---

[167] Millennials Are Selfish and Entitled, and Helicopter Parents .., http://time.com/3154186/millennials-selfish-entitled-helicopter-parenting/ (accessed October 12, 2015).

her response was frightening to say the least. This young woman's argument that the baby would be fine was that her young brother was healthy, as her mother had done crack throughout her entire pregnancy, and her brother came out fine. Well, the young woman lost her child to social services and had yet to get treatment for her addiction. In fact, she is pregnant again and still doing heroin. Sadly, this type of behavior by our young people is more prevalent than one might think.

However, there are some young people, who are exemplary in unselfishness. There are some young parents who are so devoted to their families that they sacrifice everything for their children. In fact, they have family and friends that urge them to get things for themselves, or to have a date night, for they feel like their children must always come first. There are young women who have been left with several young children because the father died in a war, and they managed the households, worked more than one job, never getting anything for themselves, like new clothes, recreation, or going out on a date. These women were consumed with the need to provide their children a future. At the end of the day, lying in their beds exhausted, what reward did they have? They could feel the love and gratitude of their children, knowing that they had a future because of their mother. These parents saw the results when the report cards came home, or the children won some sports championship, or they received a scholarship to a good university. The mothers had the joy of giving rather than receiving.

We feel far more joy when we watch a loved one open our present, seeing the smile and joy on their face; than we do in receiving a present ourselves. Why? This is because our Creator made us in his image and likeness, and there is no one more selfless than he is. Our heaven Father gave us an inner moral code, which enables us to determine what is right and what is wrong. However, he went a step further by also endowing us with the ability to feel good about justice. We feel happy, content when we do what is right, and it works out for the better in one's life.

Hence, the famed English jurist Blackstone stated that God has "so intimately connected, so inseparably interwoven the laws of eternal justice with the happiness of each individual, that the latter [happiness] cannot be attained but by observing the former [justice]; and, if the former be punctually obeyed, it cannot but induce the latter."[168] This is certainly true that we cannot have happiness without first having justice.

---

[168] The Pursuit of - Not the Right to - Happiness -- KEVIN CRAIG .., http://kevincraig.us/pursuit.htm (accessed October 15, 2015).

Moreover, the same is true of selflessness. We cannot have true and pure joy and happiness without first living an unselfish life.

Godly Qualities versus Inherited Sin

It should be noted that the godly qualities that we have been by our Creator are in every one of us, even in our imperfection. However, we do have another inner desire that wars against our desires to follow the qualities that God has instilled in us. Because of our imperfection, we are mentally bent toward evil. (Gen. 6:5; 8:21; Ps. 51:5, AT) Moreover, our heart (inner person, seat of motivation) 'is deceitful above all things, and desperately sick; which we cannot understand.' (Jer. 17:9) Therefore, if we are going to maintain and develop the quality of putting other people's needs, interests, or wishes before our own, we must cultivate our selfless side. This is especially true within the family because if one person is a selfish person, it will be a life of pain and suffering for everyone else. The reality is, it was the selfishness of Satan, Adam and Eve that has humankind living in imperfection, pain, suffering, old age and death. Sadly, every argument between family and friends, every conflict between leaders, every war between nations, every dispute between employer and employee, and every crime is the result of selfishness. Our concern with our own interests, needs, and wishes while ignoring those of others will ruin our life and any relationship we might ever hope to have.

What motivates us to be selfless? It is another human quality, empathy, the ability to identify with and understand somebody else's feelings or difficulties. When we do something for another, like pay for a military person's meal at a restaurant, we are empathizing with what he gave up so we have the freedom we have. This brings us to another quality, gratitude, i.e., being thankful for what others have done. Imagine, the traffic is moving slowly and we are laying on our horn because we are in a hurry. Soon, we see several ambulances ahead. As we drive by a car wreck, we see a teenage girl being zipped up in a black body bag. Suddenly, our heart is beating heavily, we feel the pain of that child, the pain of the mother, and our being late for a meeting is the furthest thing from our mind. If we have never pondered whether we carry out selfless acts, we might start with something small. We might focus on getting the door for people, offering better tips for service, helping someone in a small way, considering how others might feel, and seeing how we react to inconveniences. When we see how others react to our small acts of kindness, will help us to develop our selfless side further.

The apostle Paul wrote, "Let no one seek his own good, but the good of his neighbor." (1 Cor. 10:24, ESV) On this verse, Bible scholar David E. Garland writes, "Paul's command that one "not seek that which is one's own" leaves indefinite what they are not to seek.² We can fill in the blank with words such as "advantage," "interest," "good," "ends," "enjoyment," "needs." Instead of selfish things, they are to seek the interests of the other ... This "other" is not restricted to the fellow believer who might have a weak conscience, as in 8:11, but also includes the unbeliever who might offer an invitation to dinner (10:27). His concern in this section is not the effect of their behavior on other believers but its effect on nonbelievers. The overarching hermeneutical principles that govern his practical advice are these: What course of action will bring glory to God, and what course of action will be "the most effective witness to Christ?" (Ruef 1977: 103). Paul expects the Corinthians to do all things to bring glory to God (10:31) and to seek the best interests of others so that they might be saved (10:33)." (Garland 2003, p. 489)

Jesus' half-brother James wrote, "Religion that is pure and undefiled before God, the Father, is this: to visit orphans and widows in their affliction, and to keep oneself unstained from the world." (Jam. 1:27, ESV) On this, the *CPH New Testament Commentary* says, "James specifically mentions that these people were to be visited in their times of distress. The word in Greek used here for distress is *thlipsis* and it means 'pressure or a pressing together.' (Vine, 1996, pg. 17) James is not saying they were to be helped when they had no more troubles but rather it was *in the midst of* their troubles. They were to be helped as they were going through the pressures of life that were coming against them. This could include clothing, feeding, and giving them shelter, and show the love of Christ to them. James echoes what John wrote in I John 3:16-18, 'We know love by this, that He laid down His life for us; and we ought to lay down our lives for the brethren. But whoever has the world's goods, and sees his brother in need and closes his heart against him, how does the love of God abide in him? Little children, let us not love with word or with tongue, but in deed and truth.' Several Scriptures point to the fact that God has a great concern for the orphans and widows.¹⁶⁹" (Calloway 2015, p. 44)

There is little doubt that world of humankind alienated from God has entered its most selfish era in its history. While every human would

---

[169] See Deuteronomy 10:18; 14:28–29; 16:11; 24:17; 26:12; Jeremiah 22:3; Zechariah 7:8–10; Malachi 3:5; cf. Acts 6:1; 1 Timothy 5:16

say they want joy and happiness in their life, yet most are seeking to receive as opposed to giving. The reality is that we can never have true happiness and joy without developing the mentality of being selfless from the heart. This means that we are selfless; we do good to others naturally, as each and every opportunity presents itself. We do these things to family, friends, coworkers, neighbors, strangers, and even our enemies. Our greatest joy comes from sharing the good news with others, helping someone to cross over from death to life. Jesus said, "Truly, truly, I say to you, whoever hears my word and believes him who sent me has eternal life. He does not come into judgment, but has passed from death to life." (John 5:24, ESV; See 1 John 3:14) In our sharing of God's Word, we need to apply Jesus words, "Freely you have received; freely give." – Matthew 10:8, LEB.

We would be remiss if we did not offer a word of caution at the end. Our desire to be selfless does not mean that we must also be foolish or naive. Many of those who are selfish will take advantage of those who are selfless. Therefore, let us be weary of helping such ones. Moreover, women need to be cautious in helping men. For example, they should never give a male hitchhiker a ride. The world is full of evil and our having to end such a positive chapter on a negative note is a reminder of that.

Review Questions

- What is the state of our young people today?

- What can we say of some of young ones ans selflessness?

- What has God instilled in us and why must it be cultivated?

- What motivates us to be selfless?

CHAPTER 14 You Must Love the Truth

2 Thessalonians 2:3-12 Updated American Standard Version (UASV)

3 Let no one deceive[170] you in any way, for it will not come unless the apostasy[171] comes first, and the man of lawlessness is revealed, the son of destruction, **4** who opposes and exalts himself against every so-called god or object of worship, so that he takes his seat in the temple of God, showing himself as being God. **5** Do you not remember that while I was still with you, I was telling you these things? **6** And now you know the thing restraining him, so that in his time he will be revealed. **7** For the mystery of lawlessness is already at work; but only until the one who is right now acting as a restraint is out of the way. **8** Then the lawless one will be revealed, whom the Lord Jesus will do away with by the spirit of his mouth, and wipe out by the appearance of his presence, **9** but the one whose coming is in accordance with the activity of Satan, with all power and signs and false wonders, **10** and with every unrighteous deception[172] for those who are perishing, because **they did not receive <u>the love of the truth</u>** so as to be saved. **11** For this reason God is sending upon them a working of error[173] so that they will believe the lie, **12** in order that they all may be judged because **they did not <u>believe the truth</u>** but took pleasure in unrighteousness.

Those in the Thessalonica Christian congregation had thought the day of the Lord was already upon them. However, Paul begins chapter 2 by offering them a word of comfort and caution. He says, "Now we request you, brothers, with regard to the presence of our Lord Jesus Christ and our gathering together to him, that you not be quickly shaken from your composure or be disturbed either by a spirit or a word or a letter as if from us, to the effect that the day of the Lord has come." – 2 Thessalonians 2:1-2.

[2:3, 8] *Who is "the man of lawlessness," and what does it mean that the Lord Jesus will do away with him by the spirit of his mouth?*

---

[170] Or *seduce*

[171] Namely, to stand off from the truth, i.e., to not only fall away from the faith, but to then turn on the faith, rebellion.

[172] Lit *seduction*

[173] Or *a deluding influence*

Many Bible scholars would agree with Knute Larson, who says, "The **man of lawlessness** will be a person so given to sin that he will become the embodiment of it. Here is a man so overcome with evil that no flicker of light can be detected. It is hard to imagine how horrible that will be, especially in light of some of the diabolical figures throughout history which this man will overshadow." (Larson 2000, p. 106) Yes, most believe that the **man of lawlessness** is one person or man, as they believe that the antichrist will be just one person. However, they are mistaken on both counts. The apostle John clearly states there are many antichrists, which is simply anyone, any group, or organization that is against Christ. Similarly, the **man of lawlessness** is a composite man, made up of many individuals from the days of the apostles up unto **the day of the Lord**. Paul said the man of lawlessness was already at work in his day. However, he also says that this lawless one will be destroyed be Jesus in the day of the Lord. (2 Thess. 2:2, 7-8) How could one human live over 2,000 years? The lawless one will be false teachers, false prophets, and atheists, i.e., anyone trying to stand in the way of **the truth**. These ones **stand off from the truth** (i.e., apostasy), to the point that it is a defection, a revolt, a planned, deliberate rebellion. Jesus does away with the composite man [many individual rebels] of lawlessness by **the spirit of his mouth**, which is a figure of speech that evidently represents his commanding call to destroy the wicked in the day of the Lord.

Apostasy Foretold

The apostasy was foretold by Jesus Christ, Paul, and Peter.

Jesus Christ himself warned of this apostasy, in his parable of the wheat and the weeds (Matt. 13:24-30, 34-43), with the wheat picturing those who are truly Christian and an enemy [i.e., Satan] sowed the weeds picturing false Christians. Speaking of the wheat [true Christians] and weeds [false Christians], Jesus said that they are both to grow together until the end of the age, namely, in the day of the Lord. However, when the two are separated, the weeds are burned, that is destroyed. (2 Thess. 1:9) Then, in the book of Acts, we have the apostle Paul warning the Ephesian elders,

Acts 20:28-30 Updated American Standard Version (ASV)

28 Pay careful attention to yourselves and to all the flock, in which the Holy Spirit has made you overseers, to care for the congregation of

God, which he obtained with the blood of his own Son.[174] **29** I know that after my departure fierce wolves will come in among you, not sparing the flock; **30** and from among your own selves men will arise, speaking twisted things, to draw away the disciples after them.

The apostle Paul's words show that the true Christian congregation would be attacked on two fronts. First, false Christians ("weeds") would "come in among" true Christians. Second, "from among your own selves," i.e., true Christians; some would become apostates [stand off from the truth, attack the truth], "speaking twisted things." These apostates will "draw away the disciples [that is, Jesus' disciples] after them," not looking to make their own disciples. The apostle Paul also wrote,

1 Timothy 4:1-3 Updated American Standard Version (UASV) **[c. 61-64 C.E.]**	**2 Timothy** 4:2-4 Updated American Standard Version (UASV) **[c. 65 C.E.]**
1 But the Spirit explicitly says that **in later times** some will **fall away from the faith**, paying attention to deceitful spirits and doctrines of demons, **2** by means of the hypocrisy of men who speak lies, whose conscience is seared as with a branding iron, **3** men who forbid marriage and command to abstain from foods that God created to be partaken of with thanksgiving by those who have faith and accurately know the truth.	**2** preach the word; be ready in season and out of season; reprove, rebuke, exhort, with complete patience and teaching. **3** For there will be **a time when** they will **not put up with sound teaching**, but in accordance with their own desires, they will **accumulate teachers for themselves** to have their ears tickled,[175] **4** and will **turn away** their ears **from the truth** and will turn aside to myths.

The apostle Peter also spoke of these things about **64 C.E.**, "there will be false teachers among you, who will secretly bring in destructive heresies ... in their greed they will exploit you with false words." (2 Pet.

---

[174] Lit *with the blood of his Own.*

[175] Or *to tell them what they want to hear*

2:1, 3) These abandoned the faithful words, became false teachers, rising within the Christian congregation, sharing their corrupting influence, intending to hide, disguise, or mislead.

These dire warnings by Jesus and the New Testament Authors had their beginnings in the first century C.E. Yes, they began small, but burst forth on the scene in the second century.

"[Paul says it] Is Already at Work"

About **51 C.E.**, some 18-years after Jesus' death, resurrection and ascension, division was already starting to creep into the faith, "the mystery of lawlessness is already at work." (2 Thess. 2:7) Yes, the power of **the man of lawlessness** was already present, which is the power of Satan, the god of this world (2 Cor. 4:3-4), and his tens of millions of demons, are hard at work behind the scenes.

There was even some divisions beginning as early as **49 C.E.**, when the elders wrote a letter to the Gentile believers, saying,

> Since we have heard that some persons have gone out from us and troubled you with words, unsettling your minds, although we gave them no instructions (Ac 15:24)

Here we see that some *within*, were being very vocal about their opposition to the direction the faith was heading. Here, it was over whether the Gentiles needed to be circumcised, suggesting that they needed to be obedient to the Mosaic Law. – Acts 15:1, 5.

As the years progressed throughout the first-century, this divisive "talk [would] spread like gangrene." (2 Tim. 2:17, **c. 65 C.E.**) About **51 C.E.**, As we already saw above, some in Thessalonica, at worst, going ahead of, or at best, misunderstanding Paul, and wrongly stating by word and a bogus letter "that the day of the Lord has come." (2 Thess. 2:1-2) In Corinth, about **55 C.E.**, "some of [were saying] that there is no resurrection of the dead. (1 Cor. 15:12) About **65 C.E.**, some were "saying that the resurrection has already happened. They [were] upsetting the faith of some." – 2 Timothy 2:16-18.

Throughout the next three decades, no inspired books were written. However, around **96-98 C.E.**, the apostle John pens three letters, wherein he tells us, "**Now** many antichrists have come. Therefore we know that it is the last hour." (1 John 2:18) These are ones, "who denies that Jesus is the Christ" and ones who do not confess "Jesus Christ has come in the flesh is from God." – 1 John 2:22; 4:2-3.

We must keep in mind that the meaning of any given text is what the author meant by the words that he used, as should have been understood by his audience, and had some relevance/meaning for his audience. The rebellion [apostasy] began slowly in the first century, and would break forth after the death of the last apostle, i.e., John. Historian, Ariel and Will Durant inform us that by 187 C.E., there were 20 varieties of Christianity, and by 384 C.E., there were 80 varieties of Christianity. Christianity would become one again, a universal religion, i.e., Catholicism. However, that oneness was a false or imitation, as it was by threat of torture and death.

Rebellion Against God

The man of lawlessness places himself in opposition against God, being used as a tool by the great resister- adversary, Satan himself. Paul warns us that this lawless one was/is "coming is in accordance with the activity of Satan." (2 Thess. 2:9) Paul also told the Thessalonians "the mystery of lawlessness is already at work." The identity of the man of lawlessness has be shrouded in mystery, with many scholars supposing it is one evil man, which will appear just before the day of the Lord. However, as was stated above and stated by Paul, the lawless one was already at work in Paul's day. Again, the lawless one is a composite man [many individual rebels], meaning anyone in opposition against God, some worse than others. Some of these lawless ones set themselves up over God by their lying and false teachings, which they place above God's Word, as well as placing themselves in opposition to those who are truly Christian. (See 2Pet. 2:10-13) This lawless one is an imitation, false Christian, who claiming that he is truly Christ, "so that he takes his seat in the temple of God, showing himself as being God." – 2 Thessalonians 2:4.

Restraining the Man of Lawlessness

What or who is acting as a **restraint** to the man of lawlessness and the apostasy? It would seem that the apostles of the first century were preventing this great apostasy **from taking hold** while they were alive. In the above, we saw Paul warning that wolf like men would be infiltrating the congregation after Paul was gone. (Ac 20:29) Paul spoke of the apostasy in many of his writings. In order to keep the congregations clean, Paul taught all over the then known world, taught people like

Timothy and Titus, whom he left behind after he was martyred, to teach other qualified men in Paul's place. Paul called "the household of God, which is the church of the living God, a pillar and buttress of the truth." (1 Tim. 3:15) Paul and the rest of the apostles grew the Christian congregation all over the then known world, going from 120 disciples at Pentecost 33 C.E. to over a million in the beginning of the second century C.E. They wanted to build the purest church possible, **to withstand** centuries of the apostasy that began in full earnest in the second century C.E.

However, the **restraint** of the apostasy and the man of lawlessness (rebels against the truth), were not the apostles alone back in the first century C.E. The restraint of the apostasy and the lawless ones has been those who are truly Christian spread through these last 2,000 years, right up unto the day of the Lord. We have had both men and women who have stood out and stood up for the truth from the time of the martyrdom of Polycarp (69 – 155 C.E.), who had been a student of the apostle John. Keep in mind that throughout the Dark Ages 500 – 1500 C.E., that they may not have taught everything that was biblically true but they were living in a world of spiritual darkness. Catholicism was the dominant influence on Western civilization from late antiquity to the dawn of the modern age (Medieval and Renaissance Periods, 4th – 17th century C.E.). The Catholic Church would like us to forget the good "seeds" of discontent that were present within their midst many years before the Waldenses of the 12th century C.E., 200 years before John Wycliffe (1330-84) and Jan Hus (1369-1415) and 350 years before Martin Luther (1483-1546) and John Calvin (1509-64). (Matt. 13:24) These seeds of men were seeking the truth even in the darkest of periods, even if it meant their life.

Pre-Reformation Seeds of Truth Seekers

- **Bishop Agobard** of Lyons, France (779-840), was against image worship, churches dedicated to saints and church liturgy that was contrary to Scripture.

- **Bishop Claudius** (d. between 827 and 839 C.E.)

- **Archdeacon Bérenger**, or Berengarius, of Tours, France (11th century C.E.), excommunicated as a heretic in 1050

- **Peter of Bruys** (1117-c. 1131), left the church because he disagreed with infant baptism, transubstantiation, prayers for the dead, worship of the cross and the need for church buildings.

- **Henry of Lausanne** (died imprisoned around 1148), spoke out against church liturgy, the corrupt clergy and the religious hierarchy.

- **Peter Waldo** (c. 1140–c. 1218) and the Waldenses, rejected purgatory, Masses for the dead, papal pardons and indulgences, and the worship of Mary and the saints.

- **John Wycliffe** (c. 1330-1384) preached against corruption in the monastic orders, papal taxation, the doctrine of transubstantiation (doctrine that the bread and wine of Communion become, in substance, but not appearance, the body and blood of Jesus Christ at consecration), the confession, and church involvement in temporal affairs.

- **Jan Hus** (c. 1369-1415) preached against the corruption of the Roman Church and stressed the importance of reading the Bible. This swiftly fetched the anger of the hierarchy upon him. In 1403, the church leaders ordered him to stop preaching the antipapal notions of Wycliffe, whose books they had openly burned. Hus, nevertheless, went on to pen some of the most hurtful impeachments against the Church and their practices, such as the sale of indulgences. He was condemned and excommunicated in 1410.

Reformation Seeds of Truth Seekers

- **Girolamo Savonarola** (1452-98) was of the San Marcos monastery in Florence, Italy, spoke out against the corruption in the Church.

- **Martin Luther** (1483-1546) was a monk-scholar, who was also a doctor of theology and a professor of Biblical studies at the University of Wittenberg. Luther disagreed with or argued against papal indulgences, power, purgatory, plenary remission of all penalties of the pope, among many others.

- **Ulrich Zwingli** (1484-1531) was a Catholic priest, who agreed with Luther in many doctrinal areas, in addition to the removal of all vestiges of the Roman Church: images, crucifixes, clerical garb, and even liturgical music. However, he disagreed with Luther's literal interpretation of the Eucharist, or Mass (Communion), as he said it "must be taken figuratively or metaphorically; 'This is my body,' means, 'The bread signifies my body,' or 'is a figure of my body.'" This one issues caused them to part ways.

- **Anabaptists** (i.e., rejected infant baptism, so rebaptized adults, *ana* meaning "again" in Greek), **Mennonites** (Dutch Reformer Menno Simons), and **Hutterites** (Tyrolean Jacob Hutter), felt that the Reformers did not go far enough in rejecting the failings of the Catholic Church.

- **John Calvin** (1509-64) published *Institutes of the Christian Religion*, in which he summarized the ideas of the early church fathers and medieval theologians, as well as those of Luther and Zwingli. His theological views would take too much space. John Calvin had Michael Servetus burned to death as a heretic. Calvin defended his actions in these words: "When the papists are so harsh and violent in defense of their superstitions that they rage cruelly to shed innocent blood, are not Christian magistrates shamed to show themselves less ardent in defense of the sure truth?" Calvin's religious extremism and personal hatred made him unwilling to see and understand the radicalness of his judgments and choked out any Christian principles.

- **William Tyndale** (1494-1536) had to flee from England, published his New Testament in 1526, and completed most of the Old Testament after his betrayal and arrest, in a dungeon. He would be strangled at the stake, and his body was burned. The 1611 King James Version was actually 97 percent Tyndale's translation. He denounced the practice of prayer to saints. He taught justification by faith, the return of Christ, and mortality of the soul.

- **Jacobus Arminius** (1560-1609), graduated from Holland's Leiden University, after which he spent six years in Switzerland, studying theology under Théodore de Bèze, the successor to Protestant Reformer John Calvin. Rather than support Calvinism, he went against it, especially the doctrine of predestination, which was at the core of Calvinism.

The Darnel[176] Seed of Catholicism

Roman Catholicism has tainted itself with its history of immorality and bloodshed, as well as its pagan-tainted religious ideas and practices. The centuries-long oppression, torture, rape, pillage, and murder of tens of millions of men, women and children cannot come from true Christianity. They were the biggest offenders of the apostasy that Paul said had to come before **the day of the Lord**.

The Good Seed Protestantism

The Reformation gave us a return to the Bible in the common person's languages, which the Catholic Church had locked up in the dead language of Latin for 500-years. The Reformers brought the common folk freedom from papal authority but also from many erroneous Bible doctrines and dogmas that had gone on for a thousand years. However, the Protestant denominations have found themselves so fragmented and divided; one can only wonder where the truth and the Way are to be found. All 41,000 plus denominations that call themselves Christian cannot be just different roads leading to the same place.

Over eighty percent of Protestant Christianity is liberal-progressive as to their biblical and social beliefs, which began in the late 18th century up until the present. This covers too much area for a summary, but to mention just a few, they treat the Bible as being from man, not inspired and fully inerrant. They prefer to explain away the Bible accounts of miracles as myths, legends, or folk tales. They do not believe in the historicity of Bible characters such as Adam, Eve, and Job. They say that Moses did not write the first five books of the Bible but that they were written by several authors from the tenth to the fifth centuries B.C.E. and were compiled after that. They say Isaiah did not author the book

---

[176] "Darnel, the weed [in Jesus' parable of the Wheat and the Weeds] (species name Lolium temulentum,) is an annual plant that grows in the same areas as wheat. Darnel is nearly indistinguishable from wheat until the ear appears. Wheat ears are heavy and make the entire plant droop downward but darnel's light ears stand up straight. Ripe wheat is light brown but darnel is black. Jesus' parable of the weeds among the wheat in Matt. 13:24-40 builds on the early stage resemblance between darnel and wheat. Hos 10:4, Matt 13:24-40" – (Logos Bible Images by Richard Myers) It should be added that in the roots of these weeds entangle themselves with the wheat, which would make it inadvisable to pull the weed early.

bearing his name in the early eighth century B.C.E., but that two or three authors penned it, centuries later. They claim that Daniel did not write his book in the sixth century B.C.E., but rather it was written in the second-century B.C.E. They claim that the Bible is full of errors, mistakes, and contradictions, as to its history, science and geography. They claim that the Antichrist is merely good versus evil and is not to be taken literally. Higher criticism has opened Pandora's Box to an overflow of pseudo-scholarly works whose result has been to weaken, challenge and destabilize people's assurance in the trustworthiness of the Bible. Who needs enemies like agnostics and atheists, when we have liberal Bible scholars? We have not even delved into their unbiblical views of social justice, gay marriage, homosexual priests, abortion, women in the pulpits and far more.

Some may ask what about the remaining twenty percent of Christian denominations. Most of those are moderate in beliefs, which cast doubt on the trustworthiness of the Scriptures, and give fodder to the liberal-progressive denominations. These are fence-riders, who have abandoned **the Truth** and the Way of true, pure worship within Christianity. Before delving into the so-called conservative parts of Christianity, let us look at the charismatics.

We have charismatic Christianity, the fastest growing segment, which emphasizes the work of the Holy Spirit, spiritual gifts, and modern-day miracles, speaking in tongues[177] and miraculous healing, even fringe groups that perform snake handling in some areas. All of this is **un**biblical and based on emotionalism.

Those who believe that charismatic Christianity is false Christianity, persons such as this author, are said to be overly critical. Supporters of Charismatic Christianity say we "should be focusing on the fact that while many in the church continue to abandon our Christian faith, the Pentecostal/Charismatic community continues to offer the church a legitimate growth mechanism."[178] I would respond that a denomination founded on, grounded in **un**biblical beliefs is not true Christianity and are the false teachers and prophets that we were warned were coming by Jesus and the New Testament writers. Therefore, charismatic Christianity is no Christianity at all, and all who are being brought in those groups, are being obscured from finding the path of true Christianity. Further, Catholicism brought in almost the whole world from 400 to 1600 C.E.,

---

[177] http://www.christianpublishers.org/speaking-in-tongues-truth

[178] http://tiny.cc/j5d7mx

based on the same false, illogical reasoning from above, this oneness would supposedly be a sign of their being genuine Christianity. However, conservative Protestant denominations would fail to give them a pass.

So-called conservative Christianity is so minuscule that it barely gets press. We should not confuse radical Christianity, such as the Westboro Baptist Church,[179] with truly conservative, fundamentalist Christianity. However, even here within conservative Christianity, we find differences doctrinally, and yes, even in the so-called salvation doctrines.

Are all of the 41,000 different varieties of Christianity just different roads leading to the same place? Are all of the various conservative churches the Truth and the Way? There is no way of knowing for certain, but we know that Christ will bring back the oneness that the first century church experienced before the day of the Lord. We need to return to the question that Jesus asked, "When the Son of Man comes, will he find faith on earth?" (Lu 18:8) Jesus would not find faith on earth at present, not at the level that one might expect, not at present. However, what he would find is many good seeds, those who are truly Christian, who are acting as a restraint against imitation, false Christianity, agnosticism, atheism and every other man of lawlessness.

Believe the Truth

2 Thessalonians 2:9-12 Updated American Standard Version (UASV)

⁹ but the one whose coming is in accordance with the activity of Satan, with all power and signs and false wonders, ¹⁰ and with every unrighteous deception[180] for those who are perishing, because **they did not receive <u>the love of the truth</u>** so as to be saved. ¹¹ For this reason God is sending upon them a working of error[181] so that they will believe the lie, ¹² in order that they all may be judged because **they did not believe the truth** but took pleasure in unrighteousness.

Here Paul is using **truth** (*aletheia*) as something *factual*, a *truth statement* that deals what a fact or reality is. Our eternal future is dependent upon whether we **love the truth**, i.e., what is true. If we do not accept and love the truth, there is no salvation for us. How can we

---

[179] www.godhatesfags.com/

[180] Lit *seduction*

[181] Or *a deluding influence*

really know whether we love the truth, or that Satan is using unrighteous deception (deluding influence) on us? (2:9) The first question is, "Can we say that we are truly seeking the truth?" Proverbs 23:23 says, "Buy truth, and do not sell it." Dave Bland writes, "To **buy the truth** (v. 23) does not mean to pay money for it. Rather it means for one to invest mental, emotional, and spiritual resources in pursuing it." (Bland 2002, p. 213) 'Buying truth' is not as straightforward as one might think. In many cases, it means that we are paying a price; it is coming at a cost to us personally.

What if we discover that a Bible doctrine that is accepted by many denominations is not **the truth**? Suppose that we have spent months, even years, privately poring over this doctrine and find that it is just not biblically true. Do we simply hide that truth and not bring it up, and if it is commented on at a meeting, do we just not participate that day? What if we are reading a verse in the KJV and we decide to compare the ESV, RSV, UASV and the NASB, to find that all of these recent translations read differently than the King James Version? Do we just drop it and ignore that fact because their reading does not support our doctrinal position, a favorite verse in our beloved KJV that we have often used? What if we do investigate and, we find two articles, one that supports the reading in the KJV and one that supports the reading in the newer translations, and we find that the article for the KJV reading seems to be rationalizing and justifying as it really misrepresents the evidence?

Remember, the apostle Paul was known by his Jewish name Saul before he ever met Jesus on the road to Damascus. Young Saul had studied under the renowned Pharisee Gamaliel, one of the greatest Jewish teachers, who may have been there in the area when Jesus was amazing the Jewish religious leaders, at the age of twelve. Gamaliel was the grandson of Hillel, the Elder (110 B.C.E.[182] – 10 C.E.), the founder of one of the two schools within Judaism. Paul describes himself as "circumcised on the eighth day, of the people of Israel, of the tribe of Benjamin, a Hebrew of Hebrews; as to the law, a Pharisee; as to zeal, a persecutor of the church; as to righteousness under the law, blameless." (Phil 3:5-6, ESV) Why was Paul so slow to accept the truth of Christianity, even to the point of his persecuting Christians, and being there when Stephen was stoned to death?

---

[182] B.C.E. years ran down toward zero, although the Romans had no zero, and C.E. years ran up from zero. (100, 10, 3, 2, 1 ◄B.C.E. | C.E.► 1, 2, 3, 10, and 100)

Paul saw Christianity as an apostate, false religion, a break off from Judaism, as it was made up of only Jews before he was converted. Paul had been part of the only true way to God, the Israelite nation, which had existed and received miraculous protection from God for 1,500 years, not to mention the 39 books of the Old Testament. He knew that Deuteronomy said that anyone hung on a tree would be accursed by God. Well, Jesus was executed by being hung on (i.e., nailed to) a wood cross. Paul knew that Daniel and other books said that Jesus would set up a kingdom that would crush all other kingdoms, and never be brought to ruin. Jesus did no such thing and was executed for treason and as a blasphemer of God. Thus, we can see why Saul/Paul was slow to be receptive to **the truth**.

Nevertheless, Paul did convert. Did Paul buy the truth? Did it cost Paul anything? Yes, Paul had studied under the renowned Gamaliel, meaning he would have been a prominent leader and teacher within Judaism, leading to much wealth. However, in Paul's own words, what did he suffer for the truth? Paul told the Corinthians that he was "in far more labors, in far more imprisonments, beaten times without number, often in danger of death. Five times, I received from the Jews thirty-nine lashes. Three times, I was beaten with rods, once I was stoned; three times I was shipwrecked, a night and a day I have spent in the deep. I have been on frequent journeys, in dangers from rivers, dangers from robbers, dangers from my countrymen, dangers from the Gentiles, dangers in the city, dangers in the wilderness, dangers on the sea, dangers among false brethren; I have been in labor and hardship, through many sleepless nights, in hunger and thirst, often without food, in cold and exposure.[183]" (2 Cor. 11:23-27, NASB; See also 6:4-10; 7:5; 12:7) Sadly, this was in 55 C.E., so Paul had ten more years of even more pain and suffering, before he would be martyred for the truth. So, yes, Paul paid a heavy price for the truth, it cost him much. Yet, concerning such a lifetime as a wealthy, prominent Pharisee, Paul wrote, "But whatever gain I had, I counted as loss for the sake of Christ. Indeed, I count everything as loss because of the surpassing worth of knowing Christ Jesus my Lord. For his sake I have suffered the loss of all things and count them as rubbish, in order that I may gain Christ." – Philippians 3:7-8.

Looking at Saul/Paul, we can establish whether we really have **love for the truth**. Do we have such love for a doctrinal truth that that we will accept it when it is contrary to what we thought was a doctrinal

---

[183] i.e., *in cold and nakedness*

truth? Do we have such real **love for the truth** when a long-held cherished belief is exposed as false?

Imagine the courage that Paul, Barnabas, Timothy, and hundreds of others must have had in the first century Christian congregation. Imagine what is needed today with a liberal-progressive world, Islam being favored over Christianity, many thousands of false Christian denominations that claim to be the truth and the way, with liberal and moderate Bible scholars aiding atheism, not to mention some conservative scholars standing on the line, refusing to take a stand. Again, Paul warned, "the time is coming when people will not endure sound teaching, but having itching ears they will accumulate for themselves teachers to suit their own passions, and will turn away from listening to the truth and wander off into myths."[184] (2 Tim. 4:3-4, ESV) He also warned, "even if our gospel is veiled, it is veiled to those who are perishing. In their case, the god of this world has blinded the minds of the unbelievers, to keep them from seeing the light of the gospel of the glory of Christ, who is the image of God." In the same letter, "And no wonder, for even Satan disguises himself as an angel of light. So it is no surprise if his servants, also, disguise themselves as servants of righteousness. Their end will correspond to their deeds." (2 Cor. 4:3-4; 11:14-15) Many false and imitation Christians prefer to take the path of least resistance, as they possess the spirit of "go along to get along," which means to conform in order to have acceptance and security, i.e., **not** standing up for the love of the truth just to avoid confrontation. Yes, they turn away from the truth of God's Word. Thus, since most are turning away from the truth, do we have the courage of Christ, of Paul, and other faithful ones, to buy the truth, to seek the trust, no matter the cost to us?

---

[184] "**4:3 not endure**. This refers to holding up under adversity, and can be translated "tolerate." Paul here warns Timothy that, in the dangerous seasons of this age, many people would become intolerant of the confrontive, demanding preaching of God's Word (1:13, 14; 1 Tim. 1:9, 10; 6:3–5). ... **their own desires** . . . **itching ears**. Professing Christians and nominal believers in the church follow their own desires and flock to preachers who offer them God's blessings apart from His forgiveness, and His salvation apart from their repentance. They have an itch to be entertained by teachings that will produce pleasant sensations and leave them with good feelings about themselves. Their goal is that men preach "according to their own desires." Under those conditions, people will dictate what men preach, rather than God dictating it by His Word. **4:4 fables**. This refers to false idealogies, viewpoints, and philosophies in various forms that oppose sound doctrine." – MacArthur, John (2005-05-09). *The MacArthur Bible Commentary* (Kindle Locations 60854-60860). Thomas Nelson. Kindle Edition.

In addition, we can tell if we have a **love for the truth** by our heart attitude. The truth should appeal to both our heart and our head. The disciples of Jesus said to each other, "Did not our hearts burn within us while he talked to us on the road while he opened to us the Scriptures?" (Lu 24:32, ESV) It is only when we have true love for the truth; we will follow it no matter where it leads, and regardless of who is on the other side of the truth. If our hearts, like the disciples of Jesus Christ, burn within us, we will be motivated to action, because our salvation is dependent upon whether we really **love the truth**.

Walk in the Truth and Be Taught

Psalm 25:5 Updated American Standard Version (UASV)

⁵ Lead me in **your truth** and teach me,
for you are the God of my salvation;
for you I wait all the day long.

Mounce's *Complete Expository Dictionary of Old & New Testament Words* defines the Hebrew term (ᵉmet) "truth" as "faithfulness, reliability, trustworthiness; truth, what conforms to reality in contrast to what is false." (Mounce 2006, 896) Jehovah God, the Creator of heaven and earth is our only true source of information as to the truth of humanity's current circumstances (i.e., our imperfect condition). He has complete understanding of everything that he has created, which includes humankind. He knows our design, which means our optimum circumstances for enjoying the life that he gave us. He is also well aware of how to deal with the rebellion of our first parents, Adam and Eve. He is also aware of what the future holds as well.

Psalm 31:5 Updated American Standard Version (UASV)

⁵ Into your hand I commit my spirit;
you have redeemed me, O Jehovah, **God of truth**.

Jesus himself said to the Father in a prayer of the disciples, "Sanctify them in the truth; your word is truth." (John 17:17) Since we are able to place complete trust in every word God has inspired, we need to heed his direction about human behavior, as it is entirely trustworthy. Young Prince Hezekiah says of Jehovah, "all your commandments are true." (Ps. 119:151) The promises that he lays out with his Word the Bible are dependable. After a lifetime of trusting Jehovah, Joshua said, "nothing failed from all the good things that Yahweh promised to the house of Israel; everything came to pass." (Josh. 21:45) Thus, from the books of

Moses to the book of Revelation, we see that God is 'righteous and true in all his ways.' –Revelation 15:3.

Walking In the Truth

Adam and Eve were created in the image of God and were a reflection of his qualities and attributes. Even after the fall, in humanities state of imperfection, we still maintain a good measure of that image. For that reason, there is little surprise that the Creator of humankind would expect us to continue to walk in his truth, or that the **lovers of truth** would want to walk in his truth. How are we to accomplish this in our imperfection? The Apostle Paul provided that answer when he wrote, "this is good and acceptable before God our Savior, who wants all people to be saved and to come to an accurate knowledge[185] of the truth." (1 Tim. 2:4) We need to acquire an accurate knowledge of who God is, why he created the earth, humans, and his will and purpose for us and the earth. What does he expect of us, his followers? (John 17:3; 1 John 2:3-4) Walking in the truth is far more than mere head knowledge of who, what, where, why and how of things. This knowledge will lead to what Luke called the early Christians, "the Way." (Acts 9:2) This taking in knowledge of the Father and the Son will be life altering, to the point where it becomes a Way of life.

Certainly, what is true of our human parents would be even more accurate of our heavenly Father as well. God finds great joy, satisfaction and happiness when imperfect humans choose to imitate his qualities and attributes over their fleshly desires, which lean toward wrongdoing, and over the god of this system of things, Satan the Devil. (Gen. 1:26-27; Pro. 23:24-25) As the Creator and Designer of us, 'he teaches us what is best for us, leads us in the way you should go.' (Isa. 48:17) It is a privilege to work with hundreds of millions of others that want to walk in the truth, to be used in the Great Commission, helping millions more to move from death to life. – Matthew 28:19-20; John 5:24.

We also bring glory to God when we **walk in the truth**. His sovereignty, the rightfulness of his rulership was challenged by Satan, and our choosing to walk with him, means we support him as ruler. (Gen. 3:1-4; Rev. 12:9) Part of Satan's challenge was that created persons would only love him for what they can get out of him, if opposition to their loyalty arises, they will abandon him. (Job 1:6-12) Thus, our continuously,

---

[185] Greek *epignosis*, accurate or full knowledge

steadfastly walking in the truth, evidence that lie, because we refuse to compromise what is right for some immediate gratification. (Pro. 27:11) For those who have chosen not to walk in the truth, but have followed the path of independence, like Adam and Eve, they unwittingly align themselves with Satan. He is the "father of the lie," "who deceives the whole world," as he is "the god of this age [and] has blinded the minds of the unbelievers." (Jn. 8:44; Rev. 12:9; 2 Cor. 4:4) These have a closed heart and mind and are unable to see the path of truth. May we maintain the mindset of the Psalmist and the prophet Samuel,

Psalm 25:4-5 Updated American Standard Version (UASV)

4 4 Make me to know your ways, O Jehovah;
teach me your paths.
5 Lead me in your truth and teach me,
for you are the God of my salvation;
for you I wait all the day long.

1 Samuel 12:21 Updated American Standard Version (UASV)

21 You must not turn aside, for then you would go after futile things which cannot profit or deliver, because they are futile. 24 Only fear Jehovah, and serve him faithfully with all your heart, for see what great things he has done for you.

Written for Our Instruction

We can learn some object lessons from what God has disclosed to us in his Word. Paul told the Corinthians "these things happened to those people as an example but are written for our instruction." (1 Cor. 10:11) He also told the congregation in Rome, "For whatever was written beforehand was written for our instruction, in order that through patient endurance and through the encouragement of the scriptures we may have hope." (Rom. 15:4) Israelite history is a great opportunity for us to learn. God personally chose Abraham, Isaac and Jacob, because they were walking with him while others chose to abandon him. The nation of Israel was the descendants of Jacob's 12 sons.

The Israelites became God's chosen people, of whom he made a covenant, to which they agreed to follow. If they walked in the truth, they would be blessed by God's presence. If they abandoned that walk like the pagan nations, they would lose his presence, resulting in the difficulties that came with living in this fallen world. Whilst they maintained their loyalty, they never became victims to enemy nations.

(Deut. 28:7) Furthermore, they could depend on crop growth that was exceptional year after year, as well as their flocks of animals. (Ex. 22:1-15) Additionally, they had no reason to build jails to house criminals, because they had the perfect social system. (Ex. 22:1-15) In addition, they did not suffer from diseases like other nations (Deut. 7:15). Moreover, while they had an army, if they had obeyed, it would have never needed to be used because God fought in their behalf. (2 Ki 19:35)He promised them that they would "be blessed more than all of the peoples," and when they walked in the truth, this proved to be true.

Deuteronomy 7:14 Updated American Standard Version (UASV)

14 You shall be blessed above all peoples; there will be no male or female barren among you or among your cattle.

We all have the history before us of how Israel just **refused to walk in the truth**. They would walk in the truth for a number of years, and then they would abandon that truth until life was impossibly difficult, moving them to return to the Father. This walking in the truth, abandoning the truth, and repenting to return to the truth, went on for some 1,500 years. The final difficulty in this back and forth was their rejection of the Son of God. His words to them were quite clear:

Matthew 21:43 Updated American Standard Version (UASV)

43 Therefore I say to you, the kingdom of God will be taken away from you and **given to a nation**,[186] producing the fruit of it.

Matthew 23:37-38 Updated American Standard Version (UASV)

37 "Jerusalem, Jerusalem, who kills the prophets and stones those who are sent to her! How often I wanted to gather your children together, the way a hen gathers her chicks under her wings, and you were unwilling.

38 Behold, your house is being left to you desolate!

Just who are **the people or nation** that the Kingdom was to be given to after the Israelites fell out of favor with God? He chose for himself a new spiritual nation, which became the Christian congregation that Jesus established between 29 and 33 C.E. He no longer had the descendants of Abraham, Isaac and Jacob as his chosen people, by which other nations would bless themselves.

---

[186] Or *people*

Acts 10:34-35 Updated American Standard Version (UASV)

[34] So Peter opened his mouth and said: "Truly I understand that God shows no partiality, [35] but in every nation anyone who fears[187] him and works righteousness[188] is acceptable to him.

Acts 13:46 Updated American Standard Version (UASV)

[46] And Paul and Barnabas spoke out boldly and said, "It was necessary that the word of God be spoken to you first; since you thrust it aside and judge yourselves unworthy of eternal life, behold, we are turning to the Gentiles.

Did this mean that no Jewish person could be a part of the Kingdom? Hardly! The first disciples of that Kingdom for seven years, 29 C.E. to 36 C.E. were only Jewish people. After 36 C.E., and the baptism of the first Gentile, Cornelius, anyone, including the Jews, could be a part of this Kingdom, as long as they accepted the King, Jesus Christ. Jesus said, "I am the way, and the truth, and the life. No one comes to the Father except through me." (John 14:6) At Jesus' Baptism, there was a voice from heaven saying, "This is my beloved Son, with whom I am well pleased." (Matt.3:16-17) Jesus' teaching, miraculous signs, his ransom sacrifice and resurrection, established him as the truth, having the authority and power of the Father.[189] The Christians in the first century were given the position of being God's chosen people. (Acts 1:8; 2:1-4, 43) **The truth** would now flow through Jesus to the Christian congregation. As Paul told the Corinthians, "For to us God has revealed them through the Spirit. For the Spirit searches all things, even the depths of God." (1 Cor. 2:10) It happened just as Jesus had said it would, "I praise you, Father, Lord of heaven and earth, because you have hidden these things from the wise and intelligent, and have revealed them to young children." – Matthew 11:25.

However, more truth was on the horizon with the birth of the Christian congregation. There had been 39 books written by the Jewish writers of the Hebrew Old Testament (2 Tim. 3:16-17), and now there was to be added an additional 27 books by Jewish Christians, making up the Greek New Testament (2 Peter 2:15-16). Thus, there were 66 small

---

[187] This is a reverential fear of displeasing God because of one's great love for him. It is not a dreadful fear.

[188] I.e., *does what is right*

[189] Matt. 15:30-31; 20:28; John 4:34; 5:19, 27, 30; 6:38, 40; 7:16-17; 17:1-2; Acts 2:22

books, written over a 1,600-year period that would make one book, which we hold today in our modern-day translations. Yes, some 40 plus Bible writers were, as Peter put it, "men carried along by the Holy Spirit spoke from God." – 2 Peter 1:21.

True and False Disciples

The question that begs to be asked is, 'how do we know, who is walking in the truth and who only appears to be walking in the truth?' Who truly is the dispenser of truth these days? As has been mentioned, we have some 41,000 different denominations that all claim to be Christian, and each would argue that they are doing just that.

Matthew 7:21-23 Updated American Standard Version (UASV)

²¹ "Not everyone who says to me, 'Lord, Lord,' will enter the kingdom of heaven, but **the one who does the will of my Father** who is in heaven. ²² On that day many will say to me, 'Lord, Lord, did we not prophesy in your name, and cast out demons in your name, and do many mighty works in your name?' ²³ And then I will declare to them, 'I never knew you; depart from me, you who practice lawlessness.'[190]

The primary concern of any true disciple of Christ is that he is "**one who does the will of my Father.**" Many times we hear Christians saying, "I think, I feel, I believe," when in reality this is not the right path. We need to establish what the will of the Father is, as opposed to our will, or the will of our pastor, or the will of the people, or the popular will. Maybe we are accomplishing some very good deeds that are done in the name of Christ, but if it is not the will of the Father; then, it is being

---

[190] **7:21 Not everyone who says . . . but he who does**. The faith that says but does not do is really barren unbelief (cf. v. 20). Jesus is not suggesting that works merit salvation but that true faith will not fail to produce the fruit of good works. This point is also precisely the point of James 1:22–25; 2:26. 7:22 **7:22 have we not prophesied . . . cast out demons . . .** and done many wonders. Note that far from being totally devoid of works of any kind, these people were claiming to have done some remarkable signs and wonders. In fact, their whole confidence was in these works—further proof that these works, spectacular as they might have appeared, could not have been authentic. No one so bereft of genuine faith could possibly produce true good works. A bad tree cannot bear good fruit (v. 18). **7:23 lawlessness**. All sin is lawlessness (1 John 3:4), i.e., rebellion against the law of God (cf. 13:41). – MacArthur, John (2005-05-09). *The MacArthur Bible Commentary* (Kindle Locations 39114-39118). Thomas Nelson. Kindle Edition.

done in vain. We need to appreciate that the Father has placed all authority into the hands of the Son.

John 17:1-3 Updated American Standard Version (UASV)

¹ Jesus spoke these things; and lifting up his eyes to heaven, He said, "Father, the hour has come; glorify your Son, that the Son may glorify you, ² just as **you have given him authority over all flesh**, so that he may give eternal life to all those whom you have given to him. ³ This is eternal life, that they may know you, the only true God, and the one whom you sent, Jesus Christ.

Matthew 28:18-20 Updated American Standard Version (UASV)

¹⁸ And Jesus came up and spoke to them, saying, "**All authority has been given to me** in heaven and on earth. ¹⁹ Go therefore and **make disciples** of all the nations, baptizing them in the name of the Father and the Son and the Holy Spirit, ²⁰ **teaching them** to observe all that I commanded you; and behold, I am with you always, even to the end of the age."

Matthew 24:14 Updated American Standard Version (UASV)

¹⁴ And this gospel of the kingdom **will be proclaimed in all the inhabited earth**[191] as a testimony to all the nations, and then the end will come.

John 6:38 Updated American Standard Version (UASV)

³⁸ because I have come down from heaven not that I should do my will, but the will of the one who sent me.

John 5:24 Updated American Standard Version (UASV)

²⁴ Truly, truly, I say to you, whoever hears my word and believes him who sent me has eternal life. He does not come into judgment, but has **passed from death to life**.

What do we learn from the above texts? **(1)** We need to do the will of the Father, if we are to be walking in the truth. **(2)** The Father gave all authority to the Son. **(3)** The Son, Jesus, does not do his will, but the will of the Father. **(4)** Therefore, to do the will of the Father is to obey the Son, who is doing the will of the Father. Jesus specifically told his disciples before his ascension that he had "all authority in heaven and on earth."

---

[191] Or *in the whole world*

Then, he gave them one commission to obey, which was to preach, to teach, and make disciples. In other words, a disciple walking in the truth is one, who is being used as a tool to bring people from all nations over from death into life.

Faithfully Walking in the Truth

3 John 1:4 Updated American Standard Version (UASV)

4 No greater joy do I have than this, to hear of my children walking in the truth.

The Apostle John penned these words about 96-98 C.E., when he was almost 100 years old. He had spent a lifetime of making disciples, and helping them to maintain their walk in the truth. This writer has spoken many times about the number of denominations today, numbering around 41,000. Those denominations that are walking in the truth today are those that reflect Scripture, as though it were a fingerprint. When a detective lifts a fingerprint from a crime scene, and there is a match to a criminal, it is done by determining how many points within the print match up. We can use this as an analogy for those who are walking in the truth. If we use the Bible as lines in a fingerprint, how many points match up? However, for the sake of argument, let us assume that the reader is in a denomination that highly reflects the Bible, and first century Christianity. How can we be certain that we will be able to maintain our walk in the truth?

There are many difficulties in this life, which can sap us of our strength to continue our walk. Maybe we have grown discouraged because of serious health problems, or family difficulties. Then, there are those that have become distracted chasing after the lifestyles that this world has to offer. What can we do, so as not to drift away, fall away, turn away, refuse, or become sluggish in our walk in the truth?

Consider Jesus Christ

Jesus did not live in an ideal time. He lived under the Roman Empire that expected taxes from its citizen, and he lived under the Jewish system, who demanded their taxes as well. Many Jews were very poor, and the Jewish Law was very oppressive on its people, because the religious leaders added so many oral traditions. When Jesus finally started his ministry, he was tempted personally by Satan. In addition, those who chose to follow him were very difficult to deal with, because Jewish pride kept them seeking their own interests. Furthermore, Jesus faced those that mocked him for his message, as well as Jewish religious leaders that were trying to kill him for that message. Moreover, he knew how things were going to end, how he was going to be betrayed by one of the twelve, arrested, beaten within an inch of his life, and executed as a blasphemer. (Matt. 4:8-11; John 6:14, 15) Regardless, of all the difficulties that came his way, Jesus continued walking in the truth. What was it that gave him the ability to persevere?

Hebrews 12:1-2 Updated American Standard Version (UASV)

[1] Therefore, since we have so great a cloud of witnesses surrounding us, let us also lay aside every weight and the sin which so easily entangles us, and let us run with endurance the race that is set before us, [2] fixing our eyes on Jesus, the author and perfecter of faith, who for the joy set before him endured the cross, despising the shame, and has sat down at the right hand of the throne of God.

Paul informs us what it was that enable Jesus to endure. It was 'the joy set before him." He knew the result of his obedience right up to the very end, and so he kept walking in the truth, as should we. We too can keep in mind the reward of eternal life. (Rev. 22:12) As we are walking through life, there may be, some very atrociously difficult times, where getting up each morning seems overwhelming. If one can focus in on the destination of this journey, it will make each step of the way, just a little easier. Therefore, we can find our walk in the truth, somewhat easier, if we see the life that awaits us.

Consider the Apostle Paul

2 Corinthians 11:23-29 Updated American Standard Version (UASV)

[23] Are they servants of Christ? I reply like a madman, I am more outstandingly one: I have done more work, been imprisoned more often, with countless beatings, and often near deaths. [24] Five times I received 40 strokes less one from the Jews, [25] three times I was beaten with rods, once I was stoned, three times I experienced shipwreck, a night and a day I have spent in the open sea; [26] in journeys often, in dangers from rivers, in dangers from robbers, in dangers from my own people, in dangers from the nations, in dangers in the city, in dangers in the wilderness, in dangers at sea, in dangers among false brothers, [27] in labor and toil, in sleepless nights often, in hunger and thirst, frequently without food, in cold and

lacking clothing.[192] **28** Besides those things of an external kind, there is what rushes in on me from day to day: the anxiety for all the congregations. **29** Who is weak, and I am not weak? Who is made to stumble, and I am not incensed?[193]

Philippians 4:11-13 Updated American Standard Version (UASV)

11 Not that I speak from want, for I have learned to be content[194] in whatever circumstances I am. **12** I know how to be made lowly, and I know also how to be abounding; in everything and in all things I have learned the secret *of* both being filled and going hungry, both to abound and to be lacking. **13** I can do all things through[195] him who strengthens me. **14** Nevertheless, you have done well to share[196] *with me* in my affliction.

We have to appreciate the power that is offered to us, just as it was offered to Jesus and Paul, and other servants from the Hebrew Old Testament (Ps. 55:12). It is not the power to fulfill our wishes or desires, but the power to carry out the will and purpose of the Father and the Son. Our ability to walk in the truth through such things as that, which Jesus and Paul walked through, does not come to us naturally. However, this power to endure is very much available to us today as well.

Isaiah 40:29-31 Updated American Standard Version (UASV)

29 He gives power to the tired one,
   and full might to those lacking strength.
30 Youths will tire out and grow weary,
   And young men will stumble and fall;
31 But those hoping in Jehovah will regain power;
   they will soar on wings like eagles;
they will run and not grow weary;
   they will walk and not tire out.

What kinds of things would be in harmony with the will and purposes of God, by which we may be empowered? The world requires so much of our strength to cover the necessities of food, housing and

---

[192] Lit *and in nakedness*

[193] Lit *I am not on fire*

[194] Or "*self-sufficient*"

[195] Lit *in*

[196] Or *have fellowship with*

clothing. We may be worn out from work, so we need the strength to carry out our daily personal Bible study, going to Christian meetings, Christian activities, and especially our evangelism of the Good News.[197] We may need strength to maintain our Christian walk in the face of temptations, discouragement, or some form of persecution. – Psalm 1:1-3; Romans 10:10; 1 Thessalonians 5:16, 17; Hebrews 10:23-25.

Satan is the god of this wicked age.' (2 Cor. 4:4) Christians are his primary targets, as we are alien residents to his world. Therefore, we should not be at all startled that there is the extra difficulty of living a righteous life in an unrighteous world. When we accept Christ, it is as though we have arrived in a new land, the land of Christianity. It is not an isolated nation, but is embedded with a world of nations that are contrary to its very essence of God. It is no easy task to pick up stakes in the land of worldliness. We must let go of old friends, and begin to discover new ones. We must learn a completely new culture. In this land, we are the minority, and most people see us as though we are a stranger in their land. As Christians, our walk in the truth can take us through many difficulties in life, but our destination, is life in a renewed world, not this wicked fallen one.

How does this analogy play out for the Christian? We must now learn how to live according to the Spirit, not the flesh, an entirely new moral code. Shortly thereafter, we will develop a new personality that is reflective of our new land of Christianity. "For at that time I will change the speech of the peoples to a pure speech, that all of them may call upon the name of [Jehovah] and serve him with one accord." (Zeph. 3:9) As a new member of Christ's Kingdom, we will have already given up our former ways.

1 Corinthians 6:9-11 Updated American Standard Version (UASV)

⁹ Or do you not know that the unrighteous will not inherit the kingdom of God? Do not be deceived; neither fornicators, nor idolaters, nor adulterers, nor men of passive homosexual acts, nor men of active homosexual acts,[198] **10** nor thieves, nor the covetous, nor drunkards, nor

---

[197] I am not of the mind of the rest of Christianity, who believe that sharing their conversion, or what God has done in their life is our "evangelism." Our evangelism is to preach the Good News, to teach Bible doctrine, and to make disciples by conversion, much of which is not being done in Christianity at this point and time.

[198] The two Greek terms refer to passive men partners and active men partners in consensual homosexual acts

revilers, nor swindlers, will inherit the kingdom of God. [11] And such were some of you; but you were washed, you were sanctified, you were justified in the name of the Lord Jesus Christ and by the Spirit of our God.

There are far more benefits to this move from the land of worldliness to the land of Christianity. First, the land of Christianity has a population of persons that live a morally clean life, who accept and love us for who we are, not who we were. (Lu 18:29-30) Second, there is the strength that we are given to cope with this new life, as an alien resident in the land of worldliness. Third, there is God's Word, the Bible, which if followed will generally lead to a far better outcome that the former days of being led by the flesh. Fourth, we now have the hope of life, while before it was the inevitability of death. (Phil. 4:8-9) Most importantly, we will now be a friend of the Creator of heaven and earth. – James 2:23; Matthew 7:13, 14; 1 John 2:15-17

Consider Your Spiritual Health

It is generally true that if we take care of your physical health, we will seldom fall ill; and should we fall ill, the recovery is easier and faster. The same is true of spiritual health. If we fall ill spiritually, the recovery will be easier and faster, if we were healthy to begin with. We need to keep the benefits that we have received from obeying Scripture, and the hope that awaits us at the forefront of our mind. Of course, we cannot completely sidestep the difficulties of this imperfect world or its people, but if we have maintained our spiritual health, they will not overcome us entirely because there is the resurrection hope, which no one can take from us.

Review Questions

- What is the apostasy that was foretold and how long was it to run?

- Who is the man of lawlessness and how will this lawless one be destroyed?

- What rebellion against God has taken place?

- Who has been acting as the restraint against the apostasy and the man of lawlessness from the first century until now?

- What two different types of seeds have grown up together?

- What is the darnel seed of Catholicism?
- What does it mean to believe the truth?
- What does it mean to walk in the truth?
- How can we know if we truly love the truth?

CHAPTER 15 You Must Be like Young Children

Matthew 18:2-3 Updated American Standard Version (UASV)

² So calling to him a child, he put him in the midst of them, ³ and said, "Truly, I say to you, unless you turn and **become like young children**, you will never enter the kingdom of heaven.

Certainly, we would be offended if someone told us, "you are acting like a child!" The irony is, when we think of a child outside of that context, he or she will bring a smile to our face because all children are adorable. However, the comment above is likely relating to their lack of maturity, experience and wisdom. (Job 12:12. *What qualities do children have that adults might want to imitate?*

Developing Childlike Humility

Frequently, Jesus was in "the presence of children around Jesus and/or his love for them is mentioned in the Gospels. See Matt. 14:21; 15:38; 18:3; 19:13, 14 (cf. Mark 10:13, 14; Luke 18:15, 16); 21:15, 16; 23:37 (cf. Luke 13:34). Undoubtedly children felt attracted to Jesus, wanted to be with him. Whenever he wanted a child there was always one present, ready to do his bidding, to come when he called him. So also here. To speculate who this child was [in 18:2-4] is useless. The point is that this was indeed a child, endowed with all the favorable and amiable qualities generally associated with childhood in any clime and at any time." (Hendriksen 1973, p. 688)

However, on this particular occasion, Jesus wanted to make a point to his disciples, and chose a child to do so. Jesus said, said, "Truly, I say to you, unless you turn and **become like young children**, you will never enter the kingdom of heaven." While "adults tend to leave childlike ways behind them (and some such ways certainly ought to be abandoned; children can manifest qualities like pride, selfishness, and temper),[199] but Jesus is pointing out that there are some things to be learned from small children. He seems to be referring to the insignificance and unimportance of children as the ancient world saw them, perhaps also to qualities like

---

[199] Fenton remarks that the child is the symbol of humility "not because a child is humble (most of them are not), but because a child has no status in society." He cites Galatians 4:1.

trustfulness and dependence.[200] Adults like to assert themselves and to rely on their own strength and wisdom. This attitude is impossible for those who wish to enter the kingdom. We should notice further that Jesus does not answer the set terms of the question. He does not concern himself with relative positions and who will have the top job when the kingdom comes: he speaks of the more basic problem of getting into the kingdom. His emphatic double negative rules out the possibility of even entering the kingdom for those seeking great things for themselves. He does not talk about eminence in the kingdom at all; without genuine humility it is impossible even to get into it, and for humility the question of personal preeminence does not arise." (Morris 1992, p. 460)

Further, "Jesus' response to the disciples showed how selfish and foolish their question was. They were thinking childishly, but Jesus showed them that mature faith is the opposite. Mature faith is childlike humility. In fact, elsewhere in the New Testament, Peter seemed to suggest that the more mature a disciple's faith becomes, the more brotherly kindness and love it demonstrates (2 Pet. 1:5–9). The child Jesus called to him served as an object lesson for the disciples. It was a memorable image to help them learn the nature of true maturity. Little children are the most helpless and powerless members of society. But Jesus infused their childlike qualities with value and greatness. Jesus' **I tell you the truth** might be translated as "Listen up!" In fact, the disciples had not been listening well when he taught the same paradoxical principles in 5:3–12 and 16:24–25. One way to summarize Jesus' first statement is to say that there is a sign on the gates of God's kingdom reading, 'No grown-ups past this point,' or 'No big-shots allowed!' Jesus was not rejecting the positive aspects of adult-hood but the self-sufficiency, pride, sophisticated denial, and self-deception that are learned with years of practice in a sinful world. These negative qualities are not the only reason for God's judgment, but they constitute the "unforgivable sin" of 12:31–32–a stubborn, self-righteous refusal to accept the forgiveness necessary for entry into God's kingdom. At the root of true maturity is simplicity, not sophistication." (Weber 2000, p. 286)

Those who are truly Christian have the heart of a servant, not that of some prominence seeking leader. Those who are truly Christian would have no problem witnessing to a homeless person, with the same love and care we would give to our neighbor or friend. While we do not seek

---

[200] Melinsky speaks of "unselfregarding trust in God, like that so shatteringly displayed by young children towards their elders."

reward, ones with such a heart condition can draw comfort in Jesus words, "Whoever receives one such child in my name receives me, and whoever receives me, receives not me but him who sent me." (Mark 9:37, ESV) When we develop, a generous, humble, childlike heart-attitude, it helps us to draw closer to the Father and the Son. (John 17:20-21; Jam. 4:8; 1 Pet. 5:5) As we learned in a previous chapter, there is more happiness in giving than thee is in receiving. (Acts 20:35) Moreover, with a humble spirit, we can contribute to "the unity of the Spirit in the bond of peace" within the congregation. (Eph. 4:1-3) What other childlike qualities might we want to emulate?

Teachable and Trusting

Mark 10:15 Updated American Standard Version (UASV)

¹⁵ Truly I say to you, whoever does not receive the kingdom of God like a child will not enter it at all."

In the above, Jesus brings to our attention another quality that adults can learn from children. While children can be humble, aware of their limitations, because of this, they are also teachable. While older ones do have a more difficult time taking in information, the brain of a child is like a sponge, soaking up information. The question is, "How do children receive gifts? They receive with anticipation. They receive joyfully and thankfully. They receive without believing they did anything to deserve the gift." (Cooper 2000, p. 167)

Thus, if we are to benefit from God's kingdom, we need to 'receive the word of God, which we heard from Matthew, Mark, Luke, John, Paul and the other authors of the Bible, which we accept not as the word of men but as what it really is, the word of God, which is at work in us believers.' (1 Thess. 2:13) 'Like newborn infants, we need to long for the pure spiritual milk, that by it we may grow up into salvation.' (1 Pet. 2:2) What are we to do if we find certain Bible teachings difficult to understand? James wrote, "If any of you lacks wisdom, let him ask God, who gives generously to all without reproach, and it will be given him." (Jam 1:5, ESV) Are we to expect that the Holy Spirit will miraculously place the understanding within our mind if we pray for it, having faith? No, we are to work in behalf of our prayers. Wise King Solomon informs us of how we will find the very knowledge of God. He wrote, "receive my words and treasure up my commandments with you, making your ear attentive to wisdom and inclining your heart to understanding; yes, if you call out for insight and raise your voice for understanding, if you seek it like silver and search for it as for hidden treasures, then you will understand the fear of the Lord and find the knowledge of God. For the Lord gives wisdom; from his mouth come knowledge and understanding." – Proverbs 2:1-6, ESV.

Verses 1-3 shows that it is up to us, as we must search God's words by seeking, "commandments, "wisdom," "understanding," and "insight." If we have watched an old western movie, we know that to search for treasures was no easy task. It called for much digging with a pickaxe and a shovel. The same is true for the Word of God, if we are to find "the knowledge of God." We must dig into the Word of God, to discover the gems of truth lying deep beneath word studies, Bible backgrounds, grammar and syntax, historical setting, and the like. We will not find the big nuggets of truth by just skimming the surface of the gold mine.

The Psalmist wrote, "How great are your works, O Lord! Your thoughts are very deep!" (Ps. 92:5) The apostle Paul wrote, "Oh, the depth of the riches and wisdom and knowledge of God! How unsearchable are his judgments and how inscrutable his ways!" (Rom. 11:33) He was not suggesting that it was impossible to discover truths about God, but it will take effort on our part. Paul also wrote, "These things God has revealed to us through the Spirit. For the Spirit searches everything, even the depths of God." (1 Cor. 2:10) Keep in mind that the Bible is inspired (literally, "God breathed"), and those who penned it were moved along by Holy Spirit. The apostle Peter had this to say about Paul's letters, "As he does in all his letters when he speaks in them of these matters. There are some things in them that are hard to understand, which the ignorant and unstable twist to their own destruction." (2 Pet. 3:15-16) We should be truly grateful for all the study tools that we have which makes digging in the Word of God, so much easier.

Babes as to Badness

1 Corinthians 14:20 Updated American Standard Version (UASV)

[20] Brothers, do not become young children in your understanding, but be babes as to badness;[201] and become mature in your understanding.

Likely, because of the times many children that we see today in movies and television are portrayed as brats. This is show that way because some there is some truth to it, but these troubled children are

---

[201] Or *young children as to badness*

reflective of their mother and father's parenting skills. Generally speaking, most young toddlers are unusually pure in heart and mind. Because of this, Paul says we are to be **babes as to badness** (i.e., young children as to badness).

Here "Paul insisted that believers should be as naive as **infants ... in regard to evil**. But Paul did not want believers to be naive about evil. Rather, Christians must be wise as serpents (Matt. 10:16). The ideal is that believers should be inexperienced in and separated from evil, and that they should not know much about it. While he found it appropriate to be innocent regarding evil, Paul insisted that believers should still be **adults ... in** their **thinking**. In other words, with respect to Christian doctrine and practice, Paul wanted the Corinthians to be mature in their perspectives. (Pratt Jr 2000, p. 248)

Think of all of the racism in the American news media of late, which has been distorted by older ones. What do I mean? While there are minor pockets of racism in every community of the world, America is not racist as it is portrayed. It is groups like the NAACP and persons such Louis Farrakhan, President Obama, Al Sharpton, and Jesse Jackson, who are race baiters.[202] However, if we drive by and grade school when children are on recess, we will see that they are colorblind. However, in time, many liberal teachers and parents will actually instill racism within the hearts and minds of young black children, having them hold onto something that happened seventy years ago in America. On the other hand, a very small number of white parents will promote racism as well. – Acts 10:34-35.

When we become a Christian, we acquire the mind of Christ and take of our old person, while putting on a whole other person. (1 Cor. 2:16; Col. 3:9-11; Eph. 4:22-24) We are 'transformed by the renewal of our mind, that by testing we may discern what is the will of God, what is good and acceptable and perfect.' (Rom. 12:2) With the help of the Father, Son and Holy Spirit, along with the Christian congregation, we can remove any stain the world has placed on us, while recapturing the

---

[202] One who insinuates that racism or bigotry is a dominant factor with regards to an event that either does not involve race or in which diverse cultures are involved are simply a minor element.

Urban Dictionary: race baiter, http://www.urbandictionary.com/define.php?term=race+baiter (accessed October 15, 2015).

beautiful qualities that grew naturally when we were children. – Ephesians 5:1.

Review Questions

- What did Jesus mean at Matthew 18:2-4?

- How can we develop childlike humility?

- How can we be teachable when so much of the Bible is difficult to understand?

- What does it mean to be babes as to badness and what does it not mean?

- What do we acquire when we accept Christ?

- What help do we have in taking off our old personality and putting on the new personality

CHAPTER 16 Hearing and Doing the Word

James 1:19-25 Updated American Standard Version (UASV)

¹⁹ Know this, my beloved brothers: let every man be quick to hear, slow to speak, slow to anger; ²⁰ for the anger of man does not achieve the righteousness of God. ²¹ Therefore, putting aside all filthiness and abundance of wickedness, and receive with meekness the implanted word, which is able to save your souls.²⁰³ ²² But be doers of the word, and not hearers only, deceiving yourselves. ²³ For if anyone is a hearer of the word and not a doer, he is like a man who looks intently at his natural face²⁰⁴ in a mirror.²⁴ for he looks at himself and goes away, and immediately forgets what sort of man he was. ²⁵ But he that looks into the perfect law, the law of liberty, and abides by it, being no hearer who forgets but a doer of a work, he will be blessed in his doing.

Know this, my beloved brothers (1:19a)²⁰⁵

James says **know this**, which is a reference to the fact that these Christians are "a kind of firstfruits of his creatures." 'Knowing this' is suggestive of action not so much an awareness, which they had. Remember, Jesus said to his disciples that "If you *know* these things, blessed are you if you do them." (John 13:17) A Christian in a righteous standing with God will act on what he knows to be true about God. The apostle John tells us, "No one who abides in him [God] keeps on sinning; no one who keeps on sinning has either seen him or known him." (1 John 3:6) As he has done previously, he calls them "**my beloved brothers**,"²⁰⁶ (1) to draw their attention to an important point (2), and to let them

---

²⁰³ Or is able to save *you*

²⁰⁴ Lit *the face of his birth*

²⁰⁵ This chapter is from the CPH Christian Living Commentary by Brent A. Calloway

http://www.christianpublishers.org/apps/webstore/products/show/5575711

²⁰⁶ "**1:19 swift to hear, slow to speak.** Believers are to respond positively to Scripture, and eagerly pursue every opportunity to know God's Word and will better (cf. Ps. 119:11; 2 Tim. 2:15). But at the same time, they should be cautious about becoming preachers or teachers too quickly (see notes on 3:1, 2; cf. Ezek. 3:17; 33:6, 7; 1 Tim. 3:6; 5:22)." – MacArthur, John (2005-05-09). *The MacArthur Bible Commentary* (Kindle Locations 63114-63116). Thomas Nelson. Kindle Edition.

know that this applies to him as well as them. In essence, James is saying, you *know* that God has made you a *kind of firstfruits* by the *word of truth*, meaning that you should feel privileged, by evidencing your new Christian personality, living up to being a disciple of Christ.

let every man be quick to hear (1:19a)

Just as '*knowing*' in the above was suggestive of an action, so too, "hearing" is suggesting obedience. (John 8:37, 38, 47) In other words, 'to hear is to obey.' Jesus said, "He who has ears to hear, let him hear." (Matt. 11:15) We should not fail to hear aright. It takes more than hearing the audio sound of what is being said, so as to hear with understanding. We are challenged to pay close attention to what the speaker has said and to ask ourselves what he meant by the words that he used. The apostle Paul wrote, "So faith comes from hearing, and hearing through the word of Christ." (Rom. 10:17) What did Paul mean? He meant that by taking in the Word of God, our faith and sureness grows in God, as we see the outworking of his promises. If we are not obeying the Word of God, then, apparently, we have not truly heard the Word of God. We want to move beyond being hearers to being doers as well. All self-importance, willfulness, preconception and personal opinion should be set aside as we humbly hear the Word of God. We should long for the Word of God, seeking it and being eager to obey.[207]

slow to speak (1:19b)

Slow to speak, means that we should ponder what we are going to say. (Prov. 15:28; 16:23) This certainly does not mean that we can never speak. We are to proclaim the Word of God, as we are to contend for the faith and defend the Word of God and to speak the Word without fear. (Matt. 24:14; 28:19-20; 1 Pet 3:15; Jude 1:3, 22-23; Phil. 1:14; 1 Thess. 5:14; Eph. 5:15-16) However, we should not use the Bible as a tool to help others until we have incorporated the Word of God in our lives first. Then we can more clearly see how we might use it to benefit another. (Rom. 2:17-24) Paul speaks to Timothy about those "desiring to be teachers of the law, without understanding either what they are saying or the things about which they make confident assertions." (1 Tim 1:7) We do not want to use God's Word to offer advice counsel, comfort, or even to console until we have first used the Word of God effectively in our lives. The reason for this is simple, the Bible is a book for all those things

---

[207] See Matthew 11:15; 13:43; Mark 4:9; 4:23; Luke 14:35; Revelation 2:7, 11; 3:6, and 13.

and more. However, it can be misused in the hands of anyone, who does not have a correct understanding of what it means and has not truly experienced its ability to transform by way of application.

slow to anger; (1:19c)

Injustices surround us in this wicked world, filled with imperfect people, who lean toward sin and are mentally bent toward evil. Yet, James counsels us to work in harmony with Scripture and prayer to keep our anger under control. Because this is in context with our being obedient to the "word" of God, clearly any analysis of the Word of God must be treated with the correct mindset and heart condition. If we are upset to the point of being angry, he will likely be blinded to the value that lies in the Word of God. (Prov. 19:3) He will not see the light while in a provoked state of mind, let alone be able to apply the counsel in his life in a balanced manner. If another has made us angry by saying something inappropriate or mistreating us in some unjust way, we need to slow down, to avoid responding to them in kind, i.e., some vicious, hostile, spiteful comeback, which will only serve to escalate the anger and the void between us and them. There are times to be angry with righteous indignation, but after that Paul warns us, "Be angry and do not sin; do not let the sun go down on your anger." (Eph. 4:26) This is why we combat the irrational thinking, which contributes to anger, with slowing down and rationalizing the situation before we respond.

for the anger of man does not achieve the righteousness of God (1:20)

No one displaying a wrathful disposition can ever have a righteous standing before God. Wrathful ones will not see the wisdom of obedience to the Scriptures. When angry, we tend to make irrational decisions that will generally not be for the good of anyone, even creating long-lasting ripples within relationships. It could even be as simple as our destroying property in a fit of rage, irrationally not caring about the cost. However, once we are calm, the realization that those seconds of rage have cost us hundreds of dollars if not thousands, maybe even an irreplaceable family heirloom, can be very depressing. Our wrath also makes the righteousness of God difficult to accept by unbelievers who see our fits of rage, as opposed to seeing the qualities of God. If we are always angry, how are we projecting the image of God in giving a witness by our behavior? Can we imagine our stumbling someone out of seeking God because they question God based on our personality? Yes, a wrathful attitude from one who claims to be a Christian blocks the righteousness of God. It will cause the unbeliever to turn away from hearing the Word of God. Solomon writes, "Whoever is slow to anger has great understanding, but he who has a hasty temper exalts folly." – Proverbs 14:29

Therefore, putting aside all filthiness and abundance of wickedness (1:21a)

Here in these passages after James has told these believers the attitudes that they were to have when they come to the Word, he now tells them the behaviors which they must put away in order to be able to accept the word of truth. James tells his audience that they are to be **putting aside all filthiness and abundance of wickedness**. Putting aside carries with it the idea of taking off filthy and dirty clothes and casting them to the side. In other words, they were to take off the old and put it out of the way to be done away with. Keep in mind, while not addressed here, it is important to replace the old with something new. If we do not fill a void, it will return to an unusual extent. If we remove unrighteous anger from our lives, it must be replaced with understanding, compassion, empathy, kindness, and things like these.

For this reason, it is important to note that James is making the point that it is a personal act of the will to do away with these things, and not God's responsibility. The first thing that James tells his readers is that they are to put aside its filthiness. The word for filthiness is *rhuparia* and means "dirty or filthy." (Vine, 1996, pg. 237) Things such as fornication, lust, adultery, immorality, and things like these would be included in the filthiness and wickedness that James is talking about. Also in the context of this verse, James could be specifically referring to anger of which he just stated does not bring about the righteous life that God desires. The reason James tells them to put aside the filth is because as long as a person lives in filth it will keep him away from the Word of truth because imperfect humans are naturally drawn to sin. If one is coming to the Word with the wrong attitudes or the wrong behaviors, then he is nullifying that which he is reading or hearing in the Word of truth.

and receive with meekness the implanted word, which is able to save your souls. (1:21b)

After this, James describes the attitude we are to have when coming to the Word, and the behavior changes we must make, he now describes the manner with which we come to the Word of God. We are to **receive with meekness the implanted word, which is able to save your souls**. Meekness is to have a teachable and willing spirit to be ready to submit to the commands that come with the Word of God. It is a condition of the spirit and heart, which means being willing to yield to the commands coming from the word of truth.

Meekness would be the key for these believers to be able to receive, understand, and apply the Word of God into their lives. James states that the Word was already implanted if they would just become humble enough to receive it. James was talking to believers who were living with the indwelling presence of the Holy Spirit. With the inward law being already written upon their heart and the Holy Spirit dwelling within, these believers knew the Word God because it was already implanted. Edward D. Andrews writes about the indwelling of the Holy Spirit,

The Holy Spirit, through the spirit inspired, inerrant Word of God is the motivating factor for our taking off the old person and putting on the new person. (Eph. 4:20-24; Col. 3:8-9) It is also the tool used by God so that we can "be transformed by the renewal of your mind, so that you may approve what is the good and well-pleasing and perfect will of God." – Romans 12:2; See 8:9.

Just how do we **renew our mind**? This is done by taking in an accurate knowledge of Biblical truth, which enables us to meet God's current standards of righteousness. (Titus 1:1) This Bible knowledge, if applied, will enable us to move our mind in a different direction by filling the void after having removed our former sinful practices, and with the principles of God's Word, principles that guide our actions, and especially ones that guide moral behavior.

The Biblical truths that lay in between Genesis 1:1 and Revelation 22:21 will transform our way of thinking, which will in return affect our mood and actions and our inner person. It will be as the apostle Paul said to the Ephesians, We need to "put off your old self, which belongs to your former manner of life and is corrupt through deceitful desires, and to be renewed in the spirit of your minds, and to put on the new self, created after the likeness of God in true righteousness and holiness. . . ." (Ephesians 4:22-24) This force that contributes to our acting or behaving in a certain way for our best interest is internal.[208]

James here is telling his readers the reason they are to accept this Word of God in humility and why they needed to come to it with proper attitude and behavior, i.e., it contained the words of eternal life, it contains the words which places them on the path of salvation. Peter in writing of the power of the word of truth wrote,

---

[208] http://www.christianpublishers.org/holy-spirit-indwelling

1 Peter 1:23 English Standard Version (ESV)

23 since you have been born again, not of perishable seed but of imperishable, through the living and abiding word of God;

In the Word of God, these believers learned of the salvation that came through Christ alone. It was the message that they, being wicked sinners at heart, can be saved through the redeeming power of Jesus Christ. This was not just some ordinary book but the very book that leads to salvation and eternal life. It has practical benefits even now, as it will guide us through our everyday lives and then preserve us for all eternity.

The apostle Paul wrote to the Christians in Rome,

Romans 1:16 English Standard Version (ESV)

16 For I am not ashamed of the gospel, for it is the power of God for salvation to everyone who believes, to the Jew first and also to the Greek.

Paul also said to the Christians in Corinth,

1 Corinthians 1:18 English Standard Version (ESV)

18 For the word of the cross is folly to those who are perishing, but to us who are being saved it is the power of God.

But be doers of the word, (1:22a)

James is telling his readers to **be doers of the word** as obedience to the Word is not optional, it is required, if one is to walk faithfully with God. Jesus pointed out: "Not everyone who says to me, 'Lord, Lord,' will enter the kingdom of heaven, but the one who does the will of my Father who is in heaven." (Matt. 7:21, 24-27) He also said, "Blessed rather are those who hear the word of God and keep it!" (Luke 11:28) The Greek verb (*ginesthe*) is an imperative in the present tense, "be you becoming," which carries the force of an exhortation for a continuous action. James is not suggesting they *become* doers, but that they *be* doers, i.e., make sure that they are continuously doers. The expression *doer of the word is* a Hebrew idiom that literally means 'makers of word.' It could mean a writer or speaker, but more likely carries the meaning of one who lives by the word, one who obeys the word, who practices the word.

and not hearers only, (1:22b)

It does not make one a Christian because they listen dutifully as one is sharing the Word of God. While it is great if a Christian attends Christian services and reads the Scriptures daily, but there is more to being a Christian. Literally hearing the Word, even understanding the Word, is not enough. In the early first-century, Jews and Christians had similar services, wherein a lecturer would read from the Scriptures regularly while also explaining what had been read. However, this alone does not lead to faith. If one is to be the type of hearer that James is speaking of here, he would have genuine faith, meaning that his faith in what he heard would result in works. (Rom. 10:17; Jam. 2:20) In other words, a Christian, who was a hearer only, would be one who lacked faith.

deceiving yourselves (1:22c)

Over 41,000 different Christian denominations today are filled with dutiful persons who regularly attend Christian services, regularly read their Bibles, and involve themselves in the social actions of the congregation. In this, they all believe that they are fulfilling their Christian obligations. However, many of these people's lives are no different from the atheist that is a good person, living by the laws, paying his taxes, and doing good to others. We are **deceiving ourselves** if our entire *life* is not inundated in our worship of God. We may not be aware of or maybe we even block out the fact that obeying the Word of God is an unnegotiable requirement. What we may not realize is that this **deceiving ourselves** is like a roadblock on our path to salvation and harder to set aside than ignorance or skepticism itself. God expects exclusive devotion from his worshipers, which encompasses every aspect of the Christian life. (1 Cor. 10:31) If our worship is merely an outward display, a going through the motions, we are falling short. We were given the great commission of proclaiming and teaching God's Word, as well as making disciples. If we are not regularly engaged in such work in our own communities, we are missing the most important act of obedience.

For if anyone is a hearer of the word and not a doer, he is like a man who looks intently at his natural face in a mirror. (1:23)

When looking into a mirror, man has his image reflected back at himself, where he can see all of his flaws and faults. The purpose of looking into the mirror is so he can see if anything is out of place, so he can make any needed corrections. Can we imagine looking into a mirror, seeing a big stain on our shirt, our hair is completely disheveled, or that we have something on our face, but we ignore them and head off to work?

The image he sees in the mirror is sent to the mind, where it is evaluated, reasoned on, considered. For this reason, by looking at the Word of God, by hearing the Word of God, we are able to see our true selves. We can see all of our imperfections, character flaws, and human weaknesses. We can also see any wrongdoings, misdeeds, even thinking that is out of harmony with the Word of God.

We must keep in mind this analogy is a negative one that is looking at a person who looks **intently at his natural face in the mirror**, sees the things that need to be corrected, but walks away ignoring them. The same is true with the Word of God. He looks into the Word, listens to the needed corrections as he reads, ignores them, and chooses to remain inactive, and fails to respond.

For he looks at himself and goes away, and immediately forgets what sort of man he was. (1:24)

When a person looks into a mirror, he is good at quickly seeing what is out of place as to his appearance. Maybe he has been unable to sleep, so he sees the yellow skin and puffy eyes and dark circles under the eyes. Maybe he sees that he has more gray hair coming in from increased age. When he looks intently into a mirror, he is aware of the things that should give him pause as to how he is living his life. Sleepless nights can cause high blood pressure, heart attacks, strokes, memory loss, diabetes, and lower libidos, and less interest in sex. Does it seem logical to ignore the physical signs of lacking sleep? Should we not consider how we could turn things around? Nevertheless, the man in James' analogy quickly forgets, once he has turned away from the mirror. It is a case of, 'out of sight, out of mind,' as he may want to forget some unwelcome features. Yes, once he has walked away from the mirror he allows the anxieties of the day to crowd out his appearance, forgetting what he may have needed to correct. (See 2 Pet. 1:9) However, the man that is a doer reacts quite differently as he looks into the perfect law.

But he that looks into the perfect law,[209] (1:25a)

James now gives a comparison to the man who not only hears the Word but also actually applies that Word to his life. James says the man who applies the word is he that looks into the perfect law, the law of liberty. The Greek word used for "looks" is the word *parakupto*, which means to "bend inside, lean over, or stoop down to look into." (Vine 1996, Volume 2, Page 378) The sense here is of one seeking to get a better look of something by leaning forward, peering at it. (See John 20:5, 11; 1 Peter 1:12) "The same verb—translated as bent over—pictures the apostle John staring into Jesus' empty tomb (John 20:5). John's look

---

[209] God's Word is the perfect law that gives freedom.

228

led to an obedient faith (John 20:8)." (Lea 1999, 267) One who is wanting to obey the law of Christ does just that, as he peers into the perfect law to inspect, examine and study it, with a heart motivated toward obedience. He is able to visualize himself as it relates to being a biblical father, husband, son, or to herself as a biblical mother, wife or daughter. The law is perfect in the sense that it is complete, everything we in our imperfect state need to walk with God, to have and maintain a righteous standing before the Father and the Son. It is a pathway to salvation through the grace of God. – Proverbs 30:5-6; Psalm 119:105, 140.

the law of liberty, (1:25b)

Jesus said to the Jews who had believed him, "If you abide in my word, you are truly my disciples, and you will know the truth, and the truth will set you free." (John 8:31-32) The Word of God frees his people from slavery to sin and death, putting them on the path of life. (Rom. 7:5-6, 9; 8:2, 4; 2 Cor. 3:6-9) This "law of liberty" is a reference not to the Mosaic Law, but to the new covenant, in which the Father declared, "I will put my law within them, and I will write it on their hearts. And I will be their God, and they shall be my people." (Jer. 31:33) Christians are under the principles behind the Mosaic Law, but not under some lengthy code of rules and regulations but rather the inspired, inerrant Word of God, which enables them to know the will of the Father. (Matt. 7:21-23; 1 John 2:15-17; Gal. 5:1, 13-14) In other words, they have a developed fine-tuned Christian conscience, which leads them in the way that they should go, not because of some fearful dread of displeasing some all-powerful being. The Christian's worship is out of love and is principally positive, not negative. – Matthew 22:37-40; see James 2:12 Galatians 2:4; 5:1, 13 1 Peter 2:16; 2 Peter 2:19 John 8:32

and abides by it, (1:25c)

James also says that the doer of the word does not just obey it occasionally but **abides in it**. The word for abide is *parameno* which means "to remain by or near" *para*, "beside," hence, "to continue or persevere in anything." (Vine 1996, Volume 2, Page 127) He is abiding in these things in the fact he is daily striving to live these truths out in a manner that is pleasing to his master who gave him these commands. This is moving beyond a mere examination of it. This one is different than the man who had looked into the mirror, being dissatisfied with what he saw, but nonetheless walking away forgetting or even losing interest in what he saw. The Christian perseveres and continues to pore over the perfect law with the mindset of keeping his life in harmony with it. (Ps. 119:9, 16,

97) We need to be immersed and engaged fully with the Word of God, as it guides us through this imperfect age.

being no hearer who forgets but a doer of a work, he will be blessed in his doing. (1:25d)

The Christian who has moved over from being a forgetful hearer into the world of being a doer, is one who has a biblical mindset. This biblical mindset leads him to every decision he makes, no matter how great or small. Before, he had been one who may have sat listening respectfully but then failed to act on the insights he gained from the Word of God. Now, he takes everything that he hears from the Word to heart (his inner person), the seat of motivation, and puts it to work in his daily life. He now has an inner joy that he had never previously known. The Word of God proves to be beneficial in ways he had never imagined. (Ps. 19:7-11; see 1 Tim. 4:8.) He draws real comfort from the fact that he has a righteous standing before God, and that God finds him pleasing.

Clean and Pure Worship

James 1:26-27 Updated American Standard Version (UASV)

26 If anyone thinks himself to be religious, and yet does not bridle his tongue but deceives his *own* heart, this man's religion is worthless. 27 Pure and undefiled religion in the sight of *our* God and Father is this: to visit orphans and widows in their distress, *and* to keep oneself unstained by the world.

If any man thinks he is religious (1:26a)

A man may think that he is religious, i.e., (1) belief in the faith, (2) belief in the teachings of the faith, and (3) living by those teachings in one's daily life. He may believe that he is a devout person, completely dedicated to God. He may be attending Christian meetings, or he may be doing some religious works, which on the surface makes him come across as a truly committed worshiper. However, there may be something in his conduct, some flaw, which would cast doubt on the validity of his truly being a religious man. If he is truly, a religious man his entire life will be in harmony with the Word of God. His Christian conscience, mind of Christ, and inner person should be led by the Holy Spirit inspired Word of God, not a mere observance to some formalities or ritualistic practices. We need to understand that it is how God perceives us, not how we perceive ourselves. – 1 Corinthians 4:4

and does not bridle his tongue (1:26b)

James brings to his readers attention one of the most difficult tasks of the imperfect human, the failure to control the tongue, i.e., what one says, namely bad things. It is of such serious concern that James spends almost all of chapter 2 on this one issue. Not controlling one's speech would include malicious gossip, slanderous talk, badmouthing, impulsive and reckless statements, flattery, using their tongues to deceive, and the like. While he may put on great airs or an appearance of being religious, his tongue (speech) convicts him of being one who pretends.

(1) He pretends to have belief in the faith,

(2) to have belief in the teachings of the faith,

(3) and to be living by those teachings in his daily life, but actually behaves otherwise when outside of the churches view.

In James' day, the Pharisees were a self-righteous lot, who used their many words to flatter, to lie, to deceive, and to seek their own glory, while speaking ill of the common Jew as though he were less than human. – Mark 12:38-40; John 7:47-48; compare Romans 3:10-18.

but deceives his heart, (1:26c)

When one begins to think more of himself than he ought, he is surely hip deep in self-deception. Our relationship with the Father and the Son necessitates that we have control over our entire body, which includes the tongue. Paul told the Corinthian congregation that they needed to bring "every thought into captivity to the obedience of Christ." (2 Cor. 10:5) Therefore, if any is living a life that seems to be religious on the surface, yet has not gotten control over the tongue that causes pain to others and to self, this is deception in the heart, i.e., inner person. Even if one has many Christian gifts that stand out, such as being a good speaker, having a warm and charismatic personality, and is generous but falls short in his speech, this is deception. This one has not realized what all is involved in truly being a religious person. (1 Cor. 13:1-3) We cannot practice any sin, and at the same time consider ourselves a genuine Christian. The apostle John makes it clear that Jesus' ransom sacrifice covers the committing of a sin not the practice of sinning, i.e., living in sin. – 1 John 2:1; 3:6, 9-10.

this person's religion is worthless. (1:26d)

First, we should understand that James is not speaking about the religious organization, but rather the type of worship that this person carries out. This one has a major flaw in his walk with God, his Christian conduct, and so he is not pleasing in the eyes of God who would view his worship (religion) as worthless. This is a case of a formalistic worship, not a true worship of God, as he has infected his relationship with his self-deception by way of his failing to control his tongue. It is worthless to the point that all he is doing is wearing out the floors of the church as he ritualistically enters and leaves each service. His worship is tainted and polluted and, therefore, pointless or useless.

Pure and undefiled religion before our God and Father is this: to visit orphans and widows in their affliction, (1:27a)

The word that James uses here for "pure" is the Greek word *katharos* and it means *"clean or unmixed."* (Vine, 1996, pg. 498) This is the kind of purity that is not mixed with anything nor tainted with anything but clear and clean. It would be like looking at a glass of water from an area that has unclean water, if one swirls the glass, he can see little particles floating around in the bottom, unlike bottled water that is pure and clean. Jesus said at Matthew 5:8, "Blessed are the pure (*katharos*) in heart, for they shall see God." James and Jesus are saying the same thing. In the Bible, "pure" can specify what is clean in a physical sense. However, the word in other contexts can apply to what is uncontaminated, i.e., **not** adulterated, stained or dirty, or corrupted, in a moral and religious sense. Jesus said in Luke 10:27, "You shall love the Lord your God with all your heart and with all your soul and with all your strength and with all your mind, and your neighbor as yourself."

The Greek word for undefiled is *amiantos* and it means "undefiled, free from contamination." (Vine, 1996, pg. 650) The word carries with it the idea that there is nothing within the inner person of a Christian, which defiles or stains him. Therefore, James is saying that the first criterion is to see if one's worship is pure and undefiled, is in the way that they use their tongue. Then, the second criterion has to do **not** just with the tongue, but also with our actions toward people. Keep in mind, James is not giving an exhaustive list here of what pure worship should be. In other words, there are more requirements than simply taking care of widows and orphans and keeping oneself unstained by the world. When listing things, no one ever gives an exhaustive list. It is usually three or four examples and the inference is *things like these*. The point is pure worship is more than mere formalism, such as following some basic rules, or of attending meetings regularly. Rather, pure worship is that worship, which gets down to the inner person, and encompasses his entire life, and which includes his love of God and neighbor. – 1 John 3:18.

James then gives what God would consider to be pure and undefiled worship is **to visit orphans and widows in their affliction.** James here is showing that true worship is more than just living by some basic Bible rules and going to Christian meetings but it involves actions. James mentions two specific groups of people who would have been very significant in his day. He specifically mentions the orphans and the widows who should be of special interest for those who claim to have pure worship. It is the actions of Christians, who are willing to help those like orphans and widows, who are truly right in God's eye because their actions show forth their true belief. It would have been the orphans and the widows, who would have been the most rejected, and most unlikely to survive the conditions in which they found themselves.

James specifically mentions that these people were to be visited in their times of distress. The word in Greek used here for distress is *thlipsis* and it means "pressure or a pressing together." (Vine, 1996, pg. 17) James is not saying they were to be helped when they had no more troubles but rather it was *in the midst of* their troubles. They were to be helped as they were going through the pressures of life that were coming against them. This could include clothing, feeding, and giving them shelter, and show the love of Christ to them. James echoes what John wrote in 1 John 3:16-18 "We know love by this, that He laid down His life for us; and we ought to lay down our lives for the brethren. But whoever has the world's goods, and sees his brother in need and closes his heart against him, how does the love of God abide in him? Little children, let us not love with word or with tongue, but in deed and truth." Several Scriptures point to the fact that God has a great concern for the orphans and widows.[210]

and to keep oneself unstained by the world. (1:27b)

This is the third and final criterion, which James presents to Christians to see if their worship is true. The first criterion dealt with their speech, the second dealt with their actions, and now this third test deals with their integrity before God, in the fact that they were **to keep oneself unstained by the world**. The word "unstained" means "spotless" or "without spot." James is saying that the one who is truly religious, pure in worship, will keep himself from being spotted and tainted by the evil and the wickedness of this world. To be stained by the world would be to allow the sinfulness of the world to engage in the evil desires of the flesh.

---

[210] See Deuteronomy 10:18; 14:28–29; 16:11; 24:17; 26:12; Jeremiah 22:3; Zechariah 7:8–10; Malachi 3:5; cf. Acts 6:1; 1 Timothy 5:16

To be stained by the world is to engage in the wicked practices that it has to offer. The word "world" here is a reference to humankind that are alienated from God, who are "lying in the power of the evil one (i.e., Satan)." (1 John 5:19) A Christian should stand out from those using Satan's world fully. (John 17:14) Are we truly separate from the violence and corruption of the world, which would also include our entertainment? Have we adopted any of its attitudes, speech or conduct that would not be in harmony with the will of God? (Matt 7:21-23) Paul warns Timothy,

2 Timothy 2:20-22 English Standard Version (ESV)

20 Now in a great house there are not only vessels of gold and silver but also of wood and clay, some for honorable use, some for dishonorable.21 Therefore, if anyone cleanses himself from what is dishonorable, he will be a vessel for honorable use, set apart as holy, useful to the master of the house, ready for every good work.

22 So flee youthful passions and pursue righteousness, faith, love, and peace, along with those who call on the Lord from a pure heart.

It is important to note that James says, "keep oneself" from being stained by the world, which signifies that sinning or being polluted by the world is always a personal act of the will. It is the personal responsibility to actively resist the evil desires of the flesh that the world has to offer. Paul said to the Christians in Rome,

Romans 12:1-2 English Standard Version (ESV)

1 I appeal to you therefore, brothers, by the mercies of God, to present your bodies as a living sacrifice, holy and acceptable to God, which is your spiritual worship.2 Do not be conformed to this world, but be transformed by the renewal of your mind, that by testing you may discern what is the will of God, what is good and acceptable and perfect.

The sacrifice that Christians regularly make would be beyond anything that unchristian people would normally consider. Yes, Christians evidence that gratefulness by a life of self-sacrifice. It is toward this that we have made our minds over.

Review Question

- [vs 19] What is involved in being quick to hear, slow to speak, and slow to anger?

- **[vs 20]** How is it that the anger of man does not achieve the righteousness of God?

- **[vs 21]** Why must we put aside all filthiness and abundance of wickedness? How is the implanted word able to save our souls?

- **[vs 22]** What does it mean to be doers of the word, and not hearers only, and how would we be deceiving ourselves?

- **[vs 23]** What does James mean when he speaks of a man who looks intently at his natural face in a mirror?

- **[vs 24]** What does a man who looks at himself and goes away, and immediately forgets what sort of man he was mean?

- **[vs 25]** What is the perfect law, the law of liberty?

- **[vs 26]** How can one's form of worship become worthless?

- **[vs 27]** Pure and undefiled religion before our God and Father is what?

CHAPTER 17 You Must Be Steadfast and Persevere

Mark 13:13 Updated American Standard Version (UASV)

¹³ You will be hated by all because of my name, but the one who **endures to the end**, he will be saved.

The last safe place for Christians was the United States of America with its conservative principles and values and a constitution grounded in Scripture. While the United States is not the Kingdom of God by any means, it has served Christians the world over well and will likely do so right up into the Great Tribulation and Armageddon. However, this is proving to be even less the case, as more and more Christians are coming under fire, taken to court, threatened by a system that has begun to grown more and more liberal by the day. This is because those who are truly Christian give their lives to God's kingdom and will not stand for liberal-progressive morals and values, e.g., same sex marriage, abortion, the legalization of drugs, weakness on crime, and many other social agendas of the liberalism.

In the above text, Jesus said, "the one who **endures** to the end, he will be saved." What did he mean by endure? The Greek verb behind our English "endure" (*hypomeno*) literally means "to stay under." According to lexicographers is means "**to maintain a belief or course of action in the face of opposition, *stand one's ground, hold out, endure.*** ²¹¹ On this Greek verb, William Barclay writes, "It is the spirit which can bear things, not simply with resignation, but with blazing hope . . . It is the quality which keeps a man on his feet with his face to the wind. It is the virtue which can transmute the hardest trial into glory because beyond the pain it sees the goal." ²¹² Thus, endurance, empowers us to stand steadfast and persevere and not lose hope in the face difficulties or hardships. (Rom. 5:3-5) When one is in the midst of pain and suffering, he is able to look beyond to the prize that awaits him. THE BOOK OF JAMES CPH CHRISTIAN LIVING COMMENTARY offers the following on James 1:12a,

---

²¹¹ William Arndt, Frederick W. Danker, and Walter Bauer, *A Greek-English Lexicon of the New Testament and Other Early Christian Literature* (Chicago: University of Chicago Press, 2000), 1039.

²¹² William Barclay, *New Testament Words*. 144-5 (Louisville, Westminster Press, 1974)

Blessed is the man who endures under trial; (1:12a)

James here continues with his progression of the person who is undergoing the difficult trials in stating **blessed is the man who endures under trial**. James calls the believers that endure the trial blessed. The word for blessed is not some joy that the world could offer to man, but rather it was a joy that only God could give to man. It is the highest good possible that only God is able to give man by his own spirit. It is an inward peace and comfort of the soul that is not determined by outward circumstances but is a continuous inner joy through all situations of life. This is the same word that Jesus used to describe the beatitudes in (Matthew 5:3-12).The word for **endures** is *hupomone* that means to *"remain under."* (Vine, 1996, pg. 200) The blessedness that James talks about only comes to the one who remains firm in his faith in the midst of the trial. (Calloway 2015, p. 22)

Hebrews 12:1 Updated American Standard Version (UASV)

[1] Therefore, since we have so great a cloud of witnesses surrounding us, let us also **lay aside every weight** and the sin which so easily entangles us, and **let us run with <u>endurance</u>** (*hypomones*) the race that is set before us,

One would not argue that the times we now live in are truly difficult, as they are violent in the extreme, designed to cater to our fleshly side, and both parents must work just to get by. All of this is by design, to cause Christians to take their eye off the one assignment that Jesus gave us. (Matt 24:14; 28:19-20; Ac 1:8) The words of the apostle Paul in the book of Hebrews is ever applicable to us as well, as we too need to **lay aside every weight, and sin which clings so closely, run with <u>endurance</u> the race that is set before us**.

"Lay aside every weight" is a reference to the Greek and Roman athletic games. "In the context of running, it could refer to burdensome clothing or excess bodily weight. Therefore, believers are to run the Christian race with **endurance**, laying aside those things that bind or weigh us down."[213] What type of weight could hinder us in the race that is set before us? We would want to set aside any constant thinking about a particular matter or persistent interest, such as fame or making as a

---

[213] Clinton E. Arnold, Zondervan Illustrated Bible Backgrounds Commentary Volume 4: Hebrews to Revelation., 75 (Grand Rapids, MI: Zondervan, 2002).

reputation for ourselves, love of money, sexual immorality or violent entertainment, excessive travel for pleasure,[214] and other material pursuits that can affect our thinking. – 1 John 2:15-17.

Constant thinking about or persistent interest, however, can wear us out emotionally, physically, and spiritually, affecting our trust in God. Paul talks about how a lack of faith is "**sin which clings so closely.**" Imperfect humans, even Christians with the new personality and mind of Christ, have a propensity at finding themselves in periods of temporary weakness of faith. In these moments, they tend to act contrary to the Spirit's lead, through deception, human weaknesses, setting their hearts on other things, which in turn grieves the Holy Spirit, ending with their stumbling spiritually. Endurance empowers one to be steadfast if the face of hurdles and adversities all the while maintaining hope.

Pay Much Closer Attention

Hebrews 2:1 Updated American Standard Version (UASV)

2 For this reason we must pay much closer attention to the things that have been heard, so that we do not drift away from it.

What and where was the very first Christian congregation? It was the Jerusalem Christian congregation, founded right after Pentecost of 33 C.E. It was made up of the 12 apostles, Jesus brothers James and Jude, Mark who wrote the Gospel that bears his name, and hundreds of other Jews that personally knew Jesus, many traveling with him. We can only

---

[214] There is nothing wrong with traveling more when you are retired, or even taking a vacation once or twice a year with your family up unto the time of retirement. However, the key word is "excessive." If John Smith truly believed that he was going to receive everlasting life; then, this life should be used to almost entirely to carry out the work Christians were given (Matt 28:19-20). Let us play with the belief and reality of everlasting life. The 70-80 years that we now live is what, when we think of say several hundred billion trillion years that lies ahead in our everlasting life. If a true believer saw it that way, this Great Commission of preaching, teaching, and making disciples would be taken more seriously. Here is how we should view pleasure and entertainment, as a means to recuperate, before getting back to our Great Commission. The commission is called great for a reason, and the analogy I gave for John smith, is like one piece of sand, in comparison to all of the sand on all of the planets in the 125 billion universes. That piece of sand, our 70-80 years of life now is not even on the scale of significance. My comment was for the wealthy Christian family, who travels for pleasure, **excessively**.

imagine how spiritually strong that congregation must have been. (Acts 2:44-47; 4:32-34; 5:41; 6:7) However, some 31 years later in 61-64 C.E., the congregation had grown tired and apathetic. Some were drifting away (2:1), others were falling away (6:6) or willfully begging off or turning away (12:25), while other had become sluggish (6:12) and some were shrinking back (10:39) from the truth that they had known from the beginning. How could this have happened? One resource writes,

> The persons addressed were in the mental and spiritual condition common in every age of the Christian church, a condition of languor [laziness] and weariness, of disappointed expectations, deferred hopes, conscious failure and practical unbelief. They were Christians but had slender appreciation of the glory of their calling, misconstrued their experience, and had allowed themselves to drift away from boldness and hope and intensity of faith.[215]

The comment from above, "the mental and spiritual condition common in every age of the Christian church," is the reason, we are going to review what the author of Hebrews wrote, to pull that first Christian congregation out of their spiritual stupor. The first seven years of Christianity, from 29 C.E., when the founder Jesus Christ was baptized, to 36 C.E., when the first Gentile was baptized, the Christian congregation was made up of Jews only. Some of these ones were very slow in getting over that there was a new way to God, through Jesus Christ. It was deeply embedded in their mind and heart that the only way to God for 1,500 years was through the Israelite nation, and the Mosaic Law. The system of worship that they had known throughout their entire life was now replaced with a new one. They had, under the old Jewish system, an extraordinary system of worship, priesthood, regular sacrifices, and a temple in Jerusalem that could be viewed as the ninth wonder of the world. Many Jewish Christians were unable to make the transition, as they walked aimlessly because of an inability to see how the Christian system was better than the Jewish system of the past, failing to getting in the race for life.

Romans 10:4 Updated American Standard Version (UASV)

4 For Christ is the end of the law for righteousness to everyone who believes.

---

[215] W. Robertson Nicoll, The Expositor's Greek New Testament, Volume Four, 236 (Peabody: Hendrickson, 2002).

On Romans 10:4, Kenneth Boa and William Kruidenier, write, "As the **end of the law**. Christ made it possible for **everyone who believes** to attain a righteous standing before God. As the **end** (*telos*) **of the law**. Christ was its fulfillment (Matt. 5:17; Rom. 10:4), not its chronological termination (Rom. 6:15). However, it was his fulfillment of the law's requirements, and his resulting confirmation in righteousness, that cast the law aside as a tormentor of all who bore the guilt of not keeping it."[216]

What about today, with Christians coming out of the world into the Christian congregation, is it not similar? The world is full of wonderment, powerful leaders, exciting innovations, scientific advancements, stimulating opportunities, and it is specifically designed to lure the unsuspecting one into its ways of thinking, and to retain them once they have them, as well as pull them back in if they ever choose to leave. It has generated a generation of **selfish, me-first people** that set aside God's Word, because they develop a wall of disbelief, setting impossible standards for the Bible, while lowering the standards of secularism,[217] which enables them to feel good about being in the world, or returning to the world. Then, there are the Christians who are **halfhearted**, having little enthusiasm, interest, support, or conviction in their worship of God. – Psalm 119:113; Revelation 3:16.

Finally, there are those, who possess "**a double heart**" (Literally "a heart and a heart").[218] (Ps 12:2) In other words, these ones, go to every congregation meeting, are very active in their congregation, and at the same time, they are living a very worldly life outside of the congregation. It might be that they are materialistic, or they are morally unclean (1 Pet 2:12; He 4:13; 1 Cor. 6:9-11), mentally unclean (Phil 4:8; Matt 15:18-20), unclean in speech (Eph. 4:25, 29, 31; 5:3; Rev 21:8), and so on. They may lie, gamble, or steal by cheating on their taxes, or dishonest business practices. (Pro 6:16-19; Cols 3:9, 10) They may have fits of anger, and are abusive to their wife, or children. (Ps 11:5; Proverbs 22:24, 25) They may be heavy drinkers and drunkards, which leads to their household problems. (1 Cor. 5:11-13; 1 Tim. 3:8) These ones are those who are deceptively presenting themselves as one thing to the Christian

---

[216] Kenneth Boa and William Kruidenier, *Romans*, vol. 6, Holman New Testament Commentary (Nashville, TN: Broadman & Holman Publishers, 2000), 309.

[217] Secularism is the rejection of religion or its exclusion from a philosophical or moral system.

[218] Footnote, Lexham English Bible

congregation, while living an entirely different life outside of the congregation. – Matthew 15:7-8.

So again, we revisit Paul's words to this Jewish congregation, "**Therefore**, we must **pay much closer attention** to what we have heard, lest we **drift away** from it." (Heb. 2:1)

Therefore is an adverb that introduces a statement that is a consequence of the previous statement. Chapter 1 of Hebrews was/is about the supremacy of God's Son. Chapter 3 is similarly about Jesus being greater than Moses is while chapter 4 demonstrates that Jesus is a superior high priest than in the Aaronic priesthood, and chapters 5 through 7 cover the superiority of Jesus to Melchizedek.[219] Thus, the "therefore," that begins chapter 2 is expressing that there is a serious need to consider the greatness of Christ, and to learn more about Jesus. However, they needed to **pay much closer attention** to what we have heard, better appreciating the superiority of Jesus, and to negate the impressive Jewish system that had been their way for so long.

The idea of **drifting away** was a reference to ship sailing, which was a common mode of transportation in the first-century C.E. Roman Empire. If the captain of a ship does not keep his mind on the wind and current, he will risk running his ship past a safe harbor and onto rocky seashore. These Jewish Christians needed to pull themselves out of their apathetic stupor. In the same way, if we are not heeding the Word of God, by way of a regular, deep personal Bible study, preparing for our Christians meetings, so as to participate, sharing our faith with others, we too will drift ashore, experiencing spiritual shipwreck. Sadly, some shipwrecks are beyond recovery, and some crashes of one's faith places them beyond repentance. In other words, nothing will ever move them to repent. Just like a captain, who is not paying attention, we may not wake up until it is too late. Thus, let us catch any spiritual stupor before it becomes serious.

An Evil and Unbelieving Heart

Hebrews 3:12-13 Updated American Standard Version (UASV)

[12] Take care, brothers, lest there be in any of you an evil, **heart of unbelief**, leading you to **fall away** from the living God. [13] But exhort

---

[219] A priest and king of Salem who blessed Abraham, and in essence, blessed the Aaronic priesthood that was in his loins.

one another every day, as long as it is called "today," that none of you may be **hardened** by the deceitfulness of sin.

We cannot remain "pure in heart" (Matt 5:8), if we develop an evil **heart of unbelief**. An evil heart of unbelief (*kardia ponera apistias*) is "a remarkable combination. Heart ([kardia]) is common in the LXX[220] (about 1,000 times), but "evil heart" only twice in the O.T. (Jer. 16:12; 18:12). "[Apistias] is more than mere unbelief, here rather disbelief, refusal to believe, genitive case describing the evil heart marked by disbelief which is no mark of intelligence then or now."[221]

What beliefs have the world of mankind spread that would undermine one's faith in God to such an extent? **(1) Evolution** is the theoretical process by which all species develop from earlier forms of life. **(2) Relativism** is the belief that concepts such as right and wrong, goodness and badness, or truth and falsehood are not absolute but change from culture to culture and situation to situation. **(3) Limited inerrancy** as oppose to full inerrancy has caused many to lose their faith. Full inerrancy affirms that the original Scriptures contained no errors at all. Limited inerrancy on the other hand affirms that Scripture is without error in matters of salvation doctrine, but not history, science, or geography. **(4) Secularism** is the rejection of religion or its exclusion from a philosophical or moral system. **(5) Atheism** is disbelief in the existence of God or deities. **(6) Biblical criticism** is known as the historical-critical method of Bible study, such as the study of historical criticism, literary criticism, form criticism, tradition criticism, redaction criticism, structuralist criticism, among others. This is known as the new way of biblical interpretation, and it undermines the trustworthiness of Scripture, a pseudo-scholarship. **(7) Empiricism** is the philosophical belief that all knowledge is derived from the experience of the senses, to the exclusion of revelatory knowledge, such as the Word of God. **(8) Existentialism** is a philosophical movement begun in the 19th century that denies that the universe has any intrinsic meaning or purpose. It requires people to take responsibility for their own actions and shape their own destinies. **(9) Pragmatism** is the position that "those beliefs are true which it is expedient for us to act upon and believe." **(10) Religious Liberalism** is a

---

[220] LXX is the Greek Septuagint, a Greek translation of the Hebrew Bible made between 280 to 150 B.C.E. to meet the needs of Greek-speaking Jews outside Palestine.

[221] A.T. Robertson, Word Pictures in the New Testament, Heb 3:12 (Nashville, TN: Broadman Press, 1933).

movement in Protestantism stressing intellectual freedom and the moral content of Christianity over the doctrines of traditional theology. The abandonment of "the traditional view of authority and truth in order to substitute a newer source of authority, typically based on experience or intellectual conclusions."[222] This list could go on for some time, but I believe you have gotten the point. The Word of God, true Christianity, and truth has been under an ever-greater attack throughout the 20th and into the 21st century, the pinnacle of the enlightenment age that got its start in the late 17th century with René Descartes. We must not let ourselves be caught off guard by such death-dealing beliefs.

What is the result of an unbelieving heart that has been infected with the thinking of man? It leads one to **fall away** (Gr., *apostenai*, "to stand off") from the living God. Just how serious is this? You will notice that earlier, Paul spoke of '**drifting away**' because of not paying attention to one's spiritual needs. (Heb. 2:1; Matt 5:3) However, the Greek term *apostenai* rendered "fall away," which is more of a willful drawing away, means "to stand off" and is related to the word "apostasy." This is standing off from the truth that was once accepted. It signifies a willful and purposeful resisting, withdrawing, and abandoning, with a measure of disdain added. One New Testament word study book offered,

> The word "departing" deserves special attention. It is *aphistemi* which is made up of *apo* "off," and *histemi* "to stand," the compound word meaning "to stand off from." This was exactly the position of these Hebrews. They were standing aloof from the living God. The idea is not that of departing, but of standing off from. Our word "apostasy" is derived from a form of this Greek word. Apostasy is defined as the act of someone who has previously subscribed to a certain belief, and who now renounces his former professed belief in favor of some other, which is diametrically opposed to what he believed before. In other words, his new belief is not merely a new system of faith, but one, which at every point negates his former belief.[223]

As was stated, the **drifting away** of Hebrews 2:1 is the result of being inattentive to one's spiritual needs, and bears repeating. In that

---

[222] Hindson, Ed (2008-05-01). The Popular Encyclopedia of Apologetics (Kindle Locations 11777-11778). Harvest House Publishers. Kindle Edition.

[223] Kenneth S. Wuest, Wuest's Word Studies from the Greek New Testament: For the English Reader, Heb 3:12 (Grand Rapids: Eerdmans, 1997).

circumstance, there is no real effort involved to end up spiritually shipwrecked. However, this **falling away** is the result of someone taking action. This one is willfully "falling away from the living God." Why? Paul gives us the answer, an evil, **heart of unbelief**. This evil heart of unbelief is **not** the result of not being a student of the Bible, nor having sufficient knowledge of Scripture, or even an incorrect understanding of Scripture. Paul goes on to quote the occasion of the Israelites at Exodus 15, which is also referenced at Psalm 95:8, "do not harden your hearts as in the rebellion" at Meribah. The Israelites had enjoyed Jehovah's God's love, protection, and saw his "works for forty years" while in the wilderness. (Heb. 3:7-11) However, these very ones hardened their hearts against him.

In the same sense, Christians today, need to "consider how to stir up one another to love and good works, not neglecting to meet together, as is the habit of some, but encouraging one another" (Heb. 10:24-25), so that "none of you may be **hardened** by the deceitfulness of sin." What we have learned thus far? **(1)** We do not want to neglect personal Bible study. **(2)** We should be well prepared for congregation meetings **(3)** We should have mercy on those who have begun to doubt because they have fed their minds on literature from Bible critics; and we should have the ability to reason from the Scriptures, to help them overcome their doubts. **(4)** In addition, we stir up one another to love and good works, not neglecting to meet together. – Hebrews 10:24-25.

Am I suggesting that Christians should never read a book by a Bible critic? No. However, would you venture into any unsafe place in life without preparing for it first? Let me offer an illustration. A prosecuting attorney goes to the best law school in the US, studies under one of the greatest legal minds, and he may have 30-years of experience. He puts on the state's case, we are mesmerized by his knowledge of the law, the skill with which he presents it, and we find the defendant guilty as we sit in the jury box. However, one thing is missing. What? We have yet to hear the defense attorney. Do we now have blinders to the point that it does not matter? The irony is, once the defense attorney gets up and presents his case, we are so stunned by the evidence that he presents, that we have now completely changed our position.

This is what would happen if we read the Bible critics book first. We would feel that it really cast doubts about the existence of a personal God, who created everything, and that such a being inspires the Bible is no longer true. Then, we read an apologetic Bible scholar's book that deals with the same issues, say that of Dr. William Lane Craig, concluding we did not have all the facts, and now feel saddened because we doubted in the first place. What I recommend is that we read the apologetic Bible scholar's book first, like putting in a bullet proof vest, and then read the Bible critic's book if we so desire.

Do Not Shrink Back to Destruction

Hebrews 10:39 Updated American Standard Version (UASV)

³⁹ But we are not of those who **shrink back** to destruction, but of those who have faith to the preserving of the soul.

Paul closes this section with serious confidence that they "are not of those who **shrink back** and are destroyed." Today, true Christians live in a time like no other, and are under a constant bombardment from the world that surrounds us. Like Paul and the Jewish Christians, who heeded his counsel, we too do not want to shrink back to destruction. This does not mean that we will never have a moment of fear, as we are susceptible to being afraid like any other imperfect human. The Greek *hupostello*, means "'to draw back, withdraw,' perhaps a metaphor from lowering a sail and so slackening the course, and hence of being remiss in holding the truth."[224] A Christian with faith, will not 'draw back or withdraw' from their commitment to God's will and purposes, 'slacking off in their course.' Regardless of what this wicked world, alienated from God throws at them, such as persecution, difficulties, health issues, or any other tribulation. They will face these head on, like the apostle Paul, who said, "For the sake of Christ, then, I am content with weaknesses, insults, hardships, persecutions, and calamities. For when I am weak, then I am strong." (2 Cor. 12:10) Yes, we must be steadfast in our service to God, as he is well aware of our limitations, and he makes allowances for these, "he remembers that we are dust."—Psalm 55:22; 103:14.

Do Not Grow Weary or Fainthearted

Hebrews 12:3 Updated American Standard Version (UASV)

³ For consider the one who endured such hostility by sinners against himself, so that you will not **grow weary** in your souls and give up.

---

[224] W. E. Vine, Merrill F. Unger and William White, Jr., vol. 2, Vine's Complete Expository Dictionary of Old and New Testament Words, 180 (Nashville, TN: T. Nelson, 1996).

What is it that we are not to grow weary or fainthearted from? What is it Satan would love us to get too tired to carry out? The answer is found in verses 1-2.

Hebrews 12:1-2 Updated American Standard Version (UASV)

¹ Therefore, since we have so great a cloud of witnesses surrounding us, let us also lay aside every weight and the sin which so easily entangles us, and let us **run with endurance the race** that is set before us, ² **fixing our eyes on Jesus**, the author and perfecter of faith, who for the joy set before Him endured the cross, despising the shame, and has sat down at the right hand of the throne of God.

Have you bought out the time to know why Jesus ever came to earth as a man in the first place? First, we can say that the Gospels are of his life and ministry. From this you can see that his focus was on his ministry. Jesus came to earth as a man for three reasons. **(1)** Jesus said, "For this purpose I was born and for this purpose I have come into the world—to bear witness to the truth." (John 18:37) **(2)** Peter said this to Christians, "For to this you have been called, because Christ also suffered for you, leaving you an example, so that you might follow in his steps." (1 Pet. 2:21) **(3)** Jesus tells us this, "even as the Son of Man came not to be served but to serve, and to give his life as a ransom for many." (Matt. 20:28) Jesus came to leave us an example, for us to follow in his steps, which example is his ministry that he carried out to the Jews of his day, and we are to carry out to all people. (Matt. 28:19-20) The sad irony, there are really no churches within the 39,000 denominations that I am aware of based on my personal statistical surveys, which have even begun to carry out a similar message to the nations, so there is no real reason to be tired out from this work. Oh yes, they send out missionaries here and there, but the truth is, **all Christians** are responsible for preaching, teaching and making disciples. With or without the church, we need to make progress toward maturity and improve our ministry (evangelistic) skills, so as to carry out the Great Commission we were given.

Review Questions

- Jesus said, "The one who **endures to the end**, he will be saved." What did he mean by endure?

- Why is it paramount that Christians have endurance?

- Explain what Paul meant by "pay much closer attention to the things that have been heard."

- How can Christians develop an evil unbelieving heart?
- How can Christians shrink back to destruction?
- How can Christians grow weary and fainthearted?

CHAPTER 18 You Must Walk in the Light

1 John 1:5-7 Updated American Standard Version (UASV)

⁵ This is the message we have heard from him and proclaim to you, that God is light, and there is no darkness at all in him. **⁶** If we say we have fellowship with him and yet we are **walking in the darkness**, we are lying and are not practicing the truth; **⁷** but if **we are walking in the light**, as he is in the light, we have fellowship with one another, and the blood of Jesus his Son cleanses us from all sin.

First, it should be noted that John's statement that "the blood of Jesus his Son cleanses us from all sin," does not mean that we are able to go without sinning, or that our sinful nature is miraculously removed. Rather, John meant that the blood of Jesus cleanses from "every kind of sin and shows there is no limit to the categories of sin that Christ is willing to forgive. His sacrificial death made every type of sin forgivable." (Larson 2000, p. 158)

The ultimate Source of life (genuine and ultimate life, i.e., eternal life.) is the Father, who has 'given all authority in heaven and on earth to the Son.' (Matt. 28:20) Therefore, Jesus is the source of eternal life to humans as well. The prophet Daniel foretold that 'Jesus would be given authority to rule, and glory, and a kingdom; so that those of every people, nation, and language should serve him.' (Dan. 9:7) Jesus himself specifically said, "All things have been handed over to me by my Father." (Matt. 11:27, ESV) On another occasion Jesus said, "The Father loves the Son and has given all things into his hand." (John 3:35, ESV) Paul wrote, "For "he [God] subjected all things under his [Jesus'] feet." But when it says "all things" are subjected, it is clear that the one [God] who subjected all things to him [Jesus] is not included." Our point is made by Jesus prayerful words to the Father in John 17:1-3 (ESV), "**Father**, the hour has come; **glorify your Son** that the Son may glorify you, since you have **given him authority over all** flesh, <u>to give eternal life</u> **to all whom you have given** him. And this is eternal life, that they know you the only true God, and Jesus Christ whom you have sent." Thus, the Father has given all authority in heaven and on earth to the Son, to give eternal life to all that the Father had placed in his hands. Thus, Jesus is the source of eternal life by way of the Father giving him all authority.

Passed from Death to Life

John 5:24 Updated American Standard Version (ASV)

²⁴ Truly, truly, I say to you, whoever hears my word and believes him who sent me has eternal life. He does not come into judgment, but has **passed from death to life**.

1 John 3:14 Updated American Standard Version (UASV)

¹⁴ We know that we have **passed over from death to life** because we love the brothers. The one who does not love remains in death.

Here at John 5:24, Jesus is speaking about those who are truly Christian. These ones were once spiritually dead. However, upon hearing Jesus' words and having faith in him, these ones are no longer walking in the darkness (practicing sin). They '**passed from death to life**' in that their being condemned to death has been removed from them, and they are given the hope of eternal life because of their faith in Jesus Christ.

Commenting on 1 John 3:14, David Walls and Max Anders say, "True Christians, those born of God, have love for their brothers placed in their hearts by the Lord, so that we **know that we have passed from death to life, because we love our brothers.** Loving our brothers does not give us eternal life. God does that through Christ. If we have eternal life, we will manifest it by loving our brothers. We may have difficulty loving some Christians who make it hard to love them, but a fundamental desire to love them will show through our lives. Even Jesus' disciples quarreled among themselves about who would be the greatest among them. That was an unloving thing to do. It did not, however, relegate them to the realm of the unsaved." (Walls and Anders 1996, p. 197)

Those who are truly Christian are grateful for the Father, the Source of genuine and ultimate life, namely, eternal life, as well as his having 'given the Son all authority in heaven and on earth to the Son.' What does it mean to be *walking in the darkness* and *walking in the light*? It seems that John's primary focus was on the consequences of walking in the darkness as opposed to walking in the light rather than explicitly explaining what he meant by these words. However, we can look to the Gospel of John, where he offers us the best definition,

John 3:19-21 Updated American Standard Version (UASV)

19 And this is the judgment: that the light has come into the world, and men loved the darkness rather than the light, because their works were wicked. **20** For the one who practices wicked things hates the light and does not come to the light, so that his works may not be exposed. **21** But the one who practices the truth comes to the light, in order that his works may be revealed that they are accomplished in God.

One of the themes in The First Epistle of John is the contrast between the one who is practicing sin[225] (walking in the darkness) and the one who is **not** practicing sin (walking in the light). However, even the one not practicing sin may commit a sin because of human imperfection. Nevertheless, he has the ransom sacrifice of Christ to cover over the sin. The apostle Paul tells us in the book of Hebrews, "For if we go on sinning deliberately [walking in darkness] after receiving the accurate knowledge[226] of the truth, there no longer remains a sacrifice for sins [Jesus' ransom sacrifice that covers sin]." (Heb. 10:26) Thus, 'walking in the darkness' involves living in sin unrepentant, while 'walking in the light' involves being declared righteous before God even though a sinner, who sins, but only due to human weaknesses and no serious sins. If he does commit a serious sin, he will be forgiven if he is repentant; thus, Jesus ransom sacrifice will cover that sin. Thus, as we look at the first two chapters, verse-by-verse of John's first epistle, be sure to read the Scriptures as well.

Word of Life

1 John 1:1-4 Updated American Standard Version (UASV)

1 What was from the beginning, what we have heard, what we have seen with our eyes, what we have looked at and touched with our hands, concerning the Word of Life— **2** the life was made manifest, and we have seen it, and testify to it and proclaim to you the eternal life, which was with the Father and was made manifest to us— **3** that which we have seen and heard we proclaim also to you, so that you too may have fellowship[227] with us; and indeed our fellowship is with the Father and

---

[225] I.e., living in sin

[226] See Romans 3:20 ftn.

[227] Or *a sharing*

with his Son Jesus Christ. [4] And we are writing these things so that our joy may be complete.

John is writing this first letter, sharing the joy that he and other Christians have found in their "fellowship is with the Father and with his Son Jesus Christ." Jesus is "the Word of Life." He was with the Father "in the beginning," wherein he created all things, "in heaven and on earth, visible and invisible." (John 1:1-3; Col. 1:15-16) There were apostates at the time of John's letter, who were rejecting the divinity of Jesus Christ and claiming to be sinless. However, John was one of the main apostles; the one Jesus had loved very much, who spent three and half years traveling with Jesus, saw his execution, resurrection, and ascension. John knew that the Father had "given all authority in heaven and on earth" to the Son. Thousands witnessed the life and ministry of Jesus Christ. Jesus is "the Word of Life" because "the free gift of God is eternal life in Christ Jesus our Lord," "who abolished death and brought life." – Romans 6:23; 2 Timothy 1:9-10.

The apostles and other New Testament authors 'proclaimed' that Jesus Christ was sinless, perfect, and divine. John shared these things so that other true Christians 'may also have fellowship with him and other Christians, and indeed their fellowship was with the Father and with his Son Jesus Christ.' (Ps. 133:1-3; John 17:20-21) An apostate is one who not only stands of from the truth, but also turns against those who are truly Christian. Some of these apostates actually believe that they are doing the will of the Father and that they still have a righteous standing before God. They are blinded by their self-righteousness and lack of humility. Other apostates have simply abandoned everything and do not even desire fellowship with the Father and the Son. However, they like the former spend their time attacking their former brothers and sisters.

God Is Light

1 John 1:5-7 Updated American Standard Version (UASV)

[5] This is the message we have heard from him and proclaim to you, that **God is light**, and there is no darkness at all in him. [6] If we say we have fellowship with him and yet we are **walking in the darkness**, we are lying and are not practicing the truth; [7] but if **we are walking in the light**, as he is in the light, we have fellowship with one another, and the blood of Jesus his Son cleanses us from all sin.

John's "message" is what the apostles heard from Jesus. It is "**God is light**,"[228] and there is no darkness at all [nothing unholy, immoral, untrue, or wicked] in him." Therefore, all who are truly Christian will recoil from and turn away from the practice of sin, namely, living in sin.[229] Since certain apostate Christians that accept things like homosexuality being just an alternative lifestyle, which they say God accepts while they are imperfect, these ones do not believe that their works are sinful; therefore, they walk in darkness. They claim to have the true knowledge of Scripture and in John's day, they claimed to have some secret knowledge. However, being that "God is light," hos Word makes known **the truth**. – Matthew 5:14-16; 1 Peter 2:9.

If we believe that we have a part in the fellowship with the Father and the Son but we are **walking in the darkness**, living in sin, "we are lying and are not practicing the truth." However, if are following a life course outlined by an accurate understanding of God's Word, we are **walking in the light**, as God is light. We have "fellowship with [fellow Christians]; and indeed our fellowship is with the Father and with his Son Jesus Christ." This fellowship means that we are one in the biblical truths, our biblical worldview, making disciples, as well as other facets of our pure worship.

Distinct from the apostates, those who are truly Christian, walking in the light, accept that everything that Bible outlines as sin, in fact, in addition to anything similar to those things, which may not be explicitly mentioned. For example, if Paul exhorted the Ephesian Christians, not to be getting drunk with wine (5:18), it would also apply to getting drunk with whiskey that would not have been available in Paul's day. Again, when John says that the blood of Jesus "cleanses us from all sin," he

---

[228] "**God is light**. In Scripture, light and darkness are very familiar symbols. Intellectually, light refers to biblical truth, while darkness refers to error or falsehood (cf. Ps. 119:105; Prov. 6:23; John 1:4; 8:12). Morally, light refers to holiness or purity, while darkness refers to sin or wrongdoing (Rom. 13:11–14; 1 Thess. 5:4–7). The heretics claimed to be the truly enlightened, walking in the real light, but John denied that because they do not recognize their sin. About that basic reality, they were unenlightened. no darkness at all. With this phrase, John forcefully affirms that God is absolutely perfect and nothing exists in God's character that impinges upon His truth and holiness (cf. James 1:17)." – MacArthur, John (2005-05-09). *The MacArthur Bible Commentary* (Kindle Locations 65146-65152). Thomas Nelson. Kindle Edition.

[229] See Job 24:14-16; John 3:19-21; Romans 13:11-14; 2 Corinthians 6:14; 1 Thessalonians 5:6-9

means every kind of sin. He does not mean the practice of sin. Jesus blood covers Adamic sin, inherited sin, sin from our human weaknesses, but it does not cover living in sin unrepentantly. We are extremely grateful that God make allowances for our imperfection, showing mercy on sinners, who are walking in the light. – Psalm 103:8-14; Micah 7:18-19.

Fellowship with God and the Propitiatory Sacrifice

1 John 1:8-2:2 Updated American Standard Version (UASV)

[8] If we say we have no sin, we deceive ourselves, and us. [9] If we confess our sins, he is faithful and just to forgive us our sins and to cleanse us from all unrighteousness. [10] If we say we have not sinned, we make him a liar, and his word is not in us.

2 My little children, I am writing these things to you so that you may not commit a sin.[230] But if anyone does sin, we have an advocate with the Father, Jesus Christ the righteous one; [2] and he is the propitiation[231] for our sins, and not for ours only but also for the sins of the whole world.

The apostle John informs his readers as to what is needed to be cleansed from sin. This author has had some very long conversations with a person, who claims that Jesus ransom sacrifice has perfected Christians and that they are without sin and can go without sinning. This is absolutely contrary to Scripture and no more so than right here. His claiming to me "he is without sin," is his rejecting the fact that all humans are imperfect and sinful, and "the truth is not in" him. (See 1 Ki 8:46; Eccles. 7:20; Psa. 51:5; Pro. 20:9; Rom. 3:23; 5:12) If he would 'confess his sin, God would be "faith" and 'forgive him of his sins and to cleanse us from all unrighteousness,' and the same holds true for all of us. However, we must have a repentant attitude, which would move us to turn around from and reject wrongdoing. (Pro. 28:13) Of those who are truly Christian, God says, "I will remember their sin no more." (Jer. 31:31-34; Heb. 8:7-12) As to our being forgiven, God is faithful to every promise he makes.

---

[230] Gr., *hamartete*, a verb in the aorist subjunctive. According to *A Grammar of New Testament Greek*, by James H. Moulton, Vol. I, 1908, p. 109, "the Aorist has a 'punctiliar' action, that is, it regards action as a *point*: it represents the point of entrance . . . or that of completion . . . or it looks at a whole action simply as having occurred, without distinguishing any steps in its progress."

[231] Or *an atoning sacrifice*; *a means of appeasement*

In addition, God is "righteous," at all times adhering to his **standards of justice**. A ransom is a sum of money or a price demanded or paid to secure the freedom of a slave. The basic idea of "ransom" is the act of saving somebody from an oppressed condition or dangerous situation through self-sacrifice, such as a price that *covers* or satisfies justice, while the term "redemption" is the *deliverance* that results from the ransom. In the biblical instance, "redemption" would be the *deliverance* from Adamic sin (the sins of humanity) by the ransom death of Jesus Christ for many.

Hebrew terms (*kāpar, koper, pādâ, gāʾal*), as well as a number of Greek terms (*lytron, antilytron, lytroo, agorazo*), which are translated "ransom and "redeem." They all carry the idea of a price being given or paid to result in a ransom or redemption. In these, there is the sense of an equal or corresponding, that is, a substitution is common in all of these terms. In other words, the ransom sacrifice of Jesus Christ, for example, was given for Adam, which **satisfied justice** and set matters straight between God and man.

Jesus' perfect human life was given as a price to **satisfy justice** and redeem humankind from sin and death. Paul tells us that we "were bought with a price." (1 Cor. 6:20; 7:23) Paul often begins his letters "Paul, a slave of Christ Jesus," as Jesus bought us from Satan the Devil, from condemnation and death, as Peter states, Jesus is the "the Master who bought" us. (Rom. 1:1; 2 Pet. 2.1) Jesus was 'slain, and by his blood he ransomed [bought] people for God from every tribe and language and people and nation.' (Rev. 5:9, ESV) Thus, this was a means for God's principal attribute **justice to be satisfied**.

These ones standing off from the truth, say, "we have not sinned," which then 'makes God a liar.' However, 'God cannot lie.' His Word tells us "there is not a righteous man on earth who does good and never sins" (Eccles. 7:20, ESV), "for all have sinned and fall short of the glory of God." (Rom 3:23, ESV) For any, who claim that 'they have not sinned,' this would mean that 'God's his word is not in them.' For those who are truly Christian, 'God has put his laws into their minds, and has written them on their hearts, as he is their God, and they are his people.' – Hebrews 8:10.

John's purpose in penning this letter about sin, forgiveness, and 'cleansing us from all unrighteousness,' is so that his readers may go without practicing sin. While we cannot go without sinning entirely, we can go without living in sin and committing serious sins. (1 Cor. 15:34) Nevertheless, when we do commit "a sin" and are truly repentant, "we have an advocate with the Father, Jesus Christ the righteous one," who pleads with the Father on our behalf. (Heb. 7:26; See John 17:9, 15, 20) Jesus is the propitiation (an atoning sacrifice; a means of appeasement) for our sins. Jesus death satisfied justice, which allowed God to extend mercy and remove Adamic sin for those who are truly Christian. Paul wrote, "For the wages of sin is death, but the free gift of God is eternal life in Christ Jesus our Lord." – Romans 6:23, ESV.

Observing God's Commandments

1 John 2:3-6 Updated American Standard Version (UASV)

³ And by this we know that we have come to know him, if we keep his commandments. ⁴ The one who says, "I have come to know him," and does not keep his commandments, is a liar, and the truth is not in him; ⁵ but whoever keeps his word, truly in this one the love of God has been perfected. By this we know that we are in him: ⁶ the one who says he remains in him ought himself to walk in the same manner as he walked.

If we are to continue our "walking in the light," we must "keep his commandments." Each one of us are responsible for having to 'come to know God,' correctly understanding his qualities and attributes, but also his will and purposes and his commandments. (Matt. 7:21-23) If we claim to know God and at the same time has failed to obey him, he "is a liar." The 'love of God has perfected us,' i.e., made us complete, but only if we obey God's Word. It is by this obedience that 'we know we are in him.' Each of us is obligated to 'walk in the same manner as Jesus walked.' This walking as Jesus did would include our carrying out the commission of proclaiming the Word of God, teaching it, to the point of making disciples. – Matthew 24:14; 28:19-20; Acts 1:8.

The Old and New Commandment

1 John 2:7-8 Updated American Standard Version (UASV)

⁷ Beloved ones, I am writing you, not a new commandment, but an old commandment that you have had from the beginning; the old commandment is the word that you heard. ⁸ Again, I am writing you a new commandment, which is true in him and in you, because the darkness is passing away and the true light is already shining.

John is writing 'an old commandment that his readers in 98 C.E. have had from the beginning of when they became Christians. It is "old" because Jesus gave this command fifty-five years earlier, Nisan 14, 33 C.E., when Jesus was foretelling of Peter's denial and how the disciples would abandon in his hour of need. Jesus said, "A new commandment I give to you, that you **love one another**: just as I have loved you, you also are to love one another." It was "new" command in that it went beyond the neighborly love commanded under the Mosaic Law, but now their love required that they be willing to give their life in behalf of their brothers and sisters. (Lev. 19:18; John 15:12-13) It is by this level of self-sacrificing love that Christ had and we now have that we are in alignment with this new "commandment." Thus, for us, "the darkness is passing away and the true light is already shining."

1 John 2:9-11 Updated American Standard Version (UASV)

⁹ The one who says he is in the light and hates his brother is in the darkness until now. ¹⁰ The one who loves his brother remains in the light and there is no cause for stumbling in him. ¹¹ But the one who hates his brother is in the darkness and walks in the darkness, and does not know where he is going because the darkness has blinded his eyes.

Are we truly in the light? If we say that we are "in the light" and yet, 'we hate our brother,' we are really "in the darkness until now." However, if we love our brother, we remain in the light, and for us "there is no cause for stumbling." The Greek term here, (*skandalon*) originally was "the name of the part of a trap to which the bait is attached, hence, the trap or snare itself." Thus, it is used in "1 John 2:10, "occasion of stumbling," of the absence of this in the case of one who loves his brother and thereby abides in the light. Love, then, is the best safeguard against the woes pronounced by the Lord upon those who cause others to stumble.²³² On this, the Greek-English Lexicon has "**that which causes offense or revulsion and results in opposition, disapproval, or hostility, *fault, stain*** etc.²³³ In other words, something that can contribute to one falling into sin. One who claims to be Christian and at the same time hates his brother "does not know where he is going

---

²³² W. E. Vine, Merrill F. Unger, and William White Jr., *Vine's Complete Expository Dictionary of Old and New Testament Words* (Nashville, TN: T. Nelson, 1996), 441.

²³³ William Arndt, Frederick W. Danker, and Walter Bauer, *A Greek-English Lexicon of the New Testament and Other Early Christian Literature* (Chicago: University of Chicago Press, 2000), 926.

because the darkness has blinded his eyes." (See Matthew 12:35-36) If we heed this warning, we can avoid 'walking in the darkness' by not letting any personal differences get out of control, nor heeding the lies of any who are speaking against the truth, or allow anything to hinder our brotherly love.

Reasons for Writing

1 John 2:12-14 Updated American Standard Version (UASV)

¹² I am writing you, little children, because your sins have been forgiven you for the sake of his name. ¹³ I am writing to you, fathers, because you know him who has been from the beginning. I am writing to you, young men, because you have overcome the evil one. I have written to you, children, because you know the Father. ¹⁴ I have written to you, fathers, because you know Him who has been from the beginning. I have written to you, young men, because you are strong, and the word of God remains in you, and you have overcome the evil one.

Here John explains to the "little Children" (i.e., the congregation) why we can have confidence. We can have our sins forgiven 'for the sake of the name of Jesus Christ,' for it is his name alone, by which, we may gain salvation. (Acts 4:12) Those who are truly Christians "know the Father" because they have been begotten by the Holy Spirit (a spiritual rebirth because we were spiritually dead). We see the indwelling of the Holy Spirit as Christians taking the words and ideas of Scripture into our mind and drawing spiritual strength from them. The Spirit moves persons toward salvation, but the Spirit does that, in the same way, any person moves another, by persuasion with words and ideas, i.e., through the Word of God. The "fathers that John addresses, "[knew Jesus] who has been from the beginning," were likely older ones in the congregation, who had more experience and were more mature spiritually.

This would mean, the "young men" were ones who had less experience and were less mature spiritually, yet they "had overcome the evil one." These young ones were not taken advantage by Satan, for they were not ignorant of his schemes. (2 Cor. 2:11) Young ones today should not be ignorant of Satan's schemes either. Satan has set up the world so that it caters to the fallen human flesh. For example, we have unclean entertainment in very large and excessive amounts. Young ones face music that is sensual and some music that is demonic. The internet is filled with pornographic websites. The latest fad is TV shows that portray young vampires, witches and werewolves as some romantic drama while they carry out murder, black magic, and demonic control. Other TV series have two lesbian mothers over a family of dysfunctional children. The ABC Family channel was one of the biggest offenders of using entertainment to desensitize our young ones into accepting unnatural desires and behaviors as just an alternative lifestyle, which is supposed to be accepted. All of these things can and do erode the Christian mind until it is at odds with the Word of God. To the young, the Bible becomes, a book that is outdated, and the Christian parents are viewed as just not understanding. However, those young ones who are truly Christian will also be victorious over Satan's schemes because they have used the Word of God, family, and the congregation to become spiritually healthy. As John said, "the word of God remains in you, and you have overcome the evil one." The Word of God will help us with any spiritual struggles that we may be facing. Thus, we want to do the same, taking advantage of Bible study tools, rejecting the words of opposers, and actually walking in the light.

A Love We Must Avoid

1 John 2:15-17 Updated American Standard Version (UASV)

¹⁵ Do not love the world or the things in the world. If anyone loves the world, the love of the Father is not in him. ¹⁶ For all that is in the world, the lust of the flesh and the lust of the eyes and the boastful pride of life, is not from the Father, but is from the world. ¹⁷ The world is passing away, and its lusts; but the one who does the will of God remains forever.

It does not matter our age when it comes to the love that we must avoid. John says, "Do not love the world or the things in the world." Satan is the god of this world at present. (2 Cor. 4:3-4) We need 'to keep ourselves unstained from the world,' because "friendship with the world is enmity with God." (Jam. 1:27; 4:4) At one time, "were dead in the trespasses and sins 2 in which you once walked, following the course of this world, following the prince of the power of the air, the spirit that is now at work in the sons of disobedience." (Eph. 2:1-2, ESV) If we had, the mindset or worldview like those alienated from God, or the imitation Christians, 'the love of the Father would not be in us.' Thus, we certainly need to pray on this matter.

"For all that is in the world" has nothing to do with God, or his original purpose for the earth and humans. This definitely includes "the lust of the flesh," which includes unnatural or inappropriate sexual desires.

(1 Cor. 6:15-20; Gal. 5:19-21) In addition, we want to avoid "the lust of the eyes." The tree of knowledge in the Garden of Eden had been there for some time and Eve was not tempted by it until Satan put tempting thoughts in her mind. Then, notice how she viewed the tree, "the woman saw that the tree was good for food, and that it was a delight to the eyes, and that the tree was to be desired." (Gen 3:6, ESV) The tree was no different from any of the hundreds of thousands of other fruit trees, until Satan made it something that it was not. Then, there was King David watching Bathsheba take baths from his rooftop, who failed to turn away and dismiss the thoughts, which ended up leading to his committing the serious sin of adultery and murder of her husband. (2 Sam. 11:2-17) If we are to continue our walking in the light, we must avoid taking anything into our mind that is morally corrupt. – Proverbs 2:10-22; 4:20-27.

John also spoke of "the boastful pride of life," which is also of this fallen world under satanic influence. One who is proud will boast of his wealth, possessions like house(s), car, clothes, and the like, all of which can go as quickly as it came and has no real lasting fallen when set beside eternal life. This one is seeking praise from people, which he may get, but he has no divine praise. – Matthew 6:2, 5, 16, 19-21; James 4:16.

For those who are truly Christian, they keep their eye on the fact that "the world is passing away" (i.e., the wickedness in the world) and those not walking in the light will be destroyed. Yes, the one doing the will of the Father will remain forever. – Matthew 7:21-23; Titus 2:11-14.

Guard Against Anyone In Opposition to the Truth

1 John 2:18-19 Updated American Standard Version (UASV)

[18] Little children, it is the last hour; and just as you heard that antichrist is coming, even now many antichrists have arisen; whereby we know that it is the last hour. [19] They went out from us, but they were not of us; for if they had been of us, they would have continued with us; but they went out, so that they would be revealed that they all are not of us.

We can define antichrist as anyone, any group, any organization, or any government that is *against* or *instead of* Christ, or who mistreat his people. Thus, we are not just looking for one person, one group, one organization, or one power. The Bible does not refer to just one antichrist.

We notice from 1 John 2:18 that it is "the last hour." It is the last hour, because John is almost one hundred years old, and he is the last of the twelve apostles, of the apostolic period, who could protect the Christians from the great apostasy that was coming. We also notice that John says there are "many antichrists." John refers to these collectively as "the antichrist" here in 2 John 1:7. Should Christians be looking for some future time, to identify some specific antichrist? First John was written in the last years of the first century, about 98 C.E., and yet John says that there were antichrists already in the world during his day. It is the signs of antichrists in John's day, which let him, know it was the last hour. What characteristics do the antichrists have?

Psalm 2:2 American Standard Version (ASV)

² The kings of the earth take their stand

The kings of the earth take their stand,
    and the rulers take counsel together,
    against Jehovah and against his anointed one [Messiah, or Christ, saying,

Matthew 24:24 Updated American Standard Version (UASV)

²⁴ For **false Christs** and false prophets will arise and will show great signs and wonders, so as to mislead, if possible, even the chosen ones.

1 John 2:22 Updated American Standard Version (UASV)

²² Who is the liar but the one who denies that Jesus is the Christ? This is **the antichrist**, even the one who denies the Father and the Son.

1 John 4:3 Updated American Standard Version (UASV)

³ and every spirit that does not confess Jesus is not from God; this is the spirit of the antichrist, of which you have heard that it is coming, and now it is **in the world already**.

2 John 1:7 Updated American Standard Version (UASV)

⁷ For **many deceivers** have gone out into the world, even those who do not confess the coming of Jesus Christ in the flesh. This is the deceiver and **the antichrist**.

Thus, it would be any person, group, organization, or power, who

- The antichrist denies that Jesus is the Christ,
- The antichrist denies the Father and the Son,

- Some of the antichrist have abandoned the Christian faith, and thereafter work in opposition to Christ,

- The antichrist is anti-Christian

In our main text 1 John 2:18-19, John is reminding his readers that the apostles had warned them that the antichrist is coming. The appearance of many antichrists at the end of the first-century and just before the death of the last apostle was evidence it was the last hour, the close of the apostolic period. The ones who are against Christ are a composite antichrist, just as we showed the man of lawlessness is a composite. The composite antichrist is made up of different ones who pretend to be worshipers of God, but as John said, "They went out from us, but they were not of us," as they abandoned the truth. We are not distraught over the loss of these ones, as their removing themselves or being removed from those that are truly Christian, serves as a protection of the congregation.

1 John 2:20-21 Updated American Standard Version (UASV)

²⁰ But you have been anointed by the Holy One, and you all have knowledge. ²¹ I have not written to you because you do not know the truth, but because you do know it, and because no lie is of the truth.

Those who are truly Christian 'have been anointed by the Holy One, and they all have knowledge about those who would be against Christ and his people. They have bought out the time to understand the Word of God correctly, knowing the truth as it relation to Jesus Christ. The apostates, on the other hand, have incorrect views of Christ. We know that "no lie is of the truth," all who love the Father and obey his Word reject views that are biblically **un**true and those presenting them.

1 John 2:22-25 Updated American Standard Version (UASV)

²² Who is the liar but the one who denies that Jesus is the Christ? This is the antichrist, even the one who denies the Father and the Son. ²³ Everyone who denies the Son does not have the Father; the one who confesses the Son has the Father also. ²⁴ As for you, let that remain in you which you heard from the beginning. If what you heard from the beginning remains in you, you also will remain in the Son and in the Father. ²⁵ And this is the promise which he himself promised us: eternal life.

In the end, "who is the liar but the one who denies that Jesus is the Christ," the Father's Anointed One?

As we have learned, anyone denying the Father and the Son is the antichrist. When these ones deny the truth of God's Word, we should not even associate with them, nor use them as a source on other biblical topics that they may have correct. If a Bible scholar quotes another Bible scholar as a source, when this scholar has repeatedly published material that questions full or absolute inerrancy of Scripture, it only serves to give this pseudo-scholar validity and credibility. Yes, some scholars such as agnostic Dr. Bart D. Ehrman are prominent New Testament professors in leading universities, working in a major field like New Testament textual criticism, but they should be shunned as an enemy of Christ. When you coauthor books with such ones, it gives unsuspecting Christians the beliefs that it is safe to read their books. No to mention, do we really want to coauthor a book with the antichrist?

Only true Christians "honor the Son, just as they honor the Father. Whoever does not honor the Son does not honor the Father who sent him." (John 5:23)[234] So, if we correctly 'acknowledge Jesus before men, he also will acknowledge us before my Father who is in heaven, but the apostates who deny Jesus before men, he also will deny them before his Father who is in heaven.' (Matt. 10:32-33) The first century Christians clung to what they had heard about the Son of the Father "from the beginning" of their Christian lives. If we truly 'know the only, true God, and Jesus Christ whom the Father sent, we can look forward to eternal life.' – John 17:3

Taught by God

1 John 2:26-29 Updated American Standard Version (UASV)

26 These things I have written to you concerning the ones who are trying to deceive you. **27** As for you, the anointing which you received from him remains in you, and you have no need for anyone to teach you; but as his anointing teaches you about all things, and is true and is not a lie, and just as it has taught you, you remain in him.

---

[234] Kenneth O. Gangel writes, "Anyone who does not recognize that authority in the Son has denied the authority of the Father—the very authority to give life. The phrase who sent him at the end of verse 23 is used by the Lord only of the Father" (4:34; 5:24, 30; 6:38–39; 7:16, 28, 33; 8:26, 29; 9:4; 12:44–45; 13:20; 15:21; 16:5). (K. O. Gangel 2000, p. 102)

28 And now, little children, remain in him, so that when He appears we may have confidence[235] and not be ashamed before him at his coming. **29** If you know that he is righteous, you also know that everyone who practices righteousness has been born from him.

If we are going to continue our walking in the light and not be fooled by apostates, we need to have an accurate knowledge of God's Word. Sadly, the spark of interest that was at the beginning of our walking with God grew stagnant for many, meaning that their spiritual growth died out. They had deceived themselves that they were healed from the old person, and so they grew apathetic in their prayer, personal Bible study and their application of what they were learning, as well as their Christian meeting attendance. In time, they suffered a relapse into the old person they were. In some case, they became more spiritually sick than they had been. They opened themselves up to the wiles of Satan and his demons, which are very eager to take advantage of their missteps. This should concern every one of us as we walk with God throughout this evil age we live in, as it is a battle between the light and the darkness.

The Holy Bible that we have is the inspired, inerrant Word of God, and is compared to "eye salve to anoint your eyes so that you may see." (Rev 3:18) This likely reminds of Jesus applied spit that he had mixed with dirt when he miraculously healed a blind man. (John 9:1–12). At that time, he told his opponents, "If you were blind, you would have no sin; but since you say, 'We see,' your sin remains." (John 9:41) Are we going to be like the Laodicean church, believing that we have spiritual insight, if we are spiritually weak or have grown spiritually weak? Alternatively, we could recognize our spiritual apathy, 'so that we may be filled with the knowledge of his will in all spiritual wisdom and understanding.' (Col. 1:9) Jesus prayed to the Father, "Sanctify them in the truth; your word is truth." (John 17:17) Jesus had told the Samaritan woman at the well, "true worshipers will worship the Father in spirit and truth, for the Father is seeking such people to worship him." – John 4:23.

"So God created man in his own image, in the image of God he created him; male and female he created them." (Gen. 1:27) While we are imperfect, we still reflect the qualities of God, such as wisdom, love and justice. Unlike the animals, we have the mental powers and ability to reason, which enables us to see the significance of our Creator's qualities that we too possess in a small measure and are able to use for our own

---

[235] Gr., *parresia*; Lit., "freedom of speech" "outspokenness"

good. The Scriptures describe the mental powers and ability to reason by the use of the words *mind* and *conscience*.

Having the Right Mind

The *mind* is the center of consciousness that generates thoughts, feelings, ideas, and perceptions, and stores knowledge and memories. It gives us the capacity to think, understand, and reason. It also gives us concentration, or the ability to concentrate. The Bible uses the term mind in several different ways. One such way the Bible uses the term *mind* is that of taking in knowledge, with the capacity to think, understand, and reason, helping us to arrive at certain conclusions. For example, one might say when studying this book, 'I am trying to keep my mind on You Must Love the Lord chapter.' What would we mean by that statement? We would mean that we are trying to keep our minds alert, concentrating, and observant to take in all the information contained therein. This **thought** process is the activity of thinking, i.e., ideas, plans, conceptions, or beliefs produced by the **mental activity**. In speaking of the Bereans, Paul said, "Now these Jews were more noble than those in Thessalonica; they received the word with all eagerness [Gr., *prothumias*, **readiness of mind**],[236] examining the Scriptures daily to see if these things were so." Simon J. Kistemaker in *Exposition of the Acts of the Apostles* writes,

> The reason for the openness of the Bereans lies in their receptivity to and love for God's Word. For them, the Scriptures are much more than a written scroll or book that conveys a divine message. They use the Old Testament as the touchstone of truth, so that when Paul proclaims the gospel they immediately go to God's written Word for verification. They do so, Luke adds, with great eagerness. Note well, the adjective *great* indicates that they treasure the Word of God. Luke ascribes the same diligence to the Bereans as Peter does to the Old Testament prophets, who intently and diligently searched the Word and inquired into its meaning (1 Peter 1:10).

---

[236] W. E. Vine, Merrill F. Unger, and William White Jr., *Vine's Complete Expository Dictionary of Old and New Testament Words* (Nashville, TN: T. Nelson, 1996), 508.

The Bereans open the Scriptures and with ready minds learn that Jesus has fulfilled the messianic prophecies.[237]

Another such way that the Bible uses the term *mind* is the ability store the knowledge we have taken in and reasoned upon in our memories. For example, when we such things as, "I will keep that in mind," which means that we will store them in our memory, for future recall. The apostle Paul wrote to Titus saying, "Remind them to be submissive to rulers and authorities, to be obedient, to be ready for every good work." This ability is yet another way that we are made in the image of God, as Jeremiah tells his readers,

Jeremiah 44:21 Updated American Standard Version (UASV)

21 "As for the smoking sacrifices that you burned in the cities of Judah and in the streets of Jerusalem, you and your forefathers, your kings and your princes, and the people of the land, did not Jehovah **remember** them and did not *all this* **come into his mind**?

Within our *mind* is the capacity to think, understand, and reason about the knowledge (i.e., information in mind) which we have acquired, enabling us to make decisions. It depends on the information taken in, as to whether our decision will be wise or unwise. Paul exhorted the Corinthians that they "all agree and that there be no divisions among you, but that you be made complete in the same mind and in the same judgment." (1 Cor. 1:10)[238] In other words, they were to come to the same biblical truths. Paul told the Romans, "For those who live according to the flesh set their minds on the things of the flesh, but those who live according to the Spirit set their minds on the things of the Spirit." (Rom 8:5) Those in the world, who are alienated from God, but who still have a measure of *conscience*, which can determine right from wrong, entertain wrong thinking on the fallen flesh, awakening wrong desires, which affects their course of action. If they entertain wrong thinking and follow

---

[237] http://biblia.com/books/bkrc-ac/Page.p_621

[238] "**1:10 speak the same thing.** Paul is emphasizing the unity of doctrine in the local assembly of believers, not the spiritual unity of His universal church. Doctrinal unity, clearly and completely based on Scripture, must be the foundation of all church life (cf. John 17:11, 21–23; Acts 2:46, 47). Both weak commitment to doctrine and commitment to disunity of doctrine will severely weaken a church and destroy the true unity. In its place, there can be only shallow sentimentalism or superficial harmony." – MacArthur, John (2005-05-09). *The MacArthur Bible Commentary* (Kindle Locations 53053-53056). Thomas Nelson. Kindle Edition.

wrong desires for a time, they will begin to build a mindset and a pattern of behavior. This over time, left unchecked, will eventually lead to a personality that is very much at odds with God. When an unbeliever finds God, and becomes a Christian, he will need a completely new mindset and a pattern of behavior. Concerning this, Paul said,

Romans 12:2 New American Standard Bible (NASB)	**Colossians 3:9-10** Lexham English Bible (LEB)
2 And do not be conformed to this world, but be transformed by the renewing of your mind, so that you may prove what the will of God is, that which is good and acceptable and perfect.	9 Do not lie to one another, *because you* have taken off the old man together with his deeds, 10 and have put on the new *man* that is being renewed in knowledge according to the image of the one who created him,

Humans have the capacity of having various attitudes of mind. When we think of a high-minded person, this is a prideful person. Then, again, if we are thinking of a humble-minded person, this is a person, who has a modest and unassuming in attitude about himself. The latter here is the mental attitude that Jesus had. In fact, Paul counseled the Philippians to "Have this mind among yourselves, which is yours in Christ Jesus." (Phil. 2:5) Peter also says, "Since therefore Christ suffered in the flesh, arm yourselves with the same way of thinking." (1 Pet 4:1) The word *spirit* can refer to one's will or sense of self, or somebody's personality or temperament. This is largely influenced by the mind.

Proverbs 25:28 American Standard Version (ASV)

28 He whose spirit [personality or temperament] is without restraint is like a city that is broken down and without walls.[239]

However, we are blessed with another loving gift, another mental power from our heavenly Father at the creation of Adam and Eve. Looking again at Genesis 1:27 it says, "God created man in his own image, in the image of God he created him; male and female he created them," which means that man is born with a moral nature, which creates within him a conscience that reflects God's moral values. (Rom 2:14-15) It acts as a moral law within. Even in imperfection, we are born with a measure of

---

[239] **"25:28 city broken down.** Such are exposed and vulnerable to the incursion of evil thoughts and successful temptations." – MacArthur, John (2005-05-09). *The MacArthur Bible Commentary* (Kindle Locations 25729-25730). Thomas Nelson. Kindle Edition.

that conscience, which can be developed toward good or bad. A Christian conscience is developed by the Word of God. Paul told Titus,

Titus 1:15 Updated English Standard Version (UASV)

15 To the pure [persons with a conscience guided by the Bible], all things are pure; but to those who are defiled and unbelieving, nothing is pure, but both their minds [mental power] and their consciences are defiled.

We have to appreciate and realize that even after we take on the new person that Paul spoke of, as well as the mind of Christ, we will still be affected by our inborn leanings of a sinful nature. Really, there is a battle because waging between the two.

Romans 7:21-25 Updated English Standard Version (UASV)

21 I find then the law in me that when I want to do right, that evil is present in me. 22 For I delight in the law of God according to the inner man, 23 but I see a different law in my members, warring against the law of my mind and taking me captive in the law of sin which is in my members. 24 Wretched man that I am! Who will deliver me from this body of death? 25 Thanks be to God through Jesus Christ our Lord! So then, I myself serve the law of God with my mind, but with my flesh, I serve the law of sin.

The good news is that if a person is walking with Christ and according to Scripture, he will no longer be a slave to sin. The sinful leaning will be there, but as long as it is not fed, it will not dominate his life. He will no longer have a life that feeds the beast, such as inappropriate music, television, internet viewing, associations, thinking, and so on. This will give him a clean conscience before God, knowing that he now has a righteous standing, and all his past has been forgiven, cast behind the back of God. There may come times in his life when his sinful nature will attempt to reassert itself, and he will have to take steps of dismissing any wrongful thinking, replacing it with rational Scriptural thinking, as well as intensive prayer, even speaking with a spiritually mature one within the congregation.

Having the Right Heart

The term *heart* as it is commonly used in the Bible is very much related to this discussion. God is not interested in our outward appearances, but rather the inner man and woman. (1 Sam. 16:7) God's

Word tells its reader, "The refining pot is for silver and the furnace is for gold, and Jehovah **tests hearts**." (Pro. 17:3) If we want to be clean in the eyes of the one who examines our heart; then, we must guard against what we take into our heart. Proverbs also says, "If you say, 'Behold, we did not know this,' does not he who **weighs the heart** perceive it? Does not he who keeps watch over your soul know it, and will he not repay man according to his work?" (Pro. 24:12) God can examine our hearts, and he can read our minds, as he knows our very thoughts, and he will know if we are indifferent toward him. The Scriptures also counsels, "Keep your heart [inner person] with all diligence, for out of it flow the springs of life." (Pro. 4:23) The feelings of love, hate, and everything in between, flow from the human heart, which is the inner person, meaning it is about "life" and death. In other words, how we develop our heart, will be indicative of whether we receive eternal life or not.

The Bible also uses the word "heart" in such a context that it is referring to our *mental power*. Moses pressed the Israelites, "Lay it to your heart [your mind] that Jehovah is God." In addition, later he told them, "Jehovah has not given you a heart [mind] to know." (Deut. 4:39; 29:4) Whether we are talking about the Hebrew Old Testament or the Greek New Testament, the *heart* is associated with our intellect and thinking. Speaking to some of the scribes, "Jesus, knowing their thoughts, said, 'Why do you think evil in your hearts?'" (Matt 9:4) We are told by Mark 2:6, "some of the scribes were sitting there and reasoning in their hearts." Mark 6:52 says, "For they did not understand about the loaves, but their hearts were hardened."

An overview of Scripture would reveal that God in the Old Testament was searching for right-hearted ones (Enoch, Noah, Abraham, Moses, Joshua, Daniel, Jeremiah, etc.), and in the New Testament he has his disciples searching for right-hearted ones, ones with a receptive heart (Cornelius, Lydia, Onesimus, etc.). He is very much interested in our intentions of the heart, love, reasons, steadfast-faith and affection. When we feed our minds on the Word of God, in serious personal Bible study, of the deeper things of God, as we are doing now, we are planting seeds in the soil of our heart (Matt 13:23). This strengthens us against our own imperfect flesh, the world that caters to that flesh, and against Satan and his horde of demons. When the Spirit inspired, inerrant Word of God grows in our heart, it develops the fruitage of the Spirit (Gal. 5:22-23). What may be grown in our hearts in personal Bible study, in preparation for our meetings, and the attendance of meetings, will grow twentyfold if we are actively sharing Bible truths with others. Seeds of truth are reinforced and planted even deeper, so doubt cannot get at them (Jude

1:3, 22). The Psalmist tells us, "Be strong, and let your heart take courage, all you who hope in Jehovah." (Psa. 31:24, ASV) Spiritual strength and maturity are not instantaneous, like being born again; rather they are based on our buying out the time to develop them. – Proverbs 2:1-6.

Those who allow themselves to remain spiritual babes (Heb. 5:12-6:1) are (1) making themselves vulnerable to Satanic attacks, (2) deviation from the faith by way of human weaknesses, and (3) doubt, i.e., spiritual sickness. While it is true that "the god of this world has blinded the minds of the unbelievers," he also has **the ability to close the mind of** believers (1 Pet. 5:8), if he is given entry through the wall that protects us, a wall of protection, which exists only through the Father, the Son and the Holy Spirit. (Job 1:10-12) We 'were once alienated and hostile in mind, doing evil deeds,' have now been reconciled to God (Col. 1:21), "to present you holy and blameless and above reproach before him." (Col. 1:22) Remember Adam and Eve, who were perfect in mind and body, and had the natural desire toward good. Yes, we do well to heed the words of Paul to the Corinthians and the Ephesians,

---

2 Corinthians 11:3 Updated American Standard Version (UASV)

3 But I am afraid that, as the serpent deceived Eve by his craftiness, your minds will be led astray from a sincerity and pure devotion to Christ.

Ephesians 6:14 Updated American Standard Version (UASV)	**Ephesians 6:17** Updated American Standard Version (UASV)
14 Stand firm, therefore, with your loins girded[240] about with truth, and having put on the breastplate of righteousness,	17 And take the helmet of salvation, and the sword of the Spirit, which is the word of God.

Psalm 139:23-24 Updated American Standard Version (UASV)

23 Search me, O God, and know my heart;
 Examine me, and know my anxious[241] thoughts;

---

[240] (an idiom, literally 'to gird up the loins') to cause oneself to be in a state of readiness—'to get ready, to prepare oneself.'—GELNTBSD

[241] Or *disquieting*

24 And see whether there is in me any painful way,[242]
And lead me in the everlasting way

Review Questions

- Does Jesus' blood enable us to go without sinning?

- Who is the ultimate source of life?

- What does it mean to pass over from death to life? Does this mean that it will be fast and easy to give up our old ways?

- What is needed in order to be cleansed from sin?

- How has justice been satisfied?

- Why is a person's claim to be a Christian false if he hates his brother?

- Why can we have confidence?

- What love must we avoid and why?

- What is the correct understanding of the antichrist?

- How should we view Bible scholars and teachers that work with apostates?

- How are we taught by God?

- What is meant by having the right mind?

- What does it mean to have the right heart?

- What can happen if we are not working toward doing the things[243] that will help us maintain our spirituality?

- What is one way that the Bible uses the term mind?

- What is another way that the Bible uses the term mind?

---

[242] Or *hurtful way*

[243] Paul said that we "work out our salvation" (Phil. 2:12), James said, "a person is justified by works and not by faith alone" (Jam 2:24), and he said, "faith apart from works is dead." (Jam 2:26) This of course, does not mean that we earn our salvation through works, but that our works are an evident demonstration of our faith. We cannot have faith without having works.

- What determines whether we will make a good or bad decision?

- How do those in the world end up with a personality that is very much at odds with God?

- Of the various attitudes of mind, which one should we imitate?

- As imperfect humans, we lean toward sin. What will enable us to avoid sinning?

- What role does the heart play in this discussion?

- How are we to understand Proverbs 4:23?

- Who reads our hearts? How are our figurative hearts strengthened?

- Who is Satan seeking?

- What strengthens our minds and hearts?

CHAPTER 19 You Must Repent

Luke 5:32 Updated American Standard Version (UASV)

³² "I have not come to call the righteous but sinners to repentance."

Repentance is a fundamental teaching within God's Word, along with such basics as faith, baptism, and atonement. The importance of repentance is seen in the fact that one cannot receive the gift of salvation without it. – Hebrews 6:1-2.

According to the *Encarta Dictionary*, repents means "to recognize the wrong in something you have done and be sorry about it," or "to feel regret about a sin or past actions and change your ways or habits." The *Holman Illustrated Dictionary* has,

> Change of mind; also can refer to regret or remorse accompanying a realization that wrong has been done or to any shift or reversal of thought. In its biblical *sense* repentance refers to a deeply seated and thorough turning from self to God. It occurs when a radical turning to God takes place, an experience in which God is recognized as the most important fact of one's existence.
>
> **Old Testament** The concept of a wholehearted turning to God is widespread in the preaching of the OT prophets. Terms such as "return," turn," or "seek" are used to express the idea of repentance.
>
> In Amos 4–5 the Lord sends judgment in order for the nation to return to Him. Corporate repentance of the nation is a theme in Hosea (Hos. 6:1; 14:2) and the result of Jonah's preaching to Nineveh (Jon. 3:10). Classic calls to repentance are found in Ezek. 18 and 33 as well as Isa. 55. The shift toward an emphasis on individual repentance can be seen in Ezek. 18.
>
> **New Testament** Repentance was the keynote of the preaching of John the Baptist, referring to a complete turn from self to God. A note of urgency is attached to the message, "The kingdom of heaven has come near!" (Matt. 3:2 HCSB). Those who were prepared to make such a radical reorientation of their lives demonstrated that by being baptized (Mark 1:4). This complete redirection of their lives was to be demonstrated by profound changes in lifestyle and relationships (Luke 3:8–14).

The emphasis upon a total life change continues in the ministry of Jesus. The message of repentance was at the heart of His preaching (Mark 1:15). When describing the focus of His mission, Jesus said, "I have not come to call the righteous, but sinners to repentance" (Luke 5:32 HCSB).

The call to repentance is a call to absolute surrender to the purposes of God and to live in this awareness. This radical turning to God is required of all people: "Unless you repent, you will all perish" (Luke 13:3). Those who had witnessed the ministry of Jesus, the reality of God, and His claims on their lives faced serious jeopardy if they failed to repent. Jesus warned of serious consequences for those where His ministry had been rejected: "He proceeded to denounce the towns where most of His miracles were done, because they did not repent" (Matt. 11:20 HCSB). On the other hand, for the one sinner who repents, there is great "joy in heaven" (Luke 15:7). In His final words to the disciples, Jesus demanded that the same message of repentance He had preached would be preached to all nations (Luke 24:47).

What Truths and Principles

If we are going to appreciate fully what all is involved in repentance, as far as God is concerned, we have to get at the truth and principles of biblical repentance. **The first task** of those who are truly Christian is to accept, based on an accurate knowledge and understanding that God does exist, and he is the Creator and owner of his people. Moreover, he is the Sovereign of the universe, the Most High, the Judge, the Lawgiver, and so justice must always be satisfied. This should not be frightening, as if we are before an earthly judge, governor, or world leader, with their fickle emotions. Some of the other major qualities of our Creator are love, kindness, mercy, and patience, to mention just a few. Nevertheless, we are accountable to our Creator as should be expected. Being that we were given free will, as well as an internal conscience that enable us to distinguish between right and wrong, we are accountable for our actions, as well as our thoughts and feelings that lead to our actions. In other words, God is so far more superior than his angelic creation, it is not even really conceivable to the human creation, which is far more inferior than the angels just how infinite our Creator's qualities are. Therefore, if some human government has the capacity to determine laws that hold us morally accountable, how much more so would this be true of God? This basic truth seems to escape the agnostic and atheist.

The second task of those who are truly Christian is to come to terms with the fact that humanity has inherited sin from Adam, and just what his sinful condition entrails. Adam and Eve in the Garden of Eden had free will but chose to abuse it and to rebel against their Creator. God had created them perfect; they lacked nothing. They need not fear any illnesses, hunger, death, any form of difficulty that plagues man today. The only requirement that they had was to live out their freedom under the sovereignty of God, i.e., the righteous rule of God, and the laws that the Creator would introduce, including the laws of nature.

One such natural law was that they would grow hungry if they did not eat, thus the need to obey the law to eat. The same would hold true for water as well, and the need to drink. Then, there was a need for sleep. Outside of these natural laws, God gave them work to accomplish within Eden, yet we will note in the texts below, there were not innumerable details, rules, and regulations. They had the freedom to fulfill the work that was assigned, as long as it was fulfilled.

However, one must recognize that the freedom given to a child to make decisions on their own means they are given responsibilities, and they are trusted to carry out those responsibilities. Moreover, it does not mean that the act of decision making alone, for the sake of making them, are going to end with good results. A child must learn and grow from being taught by their father and mother, and as they demonstrate that, they are ready for more freedom and responsibility; then, they will receive it. God did not create Adam and Eve so that there was no need for growth, no need to learn. He gave both man and woman intelligence so that they could grow in knowledge and understanding, wisely making application to what they were learning. Of both Adam and Eve God said, "Let us make man in our image, after our likeness." This means that the inner person within the first human pair would have possessed the same qualities in their decision-making skills as their Creator. If their love and respect for God and all he had done grew, it would have only been natural that they would have wanted to please him.

There was one law that the first couples was given, which would allow them to evidence their love and appreciation, as well as grow from their experience of obeying this law. "And Jehovah God commanded the man, saying, 'From every tree of the garden you may freely eat, but of the tree of the knowledge of good and evil you shall not eat, for in the day that you eat of it, you shall surely die.'" (Gen. 2:16-17) They had an entire Garden of trees to eat from, as "God caused to grow every tree that was pleasing to the sight and good for food." (Gen. 2:9) What did this mean? It meant that they lacked nothing regardless of this one restricted tree. It also meant that to obey or not obey was within their free will, and they were no lacking of anything that would have contributed to their disobeying. Nevertheless, Adam, who was to be the father of humankind, meaning that he had to learn that while he was given the earth as his domain, it still belonged to God as the rightful Ruler. – Psalm 24:1, 10.

Born Into Slavery: Did you know that we are all born slaves? The facts are quite staggering to the first-time hearer; all humans were/are slaves and born of slaves. Each of us must face the facts, by looking honestly at the truthful evidence before us, which will help us to appreciate many things about man that have only been a mystery before first century Christianity. More importantly, it will help each of us to understand that while we may be born into slavery, a provision has paid that will release us from this bondage.

When the first man Adam willfully chose to disobey God's law, he gave up possession of perfect control of himself, gave into his selfish desire to continue with his wife, and placed her above his Creator, Jehovah God. His giving into this sinful desire made it and the result thereof, sin, his taskmaster, leading him as a slave. (Rom 6:16; James 1:14-15) In essence, he chose to place himself under sin. Sadly, all of humankind was yet to be born; therefore, Adam sold his future descendants under sin. It is for this reason that the Apostle Paul could write: "For we know that the law is spiritual, but I am of the flesh, sold under sin." (Rom 7:14) It is for this alone that humans were without a means of returning to perfection, unable to keep God's righteous Law given through Moses. The Apostle Paul put it this way: "The very commandment that promised life proved to be death to me." (Rom 7:10) What the Mosaic Law had accomplished was to highlight their inability to keep this law perfectly, labeling them as slaves to sin (missing the mark of perfection), and deserving death. Exactly, what is sin though? Sin is anything not in harmony with God's personality, standards, ways, will, and purpose.[244]

The lost opportunity for eternal life on a paradise earth, humankind walking with God in peace, took place when the first man, Adam, in an

---

[244] (See Job 2:10; Psa. 39:1; Lev. 20:20; 2 Cor. 12:21; Pro 21:4; Rom. 3:9-18; 2 Pe 2:12-15; Heb. 3:12, 13, 18, 19)

act of disobedience and rebellion, sinned against God. However, all was not lost, because there was one perfect man, who could recover this walking with God in peace, and the hope of eternal life, Christ Jesus, the second Adam, regaining through obedience, what Adam had lost through disobedience.

- Death by One Man (Rom. 5:12)

- From Adam to Moses (Rom. 5:13-14)

- Adam's Sin Contrasted with the Gift of Christ (Rom. 5:15)

- Adam's Condemnation Contrasted with the Righteousness of Christ (Rom. 5:16)

- The Reign of Death Contrasted With the Reign of Life (Rom. 5:17)

As with the ripple effect of a rock thrown into a pond, it took one man to create the ripple effect of all of humankind being placed into slavery, sold, sinful, ending with death. Fortunately, two of God's cardinal attributes is wisdom and power, using these; he was able to make the needed arrangements of offering another Adam, Jesus Christ, as a means of repurchasing humankind. It is here in verses 12–18 that we see his third chief attribute of justice being used in bringing into balance one man against another man in this repurchasing process, maintaining just all along the way.

This one act of disobedience to his God was a transgression, a sinning by "overstepping," 'sidestepping,' "bypassing," or 'passing beyond' (Heb., 'avar) God's covenant or specific orders.[245] (See Num. 14:41; Deut. 17:2, 3; Josh 7:11, 15; 1 Sam 15:24; Isa 24:5; Jer. 34:18) Therefore, Adam was guilty of sin. It is by means of inheritance that the descendants of Adam came into sin. From the time of the birth of Adam's firstborn son up unto the giving of the Mosaic Law, there was no law code; therefore, man was unable to transgress in the way of Adam.

From Genesis up unto the baptism of Christ Jesus, there was a mystery of who the prophesied seed would be. (Gen 3:15) It was not until the apostle Paul that Jesus was truly disclosed as this 1,500-year-old mystery. We find that Jesus is the second Adam, who bore some

---

[245] Harris, R. Laird; Harris, Robert Laird; Archer, Gleason Leonard; Waltke, Bruce K.: *Theological Wordbook of the Old Testament*. electronic ed. Chicago: Moody Press, 1999, c1980, S. 640

resemblance to the first, in that both were perfect humans. The first Adam committed a trespass when he very well could have chosen not to, which lead to sickness, old age, and death. On the other hand, the second Adam [Jesus] was perfectly obedient under much more severe trials, which would lead to any who trust in him receiving an unearned righteous standing for an imperfect person, and the hope of eternal life, two entirely different courses.

As was already stated, the first Adam committed his one "trespass" in the Garden of Eden, causing the death sentence of all his descendants up unto the first century C.E. It is here that man receives the unearned, the undeserved gift of "that one man Jesus Christ." By means of this "one man," God's righteous requirement of justice is met, giving many an opportunity once again to walk with Him in an approved condition. This undeserved gift was so effective that even Enoch and Noah could be spoken of as though they were walking with God based on their faith in this coming one. Here is the similarity, for both have an impact on the many.

In other words, the judgment of condemnation by God came from Adam's one trespass. This one trespass brought Adam and all who were yet to be born under the condemnation of death. In Galatians 3:19, the Apostle Paul informs us that the law "was added because of transgressions until the offspring should come to whom the promise had been made." In other words, the Mosaic Law was added to highlight the sinful nature of man and the need for a greater sacrifice. When God gave the Law to Moses, there were "many trespasses" on the part of the Israelites, establishing that humankind is sinful and in need of something more than animal sacrifices. The "free gift" allowed God's justice to be met, offering all who has an active faith [i.e., complete trust] in that gift, to be declared righted, although imperfect.

The "trespass of the one man" is a sin of encroaching on his Creator's righteous standards of right and wrong, to decide for him what is right and wrong, rejecting the sovereignty of the one who created him. The penalty of death was made clear to this "one man." The trespass of Adam in the Garden of Eden brought the reign of death to not only himself, but also all who would come out of his loins. On the opposite end of the scale is the unearned, undeserved gift of God, the free gift of righteousness, pulling any who accepted this free gift out of the quagmire of sin and death! This "free gift of righteousness" enables all who accept it to "reign in life." This hope that is set before all is a result of the sacrifice of the "one man Jesus Christ."

Initially, Adam and Eve's mental disposition or inclination was not toward evil or bad, sin. Hence, while imperfect humans are inclined, lean toward wrongdoing, it was just the opposite for our first human parents; their natural inclination was toward doing good. This is just the opposite of their descendants, for we have inherited the disease of sin, missing the mark, or standard of perfection. (Gen. 6:5, AT) "When the Lord saw that the wickedness of man on the earth was great and that the whole bent of his thinking was never anything but evil ..." (Gen. 8:21, AT) " ... the bent of man's mind may be evil from his very youth ..." (Jer. 17:9) "The heart is deceitful above all things, and it is exceedingly corrupt: who can know it?"

The Man We Are Inside

(John 13:35) [35] By this all people will know that you are my disciples, if you have love for one another." "Disciple," "pupil," "student" and "learner: (One who loves discipline) *mathetes*

(1 John 1:8) [8] If we say we have no sin, we deceive ourselves, and the truth is not in us. "Sin," "miss" hamartia (Missing the mark of perfection)

(Rom 7:22) [22] For I delight in the law of God, in my inner being. "The inside man," "the man I am within," "inward being," "inward man" *ton eso anthropos*

(Eph. 4:23) [23] and to be renewed in the spirit of your minds. Lit. "The spirit of the mind" "made new in the force actuating your mind," "renewed in the spirit of your mind,"

(Eph. 2:15) [15] by abolishing the law of commandments expressed in ordinances, that he might create in himself one new man in place of the two, so making peace. Lit. "New man," "new self," "new personality"

(1 Co 2:14) [14] The natural person does not accept the things of the Spirit of God, for they are folly to him, and he is not able to understand them because they are spiritually discerned. (The natural person seeks only the desire of his fallen flesh, ignoring his spiritual needs.)

(Rom 8:6-7) [6] For to set the mind on the flesh is death, but to set the mind on the Spirit is life and peace. [7] For the mind that is set on the flesh is hostile to God, for it does not submit to God's law; indeed, it cannot. Lit, "minding," 'way of thinking, mindset, aim, aspiration, striving.' *phronema*

When we couple our leaning toward wrongdoing with the fact that Satan the devil, who is "the god of this world," (2 Co 4:4) has worked to entice these leanings, the desires of the fallen flesh; we are even further removed from our relationship with our loving heavenly Father. During these 'last days, grievous times' has fallen on us as Satan is working all the more to prevent God's once perfect creation to achieve a righteous standing with God and entertaining the hope of eternal life. – 2 Timothy 3:1-5.

Our conscience thinking (aware) and subconscious thinking (present in our mind without you being aware of it) originates in the mind. For good, or for bad, our mind follows certain rules of action, which if entertained one will move even further in that direction until they are eventually consumed for good or for bad. In our imperfect state, our bent thinking will lean toward wrong, especially with Satan using his world of fallen humans, with so many forms of entertainment that merely feeds the flesh. – James 1:14-15.

Scriptural repentance demanded that there was some provision by which or some basis upon which God can make certain that justice is satisfied and yet take awareness of repentance, for God's attributes like love, power, wisdom and justice do not change. (Mal. 3:6) If God simply forgave indiscriminately, there would be no reason to respect him and his laws or love him to the point of fearing to displease him. The provision that the Father made was his only-begotten Son, Jesus Christ. Paul wrote, "For all have sinned and fall short of the glory of God, and are justified by his grace as a gift, through the redemption that is in Christ Jesus, whom God put forward as a propitiation by his blood, to be received by faith. This was to show God's righteousness, because in his divine forbearance he had passed over former sins. It was to show his righteousness at the present time, so that he might be just and the justifier of the one who has faith in Jesus." – Romans 3:23-26, ESV.

Lastly, we need to understand the issues that were raised in the Garden of Eden and those brought out during Satan and God's discussion over Job. God allowing sin to enter into the world for a time has settled these issues. When people ask about why God allows pain and suffering, these issues that were raised are the answer as to why.[246] – Genesis 2:17; 3:1-6; Job 1:6-11; 2:4-5.

---

[246] **Suffering & Evil - Why God?**

http://www.christianpublishers.org/suffering-evil-why-god

The Issues at Hand

(1) Satan called God a liar and said he was not to be trusted, as to the life or death issue.

(2) Satan's challenge, therefore, took into question the right and legitimacy of God's rightful place as the Universal Sovereign.

(3) Satan also suggested that people would remain obedient to God only as long as their submitting to God was to their benefit.

(4) Satan all but said that humankind was able to walk on his own, there being no need for dependence on God.

(5) Satan argued that man could be like God, choosing for himself what is right and wrong.

(6) Satan claimed that God's way of ruling was not in the best interests of humans, and they could do better without God.

True Repentance

For more than 1,500 years, there were "times of ignorance God overlooked, but now he commands all people everywhere to repent, because he has fixed a day on which he will judge the world in righteousness by a man whom he has appointed; and of this he has given assurance to all by raising him from the dead." (Ac 17:30-31, ESV) The apostle Peter tells us, "The Lord is not slow to fulfill his promise as some count slowness, but is patient toward you, not wishing that any should perish, but that all should reach repentance." – 2 Peter 3:9, ESV.

The apostle Paul tells us, "Without faith it is impossible to please him, for whoever would draw near to God must believe that he exists and that he rewards those who seek him." (Heb. 11:6, ESV) The prophet Micah informs us as well when he writes, "He has told you, O man, what is good; and what does the Lord require of you but to do justice, and to love kindness, and to walk humbly with your God?" For us in our imperfection to approach God and find ourselves in a righteous standing before him, we must repent and turnaround from our former ways. As we draw closer to God and learn of his righteous requirements, we must fully understand our sinful condition as was mentioned above and be aware of our spiritual needs. – Luke 18:13; Ezra 9:3-15; Matt. 26:75.

The apostle John says, "If we confess our sins, he is faithful and just to forgive us our sins and to cleanse us from all unrighteousness." (1 John

1:9) He goes on to say, "My little children, I am writing these things to you so that you may not commit a sin.[247] But if anyone does sin, we have an advocate with the Father, Jesus Christ the righteous one." (1 John 2:1) Jesus is "the Lamb of God who takes away the sin of the world!" – John 1:29. If we are truly repentant, there will be godly sorrow, based on our love for God and our love of his attributes like justice, righteousness, not simply because we are afraid that we will be punished otherwise. Paul tells us, "For godly grief produces a repentance that leads to salvation without regret, whereas worldly grief produces death." (2 Cor. 7:10, ESV) In fact, it is 'God's kindness that is meant to lead us to repentance.' – Romans 2:4.

Fruit Worthy of Repentance

To those Jews who traveled out to see John the Baptist, the man who prepared the way for Jesus Christ, he said, "produce fruit worthy of repentance!" (Lu 3:8, LEB) As James tells us, "the body apart from the spirit is dead, so also faith apart from works is dead." (Jam 2:26, ESV) What are the fruits that are "worthy of repentance"?

The apostle Peter gives us the first fruit, "Repent therefore, and turn back, that your sins may be blotted out." (Ac 3:19, ESV) "This refers to a change of mind and purpose that turns an individual from sin to God (1 Thess. 1:9). Such change involves more than fearing the consequences of God's judgment. Genuine repentance knows that the evil of sin must be forsaken and the person and work of Christ totally and singularly embraced. Peter exhorted his hearers to repent, otherwise they would not experience true conversion (see note on Matt. 3:2; cf. 3:19; 5:31; 8:22; 11:18; 17:30; 20:21; 26:20; Matt. 4:17)."[248] After we have repented and turned ourselves back, we are to "live for the rest of the time in the flesh no longer for human passions but for the will of God." (1 Pet. 4:2, ESV) Yes, the fruitage of repentance demands that we dedicate ourselves to doing the will of the Father and following in the footsteps of the Son,

---

[247] Gr., *hamartete*, a verb in the aorist subjunctive. According to *A Grammar of New Testament Greek*, by James H. Moulton, Vol. I, 1908, p. 109, "the Aorist has a 'punctiliar' action, that is, it regards action as a *point*: it represents the point of entrance . . . or that of completion . . . or it looks at a whole action simply as having occurred, without distinguishing any steps in its progress."

[248] MacArthur, John (2005-05-09). *The MacArthur Bible Commentary* (Kindle Locations 49041-49044). Thomas Nelson. Kindle Edition.

Jesus Christ. The first step that a new one would follow would to make a public display of his or her dedication to God, by being baptized.

One major fruit of repentance is our proclaiming the good news to others. If we do not witnessing about God's Word, our repentance would be meaningless. Paul wrote, "For with the heart one believes and is justified, and with the mouth one confesses and is saved." (Rom. 10:10) MacArthur writes, "**confession**. This Greek word basically means to say the same thing, or to be in agreement with someone. The person who confesses Jesus as Lord (v. 9) agrees with the Father's declaration that Jesus is Savior and Lord." (MacArthur, The MacArthur Bible Commentary 2005, L. 52254-5)

If we are going to have works that befit repentance, we must no longer practice any sin, i.e., live in sin. Peter writes of our former course of conduct, "For the time that is past suffices for doing what the Gentiles want to do, living in sensuality, passions, drunkenness, orgies, drinking parties, and lawless idolatry. 4 With respect to this they are surprised when you do not join them in the same flood of debauchery, and they malign you." (1 Pet 4:3, ESV) Rather we are to carry on "the fruit of the Spirit, [which] is love, joy, peace, patience, kindness, goodness, faithfulness, gentleness, self-control; against such things there is no law." – Galatians 5:22-23.

If we are demonstrating fruitage of repentance, we must "also have forgiven our debtors." Jesus said to Peter who thought forgiving seven times was enough, "I do not say to you seven times, but seventy-seven times." – Matthew 6:12; 18:22, ESV.

However, we need to understand that we are sinners, living in perfection, so we are not going to go through life never sinning again. Thus, while we should feel the appropriate measure of remorse when we fall short, depending on the sin (say lying versus adultery), we should not be grieved to a state of irrational thinking (i.e., "I am worthless," "I am no good, etc.). Remember our previous chapter and John's words, "But if we walk in the light, as he is in the light, we have fellowship with one another, and the blood of Jesus his Son cleanses us from all sin." (1 John 1:7, ESV) We need to consider how God views us after we genuinely repent from falling short. "Blessed is the one whose transgression is forgiven, whose sin is covered." (Psa. 32:1, ESV) When we consider all that is involved in fruitages of repentance, we can be certain that there is no such thing as deathbed repentance. Hollywood movies and television shows are famous with Catholic priests who absolve people of their sins on their deathbed. First, only Jesus Christ can forgive sin. Second, there is no way one can store up treasures in heaven by fruitage to God and compliance with Christ's commands, and last minute regrets cannot ransom anyone. It is like the criminal that enjoyed his crime spree until he is caught and now he regrets his actions. For some, there attempts at deathbed repentance will come at Armageddon, where they will realize that God is real and they have missed the opportunity at eternal life.

If we are in the Christian faith, we need to spend time building up our faith, not becoming complacent. We do this by having a regular prayer life. (Phil. 4:6; Col. 4:2) It is imperative that we have a daily personal Bible study and a weekly family study if we have a family. (Matt. 4:4; 2 Tim. 3:17) We need also to prepare for all of our Christian meetings, to participate and build others up. (1 Cor. 12:12-27; Heb. 10:23-25) If there are any who are truly Christian, finding that they are overtaken in gross sin, they should quickly repent of their wrong conduct. They should go to God in prayer first, and then to those taking the lead in the congregation.

First to God and then to the responsible ones in His visible organization he should make open confession of his wrong, express his repentance and earnestly seek forgiveness, expressing their godly sorrow.

Review Questions

- What is repentance, how does it differ from the OT to the NT and just how significant is it?

- What are the truth and principles in biblical repentance?

- What is sin and how did it enter into humanity?

- What is the extent of our inherited imperfection?

- What issues have been raised by Satan that needed to be settled?

- What is true repentance?

- What are some fruitages of repentance?

CHAPTER 20 You Must Fight the Good Fight

2 Timothy 4:7 Updated American Standard Version (UASV)

⁷ I have fought the good fight,[249] I have finished the course, I have kept the faith;

Imagine a soldier in the Iraq or Afghanistan war over the past 14 years being given the command: "Head home and spend some time with your family." Most would be overjoyed at such an opportunity.

Well, we have an example of this in Scripture, where King David of Israel ordered, Uriah one of his foreign warriors, to return home, where his young beautiful wife Bathsheba awaited him. Yes, it is true that King David had slept with Bathsheba, committing adultery, and impregnated her, so he wanted Uriah to have relations, so that he would believe it was his child. Setting aside David's serious sin, we must note Uriah was unaware of all of this that was playing out behind the scenes. Therefore, we note Uriah refused repeatedly to go to his house. He was eventually asked why? Uriah replied, "The ark and Israel and Judah dwell in booths, and my lord Joab and the servants of my lord are camping in the open field. Shall I then go to my house, to eat and to drink and to lie with my wife? As you live, and as your soul lives, I will not do this thing." – 2 Samuel 11:8-11, ESV.

The conduct of Uriah is important to us because those who are truly Christian are presently facing a time of war as well. Are we going to be more focused on family, friends, our station in life, wealth, or are we going to overwhelmingly seek first the kingdom of God. We are in a war that has been raging for 2,000 years and looks to be entering critical times that will be very hard to deal with, unlike anything we humanity has every experience before, and it will only go from bad to worse. The signs that Jesus gave in Matthew chapter 24, Mark chapter 13 and Luke chapter

---

[249] "The form of the three Greek verbs 'have fought, have finished, have kept,' indicate completed action with continuing results. Paul saw his life as complete. He had been able to accomplish, through the Lord's power, all that God called him to do. He was a soldier (2:3, 4; 2 Cor. 10:3; 1 Tim. 6:12; Philem. 2), an athlete (1 Cor. 9:24–27; Eph. 6:12), and a guardian (1:13, 14; 1 Tim. 6:20, 21). the faith. The truths and standards of the revealed Word of God." – MacArthur, John (2005-05-09). *The MacArthur Bible Commentary* (Kindle Locations 60887-60890). Thomas Nelson. Kindle Edition.

21 were to lead into "a great tribulation, such as has not occurred since the beginning of the world until now, nor ever will." (Matt. 24:21, NASB) Of course, at the culmination of the great tribulation is Jesus return with his angelic army at the war of Armageddon. Whether this is a year away, five years, or fifty years, we do not know.

No One Knows That Day and Hour

Matthew 24:36 English Standard Version (ESV)

[36] "But concerning that day and hour no one knows, not even the angels of heaven, nor the Son, but the Father only.

While none of us can know the precise time of Jesus' return, we do know that we are to be busy in the work that he has given us. Regardless of the time left, how will you use it? Here is how we should use our time before Christ's return. We should **live as though it is tomorrow**, but **plan as though it is 50-years away**. What do we mean by this? We **live as though** Christ is returning tomorrow, by walking with God, having a righteous standing before him. We **plan as though** it is 50-years away by living a life that has strategies for a long-term evangelism that fulfills our end of the great commission. – Matthew 24:14; 28:19-20; Acts 1:8.

Our sinful nature would not do well if we knew the exact day and hour. We do badly enough when we simply think Christ's return is close. You have had religions that have set dates for Christ's return, or are constantly saying, 'the end is near!' The ones who set actual dates for Christ's return: quit their jobs, sell their homes, take all their money out of the bank, and take their kids out of school, either (1) to have a good time before the end, or (2) to spend the last couple years yelling from the rooftops that "the end is coming!"

Those who are constantly saying, 'the end is near,' are similar, in that they do not take job promotions, because it would cut into their evangelism, they do not allow their children to have university educations or plan careers, because to them the end is near. Nevertheless, these groups are at least concerned about their evangelism, but fail to realize, we do not know when the end is coming. We do know one thing about the end as it draws near. We know that true Christians and Christian will be under critical unlike anything ever experienced in the past, and it will only worsen as the end closes in on us. We will talk more on this in a moment.

We need to find a way in the time that remains, be it 5 years or 50 years, to encourage and foster "sincere brotherly love," and to display "obedience to the truth." What do we need to be obedient to? **(1)** We need to clean up the household of Christianity. **(2)** We need to then, carry out the great commission that Jesus assigned, to preach, to teach, and to make disciples! (Matt 24:14; 28:19-20; Ac 1:8) It is our assignment, in the time remaining, to assist God in helping those with a receptive heart, to accept the good news of the kingdom. Yes, we are offering those of the world, the hope of getting on the path of salvation, an opportunity at everlasting life. Just because we do not know the day or the hour, does not mean that we should be less urgent about this assignment. Remember Jesus' illustration,

Matthew 24:43 English Standard Version (ESV)

[43] But know this, that if the master of the house had known in what part of the night the thief was coming, he would have stayed awake and would not have let his house be broken into.

Moreover, remember Jesus' question,

Luke 18:8 English Standard Version (ESV)

[8] I tell you, he will give justice to them speedily. Nevertheless, when the Son of Man comes, will he find faith on earth?"

The Christian War

The Christian war that has now entered a new era of difficulties will grow increasing hostile, of which all true Christians are involved, and must endure to the end. The risks and dangers are great and the enemy is formidable. In the Christian war, no shots are fired by some Christian military, no bombs will be dropped on our enemies, but our war strategy will be no less intense.

In any earthly war, one must know what is morally right and what is being fought for before taking up arms against another country. Is the end goal worth the casualties suffered: lives, money and property? We need to ask ourselves the same questions before entering this Christian war. The apostle Paul tells us, "Fight the good fight of the faith." Yes, our war is not to protect the United States of America, or some physical property, but rather "the faith," i.e., the Biblical truths revealed in the Word of God. If we are going to give our lives for "the faith," that is these 'truths,' there must be no doubt, if we intend to finish the course. – 1 Timothy 6:12, ESV.

A wise, careful, cautious, farsighted warrior will know the enemy he faces. The enemy we Christians face are liberal, atheistic governments, radical Islam, but even more dangerous, a superhuman being. This enemy is invisible to the eye, having superior intellect, with thousands of years of fighting experience, possessing millions of other superhuman soldiers, with superior weapons. This enemy knows every word that we have ever uttered, every action we have ever taken, which allows him to strategize just how to take us out. He is malicious, ferocious and powerful, and wicked and deceitful; he is Satan. The apostle Peter warns us, "be on the alert. Your adversary, the devil, prowls around like a roaring lion, seeking someone to devour." (1 Pet 5:8, NASB) There is not one human weapon that can be used against this enemy, nor will human cunning and trickery having any impact against this opponent. (2 Cor. 10:4) What can Christians use to wage a war against such an adversary?

The Whole Armor of God

Ephesians 6:10-19 Updated American Standard Version (UASV)

[10] Finally, be strong in the Lord and in the strength of His might. [11] Put on the full armor of God, so that you will be able to stand firm against the schemes of the devil. [12] For our struggle[250] is not against flesh and blood, but against the rulers, against the powers, against the world-rulers of this darkness, against the wicked spirit forces in the heavenly places.

[13] Therefore, take up the whole armor of God, so that you will be able to resist in the evil day, and having done everything, to stand firm. [14] Stand firm, therefore, with your **loins girded**[251] about with truth, and having put on the **breastplate of righteousness**, [15] and with your **feet shod** with the preparation of the gospel of peace; [16] in all things, taking up the **shield of faith** with which you will be able to extinguish all the flaming arrows of the evil one. [17] And take the **helmet of salvation**, and the sword of the Spirit, which is the word of God.

---

[250] Lit., "wrestling."

[251] (an idiom, literally 'to gird up the loins') to cause oneself to be in a state of readiness—'to get ready, to prepare oneself.'–GELNTBSD

18 Through all prayer and petition praying at all times in the Spirit, and with this in view, keep awake with all perseverance and making supplication for all the holy ones. **19** Pray also for me, that the words may be given to me when I open my mouth, so that I may be able to speak boldly in making known the mystery of the gospel, **20** for which I am an ambassador in chains;[252] that in it I may speak boldly, as I ought to speak.

You may be thinking that it seems very unlikely that any human can be at odds with a demonic spirit creature, and come out victorious as they have unimaginable superhuman abilities. It is only possible by our reliance on Christ Jesus. We must have a complete grasp of God's Word, and apply it in a balanced manner in our lives each day. Only by doing so, can we be freed from the bodily, moral, emotional and mental harm that those under demonic or satanic control have gone through. Only by doing so may we compete with the human element that Satan will use against us as well. – Ephesians 6:11; James 4:7.

Defending the Loins, the Breast, and the Feet

Girding Your Loins with Truth

The loins are the area on each side of the backbone of a human between the ribs and hips. At the time that the apostle Paul wrote this to the Ephesians, soldiers wore a belt or girdle-like you see in the image of Roman soldiers. It was 2 to 6 inches in width. This belt served a double duty: (1) to protect the soldier's loins, (2) but it also serve in supporting his sword. When a soldier girded up his loins, this meant he was getting ready to go into battle. This soldier and his belt served as the perfect analogy, of how a Christian is to put on the belt of biblical truth, to protect his life. The truths of Scripture should be pulled tight around us, helping us to live a life that is reflective of that truth. Thus, we can use that Bible truth to defend the faith, contend for the faith, and save those who doubt. (1 Pet. 3:15, Jude 3, 21-22) If we are to accomplish these tasks, we will have to study the Bible carefully and consider its contents. Prophetically, it was said of Jesus, "your law is within my heart." (Ps. 40:8) If Jesus came under attack by the enemy of

---

[252] Lit *a chain*

truth, he was able to refer to biblical truth from memory. – Matthew 19:3-6; 22:23-32.

Isaiah 30:20-21 Updated American Standard Version (UASV)

20 And though Jehovah[253] give you the bread of distress and the water of oppression, yet your Teacher[254] will no longer hide himself, but your eyes shall behold your Teacher. **21** And your ears shall hear a word behind you, saying, "This is the way, walk in it," when you turn to the right or when you turn to the left.

> **Stand therefore.** For the third time (see vv. 11, 13), the apostle calls Christians to take a firm position in the spiritual battle against Satan and his minions. Whether confronting Satan's efforts to distrust God, forsaking obedience, producing doctrinal confusion and falsehood, hindering service to God, bringing division, serving God in the flesh, living hypocritically, being worldly, or in any other way rejecting biblical obedience, this armor is our defense. girded . . . with truth. The soldier wore a tunic of loose-fitting cloth. Since ancient combat was largely hand-to-hand, a loose tunic was a potential hindrance and danger. A belt was necessary to cinch up the loosely hanging material. Cf. Exodus 12:11; Luke 12:35; 1 Peter 1:13. Girding up was a matter of pulling in the loose ends as preparation for battle. The belt that pulls all the spiritual loose ends in is "truth" or better, "truthfulness." The idea is of sincere commitment to fight and win without hypocrisy—self-discipline in devotion to victory. Everything that hinders is tucked away. Cf. 2 Timothy 2:4; Hebrews 12:1.[255]

Breastplate of Righteousness

The breastplate of the soldier was a piece of armor that covered the chest, protecting one of the most important organs, the heart. As all Christians likely know, we have a figurative heart, which is our inner person, and it needs special protection because it leans toward wrongdoing. (Gen. 8:21) Therefore, we must cultivate a love for God's Word and the standards and values that lie within. (Ps. 119:97, 105) Our

---

[253] One of 134 scribal changes from *YHWH* to *Adhonai*.

[254] Lit *your teachers*. The Hebrew verb is plural to denote grandeur or excellence.

[255] MacArthur, John (2005-05-09). *The MacArthur Bible Commentary* (Kindle Locations 57513-57520). Thomas Nelson. Kindle Edition.

love for the Word of God should be to such a depth that we would reject "the desires of the flesh and the desires of the eyes and pride of life." (1 Jn. 2:15-17) In addition, once we have developed such a desire for right over wrong, we will be able to avoid paths that would have otherwise led us to a ruination. (Ps. 119:99-101; Am. 5:15) Our greatest example in everything, Jesus Christ, evidenced this to such an extent that Paul could say, "You have loved righteousness and hated wickedness."–Hebrews 1:9.

the breastplate of righteousness. The breastplate was usually a tough, sleeveless piece of leather or heavy material with animal horn or hoof pieces sewn on, covering the soldier's full torso, protecting his heart and other vital organs. Because righteousness, or holiness, is such a distinctive characteristic of God Himself, it is not hard to understand why that is the Christian's chief protection against Satan and his schemes. As believers faithfully live in obedience to and communion with Jesus Christ, His own righteousness produces in them the practical, daily righteousness that becomes their spiritual breastplate. Lack of holiness, on the other hand, leaves them vulnerable to the great enemy of their souls (cf. Is. 59:17; 2 Cor. 7:1; 1 Thess. 5:8).[256]

Shod Your Feet with the Preparation of the Gospel of Peace

Roman soldiers needed suitable footwear, which (1) kept their footing sure in battle, and (2) allowed them to march some 20 miles during a campaign, while wearing or carrying some 60 pounds of armor and equipment. Thus, Paul's ongoing analogy of the armor of a Roman soldier was right on target, as the appropriate footwear for the readiness of a Christian minister active in spreading the gospel message is even more important. Paul shows the importance again in his letters to the Roman congregation. There he asks how will the people get to know God if the Christian is not willing and ready to bring it to him, as he preaches and teaches?–Romans 10:13-15.

Once again, we must look to our example Jesus Christ, as he says to the Roman Governor Pontius Pilate, "For this purpose I was born and for this purpose I have come into the world, to bear witness to the truth. Everyone who is of the truth listens to my voice." For three and a half years, Jesus walked throughout the land of Palestine, preaching to all who would listen, giving the ministry top priority in his life. (John 4:5-34;

---

[256] IBID

290

18:37) If we, like Jesus, are eager to declare the good news, we will find many opportunities to share it with others. Furthermore, our being absorbed in our ministry will help keep us spiritually strong. – Acts 18:5.

shod . . . with . . . the gospel of peace. Roman soldiers wore boots with nails in them to grip the ground in combat. The gospel of peace pertains to the good news that, through Christ, believers are at peace with God and He is on their side (Rom. 5:6–10). It is that confidence of divine support which allows the believer to stand firm, knowing that he is at peace with God and God is his strength (see Rom. 8:31, 37–39).[257]

The Shield of Faith, the Helmet of Salvation, and the Sword of the Spirit

Thureon is the Greek word rendered "shield," which actually refers to a shield that was "large and oblong, protecting every part of the soldier; the word is used metaphorically of faith."[258] This shield of faith would and will protect the Christian from the "the fiery darts of the evil one." In ancient times, the darts[259] of the soldiers were often hollowed out having small iron receptacles, which were filled with a clear colorless flammable mixture of light hydrocarbons that burned. This was one of the most lethal weapons as it caused havoc among the enemy troops, unless the soldiers had the large body shields that had been drenched in water and could quench the fiery darts. In fact, the earliest manuscripts repeat the definite article, literally "the darts of the evil one, the fiery (darts)," emphasizing the fact that they were above all destructive. If the soldier's shield caught fire, he would be tempted to throw it down, leaving himself open to the enemy's spear.

What does the highly metaphorical language of the fiery darts depict and how does this weaken or undercut our faith? It may come in the form of minor persecution if we live in the Western world, such as being ridiculed for our Christian faith, even verbally assaulted by Bible critics.

---

[257] IBID

[258] W. E. Vine, Merrill F. Unger and William White, Jr., vol. 2, Vine's Complete Expository Dictionary of Old and New Testament Words (Nashville, TN: T. Nelson, 1996), 571.

[259] 6.36 belos, ous n: a missile, including arrows (propelled by a bow) or darts (hurled by hand)—'arrow, dart.' In the NT belos occurs only in a highly figurative context, to bele … peporomena 'flaming arrows (or darts)' Eph 6:16, and refers to temptations by the Devil.—Louw and Nida 6.36.

Another fiery dart may be the temptation to put money over ministry. Then, there is the constant temptation from Satan's world to lure us into immorality. You would have to be literally blindfolded to not see sexually explicit images hundreds of times per day, as it is used to sell everything. It is not only the images, but also the mindset. I will give you just one example, and please excuse the graphic nature. The modern day junior high school children (13 and 14 years old); literally view oral sex as being no different than kissing one another on the lips.

If we are to protect our Christian family, our congregation of brothers and sisters, and ourselves, we must possess **"the shield of faith."** Faith is not a simple belief in Jesus Christ as some misinformed ones might tell us; rather it is an active faith in Jesus Christ. James tells at 1:19 "You believe that God is one; you do well. Even the demons believe, and shudder!" The demons and Satan believe in the existence of Jesus Christ, and yet this brings them no salvation whatsoever. Faith comes from taking in an active knowledge of the Father and the Son, to the point of building a relationship, a friendship based on the deepest love, and the committing of oneself to the point of turning your life over completely. It is regular prayerful communication, understanding and valuing how he protects us. – Joshua 23:14; Luke 17:5; Romans 10:17.

Yet again, we turn to our great exemplar, Jesus Christ, who demonstrated his faith throughout some very trying times. He completely trusted the Father to accomplish his will and purposes. (Matthew 26:42, 53, 54; John 6:38) A great example of this trust can be found when Jesus was in the garden of Gethsemane. He was in great anguish because he knew that he was going to be executed as a blasphemer of his Father, and even then, he fell with his face to the ground and prayed, "My Father, if it is possible, may this cup be taken from me. Yet not as I will, but as you will." (Matthew 26:39) Not that he was backing out of the execution, the ransom that is, but he wanted to be executed for another reason, other than a blasphemer. Jesus was an integrity keeper, which brought great joy to the Father. (Proverbs 27:11) As we face difficult times in the world that is alienated from God, we will do well to imitate Jesus great faith, and not give our under the pressures of a world that lies in the hands of the evil one. Moreover, our faith will be refined if we trust in God, evidencing our love for him, by applying his Word in our daily walking with him. (Psalm 19:7-11; 1 John 5:3) The immediate gratifications that this world has to offer could never compare with the blessings that lie ahead. – Proverbs 10:22.

6:16 the shield of faith. This Greek word usually refers to the large shield (2.5 ft. x 4.5 ft.) that protected the entire body. The faith to which Paul refers is not the body of Christian doctrine (as the term is used in 4:13) but basic trust in God. The believer's continual trust in God's word and promise is "above all" absolutely necessary to protect him from temptations to every sort of sin. All sin comes when the victim falls to Satan's lies and promises of pleasure, rejecting the better choice of obedience and blessing. **fiery darts**. Temptations are likened to the flaming arrows shot by the enemy and quenched by the oil-treated leather shield (cf. Ps. 18:30; Prov. 30:5, 6; 1 John 5:4).[260]

Not long ago, those trying to curb the use of drugs within the American youth had the saying, "the mind is a terrible thing to waste." Our next piece of armor of God would be a very useful tool for protecting the Christian mind, **the helmet of salvation**. The Apostle Paul said to the Thessalonians, "we must stay sober and let our faith and love be like a suit of armor. Our firm hope that we will be saved is our helmet," because it protects our Christian mind. (1 Thessalonians 5:8) Even though we may have accepted Christ, and have entered onto the path of salvation, we still suffer from imperfect human weaknesses. Even though our foremost desire is to do good, our thinking can be corrupted by this fleshly world that surrounds us. We need to **not** be like this world, but rather openly allow God to alter the way we think, through his Word the Bible, which will help us fully to grasp everything that is good and pleasing to him. (Romans 7:18; 12:2) You likely recall the test that Jesus faced, where Satan offered him "all the kingdoms of the world and their glory." (Matthew 4:8-10) Jesus response was to refer to Scripture, "Be gone, Satan! For it is written, 'you shall worship the Lord your God and him only shall you serve.'" Paul had this to say about Jesus, "looking to Jesus, the founder and perfecter of our faith, who for the joy that was set before him endured the cross, despising the shame, and is seated at the right hand of the throne of God." – Hebrews 12:2.

We need to understand that the above examples of faith, does not come to us automatically. If we focusing on what this current system of things has to offer, as opposed to focusing on the hopes that are plainly laid out in Scripture, we will be weak in the face of any difficult trial. After a few stumbles, it may be that we suffer spiritual shipwreck, and lose

---

[260] IBID

our hope altogether. Then again, if we frequently feed our minds, or concentrate the mind on the promises of God, we will carry on delighting in the hope that has been offered us. Romans 12:12.

6:17 the helmet of salvation. The helmet protected the head, always a major target in battle. Paul is speaking to those who are already saved, and is therefore not speaking here about attaining salvation. Rather, Satan seeks to destroy a believer's assurance of salvation with his weapons of doubt and discouragement. This is clear from Paul's reference to "a helmet the hope of salvation" (Is. 59:17; see note on 1 Thess. 5:8). But although a Christian's feelings about his salvation may be seriously damaged by Satan-inspired doubt, his salvation itself is eternally protected and he need not fear its loss. Satan wants to curse the believer with doubts, but the Christian can be strong in God's promises of eternal salvation in Scripture (see John 6:37–39; 10:28, 29; Rom. 5:10; 8:31–39; Phil. 1:6; 1 Pet. 1:3–5). Security is a fact; assurance is a feeling that comes to the obedient Christian (1 Pet. 1:3–10).[261]

If we are to keep our Christian mind on the hope that lies ahead, we need to possess **the Sword of the Spirit.**[262] The loving letter from our heavenly Father, his Word, the Bible is stated to be "living and active, sharper than any two-edged sword, piercing to the division of soul and of spirit, of joints and of marrow, and discerning the thoughts and intentions of the heart." This Word, if understood correctly, applied in a balanced manner, can transform our lives, and help us avoid or minimalize the pitfalls of this imperfect life. We can depend on that Word when we are overwhelmed, or temple to give way to the flesh, and when the Bible critics of this world attempt to do away with our faith. (2 Corinthians 10:4-5) We need to heed the words of the Apostle Paul to his spiritual son, Timothy:

2 Timothy 3:14-17 Updated American Standard Version (UASV)

[14] You **[Timothy]**, however, continue in the things you have learned and were persuaded to believe, knowing from whom you have learned

---

[261] IBID

[262] **the sword of the Spirit.** As the sword was the soldier's only weapon, so God's Word is the only needed weapon, infinitely more powerful than any of Satan's. The Greek term refers to a small weapon (6–18 in. long). It was used both defensively to fend off Satan's attacks, and offensively to help destroy the enemy's strategies. It is the truth of Scripture. – IBID

them **[Paul, who Timothy traveled with and studied under for 15 years]**, ¹⁵ and that from infancy[263] you have known the sacred writings **[the whole Old Testament]**, which are able to make you wise for salvation through trust[264] in Christ Jesus. ¹⁶ All Scripture is inspired by God and profitable for teaching, for reproof, for correction, for training in righteousness; ¹⁷ so that the man of God may be fully competent, equipped for every good work.

On these verses, New Testament Bible scholar Knute Larson writes,

3:14–15. Each of us is susceptible to this dangerous trap of deception unless we obey Scripture vigilantly. Following Christ is more than a one-time decision or an occasional church service or kind act. True Christianity involves continual dependence and obedience to Christ the king. Paul told Timothy to **continue in what you have learned and have become convinced of**. Our faith is proved by its endurance.

Two elements are necessary for faithful living. First, we must possess knowledge of the truth. Truth enlightens a person about what is right and wrong, what constitutes purpose and happiness. We cannot trust or love which we do not know. The second element is conviction or belief. We express our belief system in the daily decisions we make and the behaviors in which we engage. No one acts contrary to belief (though we may act contrary to our professions of belief).

Paul also wanted Timothy to consider **those from whom you learned [truth], and how from infancy you have known the holy Scriptures**. Once again he had Timothy's mother and grandmother in mind (see 2 Tim. 1:5). Timothy was schooled in the Old Testament writings and had learned the need for forgiveness, the provision of God, and the necessity of faith. He had also been discipled by Paul, learning Christ and the church. In each case, Timothy had not only been given knowledge; he had been witness to godly lives.

---

[263] *Brephos* is "the period of time when one is very young–'childhood (probably implying a time when a child is still nursing), infancy." – GELNTBSD

[264] *Pisteuo* is "to believe to the extent of complete trust and reliance—'to believe in, to have confidence in, to have faith in, to trust, faith, trust.' – GELNTBSD

These people served as examples to Timothy about the truth of God, the need for endurance, and the reward of faithfulness. Each person had staked his or her life on the revelation of the Scriptures which, according to Paul, **are able to make you wise for salvation through faith in Christ Jesus.** (Larson 2000, 306)

The apostle Paul stressed the significance of God's Word when he wrote to Timothy, "Continue in what you have learned and have firmly believed." "The things" that Paul revealed are Bible truths, which moved Timothy to grow into having faith in the gospel. These same truths, along with the entire Word of God (i.e., "All Scripture), can affect us today in the same way, making us "wise for salvation through faith in Christ Jesus."

Enemy Strategies

To fight with, struggle against, or deal with the world of mankind alienated from God or Satan and his demons is like walking through a field sown with landmines. An attack against our faith can come from any quarter, and our enemies try to catch us by surprise. However, rest assured, "No temptation has overtaken you that is not common to man. God is faithful, and he will not let you be tempted beyond your ability, but with the temptation he will also provide the way of escape, that you may be able to endure it." – 1 Corinthians 10:13.

The most straightforward **attack** the past thirty years has been **against Bible truths that are fundamental to our faith.** The problem is that Christianity was slow to respond to the threat. For a time the atheist and agnostic was penning books written on a layman's level, while Bible scholars were busy penning academic books that the average churchgoer would have no interest. The modern day Bible critic is better prepared as well because he has been devouring the Bible critic books.[265]

---

[265] **HERE ARE A FEW BOOK BY THE BIBLE CRITIC**

The God Delusion by Richard Dawkins

Why There Is No God: Simple Responses to 20 Common Arguments for the Existence of God by Armin Navabi and Nicki Hise

God Is Not Great: How Religion Poisons Everything by Christopher Hitchens

Misquoting Jesus: The Story Behind Who Changed the Bible and Why by Bart D. Ehrman

Christians on the other have been caught unawares because they do not devour Christian apologetic books with the same vigor.[266] The Bible critics use smooth words and twisted words, misrepresenting the facts, in an effort to cause spiritual shipwreck. Proverbs 11:9 notes, "With his mouth the godless man would destroy his neighbor, but by knowledge the righteous are delivered."

It would be a mistake to tell Christians to not read books by Bible critics; this gives the impression that you are hiding something from them. The better approach would be to have the Christian read a few Christian apologetic books, opening their eyes, and then have them read the Bible critic books. This way, with the knowledge they took in they will be able to identify the lies, the misleading, and the misrepresenting of the Bible critic.

Another tool of Satan is **entertainment**. Another measure that needs to be taken is the fleeing from anything that will generate wrong desires, which lead to wrong actions. This means keeping our eyes and ears away from pornography and homosexual advocates. (Col. 3:5) We need to understand that the Bible's moral values are not respected in today's world.

Parents, teachers, couches, and the like influenced the youth of the 1950s and 1960s. Most young people today are very much influenced by hip-hop, rap, and heavy metal music, as well reality television, celebrities, movies, video games, and the Internet, especially social media. Parents are now allowing their children to receive life altering opinions, beliefs, and worldviews from the likes of Snooki, a cast member of the MTV reality show *Jersey Shore*. Kim Kardashian and her family rose to prominence with their reality television series, *Keeping Up with the Kardashians*.

---

[266] **HERE ARE A FEW BOOK BY CHRISTIAN APOLOGISTS**

Misquoting Truth: A Guide to the Fallacies of Bart Ehrman's "Misquoting Jesus" by Timothy Paul Jones

Defending Your Faith: An Introduction to Apologetics by R. C. Sproul

Holman QuickSource Guide to Christian Apologetics (Holman Quicksource Guides)

On Guard: Defending Your Faith with Reason and Precision by William Lane Craig and Lee Strobel

The ABC Family channel (owned by Disney) comes across as a channel that you would want you children watching. However, most of the shows are nothing more than dysfunctional families, promotions of homosexuality as an alternative lifestyle, and young actors and actresses that are playing underage teens in high school, running around killing, causing havoc, and having sexual intercourse with multiple characters on the show. In August 2006, an all-new slogan and visual style premiered on ABC Family: A New Kind of Family. The channel shows such programming as Pretty Little Liars, Twisted, The Fosters, Melissa & Joey, Switched at Birth, The Lying Game, Bunheads and Baby Daddy.

The world has added new words to their vocabulary, like "sexting," which is the act of sending sexually explicit messages and/or photographs, primarily between cellphones. The term was first popularized in 2007. Then, there is "F-Bomb," which we are not going to define fully other than to say that the dictionary considers it "a lighthearted and printable euphemism" for something far more offensive. If all of the above is unfamiliar to you as a parent, and you have a teen or preteen child, you may want to Google the information.

Regardless of the degree of the relationship, these relationships often influence the thinking of a young life. It is important that you do not allow the wrong persons to influence you or your children. The truth is our thinking, and our actions are a direct result of bad associations, be it the wrong friends, music, celebrities, video games, or social media. The same holds true of good associations, like our parents, teachers, coaches, and good friends. Paul warned, "For there are many **rebellious men**, **empty talkers** and **deceivers**," from whom we should watch out! – Titus 1:10.

In the end, with help from God's Word, the Christian congregation, the pastor, family, and Christian counseling, you have a reasonable expectation that you will not act on the same sex desires. Moreover, there is the possibility that you may be one of the few that begins to alter oneself to the point that the desires are no more. If not, self-control will be the way of things until God brings this wicked age to an end. The final warning offered herein is this. Do not allow charismatic religious rhetoric to suggest that the laying on of hands can heal you. This will only leave you vulnerable, as you will then let down your guard, and not seek the help that you need. What they espouse is just not how it works and is unbiblical.

Another strategy used by the enemy is the **love of money**. Paul wrote, "For the love of money is a root of all kinds of evils. It is through this craving that some have wandered away from the faith and pierced themselves with many pangs." (1 Tim. 6:10, ESV) Commenting on 1 Timothy 6:10, MacArthur writes, "Lit. "affection for silver." In the context, this sin applies to false teachers specifically, but the principle is true universally. Money itself is not evil since it is a gift from God (Deut. 8:18); Paul condemns only the love of it (cf. Matt. 6:24) which is so characteristic of false teachers (see notes on 1 Pet. 5:2; 2 Pet. 2:1–3, 15). strayed from the faith. From the body of Christian truth. Gold has replaced God for these apostates, who have turned away from pursuing the things of God in favor of money."[267]

If a soldier loses his moral, he will become easy target for the enemy. "If you are slack [discouraged] in the day of distress, Your strength is limited." (Pro. 24:10, NASB) **Discouragement** is another strategy of Satan. The apostle Paul wrote, "But since we belong to the day, let us be sober, having put on the breastplate of faith and love, and for a helmet the hope of salvation." (1 Thess. 5:5) Wearing "a helmet the hope of salvation," will help us fight discouragement. MacArthur writes, "Paul pictured the Christian life in military terms as being a life of soberness (alertness) and proper equipping. The breastplate covers the vital organs of the body. Faith is an essential protection against temptations, because it is trust in God's promise, plan, and truth. It is unwavering belief in God's Word that protects us from temptation's arrows. Looking at it negatively, it is unbelief that characterizes all sin. When believers sin, they have believed Satan's lie. Love for God is essential, as perfect love for Him yields perfect obedience to Him. Elsewhere, the warrior's breastplate has been used to represent righteousness (Is. 59:17; Eph. 6:14). Faith elsewhere is represented by a soldier's shield (Eph. 6:16). The helmet is always associated with salvation in its future aspects (cf. Is. 59:17; Eph. 6:17). Our future salvation is guaranteed, nothing can take it away (Rom. 13:11). Paul again combined faith, love, and hope (cf. 1:3)."[268]

Do Not Give Up the Fight

Some of us may have been fighting doubts, health problems, old age, the loss of loved ones and we may be growing weak, and, therefore, not fighting with the vigor that we once fought. Thomas D. Lea addresses the need to stay in the fight based on Hebrews 10:32-34,

---

[267] MacArthur, John (2005-05-09). *The MacArthur Bible Commentary* (Kindle Locations 60376-60380). Thomas Nelson. Kindle Edition.

[268] IBID, (Kindle Locations 59233-59240)

10:32–33. These verses urged the readers to remember the days after their conversion when they stood their ground while they faced threats to their faith. They were to remember their previous record. What a positive record it had been!

They had refused to compromise when they faced persecution for their faith. Sometimes they had become **publicly exposed to insult and persecution.** They had endured scorn and threats from crowds. The words of 12:4 suggest that they had not yet suffered martyrdom.

Sometimes they **stood side by side** with friends who were insulted and abused. They suffered because of their association with others. They found it a privilege to share in the sufferings of others.

10:34. The general description of persecution in verse 33 becomes specific in this verse. Facing hardship involves two matters. First, they had **sympathized with those in prison.** It was common in those days for Christians to receive imprisonment for their commitment to Christ (note Paul's imprisonments mentioned in 2 Cor. 11:23). Probably at least some of the recipients of Hebrews had suffered imprisonment because of their Christian confession. Visiting these imprisoned believers openly identified some of the readers as Christians and made them subject to arrest and persecution. They had endured public shame because of their encouragement to imprisoned Christians.

Second, the readers had experienced the loss of their property. They took the loss with joy. They were so convinced of the truth of Christianity that they submitted joyfully to the loss of their possessions. How could they do this?

The readers had learned that in Christ they had **better and lasting possessions.** They could never lose their possessions in Christ because these possessions lasted (see Matt. 6:20). Heaven's treasures had greater appeal than the temporary blessings of earth.

As we carry on in our fight for the faith, remember Jesus' words, "These things I have spoken to you, so that in Me you may have peace. In the world you have tribulation, but take courage; I have overcome the world." (John 16:33, NASB)

Review Questions

- How does the conduct of Uriah help us?

- How should we live our lives when we do not know the day or the hour of Jesus' return?

- Who are our enemies in our Christian war? Who is the most dangerous one of them all?

- Why is it important that a soldier know his enemy?

- Explain each piece of the armor of God.

- What are the enemy's strategies?

- What may happen to the fight in us over time, and how can we get it back?

APPENDIX A Those Who May Dwell with God

Is that even possible? What does it mean to dwell with Jehovah God anyway? It means that you can be God's friend. Jesus half-brother James tells us in his letter, "Abraham believed God, and it was counted to him as righteousness, and he was called a friend of God." (James 2:23, ESV) The above chapter title is figurative language that means all have the opportunity of developing such a relationship with God that he or she has access to God in prayer and worship. Let us start by meditatively reading the Psalm 15:1-5 in its entirety, and then we will do a verse-by-verse discussion of the Psalm. Read it first meticulously, emphatically hitting the ten dos and the don'ts, or conditions that give ones access to God as a friend, enabling them to approach him freely in their prayer and worship.

Psalm 15 Updated American Standard Version (UASV)

A Psalm of David.

15

O Jehovah, who may be a guest[269] in your tent?
Who shall dwell on your holy mountain?

² He **who walks blamelessly** and **does what is right**
and **speaks truth** in his heart;
³ who **does not slander** with[270] his tongue
and **does no evil** to his neighbor,
nor takes up a reproach against his friend;
⁴ in whose eyes **a vile person is despised**,
but who[271] **honors those** who fear Jehovah;
who **swears to his own hurt** and does not change;
⁵ who does **not put out his money at interest**,[272]
and does **not take a bribe** against the innocent.
He who does these things shall never be shaken.

---

[269] Lit *sojourn*

[270] Lit *according to*

[271] Lit *he*

[272] I.e. **not** to the destitute

We Walk Blamelessly and Do What is Right

The Hebrew word rendered "blameless" is *tamim*, is not a reference to a perfect condition, one without sin; it is simply living an exemplary moral life, a life that is whole or sound. When the *tamim* is used in reference to humans that live during this time of imperfection, it is meant in a relative sense, not as an absolute. If we look at all of the good characteristics and qualities of the Bible, which all Christians are subject to possessing, it must be in a balanced manner. He is not expected to be perfect in all of them. He is expected to meet a certain level of competence of each, not being out of balance. He would not be kind in the extreme to others, but lack self-control in private. What does "walking" signify here? It is used in a figurative sense of following a certain course of action, life course, which is outlined in God's Word, to the extent that he finds favor in God's eyes. – Psalm 1:1; 3 John 1:3-4.

We Speak the Truth in Our Heart

How does a Christian 'speak the truth in his heart?' It means that he is consistent in what he says, he is not double hearted (Psalm 12:2), (literally, with a heart and a heart), attempting to live one way in an outward sense, while concealing another life, or deceptively saying one thing, while in his mind, he is thinking something else entirely. – 1 Chronicles 12:33

Some Christians might not out and out lie, but they speak half-truths, to avoid and discomfort that may come from telling the complete truth. Christian students cheat on their tests while their Christian parents alter the figures on their taxes to make the bottom line look better. These fall short in that they are not whole or sound when it comes to the truth. The apostle Paul said, "Do not lie to each other, since you have taken off your old self with its practices and have put on the new self, which is being renewed in knowledge in the image of its Creator." (Colossians 3:9, 10) We must ask ourselves, are we completely honest in our dealings with others? Moreover, are we completely honest with ourselves? If we are, this will affect the next condition that must be met in order to be able freely to approach God in our prayers and worship.

We Do Not Slander With Our Tongue

To slander someone is to say something false or malicious (intentionally harmful) that damages somebody's reputation. The Hebrew verb ragal is a reference to the lowest part of the leg, the body part upon which a person or animal stands, the foot (regel). It is used both literally and figuratively. It has the meaning "to foot it," in other words, "to go about." The Israelites were commanded, "You shall not go about with slander among your people." (Lev. 19:16) We are robbing a person of his good name if we slander him, deliberately trying to do harm to his or her reputation. We can help to bring slander to a halt, by refusing to listen to it, and especially not spreading it on to another. If it is of such paramount importance that we control our speech, is it not, much more important that we control what we do?

We Do No Evil to Our Neighbor

We will fare far better in life if we apply the words of Jesus, which are in harmony with Psalm 15:3: "In all things, whatever you want that people should do to you, thus also you do to them." (Matt 7:12, LEB) It is simple, we must avoid doing anything bad to other people, but it must also be a heart condition of how we feel. The Psalmist said, "O you who love Jehovah, **hate evil**: He preserves the souls of his saints; He delivers them out of the hand of the wicked."(Ps 97:10, ASV) Therefore, if we are to be a friend of God like Abraham and many other holy ones of the past, we must live by the moral standards that he created within us.

This removing of bad from our lives would fall to not doing anyone wrong when we have dealings with them. This would include what we say, as well as what we do, in our dealings with others, doing nothing to bring them any kind of harm. That is avoiding the bad, but we also need to embrace doing the good for the people that enter our lives as well. This can be as small as driving in a courteous way when we are on the road. Are we in such a hurry that we do not pause to let another driver in our lane, or out of a parking lot into traffic. We can also do good by helping the elderly, help raise the spirits of the downhearted, comfort the grieving. What does the Psalmist address next?

We Do Not Reproach Our Friends

Bringing reproach on another is criticizing him or her to another for something they may have done wrong. Each of us makes mistakes, and we would hope that our friends would overlook these small imperfect moments in our lives. It is ironic, if we make a mistake, we hope the friend ignores it and does not share it with others. However, when others are the ones that make a mistake, we can be quick to share that moment of imperfection with others. There are some in the Christian congregation, who will share minor embarrassing weaknesses of others, to sidestep their own issues, or to build themselves up, while tearing down others. However, this type of spirit does not belong to a friend of God, who throws our transgressions into the sea (so that they are so far down that they will never be seen again). One who casts our transgressions as far off as the sunrise is from the sunset (the greatest distance possible), who throws our transgressions behind his back (so he is unable to see them).-- Micah 7:19; Psalm 103:12; Isaiah 38:17

Proverbs 17:9 Updated American Standard Version (UASV)

⁹ Whoever covers a transgression seeks love,
but he who repeats a matter separates close friends.

We are to Despise Vile Persons

A vile person is one who would have no value in the life of the true worshipers, who is unclean, lacking honesty or moral integrity, or morally corrupts. A true worshiper has to have dealings with those who practice sin in this world, but does not bond with such a person in any kind of social setting or friendship. He realizes that such an association would defile him. When a man with a white glove shakes hands with a man wearing a glove that is covered in dirt, the clean white glove does not rub off on the dirty glove; it is always the dirt coming off onto the clean glove.--1 Corinthians 5:6; 15:33

There is a tendency to overlook the defiled man if he is wealthy, famous, in a position of power. (Jude 16) We must come to the realization that friendship with God is impossible for those who become friends with those who are vile (wicked in their ways). We are to hate the wicked ones ways, anything that is contrary to the moral standard of God. (Rom. 12:9) So bad was Israel's king Jehoram that the prophet Elisha told him:

2 Kings 3:14 Updated American Standard Version (UASV)

¹⁴ And Elisha said, "As the Lord of hosts lives, before whom I stand, were it not that I have regard for Jehoshaphat the king of Judah, I would neither look at you nor see you.

If we want to be considered a friend of God, then, we will adopt his values and morals to the extent that we are uncomfortable around wrongdoers. We will have dealings only to the extent that we have to because we live in this world. As Paul said 'we must live in this world, but we need not be a part of it.' On the other hand, those we invite into our lives, as friends should be chosen based on their walk with God, not because they are wealthy, popular, or influential. We will choose our friends based on the love we have for our heavenly Father because we fear the idea of ever hurting him.

We Honor Those Who Fear God

This fear of God is not the dread that we would have of say being dangled over the edge of a cliff, or cowering in a closet as our house is being robbed by several criminals, or having a cruel employer that makes our life a living torture chamber. No, the fear of Jehovah is a reverential fear of displeasing him, because our love for him is like that of a loving father, but only greater. It is like a son, who imitates his father, so too we want to be like our heavenly Father, as we are made in his image.

Proverbs 1:7 Updated American Standard Version (UASV)

⁷ The fear of the Lord is the beginning of knowledge; fools despise wisdom and instruction.

This love for him, moves us to apply his Word more fully in our lives, it serves as a daily guide in all that we do. We realize that the values and morals that he has placed in our conscience are refined by his Word, and will help us be able to determine between what is good and what is bad. For example, one who lives by these values would apply all the Bible principles that would make him an excellent worker, meaning he would be productive, honest, and looking to be of help to all on the job site. Fellow workers may view this as attempts at seeking favor with management, looking to get ahead, so they ridicule this one. Others may feel that he is making them work harder, or look bad in the boss's eyes, so they despise him. What they do not realize is that these are his qualities as a person of God, and he has none of the evil intentions that fellow workers may suspect. Are we honoring persons like this, persons who fear God?

We Keep Our Promises Regardless of the Cost

We keep our promises that we make to Jehovah God himself, as well as to our neighbor, friends, family, employer, and so on, not allowing one word to fail, as this is what God would have done. (1 Kings 8:56; 2 Corinthians 1:20) We do this even if after having made a promise, it turns out that it is going to be more complicated, or more involved than we had originally thought. If we swear to help a neighbor one weekend and then a friend offers us a chance to go to once in a lifetime event, we keep our word. If we promise our wife that we will get something done, we get it done. Even when Joshua was tricked into giving his word to the Gibeonites, he still kept that word once he found out.

Joshua 9:16-19 Updated American Standard Version (UASV)

[16] At the end of three days after they had made a covenant with them, they heard that they were their neighbors and that they lived among them.[273] [17] Then the sons of Israel set out and came to their cities on the third day. Now their cities were Gibeon and Chephirah and Beeroth and Kiriath-jearim. [18] The sons of Israel did not strike them because the leaders of the congregation had sworn to them by Jehovah the God of Israel. And the whole congregation grumbled against the leaders. [19] But all the leaders said to all the congregation, "We have sworn to them by Jehovah, the God of Israel, and now we cannot touch them.

Thus, if we make a commitment to another, we are obligated to that promise, and it is our integrity on the line, as well as God's good name, because when we fail to keep a promised, we bring reproach on ourselves, as well as the God that we represent. Jesus said, "Let what you say be simply 'Yes' or 'No'; anything more than this comes from evil." (Matthew 5:37) Especially should all who have dedicated their lives to Christ be ever determined to live up to their promise to be his disciple?

---

[273] Or *within their land*

We Lend Our Money without Charging Interest

Of course, money lent for business purposes is an exception to this principle. David in this Psalm was referring to when we give money to those living or falling into poverty. Exodus 22:25 specifically says, "If you lend money to any of my people with you who is poor, you shall not be like a moneylender to him, and you shall not exact interest from him." We also find an account in Nehemiah where he discovered the poor being taken advantage of by others who were using them for ill-gotten gains, and he brought this to a stop.--Nehemiah 5:1-13.

As an aside, of interest is David's choice of words, for the Hebrew word he used is a derivative of another one that signifies "to bite." In other words, those greedy usurers were chewing up and devouring the destitute to line their pockets. We should rather live by the principles that Jesus outlined for us at Luke 14:12-14, "When you give a dinner or a banquet, do not invite your friends or your brothers or your relatives or rich neighbors, lest they also invite you in return, and you be repaid. But when you give a feast, invite the poor, the crippled, the lame, the blind, and you will be blessed, because they cannot repay you. For you will be repaid at the resurrection of the just." If it is our desire to be a friend of God and to dwell with him, we should never take advantage of those who are struggling financially.

We Do Not Take Bribes that Hurt the Innocent

A bribe is to give somebody money or some other incentive to do something, especially something illegal or dishonest, and this has a demeaning and shameful effect. We are told at Deuteronomy 16:19, "You shall not pervert justice. You shall not show partiality, and you shall not accept a bribe, for a bribe blinds the eyes of the wise and subverts the cause of the righteous." We are to be about just and justice alone, not perverting justice. We would never want to accept any incentive to do an innocent person wrong, which deserves justice. The greatest injustice since the fall of man had been when Judas Iscariot accepted a Bribe to betray Jesus Christ! Matthew 26:14-16.

We may believe that we are innocent under this provision, but if we have ever tried to influence another to avoid justice, in any way, we are guilty. The prophet Samuel sets the example for us to follow, "Here I am; testify against me before [Jehovah] and before his anointed. Whose ox have I taken? Or whose donkey have I taken? Or whom have I defrauded? Whom have I oppressed? Or from whose hand have I taken a bribe to blind my eyes with it? Testify against me, and I will restore it to you." They said, 'You have not defrauded us or oppressed us or taken anything from any man's hand.'" (1 Samuel 12:3, 4)

If We Do These Things We Will Stand Firm

King David closes this list of standards or criterion that we are to live by, with "he who does these things shall never be moved." The New Living Translation reads, "Such people will stand firm forever." This is not an absolute; it is relative to the imperfect condition we are in and the imperfect world in which we live. All of these kinds of statements in the Bible, if you do "A" you will get "B" are best understood if you these phrases before the statement: generally speaking, "on the whole," "by and large," or "as a rule" in the front of the verse. "Generally speaking, such people will stand firm forever." Unlike those in the world, who have their flesh as their god, we will fair far better if we do these things to the best of our Christian ability.

Of course, there is far more to being God's friend than what we have covered here in Psalm 15. Jesus brought the servant of God new spiritual light, such as what he said at John 4:23-24 "But the hour is coming and is now here, when the true worshipers will worship the Father in spirit and truth, for the Father, is seeking such people to worship him. God is spirit, and those who worship him must worship in spirit and truth." By following the Bible study program that we have outlined here in this publication, you will discover the deeper things of God, which will enable to draw closer, and become God's friend.

Review Questions

- Who are morally qualified so that may dwell with God?
- If you are to be God's friend, what must you be free of?
- Are you completely honest with yourself and others, speaking the truth in your heart?
- Who should we refuse to listen to?
- What does avoiding evil include?
- How does a Christian look upon upright persons?

APPENDIX B Walk Humbly With Your God

Micah 6:8 Updated American Standard Version (UASV)

⁸ He has told you, O mortal man, what *is* good,
   and what does Jehovah require of you
but to do justice, and to love kindness,
   and to walk humbly with your God?

It is certainly a difficult thing, trying to picture a puny human walk with the Creator of heaven and earth. It would be like setting a piece of sand next to the biggest bolder on earth, and this would not even be close. Of course, we are talking about a metaphorical walk, a life course that a Christian follows, one that is in harmony with Jehovah's values, will and purposes.

Others have done just that, as we learn from Scripture that "Enoch walked with God" and "Noah walked with God." If we truly are a friend of God, like Abraham, we will be living a life that is reflective of that friendship. Jehovah expects nothing less of his servants, than that they 'walk humbly with him.' – Genesis 5:22; 6:9; Malachi 2:4, 6; Micah. 6:8

If we are to walk with God in a system of things that is run by Satan, possessing a mind and body that leans naturally toward sin, it will be necessary for us to have a very close relationship, closer than any human relationship that we may have ever had. We read of Moses that it was, "by faith he left Egypt, not fearing the anger of the king, for he persevered as if he saw the invisible one." (Heb. 11:27) Even though King David had many bumps in his relationship with God, it is said that his "eyes are continually toward Jehovah." Yes, David said, "I have set Yahweh before me always. Because he is at my right hand I will not be shaken." – Psalm 25:15; 16:8, LEB.

Why should we walk with God? First, we do so because he is the giver of life, and the sovereign of the universe. Second, as our Creator, he designed us not to walk alone. How has that been working out for humanity over the past 6,000 plus years? "I know, O [Jehovah], that to the human is not his own way, nor to a person is the walking and the directing of his own step." (Jer. 10:23, LEB) Yes, we were designed to be under the umbrella of his sovereignty, possessing free will, but best served by following his lead. Therefore, our eternal happiness is dependent upon our walking with him.

We can draw comfort from the fact that God created us out of his endless love, making us in such a way, to enjoy life to the fullest extent. It was Adam who rebelled, placing us in this difficult situation. Now Jehovah is moving heaven and earth to get us back to his intended purpose. Jehovah is omniscient (all knowing), which means he knows what is best for us. Having him walk us through this difficult period in human history is the safest way to the end of this wicked system of things. – Proverbs 2:6-9; Psalm 91:1

Further, walking with God should come out of our love for him, not what we can gain from him. We should find true happiness in our friendship with him; otherwise, our motives are not pure. The Scriptures are quite clear about how he feels about our love for him, as he tells us to "Be wise, my child, and make my heart glad, and I will answer him who reproaches me with a word." – Proverbs 77:11, LEB.

Threefold Resistance

When we enter the pathway of walking with our God, we will certainly come across resistance from three different areas. **Our greatest obstacle** is **ourselves**, because we have inherited imperfection from our first parents Adam and Eve. The Scriptures make it quite clear that we are mentally bent toward bad, not good. (Gen 6:5; 8:21, AT) In other words, our natural desire is toward wrong. Prior to sinning, Adam and Eve were perfect, and they had the natural desire of doing good, and to go against that was to go against the grain of their inner person. Scripture also tells us of our inner person, our heart.

Jeremiah 17:9 Updated American Standard Version (UASV)

⁹ The heart is more deceitful than all else,
and desperately sick;
who can understand it?

Romans 7:21-25 Updated American Standard Version (UASV)

²¹ I find then the law in me that when I want to do right, that evil is present in me. ²² For I delight in the law of God according to the inner man, ²³ but I see a different law in my members, warring against the law of my mind and taking me captive in the law of sin which is in my members. ²⁴ Wretched man that I am! Who will deliver me from this body of death? ²⁵ Thanks be to God through Jesus Christ our Lord! So then, I myself serve the law of God with my mind, but with my flesh, I serve the law of sin.

1 Corinthians 9:27 Updated American Standard Version (UASV)

27 but I discipline my body and make it my slave, so that, after I have preached to others, I myself will not be disqualified.

The **second greatest obstacle** is the **world of humankind that is alienated from God**. Its ruler, Satan, designs this world to cater to our fallen flesh. The spirit of this world comes from Satan himself, and if breathed in for too long, we will begin to adopt the same mindset, the same thinking, attitude, conduct, and speech that is opposite of Jehovah God. This poisonous air will paralyze us quite quickly if we entertain it either by thinking on it, or worse still, engaging in it. 1 Corinthians 2:11-16, LEB

1 Peter 4:3-4 Updated American Standard Version (UASV)

3 For the time that has passed *was* sufficient *to do what the Gentiles desire to do*, having lived in licentiousness, *evil* desires, drunkenness, carousing, drinking parties, and wanton idolatries, **4** with respect to which they are surprised *when* you do not run with *them* into the same flood of dissipation, *and so they* revile *you*.[274]

The **third greatest obstacle** is **Satan the Devil and his demon army**. Yes, they are so powerful that one demon could kill hundreds of thousands of humans in very short order. That is why true Christians receive a hedge placed around them by God, protecting them from Satan and the demons. Yes, God's servants receive special protection from this powerful force. (Job 1-2) The only way to weaken that protection is to

---

[274] **"4:3 lewdness . . . abominable idolatries**. Lewdness describes unbridled, unrestrained sin, an excessive indulgence in sensual pleasure. Revelries has the idea of an orgy. The Greek word was used in extrabiblical literature to refer to a band of drunken, wildly acting people, swaggering and staggering through public streets, wreaking havoc. Thus, the pleasures of the ungodly are described here from the perspective of God as despicable acts of wickedness. Though Peter's readers had indulged in such sins before salvation, they must never do so again. Sin in the believer is a burden which afflicts him rather than a pleasure which delights him.

4:4 they think it strange. One's former friends are surprised, offended, and resentful because of the Christian's lack of interest in ungodly pleasures. the same flood of dissipation. Dissipation refers to the state of evil in which a person thinks about nothing else. The picture here is of a large crowd running together in a mad, wild race—a melee pursuing sin." – MacArthur, John (2005-05-09). The MacArthur Bible Commentary (Kindle Locations 64155-64162). Thomas Nelson. Kindle Edition.

violate your conscience repeatedly, toy with demonic activities, like horror movies, rap and heavy metal music, games like the wigi-board or dungeons and dragons.

Our human imperfections and the world that caters to them is with us 24/7. True, we can get control over our vessel by putting on the new personality, gaining the mind of Christ, and the help of Holy Spirit. However, it does not take much to drift away, fall away, refuse, draw away, become sluggish, become hardened through deceptive powers, or shrink back from Christian responsibilities. We just need to entertain the wrong thoughts too long, without dismissing them, and then we are on our way. (James 1:14-15) Now, as far as Satan goes, Peter warns us in the extreme to, "Be sober; be on the alert. Your adversary the devil walks around like a roaring lion, looking for someone to devour." (1 Pet. 5:8) Paul also said that were to,

Ephesians 6:11-12 Updated American Standard Version (UASV)

[11] Put on the full armor of God, so that you will be able to stand firm against the schemes of the devil.[275] [12] For our struggle[276] is not against flesh and blood, but against the rulers, against the powers, against the world-rulers of this darkness, against the wicked spirit forces in the heavenly places.[277]

---

[275] "**6:11 Put on the whole armor of God**. Put on conveys the idea of permanence, indicating that armor should be the Christian's sustained, life-long attire. Paul uses the common armor worn by Roman soldiers as the analogy for the believer's spiritual defense and affirms its necessity if one is to hold his position while under attack. wiles. This is the Greek word for schemes, carrying the idea of cleverness, crafty methods, cunning, and deception. Satan's schemes are propagated through the evil world system over which he rules, and are carried out by his demon hosts. Wiles is all-inclusive, encompassing every sin, immoral practice, false theology, false religion, and worldly enticement. See note on 2 Corinthians 2:11. the devil. Scripture refers to him as "the anointed cherub" (Ezek. 28:14), "the ruler of the demons" (Luke 11:15), "the god of this world" (2 Cor. 4:4), and "the prince of the power of the air" (2:2). Scripture depicts him opposing God's work (Zech. 3:1), perverting God's Word (Matt. 4:6), hindering God's servant (1 Thess. 2:18), obscuring the gospel (2 Cor. 4:4), snaring the righteous (1 Tim. 3:7), and holding the world in his power (1 John 5:19)." – MacArthur, John (2005-05-09). *The MacArthur Bible Commentary* (Kindle Locations 57495-57498). Thomas Nelson. Kindle Edition.

[276] Lit., "wrestling."

[277] "**6:12 wrestle**. A term used of hand-to-hand combat. Wrestling features trickery and deception, like Satan and his hosts when they attack. Coping with

Threefold Assistance

There is a threefold defense against this threefold opposition to our walking with God. **First**, we have **the Word of God**, which should come in the way of literal translations, like the English Standard Version and New American Standard Bible. Jehovah God gave us this special revelation to guide us through this wicked time. It has the power to make us stronger spiritually, as well as fortify us to accomplish his will and purposes. The Bible should be read daily, in conjunction with our recommended Bible reading program.[278] We also need to use our Bible in all of our religious meetings. If a Scripture is being read, we need to look it up. We also need to use our Bible in our ministry, meaning that we need to formulate texts that can help us to teach others the good news of the Kingdom.

Deuteronomy 17:19 Updated American Standard Version (UASV)

[19] And it shall be with him, and he shall read in it all the days of his life, that he may learn to fear Jehovah his God by keeping all the words of this law and these statutes, and doing them,

As we work our way through the Bible in our Bible reading program, let us not rush, but make sure we understand the author's intended meaning, and how we can apply that in our lives, as well as share it with others. We should be able to see our walking with God, come to life through the historical accounts found all throughout Scripture.

Joshua 1:7-8 Updated American Standard Version (UASV)

[7] Only be strong and very courageous, being careful to do according to all the law that Moses my servant commanded you; do not turn from it to the right or to the left, so that you may have success wherever you

---

deceptive temptation requires truth and righteousness. The four designations describe the different strata and rankings of those demons and the evil supernatural empire in which they operate. Satan's forces of darkness are highly structured for the most destructive purposes. Cf. Colossians 2:15; 1 Peter 3:22. not . . . against flesh and blood. See 2 Corinthians 10:3–5. spiritual hosts of wickedness. This possibly refers to the most depraved abominations, including such things as extreme sexual perversions, occultism, and Satan worship. See note on Colossians 1:16. in the heavenly places. As in 1:3; 3:10, this refers to the entire realm of spiritual beings. – MacArthur, John (2005-05-09). *The MacArthur Bible Commentary* (Kindle Locations 57499-57505). Thomas Nelson. Kindle Edition.

[278] http://christianway.us/page/bible-reading-program

go. ⁸ This Book of the Law shall not depart from your mouth, but you shall meditate on it day and night, so that you may be careful to do according to all that is written in it; for then you will make your way prosperous, and then you will have good success.

Below in Psalm 1:1-3, you will notice in verse 1 that there is a progression of intimacy through walking in the counsel of the wicked, to standing with sinners, to sitting with scoffers. Each level is a sign of spending more time with, being more deeply involved. We should not be involved with any of these three, because this would never be in harmony with a Christian, who is walking with God. Yes, verse 2 helps us to appreciate where our delight is found, the law of Jehovah, to which we read and study in a meditative way, day and night, which simply means on a regular basis. Truly, verse 3 helps us to appreciate the result of avoiding certain ones, and cultivating a love for God's Word, endurance and a strong spiritual health. If we follow the counsel of verses 1-2, we will be able to weather any storm that may come upon us.

Psalm 1:1-3 Updated American Standard Version (UASV)

The Way of the Righteous and the Wicked

Blessed is the man
   who walks not in the counsel of the wicked,
 nor stands in the way of sinners,
nor sits in the seat of scoffers;
² but his delight is in the law of Jehovah,
  and on his law he meditates day and night.

  ³ He is like a tree
planted by streams of water²⁷⁹
that yields its fruit in its season,
  and its leaf does not wither.
In all that he does, he prospers.

Second, along with God's Word, are some of the best **Bible study tools** as well as the **Christian congregation**. Paul tells the Ephesians, "Look carefully then how you walk, not as unwise but as wise, making the best use of the time, because the days are evil." (Eph. 5:15-16) Moreover, the Apostle Paul exhorted "let us consider how to stir up one

---

²⁷⁹ "Here, David is referring to a tree that has been deliberately planted in a choice location; not something, that by chance, has sprung up just anywhere. Consideration and thought has gone into its planting. Such is the planning by God for the life of a Christian."—Bruce Prince.

another to love and good works, not neglecting to meet together, as is the habit of some, but encouraging one another, and all the more as you see the Day drawing near." (Heb. 10:24-25)

Third, we have **Holy Spirit**, which sustains us in these difficult days. We need to "Live by the Spirit and reject the deeds of the flesh." If we are to be victorious over our fallen flesh, or fallen imperfection, it will be by way of the Spirit. From our first step of entering the path of salvation, to the continuation of walking on that path of developing our new personality, and taking on the mind of Christ, that is sanctification, we are in need of the Holy Spirit.

Galatians 5:16-26 Updated American Standard Version (UASV)

16 16 But I say, walk by the Spirit, and you will not carry out the desire of the flesh. 17 For the desires of the flesh are against the Spirit, and the desires of the Spirit are against the flesh, for these are opposed to each other, so that you may not do the things you want to do. 18 But if you are led by the Spirit, you are not under the law. 19 Now the works of the flesh are evident, which are: sexual immorality, impurity, sensuality, 20 idolatry, sorcery, enmity, strife, jealousy, fits of anger, rivalries, dissensions, divisions, 21 envy, drunkenness, orgies, and things like these. I warn you, as I warned you before, that those who do such things will not inherit the kingdom of God. 22 But the fruit of the Spirit is love, joy, peace, patience, kindness, goodness, faithfulness, 23 gentleness, self-control; against such things there is no law. 24 And those who belong to Christ Jesus have crucified the flesh with its passions and desires.

25 If we live by the Spirit, let us also walk by the Spirit. 26 Let us not become conceited, provoking one another, envying one another.

Those who follow the flesh will reap the results of such a course by having unattractive fruits. On the other hand, those who follow the lead of the Spirit will have fruitage that is attractive and beneficial for themselves, family, congregation, friends, and neighbors. One thing that we have to realize by looking at other related texts is, these fruits are not the results of our efforts, are the consequence of having an active faith in Christ, which makes us receptive to them.

Godly Devotion

If we are to walk with God, we need to possess the most important ingredient, FAITH. "Now faith is the reality of what is hoped for, the proof of what is not seen." (Heb. 11:1, HCSB) "Now without faith it is impossible to please God, for the one who draws near to Him must believe that He exists and rewards those who seek Him." (Heb. 11:6, HCSB) However, before we can have the faith that we need to walk with God, we must ask, "Do two walk together unless they have met?" (Amos 3:3, LEB) Yes, if we are to truly going to get to walk with God, we must, "this is eternal life: that they may know You, the only true God, and the One You have sent, Jesus Christ." – John 17:3, HCSB.

Proverbs 2:1-6 Updated American Standard Version (UASV)

The Value of Wisdom

2 My son, if you receive my words
and treasure up my commandments with you,
² making your ear attentive to wisdom
and inclining your heart to discernment;[280]
³ For if you cry for discernment[281]
and raise your voice for understanding,
⁴ if you seek it like silver
and search for it as for hidden treasures,
⁵ then you will understand the fear of Jehovah
and find the knowledge of God.
⁶ For Jehovah gives wisdom;
from his mouth come knowledge and understanding;

Once we have studied to the point of coming to know God through knowledge, discernment, and understanding, we will begin to appreciate who he is, what he did for us, and after we had rebelled, what he did to save us. Moreover, after we have begun to live by the principles within his revelation to us, we will begin to love and appreciate him even more, as we see a life of chaos; become a life of order, blessing, and joy, even in this imperfect world. If we are truly to walk with God, we must be in harmony with his will and purposes. "Not everyone who says to me, 'Lord, Lord,' will enter the kingdom of heaven, but the one who does the will of my Father who is in heaven." (Matt 7:21, ESV) Exactly, what is the will and purpose of God? You might be thinking that it is to remove sin and death from his human creation, because of sending his Son, Jesus Christ to ransom those that are receptive to the Gospel. However, this is not the primary purpose of God; it is the vindication of the slanderous

---

[280] The Hebrew word rendered here as "discernment" (*tevunah*) is related to the word *binah*, translated "understanding." Both appear at Proverbs 2:3.

[281] See 2.2 ftn.

317

accusations made by Satan the Devil, made in the Garden of Eden, and in the book of Job. (Gen 3:1-6; Job 1-2) It is by means of his Son in the Kingdom of God that is to bring this about. The secondary purpose, which runs alongside is the vindication of his human creation.

Exodus 34:14 Updated American Standard Version (UASV)

[14] for you shall worship no other god, for Jehovah, whose name is Jealous, is a jealous God,[282]

Mark 12:30 Updated American Standard Version (UASV)

[30] and you shall love the Lord your God with all your heart, and with all your soul, and with all your mind, and with all your strength.'[283]

Matthew 6:33 Updated American Standard Version (UASV)

[33] But be you seeking[284] the kingdom of God and his righteousness, and all these things will be added to you.

Have we grown so close to God that we understand the issues behind why we were allowed to enter into this period of sin and death, as opposed to just removing those that caused the rebellion, why he has allowed pain and suffering to continue for so long?[285] Are we willing to work toward the same purpose, the vindication of God's great name and reputation, to resolve the issues that were raised? If so, we will seek out what our role in the great commission is (Matt. 28:19-20), and we will carry it out with our whole heart, soul, mind and strength.

---

[282] God is jealous for His people Israel in sense (1), that is, God is intolerant of rival gods (Exod. 20:5; 34:14; Deut. 4:24; 5:9) One expression of God's jealousy for Israel is God's protection of His people from enemies. Thus God's jealousy includes avenging Israel (Ezek. 36:6; 39:25; Nah. 1:2; Zech. 1:14; 8:2). Phinehas is described as jealous with God's jealousy (Num. 25:11, 13, sometimes translated zealous for God). Elijah is similarly characterized as jealous (or zealous) for God (1 Kings 19:10, 14). *Holman Illustrated Bible Dictionary*, ed. Chad Brand, Charles Draper, Archie England et al. (Nashville, TN: Holman Bible Publishers, 2003), 873.

[283] Quotation from Deuteronomy 6:4–5, which reads, "Hear, O Israel! Jehovah our God is one Jehovah! You shall love Jehovah your God with all your heart and with all your soul and with all your might."

[284] Gr., *zeteite*; the verb form indicates continuous action.

[285] Why Has God Permitted Wickedness and Suffering:

http://www.christianpublishers.org/suffering-evil-why-god

God's Case for Justice

If we are to walk with God, we have to be guided by his divine justice. He is holy, so we to must be holy, which means that like him, we separate ourselves from anything that would be at odds with his moral standards. In addition, while he is perfect in an absolute sense, we can do this by loving our enemies and praying for those who persecute us. Even though we are truly insignificant as we walk alongside the Creator of all things, we must be a dispenser of his brand of justice. – Micah 6:8; 1 Peter 1:16; Matthew 5:48.

We must love to do right,[286] but deplore the idea of ever doing what is bad, if we are to continue our walk with God. Satan's world has catered to the fleshly desires that lie within each of us for so long; it is not great thing for us to be tempted in a weak moment, and surrender. Therefore, our best recourse is to cultivate abhorrence for what is bad. Not one of us should ever believe that we are too strong, or that we might never stumble, because the Apostle Paul was not so bold to believe this about himself. – Isaiah 61:8; Psalm 45:7; 97:10; Romans 12:9; 1 Corinthians 9:27; 10:12.

Each of us is well aware of what our particular weakness is. The best defense against any such weakness is to identify it to ourselves outwardly in prayer, regularly. We need to understand how we fall short in this weakness, what is usually going on with us at the time we give in. We need to see if there are innocent- appearing situations that will put us in the line of fire. Once these are understood, we need to avoid them at all costs. If one is an alcoholic, it is all too clear that he would not take a job as a bartender, or rent an apartment above a bar. However, what about the convenient store where you pick up the newspaper, if it has a very large alcohol section. If our weakness has something to do with sex, we would not want to find ourselves in a compromising situation with the opposite sex, or the same sex if this is the tendency. If immoral thoughts enter our mind, they are to be immediately dismissed ("flee fornication"), followed by a prayer. We must self-talk to ourselves about the consequences, quashing all irrational thoughts. – Matthew 10:26; 2 Cor. 10:5; Isa. 52:11.

---

[286] "The Greek word "agape", which is generally translated into the all-rounder English word "love", means simply to seek the other's highest good. We can do this even for those who persecute us."—Bruce Prince.

Love Kindness

If we are to walk with God, we must love kindness. The Hebrew word *checed*, is rendered "loving-kindness, steadfast love, grace, mercy, faithfulness, goodness, devotion." "This word is used 240 times in the Old Testament, and is especially frequent in the Psalter. The term is one of the most important in the vocabulary of Old Testament theology and ethics."[287] If it were not for God's loving kindness toward his creation, at the rebellion, we would not even be here having this conversation. The Psalmist says, "How precious is your steadfast love, O God! The children of mankind take refuge in the shadow of your wings." (Ps. 26:7) Jeremiah helps us to appreciate that 'in Jehovah God is salvation." (Lam. 3:22-23) And James, the half-brother of Jesus wrote, "the Lord is compassionate and merciful." – James 5:11.

The Apostle Paul gives us the fruitage of the Spirit, "**love**, joy, peace, patience, **kindness**, goodness, faithfulness, gentleness, [and] self-control." If we can take on the quality of Loving-kindness, we will be more sympathetic, empathetic, tolerant, thoughtful, tender and supportive of others, even enemies. When we enter into a difficulty with another, we will have the ability to identify with and understand their feelings or difficulties. Even though it may appear that Jehovah God is far removed from us and our circumstances, he is very much able to identify with our circumstances, especially since he sent his Son to walk in our shoes, so to speak.

Psalm 103:6-14 Updated American Standard Version (UASV)

⁶ Jehovah performs righteous deeds
　and judgments for all who are oppressed.
⁷ He made known his ways to Moses,
　his acts to the sons of Israel.
⁸ Jehovah is compassionate and gracious,
　slow to anger and abounding in lovingkindness.
⁹ He will not always find fault,
　nor will he keep his anger forever.
¹⁰ He does not deal with us according to our sins,
　nor repaid us according to our iniquities.
¹¹ For as high as the heavens are above the earth,

---

[287] W. E. Vine, Merrill F. Unger and William White, Jr., vol. 1, *Vine's Complete Expository Dictionary of Old and New Testament Words* (Nashville, TN: T. Nelson, 1996), 142.

So great is his lovingkindness toward those who fear him.
12 As far as the east is from the west,
so far does he remove our transgressions from us.
13 As a father has compassion on his children,
so Jehovah has compassion on those who fear him.
14 For he himself knows our formation;
he remembers that we are dust.

Jesus Christ was the perfect example of an empathetic person. He chose to give up his position in heaven, to come down here and suffer with us, to walk with us, suffer a severe persecution, and a horrendous execution. Remember that Saul (Paul), prior to his conversion was persecuting the Christians and even played a part in the stoning of Stephen. The risen Christ came to Paul on the road to Damascus, as he was heading to arrest more Christians. Paul said to Jesus, "Who are you, Lord?" And he said, "I am Jesus, whom you are persecuting! (Acts 9:5) Jesus' statement means that he was putting himself in the place of those who were being persecuted. In other words, to be persecuting them, was the same as persecuting him.

Once Saul became a Christian, and started using his name Paul, we find him imitating Jesus empathic example. Paul too put himself in the circumstances of those to whom he witnessed.

1 Corinthians 9:19-23 Updated American Standard Version (UASV)

19 For though I am free from all men, I have made myself a slave to all, so that I may gain more. 20 And so to the Jews I became as a Jew, that I might gain Jews; to those under the law I became as under the law, though I myself am not under the law, that I might gain those under the law. 21 To those without law I became as without law, although I am not without law toward God but under the law toward Christ, that I might gain those without law. 22 To the weak I became weak, that I might gain the weak. I have become all things to all men, that I might by all means save some. 23 But I do all things for the sake of the gospel, that I may become a fellow partaker of it.

Walk Humbly With Your God

Imagine that the Creator of everything is willing to humble himself to walk with us. One would think that is a given (common sense) that, we would humble ourselves to walk with him. What exactly is involved in our humbling ourselves? It means that we are obedient to him as the sovereign of the universe. This should be the first thing we learn before we ever commit ourselves to him. If we are humble in our dealing, we will not be self-important. This means that a wife would recognize the headship of her husband, and that the congregation would recognize the authority of those taking the lead among them. Let us suppose that the wife of a household has better judgment than her husband has. It does not mean that she usurps his position, but then again, it does not mean that the husband is dismissive of her counsel. She can inform him, and he makes the decision based on that added knowledge.

Humility helps us to be submissive to those that have been given responsibility over us. The one with the responsibility could be a husband, a pastor in the congregation, or the superior authorities of the nation where we live. Everyone has someone who is over him or her but God. We need to keep in mind that our greatest goal is to make peace where there may be none, or to preserve peace. Another concern is our unity as a family or as a Christian congregation. Therefore, we must be wise in our dealings with others, considering much beside ourselves. If we have insight that can improve a family decision, or the congregation, it should be given at the appropriate time, and in the right way.

Certainly, if you have ever investigated the Bible a even a little, you know that the wisest course is to walk with God. However, if you have been at it for some time, you may have discovered that it is not always easy to do, when based on your human weaknesses, the wicked world that we live in, in addition to the influence of Satan and his demons. However, we know that it is not too difficult for God, who has given us his **(1)** Word, **(2)** study tools and the Christian congregation, as well as **(3)** the Holy Spirit. Then, he has opened himself up to hearing our every prayer that is in harmony with his will and purposes, giving us a chance to talk with him, especially in time of need.

Review Questions

- What does it mean to walk humbly with your God?
- What threefold resistance to we come across in our walk with our God?
- What threefold assistance do we have in our walk with our God
- What is Godly devotion?
- What do we mean by God's case for justice?
- What does it mean to love kindness?

- What does it mean to walk humbly with your God?

OTHER Books By Edward D. Andrews

Christian Publishing House
ISBN-13: 978-0692562314
ISBN-10: 0692562311

http://www.christianpublishers.org/apps/webstore/products/show/63
38461

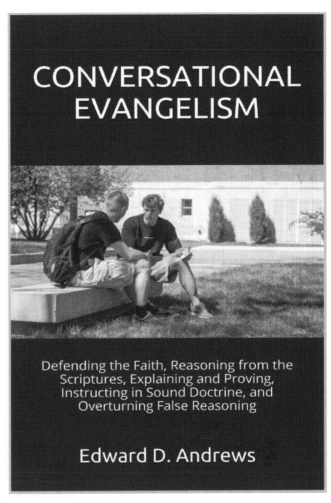

CONVERSATIONAL
EVANGELISM

Defending the Faith, Reasoning from the
Scriptures, Explaining and Proving,
Instructing in Sound Doctrine, and
Overturning False Reasoning

Edward D. Andrews

Christian Publishing House
ISBN-13: 978-0692472323
ISBN-10: 0692472320

http://www.christianpublishers.org/apps/webstore/products/show/57
49015

IF GOD IS GOOD

Why Does God Allow Suffering?

EDWARD D. ANDREWS

Christian Publishing House
ISBN-13: 978-0692414620
ISBN-10: 0692414622

http://www.christianpublishers.org/apps/webstore/products/show/57
86449

Bibliography

Anders, Max. *Holman New Testament Commentary: vol. 8, Galatians, Ephesians, Philippians, Colossians.* Nashville, TN: Broadman & Holman Publishers, 1999.

Anderson, Neil T. *Discipleship Counseling: The Complete Guide to Helping Others: Walk in Freedon and Gow in Christ.* Ventura: Regal Books, 2003.

Andrews, Edward D. *FOR AS I THINK IN MY HEART—SO I AM: Combining Biblical Counseling with Cognitive Behavioral Therapy.* Cambridge: Christian Publishing House, 2013.

—. *PUT OFF THE OLD PERSON WITH ITS PRACTICES And Put On the New Person.* Cambridge: Christian Publishing House, 2014.

Andrews, Stephen J, and Robert D Bergen. *Holman Old Testament Commentary: 1-2 Samuel.* Nashville: Broadman & Holman, 2009.

Arndt, William, Frederick W. Danker, and Walter Bauer. *A Greek-English Lexicon of the New Testament and Other Early Christian Literature. 3rd ed.*. Chicago: University of Chicago Press, 2000.

Arnold, Clinton E. *Zondervan Illustrated Bible Backgrounds Commentary: Matthew, Mark, Luke, vol. 1.* Grand Rapids, MI: Zondervan, 2002.

Barry, John D., and Lazarus Wentz. *The Lexham Bible Dictionary.* Bellingham, WA: Logos Bible Software, 2012.

Benner, David G. *Strategic Pastoral Counseling: A Short-Term Structural Model.* Grand Rapids: Baker Academic, 1992, 2003.

Bercot, David W. *A Dictionary of Early Christian Beliefs.* Peabody: Hendrickson, 1998.

Black, David Alan. *IT"S STILL GREEK TO ME: An Easy-to-Understand Guide t Intermediate Greek.* Grand Rapids: Baker Books, 1998.

Bland, Dave. *The College Press NIV Commentary: Proverbs, Ecclesiastes & Song of Songs,* . Joplin: College Press Pub. Co., 2002.

Boa, Kenneth, and William Kruidenier. *Holman New Testament Commentary: Romans, Vol. 6.* Nashville, TN: Broadman & Holman, 2000.

Boisen, Sean, Mark Keaton, Jeremy Thompson, and David Witthoff. *Bible Sense Lexicon.* Bellingham: Lexham Press, June 25, 2014.

Brand, Chad, Charles Draper, and England Archie. *Holman Illustrated Bible Dictionary: Revised, Updated and Expanded.* Nashville, TN: Holman, 2003.

Bromiley, Geoffrey W. *The International Standard Bible Encyclopedia (Vol. 1-4).* Grand Rapids, MI: William B. Eerdmans Publishing Co., 1986.

Bromiley, Geoffrey W., and Gerhard Friedrich. *Theological Dictionary of the New Testament, ed. Gerhard Kittel, vol. 4.* Grand Rapids, MI: Eerdmans, 1964-.

Calloway, Brent A. *THE BOOK OF JAMES: CPH CHRISTIAN LIVING COMMENTARY.* Cambridge: Chriwstian Publishing House, 2015.

Clinton, Tim, and George Ohlschlager. *Competent Christian Counseling; Volume One: Foundations and Practice of Compassionate Soul Care.* Colorado Springs, CO: WaterBrook Press, 2008.

Cooper, Rodney. *Holman New Testament Commentary: Mark.* Nashville: Broadman & Holman Publishers, 2000.

Easton, M. G. *Easton's Bible Dictionary.* Oak Harbor, WA: Logos Research Systems, 1996, c1897.

Edwards, Tyron. *A Dictionary of Thoughts.* Detroit: F. B. Dickerson Company, 1908.

Elwell, Walter A. *Baker Encyclopedia of the Bible.* Grand Rapids: Baker Book House, 1988.

—. *Evangelical Dictionary of Theology (Second Edition).* Grand Rapids: Baker Academic, 2001.

Elwell, Walter A, and Philip Wesley Comfort. *Tyndale Bible Dictionary.* Wheaton, Ill: Tyndale House Publishers, 2001.

Freedman, David Noel, Allen C. Myers, and Astrid B. Beck. *Eerdmans Dictionary of the Bible .* Grand Rapids, Mich.: W.B. Eerdmans , 2000.

Gangel, Kenneth O. *Holman New Testament Commentary: Acts.* Nashville, TN: Broadman & Holman Publishers, 1998.

Gangel, Kenneth O. *Holman New Testament Commentary, vol. 4, John .* Nashville, TN: Broadman & Holman Publishers, 2000.

Garland, David E. *1 Corinthians, Baker Exegetical Commentary on the New Testament.* Grand Rapids, MI: : Baker Academic, 2003.

Green, Joel B, Scot McKnight, and Howard Marshall. *Dictionary of Jesus and the Gospels.* Downers Grove, IL: InterVarsity Press, 1992.

Guralnik, David B. *Webster's New World Dictionary, 2d college ed.* New York, NY: Simon and Schuster, 1984.

Hastings, James, John A Selbie, and John C Lambert. *A Dictionary of Christ and the Gospels.* New York, NY: Charles Scribner's Sons, 1907.

Hendriksen, William. *Baker New Testament Commentary: Matthew.* Grand Rapids: Baker Book House, 1973.

Kittel, Gerhard, Gerhard Friedrich, and Geoffrey William Bromiley. *Theological Dictionary of the New Testament.* Grand Rapids: Eerdmans, 1995, c1985.

Kollar, Charles Allen. *Solution-Focused Pastoral Counseling: An Effective Short-Term Approach for Getting People Back on Track.* Grand Rapids: Zondervan, 1997.

Larson, Knute. *Holman New Testament Commentary, vol. 9, I & II Thessalonians, I & II Timothy, Titus, Philemon.* Nashville, TN: Broadman & Holman Publishers, 2000.

Lea, Thomas D. *Holman New Testament Commentary: Vol. 10, Hebrews, James.* Nashville, TN: Broadman & Holman Publishers, 1999.

Lukaszewski, Albert L., Mark Dubis, and Ted J Blakley. *The Lexham Syntactic Greek New Testament.* Bellingham: Logos Bible Software, 2013.

MacArthur, John. *Counseling: How to Counsel Biblically.* Nashville, TN: Thomas Nelson, Inc., 2005.

—. *The MacArthur Bible Commentary.* Nashville: Thomas Nelson, 2005.

Marshall, Alfred. *THE NASB-NIV INTERLINEAR GREEK-ENGLISH NEW TESTAMENT.* Grand Rapids: Zondervan, 1993.

McMinn, Mark R. *Psychology, Theology, and Spirituality in Christian Counseling (AACC Library).* Carol Stream, IL: Tyndale House Publishers, 2010.

Microsoft. *Encarta ® World English Dictionary.* Redmond: Microsoft Corporation, 1998-2010.

Mirriam-Webster, Inc. *Mirriam-Webster's Collegiate Dictionary. Eleventh Edition*. Springfield: Mirriam-Webster, Inc., 2003.

Morris, Leon. *The Gospel According to Matthew*. Grand Rapids, MI: Inter-Varsity Press, 1992.

Mounce, William D. *Mounce's Complete Expository Dictionary of Old & New Testament Words*. Grand Rapids, MI: Zondervan, 2006.

Myers, Allen C. *The Eerdmans Bible Dictionary* . Grand Rapids, Mich: Eerdmans, 1987.

Pratt Jr, Richard L. *Holman New Testament Commentary: I & II Corinthians, vol. 7*. Nashville: Broadman & Holman Publishers, 2000.

Swanson, James. *A Dictionary of Biblical Languages - Greek*. Washington: Logos Research Systems, 1997.

Vine, W E. *Vine's Expository Dictionary of Old and New Testament Words*. Nashville: Thomas Nelson, 1996.

Walls, David, and Max Anders. *Holman New Testament Commentary: I & II Peter, I, II & III John, Jude*. Nashville: Broadman & Holman Publishers, 1996.

Weber, Stuart K. *Holman New Testament Commentary, vol. 1, Matthew*. Nashville, TN: Broadman & Holman Publishers, 2000.

Whitney, Donald S. *Spiritual Disciplines for the Christian Life with Bonus Content (Pilgrimage Growth Guide)*. Colorado Springs, CO: Navpress, 1991.

Wilkins, Michael, and Craig A. Evans. *The Gospels and Acts (The Holman Apologetics Commentary on the Bible)*. Nashville: B & H Publishing Group, 2013.

Wood, D R W. *New Bible Dictionary (Third Edition)*. Downers Grove: InterVarsity Press, 1996.

Zodhiates, Spiros. *The Complete Word Study Dictionary: New Testament*. Chattanooga: AMG Publishers, 2000, c1992, c1993.

Printed in Great Britain
by Amazon